CANADIAN POLICE WORK

FOURTH EDITION

CURT T. GRIFFITHS

SIMON FRASER UNIVERSITY

NELSON

NELSON

Canadian Police Work, Fourth Edition
by Curt T. Griffiths

Vice President, Editorial Higher Education:
Anne Williams

Publisher:
Leanna Maclean

Marketing Manager:
Terry Fedorkiw

Developmental Editor:
Suzanne Simpson Millar

Photo Researcher/Permissions Coordinator:
Jessie Coffey

Senior Production Project Manager:
Imoinda Romain

Production Service:
Cenveo Publisher Services

Copy Editor:
Michael Kelly

Proofreader:
Pushpa V. Giri

Indexer:
BIM Publishing Services

Design Director:
Ken Phipps

Managing Designer:
Franca Amore

Interior Design:
Andrew Adams

Cover Design:
Sharon Kish

Cover Images:
(Top) MarekPiotrowski/Shutterstock; (bottom) Courtesy of Winnipeg Police Service

Compositor:
Cenveo Publisher Services

Printed and bound in Canada
3 4 5 6 21 20 19 18

For more information contact Nelson Education Ltd., 1120 Birchmount Road, Toronto, Ontario, M1K 5G4. Or you can visit our Internet site at nelson.com

Library and Archives Canada Cataloguing in Publication

Griffiths, Curt T. (Curt Taylor), 1948–, author
Canadian police work/ Curt T. Griffiths (Simon Fraser University). — Fourth edition.

Includes bibliographical references and index.
ISBN 978-0-17-658293-7 (paperback)

1. Police—Canada. 2. Police administration—Canada. 3. Law enforcement—Canada. I. Title.

HV8157.G756 2015
363.2'30971 C2015-903527-9

ISBN-13: 978-0-17-658293-7
ISBN-10: 0-17-658293-2

TO ADDISYN LEIGH AND BRAXTON TAYLOR – MAY THEY
INHERIT A JUST AND PEACEFUL WORLD

AND TO

DR. MARK I. SINGER AND DR. MOHAMMED KASHANI-SABET,
SUTTER PACIFIC MEDICAL FOUNDATION, SAN FRANCISCO,
FOR SAVING MY LIFE

Brief Contents

Contents

Preface to the Fourth Edition

Policing is perhaps the most high-profile, dynamic, and oftentimes controversial component of the Canadian criminal justice system. It is police officers who respond to criminal offences, disorder, and conflict in the community. How police services and police officers respond to the multifaceted demands that are placed on them affects individual citizens and their neighbourhoods and communities, as well as officers and the police services within which they work. Police are the only agents of the criminal justice system with whom most Canadians ever have contact.

In contrast to personnel in other components of the justice system, police officers work in ever-changing environments. Among their criminal justice co-workers, police officers are the most likely to be shot at, assaulted, criticized, praised, and relied on in times of crisis. Furthermore, it is police officers who are most likely to find themselves caught in personal and social conflicts, civil disobedience, conflicting and often unrealistic community expectations, and the political agendas of senior police administrators, government leaders, and community interest groups. They must often make decisions in a split second, with little time for reflection and deliberation.

These unique attributes of police work explain the ongoing popularity of movies and TV series featuring police. These same attributes also are responsible for the myths and misunderstandings that surround police work. And geography, demographics, and cultural diversity combine to make the environments in which police work is carried out more diverse in Canada than anywhere else in the world.

The decisions of police officers are highly visible, and the consequences of those decisions can be significant. The power to use lethal force distinguishes the police from most other criminal justice personnel. Canadian police have traditionally enjoyed high levels of public support, yet there are ongoing tensions between the need for the police to have sufficient authority to maintain law and order, and the rights of citizens guaranteed by the Charter of Rights and Freedoms. It is at this knife edge that many of the flashpoints of policing in Canadian society develop.

This, the fourth edition of *Canadian Police Work*, updates and extends the materials contained in the third edition. An attempt has been made to make the text more comprehensive while at the same time expanding coverage of various policing issues. This edition of the text contains a new introductory chapter, "Considering Police Work," and a new concluding chapter, "Going Forward: Critical Issues in Canadian Policing." Materials on police research have been updated in all of the chapters. In addition, there is new material on the police and persons with mental illness, the occupational stresses associated with the police occupation, the increasing role of high technology in police work, and the ongoing debate over the economics of policing. Specific attention is also given to the increasing challenges associated with ensuring that Canadians are safe and secure while at the same time ensuring their rights. In the wake of terrorist attacks in Canada, the U.S., and Europe, this is a balance that appears increasingly difficult to maintain.

The text attempts to strike a balance between being an academic treatise on the police and addressing the more applied aspects of policing. To this end, both current research findings and case examples from the field are presented. An attempt has been made to avoid the more sensational portrayals of policing so often encountered in the media and at the same time to avoid the sterility that is so often evident in academic studies. One objective of this edition is the same as in the first three editions: to close what is often a wide gap between scholarly writing on policing and the experiences of police officers.

Any examination of police work in Canada is hindered by a paucity of scholarly research. Canada lacks a robust program of research support that would facilitate field research into the many facets of police work.

A variety of techniques have been incorporated into the text in an effort to make it more "user friendly": academic and police jargon has been held to a minimum, as have notes and exhaustive citations. **Police Files** provide concise and up-to-date information on the latest research findings or present materials on actual incidents. Embedded in the chapters is a feature called **Police Perspective,** wherein Canadian police officers offer their confidential observations and experiences on the topics being discussed.

Each chapter ends with a **Key Points Review** and **Key Term Questions**. These are designed to ensure that students understand the important materials presented in each chapter. Also at the end of each chapter, there are **Critical Thinking Exercises** that challenge the reader to explore the complexities of policing, topics for **Class/Group Discussion Exercises**, and **Media Links** that enhance the materials.

CHANGES TO THE FOURTH EDITION

This edition of the text contains eleven chapters. Significant changes include the inclusion of three new chapters: Chapter 1, "Considering Police Work"; Chapter 4, "Police Ethics and Accountability"; and Chapter 11, "Going Forward: Critical Issues in Canadian Policing." Chapter 11 in the previous edition, "Police Work in a Diverse Society," has been replaced, and the materials on that topic are included throughout the text.

Chapter 1, Considering Police Work. This is a new chapter designed to set the framework for the study of police work in Canada. It provides a definition of policing, sets out contrasting perspectives on the role of police in society, and discusses the challenges of police work in a democratic society. This includes maintaining the balance between maintaining order and protecting the community while ensuring the rights of citizens. The features of policing are identified, including the various influences on the role and activities of the police, and the various contexts in which police work occurs. A number of key concepts central to the study of police work are identified and discussed.

Chapter 4, Police Ethics and Accountability. Chapter 4 is an amalgamation of materials from two chapters in the third edition: Chapter 3, "Police Governance and Accountability," and Chapter 7, "Police Ethics and Professionalism."

Chapter 11, Going Forward: Critical Issues in Canadian Policing. This chapter was conceived to provide a wrap-up for the text and to offer ideas for moving forward. It sets out a number of challenges, including meeting the threat of transnational crime and the threat of terrorism while ensuring citizens' rights; ensuring that police services are delivered as effectively and efficiently as possible within a best-practices, evidence-driven model; and making certain that new technologies are used appropriately.

In addition to these new chapters, there have been significant changes throughout the text, including the following:

Chapter 2, The Origins and Evolution of Police Work, has a section on policing morality, including a discussion of the role of the police in the surveillance and harassment of the LGBT community. A new section discusses the rise of the warrior cop, focusing on the increasing militarization of police services in North America.

Chapter 5, The Police Occupation, includes new sections on the challenges faced by Aboriginal, visible/cultural minority officers, and LGBT officers and an expanded section on post-traumatic stress disorder and suicide among police officers.

Chapter 6, Patrol and General Duty Policing, includes an expanded discussion of the police and persons with mental illness and policing special needs populations. There is also a discussion of the introduction and potential impact of body-worn cameras on the decision making of police officers.

Chapter 7, Police Powers and the Use of Force, has a discussion of the issues surrounding the police use of force in encounters with persons with a mental illness and the impact of social media and police visibility on the use of force.

The extent to which the text captures the essential dimensions of Canadian police work while also stimulating students will be determined largely by the instructors who adopt it and by the students who read it. I encourage instructors and students to provide feedback about the book and suggestions as to how it can be improved. Please send your comments, suggestions, and queries to griffith@sfu.ca.

Thanks.
Curt Taylor Griffiths
Vancouver, British Columbia
February 2015

INSTRUCTOR RESOURCES

The **Nelson Education Teaching Advantage (NETA)** program delivers research-based instructor resources that promote student engagement and higher-order thinking to enable the success of Canadian students and educators. Visit Nelson Education's **Inspired Instruction** website at http://www.nelson.com/inspired to find out more about NETA.

The following instructor resources have been created for *Canadian Police Work*, Fourth Edition. Access these ultimate tools for customizing lectures and presentations at www.nelson.com/instructor.

NETA Test Bank

This resource was written by Danielle Murdoch, Boise State University. It includes more than 200 multiple-choice questions written according to NETA guidelines for effective construction and development of higher-order questions. The Test Bank was copy edited by a NETA-trained editor. Also included are 110 true/false questions (10 per chapter) and 55 short-answer questions (5 per chapter).

NETA PowerPoint

Microsoft® PowerPoint® lecture slides for every chapter have been created by Josh Murphy, Simon Fraser University. There is an average of 11 slides per chapter, many featuring key figures, tables, and photographs from *Canadian Police Work*, Fourth Edition. NETA principles of clear design and engaging content have been incorporated throughout, making it simple for instructors to customize the deck for their courses.

NETA Instructor Guide

This resource was written by Earl Anderson, Langara College. It is organized according to the textbook chapters and outlines key learning objectives while providing additional pedagogical elements for use in the classroom. Features include suggested answers for in-text exercises, review questions, issues for discussion, and recommended activities for students to do in class and online.

DayOne

Day One—Prof InClass is a PowerPoint presentation that instructors can customize to orient students to the class and their text at the beginning of the course.

STUDENT RESOURCES

Additional group discussions and media links can be accessed online at the text's **Student Companion Website**. Visit www.nelson.com/student.

Acknowledgments

I would like to acknowledge the many people in the field of policing who have contributed information and ideas that have been incorporated into this text. Special thanks to Chief Constable Adam Palmer, Deputy Chief Constable Doug LePard, Staff Sergeant Earl Andersen, and Special Constable Ryan Prox, all of the Vancouver Police Department; Chief Constable Neil Dubord, Delta Police Department (BC); Superintendent Peter Clark, Commanding Officer, RCMP "M" Division (Yukon); Sergeant Stacy Wytinck, Winnipeg Police Service; and Tom Stamatakis, President, Canadian Police Association. Also, special thanks to Dr. Rick Parent, my colleague in the School of Criminology at Simon Fraser University, and to Nahanni Pollard, Department of Criminology, Douglas College.

I would also like to thank the external reviewers for their insightful recommendations for improving the text, many of which have been incorporated into this edition: Earl Andersen, Langara College, and Rick Parent, Simon Fraser University.

As always, it has been a pleasure to work with the professionals at Nelson, whose energy and enthusiasm helped make it happen. I would also like to thank the manuscript editor, Michael Kelly, who did a fantastic job within a very constrained timeline.

About the Author

Curt T. Griffiths is a professor and Director, Police Studies Centre in the School of Criminology at Simon Fraser University.

1 Considering Police Work

LEARNING OBJECTIVES

After reading this chapter, you should be able to:

- Provide a definition of policing
- Compare and contrast the social contract and radical perspectives on the role of the police
- Discuss the notion of political policing
- Discuss the challenges of police work in a democratic society
- Discuss the legislative framework in which the police carry out their mandate
- Discuss the basis for the exercise of authority and the use of force by police officers
- Note the features of policing that make it unique in the criminal justice system
- Identify and discuss several of the influences on the role and activities of the police
- Identify and discuss the various contexts in which policing takes place
- Identify and discuss several of the key concepts in the study of policing

Policing is perhaps the most high-profile, dynamic, and, oftentimes, controversial component of the Canadian criminal justice system. It is police officers who respond to criminal offences, disorder, and conflict in the community. How police services and police officers respond to the multifaceted demands that are placed on them affects individual citizens and their neighbourhoods and communities, as well as officers and the police services within which they work. Police are the only agents of the criminal justice system with whom most Canadians ever have contact.

In contrast to personnel in other components of the justice system, police officers work in environments that are always changing. Technological developments, most notably the prevalence of mobile phone cameras, Internet-based platforms such as YouTube, and social networking sites like Facebook, have significantly increased the visibility of police actions.[1] The pervasiveness of the media and social media ensure that critical incidents involving the police receive extensive coverage, and this has contributed to the Canadian public being more demanding and less forgiving of issues related to police misconduct.

CONTEMPORARY POLICE WORK

Police work presents challenges, risks, and rewards and requires special knowledge, skills, and abilities. Policing as an occupation is often characterized by considerable role ambiguity. The daily tasks of police officers are often difficult and at times unappealing. Officers must often search people who are dirty, neglected, or carriers of communicable diseases such as hepatitis or HIV/AIDS. Many of the people they deal with are impaired by alcohol, drugs, and/or mental illness.

Police officers in the early 21st century are highly trained, multi-skilled professionals who have a broad range of demands placed on them. This includes training to deal with at risk and vulnerable groups, cultural and ethnic minorities, newcomers, and Aboriginal peoples. The police officer in the early 21st century is a psychologist, mediator, and problem solver and has near-continuous contact with community residents.

The police occupy a unique, and important, place in the criminal justice system and in Canadian society. With a few notable exceptions, police officers are the only personnel in the justice system with the authority to arrest and detain people and to use lethal force while carrying out their legally mandated duties. Policing issues are discussed and debated every day by politicians, the media, and the community—as well as within police forces themselves.

THE IMAGE AND REALITY OF THE POLICE

There is in our culture a fascination with the police that portrays the world of police officers in a highly seductive fashion: at times extremely dangerous, at other times isolated and lonely. The media—both print and electronic—have been a major contributor to the distorted images that Canadians have of police work. Popular television shows depict policing as an action-packed occupation in which police routinely stare down death. Of all of the components of the criminal justice system, it is the police that most capture the imagination of the public.

Popular police dramas such as the *CSI* series attempt to whet what appears to be an insatiable appetite for the danger, intrigue, and excitement of police work. That these shows only distort the realities of police work is of little concern to either the producers or the viewing audience. Yet these images may have a strong impact on public perceptions of police and on the expectations that communities and victims of crime have on the ability of the police to prevent and solve crime. After all, on-screen police officers almost always solve the crime and arrest the suspects, and crime scene investigators are able to complete complex case investigations in the span of a one-hour time slot. See Critical Thinking Exercise 1.1 at the end of this chapter.

DEFINING POLICE WORK

policing
the activities of any individual or organization acting legally on behalf of public or private organizations or persons to maintain security or social order

A definition of **policing** must include both public and private police; it is the activities of any individual or organization acting legally on behalf of public or private organizations or persons to maintain security or social order while empowered by either public or private contract, regulations or policies, written or verbal.[2]

This definition is an acknowledgement that the public police no longer have a monopoly on policing, although with a few exceptions, they retain a monopoly on the use of force. An increasing role in safety and security in the community is being played by private security services and para-police officers, that is, community constables that have limited powers of enforcement.

THE LEGISLATIVE FRAMEWORK OF POLICE WORK

Police officers carry out their tasks within a number of legislative frameworks that define their roles, powers, and responsibilities. These are generally set out in provincial legislation and—in the case of the Royal Canadian Mounted Police (RCMP)—in the federal RCMP Act. When new legislation is enacted, it may result in increased demands on the police and extend the role and activities of the police. Among the more significant pieces of legislation are these:

Canadian Charter of Rights and Freedoms
a component of the Constitution Act that guarantees basic rights and freedoms

Constitution Act, 1867
legislation that includes provisions that define the responsibilities of the federal and provincial governments in the area of criminal justice

- **Canadian Charter of Rights and Freedoms**. This is the primary law of the land in Canada and guarantees basic rights and freedoms for citizens. The Charter contains specific sections on fundamental freedoms, legal rights, equality rights, and enforcement. The courts may use the Charter to strike down legislation and criminal laws as unconstitutional. No other piece of legislation has had as strong an impact on the powers and activities of the police as the Charter, specifically Sections 7 to 14, the Legal Rights section. This topic is discussed in Chapter 7.
- **Constitution Act, 1867**. This sets out the responsibilities of the federal and provincial governments in the area of criminal justice. The federal government has the sole authority to enact criminal laws and to establish the procedures to be followed in criminal cases (s. 91(14)), while the provinces are assigned responsibility for actually administering justice (s. 92(27)). If the Constitution Act were followed to the letter, the federal government would be limited to passing laws, with the provinces and

territories given the task of policing and justice administration. In reality, it's much more complex than that. The RCMP is a national police force involved in federal, provincial, and municipal policing. The federal government operates a corrections system for individuals who receive sentences of two years or more. Also, provincial and municipal governments enact their own laws; however, provincial laws and municipal bylaws are generally for less serious types of offences and are most often punished by fines. Even though bylaws are relatively minor in the overall scheme of laws, they can be the source of considerable controversy. This was illustrated when municipalities began passing bylaws that severely restricted where persons could smoke.

- **Criminal Code**. This sets out the criminal laws as well as the procedures for administering justice.
- *Other federal statutes.* These include the Anti-Terrorism Act, the Controlled Drugs and Substances Act, the Youth Criminal Justice Act, the Canada Evidence Act (which pertains to evidentiary matters in the courts), the Access to Information Act, and various privacy acts.
- *Provincial and municipal legislation.* This includes a wide range of statutes such as motor vehicle administration acts, highway traffic acts, liquor acts, and provincial/municipal police acts. All of these provide the framework within which police services are structured and delivered. As well, the various police acts set out the principles of policing, processes for filing complaints against police officers, and disciplinary procedures for police officers, besides providing for and defining the activities of police commissions and municipal police boards.
- **Royal Canadian Mounted Police Act**. This provides the legislative framework for the operations of the RCMP. It also contains provisions relating to the operations of the External Review Committee and the Civilian Review and Complaints Commission, as well as to officer grievances, discipline, discharge, and demotion.

Criminal Code
federal legislation that sets out criminal law, procedures for prosecuting federal offences, and sentences and procedures for the administration of justice

Royal Canadian Mounted Police Act
federal legislation that provides the framework for the operation of the RCMP

PERSPECTIVES ON THE ROLE OF THE POLICE

There are two competing perspectives on the role of the police, the **social contract perspective** and the **radical perspective**.

social contract perspective (on the role of the police)
a perspective that considers the police to be a politically neutral force that acts primarily to enforce the law and protect the public

The Social Contract Perspective

The social contract perspective views the police as a politically neutral force that acts primarily to enforce the law and protect the public. The power of police and their mandate to use force against citizens is justified under the social contract vision of society. The police use of force is necessary to maintain order and maximize collective good by maintaining a safe and workable society. Under social contract theory, citizens are understood to voluntarily surrender some of their power and rights and delegate them to the state and to the police force. The social contract theory of policing informs mainstream views of policing, which see police as a protective force against crime and social disorder.

radical perspective (on the role of the police)
a perspective that views the police as an instrument used by governments and powerful interests to suppress dissent, stifle protest, and help maintain the status quo

© CHRISTINNE MUSCHI/Reuters/Corbis

Police officers comfort a boy following an incident.

Given the widespread belief in the social contract theory of police and the partisan nature of media reporting, the general public is often uncritically supportive of police behaviour even where such behaviour involves high levels of force and coercion. Police violence against protesters will often be seen as legitimate even where it goes beyond the bounds of reasonable force. The materials presented throughout this text will reveal that Canadian police services have often come up short in reflecting these values.

The Radical Perspective

While the social contract perspective depicts the police as a neutral agent of the state providing for the safety and security of citizens, the proponents of the radical perspective point out that since the police support the government, which in turn supports the interests of the ruling class, the police are never politically neutral.[3]

The radical perspective on the police is captured in the following narrative:

> Policing is part of the complex technologies, or methods of control (such as corrections institutions, public health administration, public education administration and corporate management) whose primary function in history has been to consolidate the social power of the capitalist class and administer the working class and poor...[T]he police are integral to the manner in which the state controls and contains civil society in general and people in particular.[4]

The radical perspective considers police as a repressive force that is instrumental in the maintenance of an unjust social system: "The police are primarily utilised by the government to maintain the status quo and to protect the powerful against any perceived threats."[5] This includes conducting surveillance on individuals and groups who are deemed to be a threat to national security and suppressing public protests. For a radical perspective on the role of police in Canada, view the documentary film *Into the Fire (Canada Is a Police State)*, listed in Media Links at the end of this chapter.

Proponents of this perspective of the police and of Canadian society as a "police state" cite as evidence the historical record. There are numerous historical and contemporary examples presented in Chapter 2 wherein the police were used by the government to "pacify" the Canadian west so that it could be settled and developed, to break strikes and suppress citizen protests, and to monitor the activities of Canadians who were/are deemed to be a threat to the state. The persons most often the subject of government and police interest have been those involved in various political activities and/or those who had beliefs or engaged in behaviours (including sexual) that were viewed as a threat to the stability and status quo of the state. Continuing to the present, the police have spied on citizens and have engaged in activities that violated citizens' rights. Police services, particularly the

RCMP and CSIS (the Canadian Security Intelligence Service) have maintained extensive secret data files on citizens and engaged in activities that have often been determined to be illegal.

More recently, the policing of the G20 protests in Toronto in 2010 (discussed in Chapter 7) raised concerns about the neutrality of the police. Documents obtained under the Access to Information Act revealed a massive RCMP-led initiative to infiltrate activist groups across the country, conduct surveillance, and ultimately, arrest persons involved during the G20 protests.[6] This initiative involved over 500 municipal, provincial, and federal police officers and contributed to the $1 billion price tag for security for the G8 and G20 summits. See the Media Link, "Police State Canada: From the McDonald Commission to the G20," at the end of this chapter.

The Canadian scholars Reg Whitaker, Gregory Kealey, and Andrew Parnaby have labelled this phenomenon **political policing.**[7] There are numerous examples of this in Canadian history and in contemporary times. Several of these are discussed in Chapter 2 and throughout the text.

political policing
secretive police investigative activities and surveillance of persons and groups deemed to be a threat to the stability and status quo of the state

The terrorist attacks of 9/11 in the U.S. accelerated police surveillance on groups and persons identified as posing a terrorist threat. In Canada, increasing concerns with "homegrown terrorists" have led to an expansion of police powers and legislation that gives the police and security agencies even greater authority to conduct surveillance of persons and groups deemed to pose a threat. "Extremist travellers," persons intent on leaving Canada to join conflicts in other parts of the world and those returning from conflict zones with terrorist training and combat experience, have become a major focus of police services.

The attack on Parliament Hill on October 22, 2014, heightened these concerns and raised the spectre that Canadian police services will become involved in more incidents of this nature in the future. This incident provided additional impetus for expanding the powers of the police and the ability of the police to conduct surveillance on persons and groups who are deemed to pose a threat to the safety and security of Canadians. A key question is: "How much power for the police is enough or too much?" And importantly, "Will additional police powers make citizens safer or compromise rights?" This issue is discussed further in Chapter 7.

As the front line of the criminal justice system, the police have always been drawn into situations involving social disorder and public protests, including demonstrations against global capitalism. This will be revealed in the discussion of the origins and evolution of the police in Canada in Chapter 2 and of police powers in Chapter 7.

Whatever framework you bring to the understanding of the role of police in society, there is no doubt that they are a powerful force. On the one hand, the police enjoy high levels of public support; on the other, the police (along with the military and correctional officers) have a virtual monopoly on legitimate force combined with an array of weapons and tactics that provide the potential for coercion and repression.

POLICE WORK IN A DEMOCRATIC SOCIETY

The separation of powers between the police and government is considered an important tenet of liberal democracy. The separation of powers assists in ensuring that the police are not used in a partisan political way to harass and punish political opponents and dissidents. There is also a separation of roles and powers between the courts and the police. It is the police role to bring suspected offenders before the courts and the courts' role to decide on guilt or innocence and, in the case of conviction, decide on punishment. Among all of the institutions and organizations in society, it is the police that can have a direct impact on the rights and freedoms of individual citizens. This is due to the powers that police officers are given under the law.

The police mandate is at its heart contradictory: the police are expected to protect both public order *and* individual rights. There are natural tensions between the power and authority of the police and their legal mandate to maintain order, on the one hand, and the values and processes that exist in a democratic society, on the other. This tension is inevitable and, generally, irreconcilable.

The governments and the public rely on the police to prevent and respond to crime and to apprehend offenders; yet at the same time, these governments are committed to the principles of democracy and due process. It is not surprising, then, that police officers often experience conflict in carrying out their duties and that the police are often "caught in the middle." Proponents of the radical perspective of the police would contend that there is no conflict in the police role; rather, the activities of the police are primarily directed toward supporting the state at the expense of citizens' rights.

Police services are also required to monitor and control protest demonstrations involving opposing groups who support different sides in conflicts in other regions of the world. This localization of global conflicts is reflected in clashes between pro-Palestinian and Pro-Israeli demonstrators in Calgary in 2014 as a result of conflicts in the Middle East (see photo).

Given these circumstances, it is impossible for the police to avoid becoming involved in and affected by politics and other outside influences. A key issue is the extent to which this involvement, or influence, affects the ability of the police to carry out their mandate in a fair and impartial manner. There are numerous instances in which Canadian police have failed to do this.

The Law Reform Commission of Canada identified four key values that form the framework for understanding police work in Canadian society:[8]

- *Justice*. The police are to maintain peace and security in the community while ensuring that individuals are treated fairly and that human rights are respected.
- *Equality*. All citizens are entitled to policing services that contribute to their feelings of safety and security.
- *Accountability*. The actions of police services, and police officers, are subject to review.
- *Efficiency*. Policing services must be cost effective.

These are the ideal values that should underpin policing. In actuality, there are often conflicts between the role of the police in ensuring safety and security and ensuring that the rights of Canadian citizens are protected. See Critical Thinking Exercises 1.2 and 1.3, both at the end of this chapter.

Photo by Colleen De Neve. Reprinted with permission of The Calgary Herald.

Police contain a pro-Palestinian and pro-Israeli protest that had broken out at Calgary's City Hall in July 2014.

THE ROLES OF THE POLICE

The Unique Role of the Police in the Criminal Justice System

The police are only one component of the criminal justice system. While police officers have much in common with their professional counterparts in that system (e.g., they exercise considerable discretion in making decisions), they are also unique in many ways, including the following:

- Police work is carried out in diverse environments.
- Police work takes place in a wide variety of situations and circumstances, many of which may involve personal conflict, crises and chaos, biohazards, blood, and sometimes death.
- Police officers have the authority to detain people and to use force, including lethal force.
- Police work—especially community police work—involves extensive personal contact with the general public and (increasingly) the development of partnerships with communities, non-governmental organizations (NGOs), the private sector, and increasingly, international partners.
- Police work involves much more than law enforcement; it includes order maintenance, service, crime prevention, conflict mediation and dispute resolution, and public relations.
- Police work presents officers with situations in which they must make split-second decisions or decisions, often involving the use of force, based on a limited amount of information.

The Expanding Police Role

The primary activities of the police have traditionally been viewed as centring on three major areas: crime control (catching criminals), order maintenance (keeping the peace), and service (providing assistance). Police officers may view themselves primarily as peacekeepers rather than law enforcers: depending on the specific area being policed, many officers spend most of their time attending to order-maintenance activities and much less time actually enforcing laws. A large portion of police work involves officers restoring order in situations of conflict without resorting to the criminal law.[9] In carrying out these functions, the police have broad discretion. This is discussed in Chapter 6.

These components, however, may no longer accurately capture the diversity and complexity of the police role in a highly technological, globalized community. The police role has become much more multifaceted in recent years, often referred to as "diversification." Increasingly, police services are being asked to address non–law enforcement issues, such as the challenges of the mentally ill, and most police services have developed an extensive network of collaborative partnerships with agencies and community organizations to address issues related to crime and disorder.[10] The discussion in this text will reveal that the police play a multifaceted role in Canadian society, one that seems to be expanding in the early 21st century.

Police observers have argued that many of the difficulties experienced by the police in fulfilling their mandate are the result of having assumed responsibility for a broad social domain in society. This has led to unrealistic expectations on the part of the general public as to what the police can realistically accomplish in terms of crime prevention and response. And it has challenged police services to document the effectiveness and efficiency of their operations.[11]

Contributing to this has been the phenomena of "downloading," wherein the police being required to fill gaps in service that are the mandated responsibility of other agencies and organizations. For example, when governments cut the numbers of social workers and mental health workers, as well as funding for shelter beds and for specialized facilities for the mentally ill, there is a direct impact on the demands placed on the police resources. As a consequence of this, police services across the country are spending an increasing portion of their time responding to high-risk and vulnerable populations, including the mentally ill. This is discussed further in Chapter 8.

A major challenge for Canadian police, governments, and citizens is that the core functions of the police have not been clearly defined. This has resulted in the continued expansion of the police role and, with this, increased expectations of the police to effectively address a wide variety of issues that were not traditionally within their purview. See Class/Group Discussion 1.1 at the end of this chapter.

The Use of Authority

A key element of the police role in society is their use of authority. This authority includes depriving citizens of their freedom, as well as the application of physical force—in extreme circumstances, lethal force. Police observers have pointed out, however, that police officers are generally quite subtle in their exercise of authority. They often project it merely by being a uniformed presence in public settings and by soliciting information from citizens. Canadian police officers derive their authority from the Criminal Code and various provincial statutes.

The legal authority of police officers, however, does not automatically translate into *moral* authority. The latter requires officers to establish their legitimacy in the community.[12] The importance of police legitimacy is discussed in Chapter 8.

The Authority to Use Force

Another defining attribute of the police role is the authority to use force. No other personnel (except for the military and correctional officers) in the criminal justice system are invested with this authority. This authority is integral to all facets of the police role, from selection and training to operational patrol and high-risk policing situations. And while most incidents are resolved without the use of force, the potential for its use is always present. In recent years, there have been several high-profile cases involving police officers who used force in encounter situations. The police use of force and its consequences for police services, officers, suspects, and the community are considered in Chapter 7.

INFLUENCES ON THE ROLE AND ACTIVITIES OF THE POLICE

> *The demand for policing services has been increasing over the past ten years through increases in non-criminal calls for policing, continuing increases in the legal complexity of equitable handling of cases, the growing response to mental health and addiction needs, and the increases in technical demands on services.*[13*]

There are a number of factors that influence the role and activities of the police, and the ability of the police to effectively respond to community expectations and to crime and disorder in any one jurisdiction. A number of these factors are depicted in Figure 1.1. Many of these same factors will influence the decision making of patrol officers, discussed in Chapter 6.

Canadian police officers carry out their mandate and tasks in a variety of contexts. The community in which a police service operates and in which police officers carry out their tasks has a strong impact on what police do and what is expected of them, as well as on the administrative, operational, and investigative activities of the service as a whole. This environment includes the various internal organizational and external environmental contexts in which police services go about their work.

The internal context includes the organizational features of the police service, including its size and structure and the activities and attitudes of its leaders, middle managers, civilian members, patrol officers, and investigative officers. It also includes the strategic planning and research capacities of the police service—that is, the organization's ability to develop strategic plans, evaluate its own performance, and implement reforms when required.

The external environment (or task environment) of a police service includes a multitude of factors. These are certainly not limited to the following: the patterns of crime in the area; relations between the police service and other components of the justice system; the requirements imposed on the police by legislation, government policies, and court decisions; the demographics of the

*Institute for Canadian Urban Research Studies. 2014. *Economics of Policing: Complexity and Costs in Canada, 2014*, p.1. Burnaby, BC.

Figure 1.1. Influences on the Role and Activities of the Police

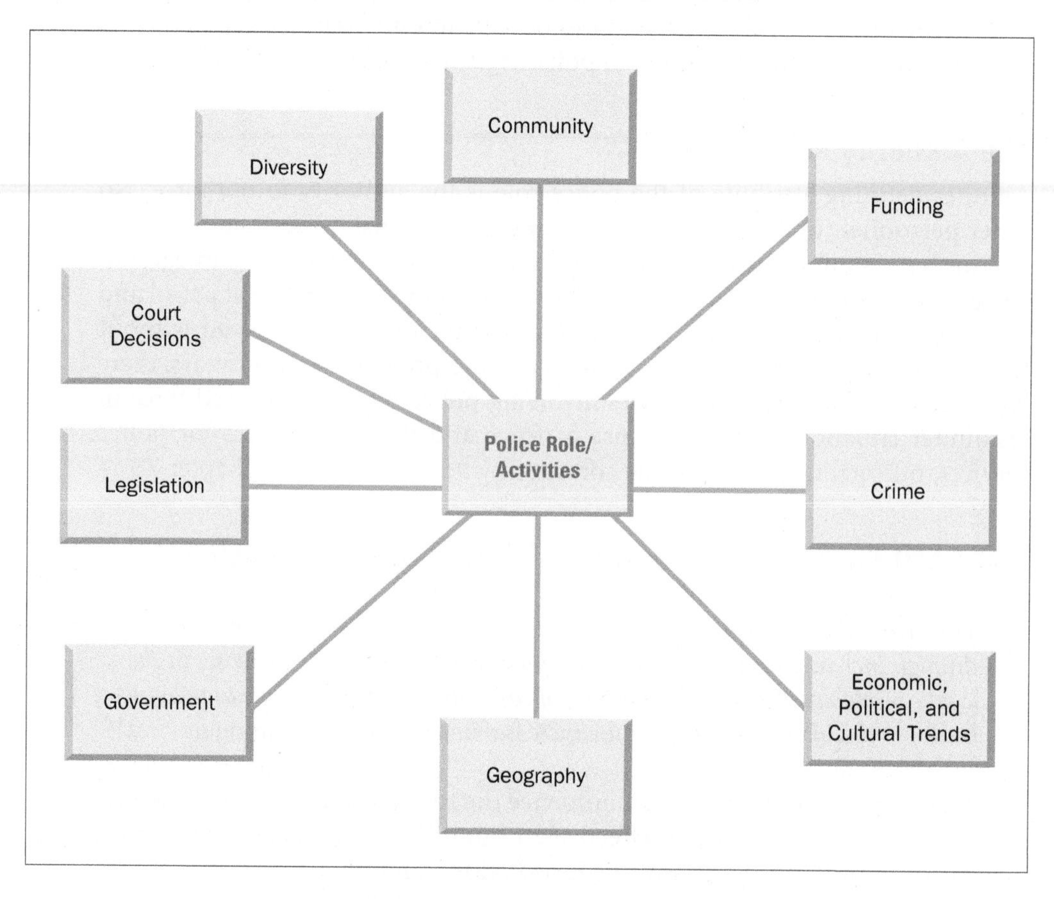

Question: Can you think of additional factors that may influence the role and activities of the police?

community; the forms of oversight and accountability faced by the service; the types of criminal activities that are present; the fiscal decisions of governments and municipal councils; the media; and the specific incidents to which officers respond and what happens during those encounters.

The environment for policing can be hostile or friendly, depending on a variety of political, economic, and socio-demographic factors and on the demands that are made on the police service.

The impact of the task environment on the decision making of police officers is discussed in Chapter 6.

The Community

The community in which the police service operates greatly affects the demands made on police officers, the role that the police assume in the community, and the patterns of relationships that exist between the community and the police (which, in turn, will determine the potential for police–community partnerships; see Chapter 8).

Communities vary on a number of important dimensions, including these: their size; their socio-economic, ethnic, cultural, and religious composition; the types and levels of crime and disorder; the attitudes toward and expectations of the police; the demands citizens make on the police; and the levels of citizen interest in becoming involved in police–community partnerships. The impact of these factors on the activities and decision making of police officers is discussed in Chapter 6.

Residents in neighbourhoods with higher levels of crime and social disorder generally place heavier demands on the police than those in quieter neighbourhoods. Police services have to tailor their crime prevention and response strategies to the needs of specific neighbourhoods.

Residents often have unrealistic and conflicting expectations of the police. Community residents often assign equal importance to crime prevention, crime control, order maintenance, and service functions and rarely provide any input into how police resources are to be allocated. Similarly, many individuals who phone the police expect an immediate response by a patrol car, no matter how minor the incident. Put simply, community residents often want the police to be all things to all people, which is an impossible goal.

Diversity

A key feature of Canada is diversity. This includes visible minorities, newcomers, indigenous peoples, religious beliefs, and sexual orientation, among others. Canada is becoming more diverse. In 2011, visible minorities composed 20 percent of the population; by 2031, it is estimated that this will rise to nearly 31 percent, and at that time, 25 percent of Canadians will be foreign-born. Currently, visible minorities comprise almost one-half of the population of the city of Toronto (see Figure 1.2).[14]

It is predicted that by 2031, 60 percent of residents of Toronto and Vancouver will belong to a visible minority. These trends have led some observers to suggest that the term "visible minority" may be obsolete or will soon be.[15]

Fifteen percent of this country's population is foreign-born, and that percentage is expected to rise in the coming years. Two-thirds of arriving immigrants settle in the megacities of Vancouver, Toronto, and Montreal, and they may have little understanding of the role of the police and/or have had negative experiences with the police in their countries of origin. A lack of English or French language skills may also be a barrier.

The challenges faced by newcomers are discussed in Chapter 8. Urban centres are also attracting increasing numbers of Aboriginal people from rural and remote areas, and this may pose challenges for police services.

This diversity has significant implications for police work. Section 15(1) of the Charter of Rights and Freedoms guarantees equality rights: "Every individual is equal before and under the law and has the right to the equal protection and equal benefit of the law without discrimination and, in particular, without discrimination based on race, national or ethnic origin, colour, religion, sex, age or mental or physical disability." Section 3(e) of the Canadian

Figure 1.2. Population Composition, Toronto, 2006 Census

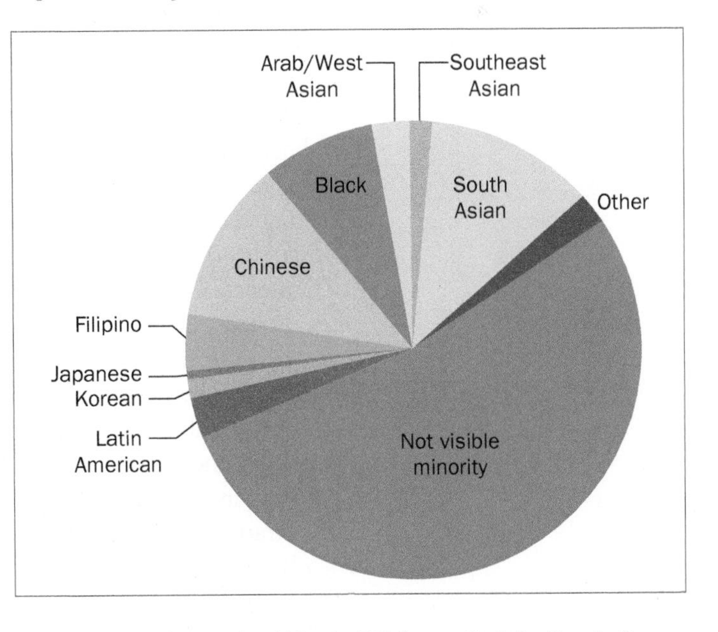

Source: *Canada's Ethnocultural Mosaic, 2006 Census*, Statistics Canada, Census year 2006. Catalogue no. 97-562-X.

Multiculturalism Act (R.S., 1985, c. 24 (4th Supp.)) states that it is the policy of the Government of Canada to "ensure that all individuals receive equal treatment and equal protection under the law, while respecting and valuing their diversity."

The Canadian Human Rights Act prohibits discrimination on the grounds of "race, national or ethnic origin, colour, religion, age, sex, sexual orientation, marital status, family status, disability and conviction for which a pardon has been granted."[16] Many provinces, including Ontario, British Columbia, Alberta, and Manitoba, have human rights codes that mirror the federal human rights code, contain sections proclaiming the right of residents to be free from discrimination, and provide for human rights tribunals.

The debate over racial profiling by the police, discussed in Chapter 6, is illustrative of the human rights issues that surround policing a diverse community.

Geography

Canada is a huge but sparsely populated country. A unique feature of Canadian police work is that Ontario Provincial Police (OPP), Sûreté du Québec (SQ), and RCMP officers are posted to northern and remote communities. RCMP officers, often working in detachments as small as three members, are responsible for policing Aboriginal and Inuit communities in Yukon, the Northwest Territories, and Nunavut. The challenges of policing in remote communities, many of which are afflicted by high rates of crime and social disorder, have remained largely unexplored by Canadian police scholars. The discussion in Chapter 6 will reveal that the officers in these communities must be highly adaptable and, in the absence of the supportive infrastructure found in larger police services, self-sufficient.

The Police Organization

Police services engage in a wide variety of activities, including establishing policies and procedures that officers must follow, setting priorities, determining how resources will be allocated, and setting standards for assessing officers' performance and career advancement, among others.

Police services also differ regarding the expectations of the communities they police, the number of officers in the department, and the perspectives of senior management. However, all police services include a senior executive, middle-management officers, patrol officers, investigative divisions (including specialty units), and various support services. General-duty policing is discussed in Chapter 6, and the work of specialty units and police investigators in Chapter 10.

Police officers in Canada work in departments and detachments that vary greatly in terms of size, structure, and activities. For example, although an RCMP officer may be posted to a three-officer detachment in a remote area, the officer is still accountable to an organizational hierarchy that stretches many kilometres from the detachment to the subdivision, to the division headquarters, and to RCMP headquarters in Ottawa. RCMP policies and procedures are formulated in Ottawa and then transmitted regularly to the detachments through the division headquarters.

The discussion throughout this text will also highlight the importance of the police organization in understanding police ethics and professionalism (Chapter 4), the occupational experience of police officers (Chapter 6), and police use of force (Chapter 7), among others.

Legislation

New laws and amendments to existing legislation can have a sharp impact on police powers, on the demands placed on police services, and on how police services set (and try to achieve) their operational priorities. Literally overnight, behaviour that was once criminal can become legal, and behaviour that was once legal can become criminalized. The Anti-Terrorism Act, for example, gives police expanded powers to deal with individuals identified as posing a threat to safety and security; it has also established a new crime—"terrorist activity." Increasing police resources are being directed toward identifying and monitoring persons who have been deemed at risk of engaging in terrorist activities.

Another piece of legislation that has impacted police resources is the Access to Information Act (1994). This allows the public to request information from the police on a variety of matters, and there are extensive requirements for the police to obtain search warrants and DNA warrants. The expectation is that police services have the capacity to fulfill these requirements.

Court Decisions

Court decisions may impact not only the powers of the police but also policing costs. The decisions of the Supreme Court of Canada have also been identified as a major reason that policing costs have increased.[17] One case that has had a significant impact on police resources is *R. v. Stinchcombe*, 1991, 3 S.C.R. 326, which established the right to full disclosure of Crown evidence. Previously, police were only required to submit information sufficient for the Crown to make a case. Now, the police are required to provide to Crown counsel and for dissemination to the defence lawyers, the following information:

> all audio and video tapes; notebook entries from all officers; reports; all source briefings; all tips (and outcomes of tips); all connected cases; all affiant material; all wiretap information; all operational plans; all surveillance notes; medical records; all analyses of telephone records or other documents; undercover operational information; information relating to investigative techniques considered; whether they were actually used or not; and, investigative team minutes of meetings or debriefings.[18]*

These requirements may be particularly onerous in cases that have involved a lengthy and complex investigation. Significant police resources may be required to assemble this information.[19] Subsequent decisions of the SCC expanded the right to full disclosure. This included the decisions in *R. v. McNeil*, 2009, SCC 3, where the court held that disclosure extended to providing information on the arresting officer, and *R. v. O'Connor*, 1995, 4 SCR 411, relating to the disclosure of medical records of the complainant under certain circumstances.

One study of police workload found that over a thirty-year period (1975–2005), the time required of the RCMP to complete all of the procedural elements had increased dramatically: for example, break and enter went from up to one hour to five to ten hours, domestic assault from up to one hour to ten to twelve hours, and driving under the influence from one hour to five hours.[20]

---

*Easton, S., H. Furness, and P. Brantingham. 2014. *The Cost of Crime in Canada* (Vancouver: The Fraser Institute).

There has also been an expansion of legal regulations and levels of accountability that has affected all facets of policing, from the conduct of officers to case investigation. The procedural requirements for investigating and processing offences have resulted in a dramatic increase in the time and resources required to complete procedural requirements.

Crime

Communities vary in terms of the amount and types of criminal activity. The nature and extent of crime in a community will have a significant impact on the demands made of the police service and its officers. Generally speaking, the severity and volume of police-reported crime rate continues its decade-long decline. Violent crime also continued to decline, with the exception of certain categories of offences, including extortion, child pornography, and aggravated sexual assault, among others. Canada's homicide rate is at its lowest level since the 1960s.[21] There are, however, crime hot spots: there are urban, rural, and remote areas of the country that have high rates of serious crime. The rates of violent crime in Canada are highest in remote, northern Aboriginal and Inuit communities, areas where there are the fewest resources.[22] The rates of crime continue to be high in the territories, particularly in the Northwest Territories and Nunavut.[23] Aboriginal peoples are more likely to be the victims of violence, and Aboriginal women have a much greater likelihood of being the victim of spousal abuse than non-Aboriginal women.[24] This poses unique challenges for police officers posted to northern and remote communities, and these challenges are discussed in Chapter 6.

Besides the more traditional types of crime (i.e., robberies, assaults, property crimes), police services are now being confronted with increasingly sophisticated criminal activities that are often international in scope.

The increasing sophistication of criminal behaviour and the rise of transnational crime have required police services to adopt new strategies and technology. These may, in turn, increase the costs of policing. Cybercrime, for example, has emerged as a major, and resource-intensive, challenge for police services, as has child exploitation on the Internet. The victims of cybercrime are generally young, and many of these crimes involve sexual violations.[25]

Figure 1.3 presents information on the costs of fraudulent e-commerce, telephone, and mail purchases in Canada.

More-sophisticated technologies are also being used by police services to combat these types of crime. These are discussed in Chapter 10.

There are a number of factors that may influence police-reported crime statistics, including legislative changes, the policies and procedures of individual police services, and public reporting

Figure 1.3. Fraudulent E-Commerce, Telephone, and Mail Purchases in Canada

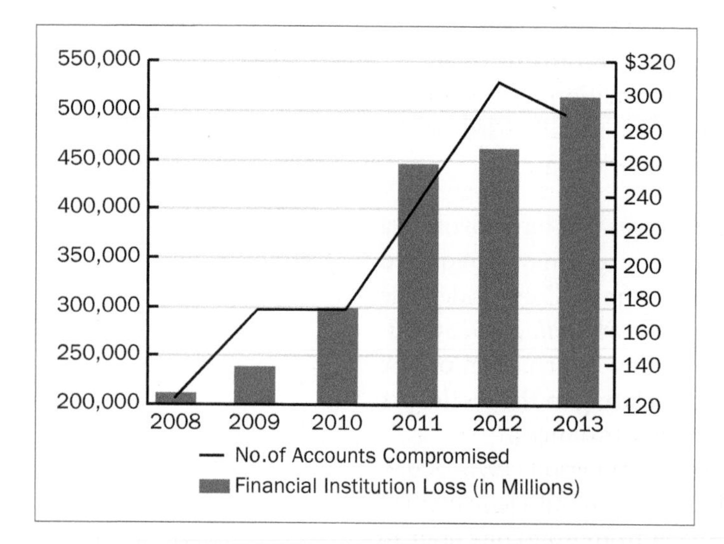

Source: From Shane Dingman, Sean Silcoff, and Rachel Greenspan (2014). "Hacked: The escalating arms race against cybercrime," *The Globe & Mail*, October 24, http://www.theglobeandmail.com/report-on-business/hacked-the-escalating-arms-race-against-cybercrime/article21305464/. © The Globe and Mail Inc. All Rights Reserved.

rates, as well as the lack of awareness that a crime has occurred, among others. This creates a **dark figure of crime**—that is, the amount of crime that for whatever reasons is not reported to the police.

dark figure of crime
the difference between how much crime occurs and how much crime is reported to or discovered by the police

Even homicides may be underreported, especially in cases involving organized crime or the deaths of individuals who live and/or work on the street. (Conversely, in cases of theft or damage when the victim has insurance, report rates are higher.) This dark figure is a result of many factors, including the unwillingness of crime victims to report to the police, the fact that some crimes have no direct victim (e.g., pollution), and the fact that many of the conflicts to which police officers respond are resolved informally without any charges being laid. Persons or organizations may also not realize they have been victimized. Cybercrime and hacking attacks may never be discovered, or only discovered years after the crime has been committed.

KEY CONCEPTS IN THE STUDY OF POLICE WORK

There are a number of key concepts that are important in any discussion of policing in the early 21st century. These are discussed throughout the text and include the following:

- The transparency and accountability of the police
- The cost-benefits of policing
- Police legitimacy
- The changing boundaries of policing
- The increasing visibility of the police

The Transparency and Accountability of the Police

There is an increasing demand that police services be transparent in their activities and accountable for the decisions they make and the resources they expend, and that there be in place structures of oversight. Transparency and accountability are required at the community and government level and best practice police services have in place capacities to provide ongoing communication and information-sharing with their key stakeholders. Ethics and accountability in policing are discussed in Chapter 4.

The Cost-Benefits of Policing

Although the crime rate decreased by approximately 27 percent between 2002 and 2012, the costs of the justice system increased by 35 percent during this same period. As of 2014, it is estimated that the total annual costs associated with crime, victimization, and the criminal justice system are approximately $85 billion.[26] The greatest increase was in policing, which recorded a 44 percent increase. A portion of this increase has been attributed to the decisions by the Supreme Court of Canada that have increased the time and resources required to prosecute cases. This has increased the "cost-per-conviction."[27]

Policing costs compose a significant portion of many municipal budgets. This is to be expected. Municipalities are responsible for police and fire/rescue. All other response services, including sheriffs, probation officers, social workers, and mental health workers, are a provincial/territorial responsibility. In the early 21st century, police services are assuming many responsibilities that fall within the mandate of other agencies and organizations. This is reflected in the challenges that police officers face in responding to persons with mental illness (discussed in Chapter 6). There are no signs that this downloading is slowing; rather, it will likely continue given the fiscal crises of governments.

The cost-benefits of policing are only now beginning to be documented by research. Studies in the U.S. have found that, all else being equal, a 10 percent reduction in the size of a typical police service has been found to lead to a 6 percent increase in robberies, a 3 percent increase in serious assaults, and a 4 percent increase in vehicle theft.[28] There is also research to suggest that specific strategies can have a significant impact on the levels of crime and the numbers of offenders (and associated expense) processed through the criminal justice system. This is discussed in Chapter 9. This economic analysis highlights the value of investing in policing and suggests that under-resourcing for police services may have a number of negative outcomes.

Police Legitimacy

police legitimacy
the collective actions taken by the police to enhance the levels of trust and confidence that citizens have in the police

A common theme in the community policing literature is that of **police legitimacy**. This has to do with the collective actions taken by the police to enhance the levels of trust and confidence that citizens have in the police.

Community policing initiatives have a much greater success, as do efforts to develop partnerships with the community, when the community trusts and has confidence in the police. Police legitimacy, however, is fragile, and can be undermined by high-profile incidents, including the misuse of force and police misconduct. This is discussed in Chapter 8.

If improperly applied, police strategies to prevent and reduce crime can also compromise the legitimacy of the police, particularly among groups who may feel they are being targeted. The discussion in Chapter 8 explores the dynamics that surround policing in the community.

The Changing Boundaries of Policing

Historically, there have been very clear boundaries between the various components of the criminal justice system. This often has resulted in agencies operating in "silos," focused only on their specific mandate and not considering the larger context of the problem of crime and disorder, specific patterns of criminal behaviour, or the needs of offenders, which are often multifaceted (i.e., addicted, mentally ill, etc.).

Recent years have witnessed the development of integrated, multi-agency teams. These teams may be focused on a specific neighbourhood or on a group of offenders and bring together police officers, social workers, mental health workers, and other community resources. This is a more holistic approach to problem solving and has the potential to effectively address the underlying issues that contribute to crime and disorder, rather than merely responding to the symptoms of these issues.

The multi-agency approach is designed to break down the silos that have traditionally existed in the justice system and between criminal justice and social service agencies and other care providers in the community. Multi-agency teams provide an opportunity to optimize information sharing and to create holistic solutions for

Police Perspective 1.1

A Deputy Chief Constable Speaks about Policing Protests

"There are often situations where different rights collide. For example, the Canadian Charter of Rights and Freedoms protects free speech and the right of assembly, but not without limits, as set out in Section 1 of the Charter (known as the 'reasonable limits clause'). We regularly deal with demonstrations and protests, including 'Critical Mass,' which is a large number of cyclists who obstruct traffic on their route to advance a certain agenda once a month. Many citizens whose commute is interfered with have a first reaction that we ought to be strictly enforcing the law. Well, we are dealing with relatively minor traffic offences but to actually enforce the law when hundreds of cyclists are involved would require a massive and expensive police response and might very well require the use of force. In that situation, we would generally manage it by making the ride as safe as possible and preventing conflicts. The exercise of free speech will trump the traffic laws requiring certain behaviour, particularly given the disproportional police response that would be required to safely intervene. What guides us is the law, our values as an organization, which include responding proportionately with the least intrusive measures necessary to provide public safety, and our Public Demonstration Guidelines, which we put on our website for all to see—that's a tool to educate the public about why we do what we do."

Source: Personal communication with author, October 2014.

the target audience. There are concerns, however, that these teams blur the mandates of the individual components of the justice system. These changing boundaries are also illustrated by the rise of tiered policing, wherein private security and parapolice are assuming functions traditionally performed by sworn police officers.

Examples of the collaboration between agencies are presented throughout the text. Although there are benefits to agencies moving outside of their silos, concerns have been expressed that, in some areas, collaboration between agencies compromises the individual mandates of the agencies. For example, collaborative initiatives between parole officers and police services may function to create an inordinate focus on surveillance and control to the detriment of the helping and assistance role of parole officers.[29]

The changing boundaries in criminal justice are also reflected in the relationships between the public and private police, which one police scholar has described as "messy and complex."[30] Many former police officers work in the private policing sector, and there may be a blurring of their role and that of public police officers. Increasingly, functions performed by the public police are being "outsourced" due to rising costs.[31]

The Increasing Visibility of the Police

The police are unique in the criminal justice system in that the majority of their activities take place on the street and away from the confines of office buildings.

Police officers have more contact with the community than other criminal justice professionals (judges, probation officers, and correctional officers, for example) who operate in relative obscurity. With the exception of occasional high-profile cases and incidents (e.g., sentencing a violent offender, a prison riot), criminal justice practitioners are relatively immune from the scrutiny that police officers receive in carrying out their day-to-day tasks. Technological developments, most notably the prevalence of mobile phone cameras, Internet-based platforms such as YouTube, and social networking sites like Facebook, have significantly increased the visibility of police actions.[32] Many police officers have complained about "trial by YouTube," with citizens judging the appropriateness of police decision making based on a video clip posted on social media.

An increasing number of police services are adopting body-worn cameras that are worn by patrol officers. These cameras have the capacity to record at least a portion of the encounters involving police officers. Body-worn cameras are discussed in Chapter 6.

Summary

The discussion in this chapter has focused on some of the roles of the police in Canadian society. A definition of policing was provided. It was noted that the police carry out their activities within a legislative framework that defines their roles, powers, and responsibilities. Two different perspectives on the role of the police—the social contract perspective and the radical perspective—were examined. There are challenges of doing police work in a democratic society that centre on protecting the community while ensuring the rights of citizens. A number of influences on the role and activities of the police were discussed. Among them are the community, diversity, the nature and levels of crime, legislation, and court decisions. Key concepts in the study of police work were identified, including the transparency and accountability of the police, the cost-benefits of policing, police legitimacy, the changing boundaries of policing, and the increasing visibility of police work.

KEY POINTS REVIEW

1. There is often a disconnect between the image and reality of policing.
2. Policing can be defined as the "activities of any individual or organization acting legally on behalf of public or private organizations or persons to maintain security or social order."
3. Canadian police operate within a legislative framework that includes the Charter of Rights and Freedoms, the Constitution Act, the Criminal Code, various police acts, and other legislation.
4. There are two major perspectives on the role of the police, one of which views the police as a politically neutral force and the other that views the police as an instrument of government and powerful interests.

5. There are natural tensions between the power and authority of the police and their legal mandate to maintain order, and the values and processes that exist in a democratic society.
6. The police play a unique role in the criminal justice system, one that has expanded in recent years.
7. The use of authority and the authority to use force are two defining components of the police role.
8. There are a variety of influences on the role and activities of the police.
9. There are several key concepts that are important in the study of police work, including the transparency and accountability of the police, the cost-benefits of policing, police legitimacy, the changing boundaries of the police, and the increasing visibility of the police.

KEY TERM QUESTIONS

1. What is the definition of **policing**?
2. Why are the **Canadian Charter of Rights and Freedoms**, the **Constitution Act**, and the **Criminal Code** important in any discussion of Canadian police work?
3. What is the **RCMP Act**?
4. Compare and contrast the **social contract perspective** on the role of the police with the **radical perspective** on the role of the police.
5. What is meant by the term **political policing** and how is this related to the study of police work?
6. What is the **dark figure of crime** and what factors contribute to it?
7. Define and discuss the notion of **police legitimacy**.

CRITICAL THINKING EXERCISES

Exercise 1.1. The Police: Public Images and Realities

Consider the views of the police that you had while growing up and in what way, if any, these views have changed over time. More specifically, consider the following:

1. What is the role of the media in projecting positive, or negative, images of the police?
2. How have your personal experiences with the police influenced your view of the police?
3. In your view, what are the positive, and negative, features of having the RCMP as a national symbol?

Exercise 1.2. Enemies of the State?

Watch the episode "Enemies of the State," presented on CBC's *Fifth Estate*. Then discuss the role of the police and the challenges of maintaining a balance between maintaining public safety and security and adhering to the rule of law and ensuring citizen rights. Are there any portions of the film that you found disturbing? What policies and procedures could be put in place to ensure that citizen rights are protected?

Exercise 1.3. The Police and Protests in Montreal

Following is a description of an event in Montreal where municipal workers, including firefighters, were protesting changes to their pension fund. In this instance, the police did not intervene.

> Dozens of Montreal firefighters and municipal employees protesting pension reforms stormed city hall Monday night, pushing past security guards trying to hold the doors closed and marauding through the city's ornate seat of power.
>
> They tossed papers throughout the building and in council chambers five minutes before city council was scheduled to begin its evening session. They threw water at city councillors who refused to leave, blew horns and whistles, and hoisted a banner in council inscribed "Coderre Voleur."
>
> Several protesters ran upstairs, trying to find Mayor Denis Coderre as security guards shuttled him from room to room to evade their pursuers. Witnesses reported protesters banged on doors trying to get in and tried to force the heavy wooden doors open. On-duty police officers, wearing their current uniform of red baseball caps and camouflage pants to show their displeasure with the Liberal government's pension reforms, stood by outside. City councillor Marc-André Gadoury said protesters threw water on him and that one punched him in the side. Witnesses said police officers were among the protesters.[33]*

Following the protest, six firefighters were fired and 57 other staff members, including 46 firefighters, were suspended for periods of time between one week and six months for their role in the melee. The head of the firefighters union was suspended, without pay, for six months.[34] No police officers were reprimanded.

Your Thoughts?

1. Do you think that police leaders and/or officers should be sanctioned when a) they do not enforce a court order, and b) they stand by while persons commit illegal activities?
2. Would these events support the social contract perspective or the radical perspective on the role of the police?
3. Read Police Perspective 1.1 earlier in this chapter. Do you agree with this police leader's perspective on policing protests?

CLASS/GROUP DISCUSSIONS

Discussion 1.1. The Priorities of the Police

It's often said that the police "cannot be all things to all people." The limited resource capacities of the police require that they prioritize their activities.

*From R. Bruemmer and K. Laframboise, 2014. "Dozens of Montreal firefighters storm city hall, throw water at councilors to protest pension reforms," Postmedia News, August 19, http://news.nationalpost.com/2014/08/19/dozens-of-montreal-firefighters-storm-city-hall-throw-water-at-city-councillors-to-protest-pension-reforms/). Material reprinted with the express permission of Postmedia News, a division of Postmedia Network Inc.

A question is, "How are police priorities to be determined?" Consider the following for class/group discussion:

Rank the following activities of the police on a scale of 0 to 10, with 0 being not important at all and 10 being extremely important. You may assign the same numerical value to multiple activities.

___ Reduce property crime

___ Reduce violence against seniors

___ Reduce violence against sex trade workers

___ Reduce domestic violence

___ Reduce violence against children

___ Reduce violence caused by gangs

___ Reduce violence caused by guns

___ Improve traffic safety by targeting speeders

___ Improve traffic safety by targeting impaired drivers

___ Improve traffic safety by increasing police presence on the street

___ Reduce street disorder

___ Arrest more violent criminals

___ Arrest more drug dealers

___ Generate more criminal charges

___ Solve more violent crimes

___ Solve more property crimes

___ Address the needs of at-risk youth

___ Develop collaborative partnerships with other agencies and with community groups and organizations

___ Respond faster to emergencies

___ Respond faster to calls for service that are not emergencies

___ Spend more time on each call for service

___ Ensure that victims of crime have adequate assistance

___ Investigate criminal incidents in a timely manner

___ More visible vehicle patrols

___ More visible foot patrols

Your Thoughts?

1. What is your rationale for the rankings you have assigned to each of the activities?
2. What do your rankings indicate about how you view the role of the police in Canadian society?
3. In your view, who should decide what the priorities of a police service should be? The police? Politicians? Community residents? All of the above working together?
4. What would be the best way to determine the priorities of the community?

MEDIA LINKS

Visit www.nelson.com/canadianpolicework4 for links to these videos and other additional content available with this text.

Into the Fire (Canada Is a Police State), Press for Truth, August 5, 2012, youtube.com

"Police State Canada: From the McDonald Commission to the G20," James Corbett, November 30, 2011, corbettreport.com

2 The Origins and Evolution of Police Work

LEARNING OBJECTIVES

After reading this chapter, you should be able to:

- Discuss the origins, structure, and evolution of policing in England
- Discuss the controversy that surrounded the creation of the first police force in England
- Identify the policing principles of Sir Robert Peel
- Describe the evolution of police work in Canada
- Identify the roles of the early municipal and provincial police and the RCMP
- Discuss the contrast between the image and the reality of the RCMP in its evolution
- Describe the role of the police in policing morality and in conducting surveillance on Canadians
- Discuss the role of the RCMP in the remote North
- Describe the attributes of Canadian policing in the early 21st century
- Discuss what is meant by the militarization of the police and its implications for policing

The development of policing in Canada was strongly influenced by the system of policing that emerged in England in the early 1800s. Canadian policing, however, has a unique history and has evolved so that its structure today is quite distinct from its counterparts in England and the United States.

THE ORIGINS OF POLICING

Full-time police forces, operating under the state's authority and enforcing sets of codified laws, are a relatively recent phenomenon. Prior to the emergence of centralized states with codified laws, order within and among groups was maintained through systems of self-policing. Personal, group, or tribal retaliation was applied against those whose behaviour contravened established folkways and customs. In these rural, agrarian societies, which were primarily concerned with day-to-day survival, there were no individuals or organizations charged with the task of enforcing law.

As societies increased in complexity, however, the effectiveness of these self-policing arrangements diminished. Systems of codified laws were enacted—the Hammurabi Code in 1200 BCE and similar codes of law during the Shang (1500 BCE) and Chou (1000 BCE) Dynasties. These codes of law, enforced by military authority, outlined prescribed rules of conduct as well as penalties for non-compliance. The enactment of these codes of law signalled a shift in the enforcement of conduct from the individual and group level to that of a centralized authority.

Centuries later, in the Greek city-states and in the Roman Empire, similar developments occurred. In Greece there emerged a system of self-policing called "kin police." Roman law was codified in the Law of the Twelve Tables (450 BCE), and officials were assigned the task of enforcing laws. At the height of the Roman Empire, there were distinct police forces. In both Greece and the Roman Empire, it was the military who were charged with policing; later on, the Romans were the first to utilize a non-military unit, the *vigiles*, whose task it was to fight fires and to help maintain order. The *vigiles* in the Roman Empire and the kin police in the Greek city-states were early examples of policing, but it was in England that policing was to evolve into an institution. Developments there would have a profound influence on Canadian policing.

The Development of Policing in England

Before the Industrial Revolution and the development of capitalism, England was a feudal village society. Policing was a community responsibility (hold this thought until we return to a discussion of policing in the early 21st century). Order was maintained under the principle of **hue and cry**, according to which every able-bodied man was responsible for assisting in the pursuit and apprehension of law violators. Failure to respond to the hue and cry could result in punishment of the derelict citizen, often equal to that imposed on the lawbreaker.

hue and cry
in early England, the requirement that able-bodied men assist the police

Law enforcement in England can be traced back to the reign of Alfred the Great (872–901). Lacking a standing army to maintain order, and lacking the funds to create a force specifically for peacekeeping, Alfred instituted the **frankpledge system**. This system was based on the principle that every individual was

frankpledge system
an early system of maintaining order in early England

responsible to his neighbours. Under the frankpledge system, every free man between fifteen and sixty was required to enroll in a grouping of ten families, called a tything. In each tything, a tythingman was responsible for keeping order. The other members were required to report crimes to the tythingman and to respond to his hue and cry (most often, "Halt! Who goes there?"). The forerunner of the English police officer, then, was the tythingman.

The tythingman was an elected community spokesman and was responsible for all aspects of local government within his community.[1] He also had the authority to collect fines from those charged with breaching the peace, as well as to demand surety or bail. Each adult male in the community was required to accept a turn as tythingman.

As villages grew, tythings were formed into "hundreds" (groups of ten tyths), each headed by a "hundredman." Constables, generally considered to be the first real police officers, were appointed by local noblemen and placed in charge of the equipment and weapons of the hundred. Hundreds were combined to form shires (parishes or counties), which were administered by officials known as shire-reeves (sheriffs). These were appointed by the king to represent his interests and to uphold the Crown's authority. The shire-reeve was invested with considerable military, civil, and judicial powers and made periodic visits to each hundred to ensure that the system of local policing was operating properly.

		Shire-Reeve	
	Hundredman	Hundredman	
Tythingman	Tythingman	Tythingman	Tythingman

This localized system of crime control was based on the concept that all individuals were responsible for one another.

The frankpledge system invested the tythingmen and hundredmen with a certain amount of authority to maintain community order. Another important attribute of this system was that it was organized "from the ground up." The tythingmen and hundredmen were locally chosen, were responsible to the community, and could be removed for dereliction of duty. This system was in sharp contrast to the policing arrangements that existed in continental Europe, where the police were directly attached to centralized autocracies.

After the Normans invaded England in 1066, the frankpledge system was continued by William the Conqueror. Around this time, though, there was movement away from community responsibility for maintaining peace (as established by the tything system) toward a concept of "state" responsibility. To help implement Norman policing, the shire-reeves were invested with considerable powers, which were often used to collect unjust and oppressive fines and taxes from the community. Military officers were made responsible for maintaining order in specific districts.

By 1252, during the reign of Henry III, the title of constable was being given to the local law enforcement officers previously known as tythingmen, and a "watch and ward" system had been introduced in communities to maintain order. The watch-and-ward system provided for two watchmen to supplement the duties of the constable: "A watch of up to sixteen men . . . was to be stationed at every gate of a walled town between sunset and sunrise, and the watchmen were given the power to arrest strangers during the hours of darkness."[2] All able-bodied men in the town were required to serve a term on watch, which reinforced their responsibility to participate in policing.

By the time the Metropolitan Police Act was passed in 1829, two important statutes had been enacted. The **Statute of Winchester**, passed in 1285, made policing a community responsibility. It called for the formation of village night watches, which were to support the local constables in their duties and to arrest those who were disruptive or who violated the law.

Statute of Winchester
a statute that made policing a community responsibility

This statute assigned to the hundred responsibility for all offences committed within it, revived the hue and cry, and reinforced the watch-and-ward system. In 1361, the **Justice of the Peace Act** centralized peacekeeping duties under justices of the peace, who were appointed directly by the king and who enjoyed stronger authority and greater powers than the constables. The justice of the peace replaced the shire-reeve as peace officer and also acted in a judicial capacity. For the first time, then, the police had been subordinated to the judiciary. This arrangement resulted in considerable injustice and corruption.

Justice of the Peace Act
centralized peacekeeping duties under justices of the peace

By the 1500s, the system of community-based policing was beginning to deteriorate, mainly because of the growth of cities such as London, the increased mobility of the population, and the beginnings of the shift from an agricultural economy to one based on industry. As communities were transformed by these events, individuals avoided serving as constables, paying others to assume their duties. This had disastrous consequences, as it was often only the unemployed and the uneducated who were willing to take on the constable's duties. The old system of community-based policing was thereby undermined.

As a consequence of the profound changes taking place in English society, the increasing corruption of the justices of the peace, and the reluctance of townspeople to serve as constables, by the 1800s many towns and cities, including London, were virtually unpoliced. Justices of the peace had corrupted the system of criminal justice, and it was obvious that the tything system, the hue and cry, and the office of constable were failing to manage the changes occurring in English society. Merchants and industrialists increasingly feared the "dangerous classes" and the threat they posed to law and order. Businessmen began to employ private police to protect their establishments and to help maintain order. It is against this backdrop—the deterioration of community-based policing, and the widening gap between the propertied classes and the landless peasantry—that modern policing as we know it developed.

The Emergence of Modern Policing

England's first organized body of police was established in the mid-1700s by Henry Fielding, a justice of the peace who was also a novelist and playwright. To enforce the decisions of his court and to address the growing problem of disorder, Fielding created the Bow Street Runners, named after the street on which his court was located. These constables, who were adequately paid so that they would not take bribes, were equipped with a baton, handcuffs, and uniforms. Although Fielding had recruited men of high calibre and paid them well, the force's efforts were not enough to stem the rising tide of social disorder and chaos generated by the emerging Industrial Revolution.

During the late 1700s and early 1800s, London faced a series of riots, many of which were started by labourers protesting rising prices and the displacement of workers by increased mechanization. Yet there continued to be strong resistance to the idea of forming an organized, twenty-four-hour police force. In 1822, the Home Secretary, **Sir Robert Peel**, set out to establish a full-time police force. His initial attempts to create a metropolitan police force were repeatedly voted down.

Sir Robert Peel
founded the first organized police service

Between 1822 and 1828, no fewer than seventeen parliamentary subcommittees studied the need to reform the system of law enforcement. One committee report stated: "In a free society, there should only be rational and humane laws, making a police force unnecessary."[3]

For all the widespread opposition to the formation of a police force, by the late 1820s—at least among the propertied classes—the fear of crime and disorder had overshadowed the potential threat to liberty inherent in an organized police unit. In 1829 the **Metropolitan Police Act** was enacted, establishing a full-time, unarmed police force of one thousand men in London.

Metropolitan Police Act
established a full-time, unarmed police force in London

Among the largely skeptical public, Peel's new officers were known derisively as "Bobbies" or "Peelers."

The public and many politicians were concerned about the power that would be vested in a formal police force, and when Peel finally won acceptance of his police plan for London, he was denounced as a potential dictator. "Reform! . . . No Peel! No new police! . . . No Standing Armies!" So chanted the crowds in 1830 as Londoners expressed their opposition to the new Metropolitan Police Force.[4] When it came time to vote on a budget for Peel's new police force in the House of Lords, one member stated: "What I really don't want to see is an efficient police, for an efficient police is a power—a power which we should not have outside the Crown itself."[5] Similar concerns were expressed in opposition to the expansion of the RCMP in Canada in the early 1900s.

Peel attempted to legitimize the new police force by arguing that the police would serve the interests of all citizens, the police would include the prevention of crime as part of their mandate, and the force's officers would be recruited from the working class. In a determined effort to create a professional police force and to reduce public suspicion and distrust of the police, he established high standards of recruitment and training and selected constables from the community. He also introduced the concept of community police stations. In contrast to the local watchmen who preceded them, the new police were to be proactive rather than reactive and were to engage in crime prevention activities. As well, the "new" police wore uniforms, and these were blue, in contrast to the red worn by the military.[6] This can be viewed as the first attempt at community policing by an organized police service.

An 1829 illustration depicting the Peelers

In addition, Peel formulated several principles for law enforcement, which even today are viewed as the basis for community policing. These principles were captured by Charles Reith in *A New Study of Police History* (see Box 2.1).[7] These principles will provide the basis for much of the discussion throughout the rest of this book.

Peel's police force was generally successful in reducing the amount of crime in London. In 1865, Parliament passed an act that required all towns in England to establish their own police forces. As these forces were established throughout the country, justices of the peace gave up their law enforcement duties and focused their efforts solely on judicial activities.

Policing in England, then, was based on community control. In contrast, European police forces tended to be centralized, nationalized, and militarized. As the Canadian police scholar Chris Murphy has written: "The public police model created in England rejected secretive and authoritarian continental policing, developing instead a police model compatible with past community policing practices and growing democratic values."[8]

Early Private Police

Private security services are hardly a modern invention. In fact, they played a major role in policing communities in these early days. Some even predated the London Metropolitan Police. For example, the Bow Street Runners were supported in part by private contracts, and one Patrick Colquhoun formed the

Box 2.1

The Principles of Sir Robert Peel

1. The basic mission of the police is to prevent crime and disorder.
2. The ability of the police to perform their duties depends upon public approval of their actions.
3. Police must secure the cooperation of the public in voluntary observance of the law in order to secure and maintain the respect of the public.
4. The degree of public cooperation with police diminishes proportionately to the necessity of the use of physical force.
5. Police maintain public favour by constantly demonstrating absolute impartial service, not by catering to public opinion.
6. Police should use physical force only to the extent necessary to ensure compliance with the law or to restore order only after persuasion, advice and warnings are insufficient.
7. Police should maintain a relationship with the public that is based on the fact that the police are the public and the public are the police.
8. Police should direct their actions toward their functions and not appear to usurp the powers of the judiciary.
9. The test of police efficiency is the absence of crime and disorder.

Source: New Westminster Police Department, "Sir Robert Peel's Nine Principles," http://www.nwpolice.org/inside-new-westminster-police-department/history/.

Thames River Police, the main costs of which were borne by merchants. Because of its success, this private police force was later converted into a public police force. See Critical Thinking Exercise 2.1 at the end of this chapter.

THE EVOLUTION OF POLICE WORK IN CANADA

Early Municipal Police

A number of important events have shaped Canadian policing. In many respects, the emergence of Canadian policing during the 19th century closely mirrored the development of systems of punishment and corrections.

In the earliest days, law enforcement in communities was carried out informally by community residents. In Halifax, for example, tavern owners were charged with maintaining order. Later, Halifax and other eastern port cities such as St. John's relied on militias and the navy, while the emptier regions of the country remained largely unpoliced. These arrangements were ultimately insufficient to meet the problems of an increasingly urbanized and industrialized society.

Newfoundland's history highlights the types of problems with law and order that existed in early settlements, as well as the solutions applied to them. In St. John's in the 1600s, criminal bands were committing crimes with impunity. Complaints by fishermen resulted in the first Court of Justice in North America, at Trinity Bay. It was headed by Captain Richard Whitbourne under the authority of the English High Court of Admiralty. This early attempt to maintain order and combat crime was a failure, so in 1634, the English authorities appointed "fishing admirals," captains of fishing vessels who were empowered to settle disputes.

This effort also largely failed. These admirals were untrained and were often as disorderly as those they sought to control: "Being untrained men, they were ill-fitted to carry out the functions of the law properly, and they abused their power by a particularly corrupt administration of the laws. In their judicial character, they would decide cases, according to their caprice, over a bottle of rum; and frequently would inflict summary punishment by flogging the culprit with a rope's end."[9]

So in 1792, a royal proclamation was issued that authorized the governor of Newfoundland to appoint justices of the peace and constables, although no regulations governing their supervision were set down until many years later.

Early police work in Canada was characterized by a considerable degree of diversity. Before Confederation in 1867, each region of the country had its own policing arrangements, which reflected the size of settlements, the characteristics of the population, and the specific needs of communities. In areas settled by the French, for example, major town centres were policed under the traditional French system of militia captains. In Upper Canada, in contrast, the British influence was clear; there, a system developed based on the common law and carried out by sheriffs, high constables, constables, and justices of the peace.

The first police constables were appointed in Quebec City around 1651;[10] in Upper Canada (now Ontario), they appeared in the early 1800s. A policing system was also introduced in Montreal in the mid-1600s, though its main purpose was to protect the settlement from attacks by the Iroquois. It is likely that the first constables in Quebec City served mainly as night watchmen.

It was not until justices of the peace were appointed in 1673 that these constables assumed law enforcement responsibilities.

The conquest of New France by the British in 1759 radically altered the French-influenced system of policing that had been developing in Lower Canada. In 1787, an ordinance was passed that authorized justices of the peace in Montreal and Quebec to appoint individuals to help carry out court orders and to maintain order. This legislation introduced the position of constable, and thus served as a model for policing throughout the province.

In Upper Canada, the British settlers implemented a legal system similar to that of England. In 1792, the English common law was made the law of Upper Canada, and in 1793, the Parish and Town Officers Act was passed by the local assembly. This act provided for the appointment of high constables for each district; these men in turn were to appoint citizens to serve as unpaid constables in each parish and township in that district. In 1858, legislation was passed in Upper Canada that authorized towns and cities to create boards of commissioners to oversee police forces.

The 1858 legislation was intended to expand the system of policing throughout Upper Canada. However, community officials and residents did not regard crime as a serious problem; nor did they view as a high priority the development of crime control structures such as police forces and jails.

In 1845, a bylaw in the newly incorporated town of St. Catharines provided for "poundkeepers and constables," citizen volunteers who would provide assistance when required. The activities of this "police force" were supervised by a police board, which also served as the town council. The volunteers were paid according to a fee schedule—for example, five shillings for issuing a summons, making an arrest under a warrant, or assisting in an arrest. Escorting a prisoner to jail paid fifteen shillings. The town hired its first full-time police officers in 1856.

When municipalities did appoint police constables, they generally had other duties as well. In Sudbury, Ontario, for example, the first constable was also the jailer, as well as a tax collector, sanitary inspector, truant officer, fire department engineer, bailiff, chimney inspector, and animal pound caretaker.[11] In 1826, Kingston appointed its first paid constable, one Henry Wilkinson, who also held the position of street surveyor.

The early municipal police forces generally had a three-part mandate: (1) to police conflicts between ethnic groups, and between labourers and their employers; (2) to maintain moral standards by enforcing laws against drunkenness, prostitution, and gambling; and (3) to apprehend criminals.[12] Records from the time indicate that the five-man Kingston police force (created in 1841) spent most of its time dealing with the drunken and the disorderly.

One George Weiss of Halifax has the dubious distinction of receiving Canada's first traffic violation ticket (great trivia question!). In 1793, he was issued a citation for "disorderly riding in the streets" and offered the option of paying a fine of ten shillings, serving four days on a highway work crew, or receiving ten stripes at the local house of correction.[13]

Townspeople were often reluctant to serve as constables. While many of the charters establishing towns required that policing systems be created, these communities were often reluctant to do so unless confronted with serious disorder.

Precisely for this reason, early attempts to establish a formal system of justice, including police, met with failure in Upper Canada and Quebec.[14] This illustrates one of the key factors in the emergence of formal policing: a general hesitancy in both England and early Canada to create police forces that had authority and power over the populace. Furthermore, when such forces were created, a great deal of criticism was often directed toward them. Similar concerns were to be expressed about the expansion of the then North-West Mounted Police (NWMP) into provincial and municipal policing.

During the early 1800s, though, concerns about crime and the "criminal classes" were growing. Whether this shift in attitude was due to an actual increase in the amount and seriousness of crime or merely a function of townspeople's perceptions that crime was increasing has been the subject of considerable scholarly debate. What *is* clear is that governments took a much more proactive approach to creating systems for controlling crime—including police forces.

Again, Newfoundland provides a good illustration of the changes occurring around this time. In the early 1800s, the police force in St. John's consisted of tavern keepers, who performed policing duties in return for their business licences. In 1848, the first night-watch system was established in the city, consisting of sixteen special constables and four constables under the supervision of a high constable. These officers were the predecessors of the Royal Newfoundland Constabulary, formed in 1872.

Similar developments were taking place in Upper Canada. By 1835, as noted earlier, Toronto had a full-time police force of six men to replace the night-watch system. Given the vast distances and sparse populations, municipal police forces developed much later in the western parts of Canada. This country's first territorial police force was established in 1858 in what is now British Columbia.

The Functions and Effectiveness of Early Municipal Police

The historical record indicates that early municipal police forces were heavily influenced by politics and patronage. Following its incorporation in 1834, for example, the power to hire police officers in Toronto was held by the city council and individual aldermen could appoint police constables for their ward. As one historian has noted, "There were no standards of recruitment and no training, and even though uniforms were first issued in 1837, it was stated at the time by one observer that the Toronto police was 'without uniformity, except in one respect—they were uniformly slovenly.'"[15] The Canadian historian, John Weaver, describes an all-too-common feature of the Hamilton (Ont.) police department of the day:

> Constable Coulter began inauspiciously. Hired in March 1878, he was fined 10 days pay that November for being found in house of ill fame. After being released from beat duty at midnight, constables Coulter, Sutherland, and Moore paid a visit to Jennie Kennedy's whorehouse and dallied for an hour. A little over a year later, Coulter fell asleep while on duty. In 1882 he paid a fine for disobedience. But he must have had an ability and straightened up, for the commission awarded him a good

> conduct badge in 1891, appointed him detective in 1895, and in 1911 made him inspector of the detective division.[16*]

In Toronto, there were no fewer than twenty-six riots between 1839 and 1860, most all of them due to conflicts between rival political factions. The police were often used by politicians as a private army to counter the efforts of opposition groups.[17] During the time period from 1870 to 1920, the Toronto Police concentrated their efforts on controlling the "dangerous classes"—lower-class working persons:

> Control of all aspects of working class people's lives was the goal set before the police . . . the force strove to curb the more unruly aspects of popular culture, prohibiting bonfires, restraining weekend revels, banning firecrackers, and curbing the activities of 'mischievous urchins' who sought to soil the crinoline dresses of ladies on national holidays. Arresting drunks and prosecuting prostitutes became a major focus of Toronto Police activity.[18**]

This focus of the Toronto police on issues related more to morals suggests that the crime-fighting role of the police was to develop much later.

In early Canada, when police officers were hired, a high premium was placed on physical attributes. The following describes the approach taken by municipal authorities in Hamilton, Ontario, in 1881:

> Applicants lined up and Judge Sinclair asked them to take off their coats. This being done, Sinclair felt "their thighs and sinews," poking them with a finger "in the manner practiced by the gentry from the rural districts when examining a prize bull." Next, the men had to walk about, turning left and right while the commissioners commented on the good and bad points about their backs and shoulders. To measure stamina, five were singled out and asked to jog around council chambers. . . . The commissioners preferred married men, claiming that they were "steadier." Married men were also less likely than single men to leave town in search of better work.[19***]

This passage suggests that, in selecting police constables, a premium was placed on physique, with little thought to providing new recruits with training in conflict resolution (see Chapter 5 for a discussion of modern-day training and recruitment, which is vastly different). The pay scale for Toronto police officers in 1886 ranged from $1.35 per day for a 3rd-class constable, to $1.90 for a 1st-class constable, up to $2.90 per day for an inspector.

When municipalities did appoint police constables, it was not unusual for those men to carry out a variety of duties besides law enforcement. Constables

---

*J.C. Weaver, *Crimes, Constables, and Courts.* (Montreal and Kingston: McGill–Queen's University Press, 1995), 101.

**P. Vronsky, "History of the Toronto Police, 1870–1920, Part 4: 'Constables as Urban Missionaries,'" (2003–4), 2.

***J.C. Weaver, *Crimes, Constables, and Courts* (Montreal and Kingston: McGill–Queen's University Press, 1995), 89.

in Calgary were responsible for inspecting buildings, roads, and fresh fruits, vegetables, and meat, as well as issuing licences and maintaining the animal pound. The first constable appointed in Regina, in 1892, was also required to serve as dogcatcher, sanitation inspector, and firefighter.[20] Today, only police officers posted to remote northern communities continue to provide a wide variety of services in addition to policing.

The first woman joined the Toronto Police Department in 1888 and fulfilled the role of matron to supervise women and children who were brought to the police station. The Vancouver Police Department hired Canada's first two women police constables on July 8, 1912. They acted as matrons in the jail, escorted women prisoners, and made regular patrols of pool halls, cabarets, dances, and other places where young people congregated.[21]

The first female police constables were hired in Winnipeg in 1916. Historical documents from Winnipeg indicate that the women were "issued a badge, a whistle, a call box key and the Book of Rules and Regulations." Their duties centred on assisting the morality squad, dealing with children, and assisting in cases where women were in distress. The women constables rarely left the police station and were always accompanied by a male officer when they did. Women officers were paid less than their male counterparts until the mid-1960s; it was not until 1987 that a woman officer was promoted to the position of sergeant.[22] The RCMP did not swear in its first women officers until 1974, the same year that women joined the uniformed ranks in the OPP. It has been argued that the first women RCMP officers were viewed in highly gendered terms and that their presence challenged the historical and cultural depictions of masculinity and manliness.[23] The challenges that continue to face women RCMP officers, discussed in Chapter 5, suggest that more change is required to the organizational culture of the RCMP.

Vancouver Police Museum Archives P03214

Vancouver policewomen, circa 1940s

Early municipal police forces were not very effective in maintaining high moral standards or catching criminals. Many departments were notoriously corrupt: "While police forces did have chiefs and men who were honest and bent on doing a good job, many were only interested in getting a share of the wealth that was floating around. Corruption became accepted as a more or less integral part of police work."[24] Police chiefs and police officers took bribes to look the other way, and as a consequence, prostitution, gambling, and crime flourished in cities such as Montreal.

These police forces were reluctant to involve themselves in labour strikes either by helping managers force employees back to work or by protecting strikebreakers who were crossing picket lines. In later years, the close ties between municipal police forces and their communities would lead the federal government to suspect that local police could not be trusted to maintain order, especially in situations involving strikes and political demonstrations. For this reason, it often sent in the RCMP as a federal police force, often with disastrous consequences. (This partly explains the long-standing transfer policy of the RCMP, under which officers are regularly moved from one posting to the next.)

It was the North-West Mounted Police (NWMP)—predecessors of the modern-day RCMP—who most often responded to the labour strikes in the early 1900s: strikes by coal miners in Nova Scotia and British Columbia, by textile workers in Quebec, by the building trades in Vancouver, and by railway workers in Winnipeg, Manitoba, and Brockville, Ontario.

See the websites of individual police services for highlights of their history. For example, for Halifax, go to http://www.halifax.ca/police/AboutHRP/history.php; for the Ontario Provincial Police, see http://www.opp.ca/museum/en/collection/historicalhighlights.php; and for the Toronto Police Service, open http://www.russianbooks.org/crime/cph3.htm and http://www.russianbooks.org/crime/cph6.htm.

The Role of the Police in the Canadian West

Police forces did not emerge in western Canada until the mid to late 1800s. In 1858, the first organized police force was created in what is now the province of British Columbia. Modelled on the Royal Irish Constabulary, it was established as a response to the increasing violence and disorder that followed the discovery of gold in the region. This force was the predecessor of the British Columbia Provincial Police (BCPP), which was formed in 1871 when the province joined Confederation. British authorities worried that the United States had territorial ambitions in the area. BCPP officers carried out policing duties, collected revenues and excise taxes, and provided emergency services in communities. Calgary hired its first constable in 1885; Lethbridge appointed its first in 1891. In the absence of police forces, most communities in Western Canada policed themselves. Aboriginal peoples, of course, already had systems of social control, as well as mechanisms for sanctioning violations of customary law. These systems were gradually displaced by British law.[25] As settlements grew, they appointed constables, who were paid a small sum for carrying out peacekeeping duties and for controlling disorder, which largely involved drinking, prostitution, and gambling.

A unique feature of policing in the Canadian West was the role played by agents of the Hudson's Bay Company (HBC). As late as 1861, the presiding judicial officer of the HBC served as coroner, jailer, sheriff, and chief medical officer. There is little doubt that it was in the best interests of the HBC to maintain peace and order in the west so as to ensure that there were no disruptions to trade and commerce.[26]

The absence of serious crime was another reason for the late development of policing systems in the west. Except for the disorder surrounding fortune seekers and the whisky traders, the west was less violent in Canada than in the United States. The landscape of the American West was littered with the victims of battles between Native people and the U.S. Cavalry, and the streets of frontier towns were often the scene of "high noon" shootouts. The Canadian West was subdued with considerably less bloodshed, although the outcome of this conflict was the same (the destruction of Aboriginal culture and communities).

However, as discussed below, there were a number of similarities between the NWMP officers who policed the Canadian West and the U.S. cavalrymen south of the border.

Early Provincial Police

The emergence of provincial police forces after Confederation was closely linked to the establishment and growth of the federal police force, now known as the RCMP. Under the Constitution Act, 1867, the federal government had the authority to enact criminal law and procedures, while the enforcement of laws and the administration of justice were delegated to the provinces. This meant that provincial governments needed to establish law enforcement agencies, courts, and correctional institutions.

Although the Constitution Act clearly gave the provinces the authority to enforce criminal law, in 1868, the federal Parliament passed the Police Act of Canada, which authorized the federal government to establish the Dominion Police Force, with Canada-wide jurisdiction. This force's primary mandate was to protect federal buildings, including Parliament, although it later became involved in enforcing counterfeiting laws and providing security for naval shipyards and other government properties. The Dominion Police Force was absorbed by the RCMP in 1920; the point is, this was the first time a police authority had been created with jurisdiction beyond the municipal level—a precedent that was to provide the basis for today's RCMP.

The Constitution Act provided that, on entry into Confederation, each province would enact legislation to create a provincial police force. Legislation was enacted to this effect in Manitoba and Quebec (1870), British Columbia (1871), Ontario (1909), New Brunswick (1927), Nova Scotia (1928), and Prince Edward Island (1930). In Newfoundland, which did not join Confederation until 1949, the Royal Newfoundland Constabulary had been operating since 1872. A second police force, the Newfoundland Company of Rangers, was formed in 1935.

All of the regions that eventually joined Confederation had police forces. However, the provincial police forces in Alberta, Saskatchewan, and Manitoba experienced a number of difficulties, including poor leadership and a lack of qualified officers. The Saskatchewan Provincial Police (SPP) was beset with so many problems that it became a major embarrassment for the provincial authorities. One police historian has noted that, while many SPP recruits were capable and experienced, others were merely "filling the gap . . . Some barely understood the words of their oath, while others would have been stumped to spell some of them."[27]

Alberta and Saskatchewan negotiated agreements with the federal government for the services of the Royal North-West Mounted Police (RNWMP). Under contracts signed between Ottawa and the governments of Alberta and Saskatchewan, the RNWMP would serve as the provincial police force under a cost-sharing agreement. There is no evidence in the historical record to indicate that this action by the two provincial governments was ever challenged, although it represented a significant departure from the intent of the Constitution Act. By the late 1920s, the provincial forces on the Prairies had been replaced by the RCMP.

Between 1917 and 1950, the Mounties assumed provincial policing responsibilities in all provinces except Quebec and Ontario, which continue to operate the only independent provincial police forces in Canada, along with Newfoundland. On October 13, 1909, an Order-in-Council authorized the immediate formation of the Ontario Provincial Police. The intent was to bring the widely dispersed policing services under one administrative umbrella.

Early Federal Policing: The Origins and Expansion of the RCMP

The North-West Mounted Police was founded in 1873 to police the vast area known as Rupert's Land, which Canada had purchased from the HBC in 1869. The NWMP was a military-style police force, modelled on the Royal Irish Constabulary rather than on the urban model of police developed by Sir Robert Peel. The allegiance of the force was to the federal government, Canadian police scholars noting that: "The RCMP was there to police the locals as an extension of the central government and its officers were only accountable to their commanding officers and not to local public or political authority."[28]

In 1904, its name was changed to the Royal North-West Mounted Police; then, in 1920, its name was changed again to the Royal Canadian Mounted Police (RCMP). It was anticipated that as Canada became more urbanized, responsibility for policing would shift to local communities. However, this did not often happen.

The reasons for the founding of the RCMP have long been debated. Some have suggested that the force was established mainly to preserve peace in the Canadian West and to protect Aboriginal people from whisky traders and overaggressive settlers. In fact, the NWMP's efforts to establish relationships of trust with Aboriginal peoples were constantly being undermined by Ottawa, which ignored the commitments it had made in its treaties with Aboriginal peoples. As one historian has observed:

> Canadian dealings with the Indian, with treaties, land surrenders, annuities, agents and land reserves, bore a close resemblance to American methods.... Pressed to reduce public spending, Ottawa officials found logical economics by reducing rations, substituting bacon for beef on the Blackfoot reserves and dismissing junior employees. The era of starvation more than the advent of white settlement cost the N.W.M.P. its former standing with the native people.[29*]

(Andrew Graybill offers an insightful comparative analysis of the role of the RCMP in the Canadian Northwest and the Texas Rangers in the U.S. in the late 19th and early 20th centuries.[30])

A number of Canadian scholars contend that the NWMP played much the same role as the Canadian Pacific Railway—that is, to establish political and economic sovereignty over the farthest reaches of the country. This included settling indigenous lands in an orderly manner (i.e., with white settlers) and guarding against perceived threats of American annexation.

* D. Morton, "Cavalry or Police: Keeping the Peace on Two Adjacent Frontiers, 1870–1900," *Journal of Canadian Studies* 12, no. 1 (1977): 27–37 at 32.

For an insightful look at the then-NWMP in the late 1880s, listen to the CBC Radio interview conducted in 1964 with then-106-year-old William Henry Walden, who joined the force in 1877. See the Media Link "North-West Mounted Police in the Late 1800s" at the end of this chapter. Also, see archival materials that include the diaries of officers in the NWMP in the late 1880s: "James Finlayson's Diary of the March West, 1874" (https://www.collectionscanada.gc.ca/canadian-west/052920/05292023_e.html) and "Fred Bagley of the Northwest Mounted Police, 1874-1946" (http://www.glenbow.org/collections/search/findingAids/archhtm/bagley.cfm).

The RCMP: Image and Reality

While there may be disagreement over the role of the Mounted Police in early Canada, there is little doubt that the RCMP has become the most widely recognized symbol of Canada throughout the world, far outdistancing the beaver, Canada's official symbol. Perhaps no other police force in the world is so closely intertwined with a nation's culture as the Mounties are with Canada.

The exploits and daring of the Mounties were immortalized by Canadian, European, and American authors in the early 20th century in books like *Morgan of the Mounted* (White, 1939), *Tales of the Mounted* (Brockie, 1949), *Yukon Patrol* (Douthwaite, 1936), and *Arctic Patrols* (Campbell, 1936). With the advent of motion pictures, these exploits soon found their way onto the silver screen; more than six hundred films have been made with a Mountie as the hero. The red-serged Mountie was one of Hollywood's favourite images.

Library and Archives Canada, Acc. No. 1995-111-803

A movie poster from the 1950s

The image of the square-jawed, stoic, strong (yet polite) Mountie has been imprinted on Canadians and others around the world. View the film "Scarlet Guardians: RCMP officers in training," produced by the CBC in 1958 and listed in Media Links at the end of this chapter. This close association between the RCMP and Canada's national identity has, historically, helped to mitigate criticisms of the sort that are generally directed toward police forces. In recent years, however, a number of high-profile incidents have served to undermine public trust in the RCMP. These are discussed throughout the text.

It is not generally known that in its early days, the RCMP faced many internal difficulties. The historical record indicates that the Mounties faced high rates of desertion, resignations, and improper conduct, including drunkenness and illicit sexual alliances with women.[31] These difficulties were ascribed to the isolation and harsh conditions on the frontier, inadequate housing and medical attention, and the failure of officers to be paid, often for months at a time. One historian has noted that there were, in fact, a number of similarities between American cavalrymen and their Mounted Police counterparts: "Pay was meager and often in arrears. Traders at military and police posts were equally rapacious. Barracks were often temporary shacks, ill-constructed, frigid in winter and sometimes unsanitary. Arms and equipment were sometimes obsolete and often inappropriate for western conditions. Political interference in both countries pervaded every sphere of administration, from forage contracts to promotions."[32]

There was also considerable hostility directed toward the RCMP by both settlers and federal MPs. Many Canadians disliked the Mounties. In 1920, the federal government's decision to found the RCMP by merging the NWMP with the Dominion Police (Canada's first federal police force) met considerable opposition, especially from Maritime province MPs. For example, Robert H. Butts, representing Cape Breton South, declared: "I have been a magistrate, sometimes I have been called a judge, of a town of between 9,000 and 10,000 people. We never had need of Mounted Police down there and we have no need of them now. . . . Do not send hayseeds from away across the plains to Nova Scotia. . . . I say that it is dangerous to send them here. I speak for 73,000 people in Cape Breton, and I can say that they will not appreciate any such intrusion."[33]

A Nova Scotia MP, J.H. Sinclair, echoed these views: "The Federal Government are assuming a duty that they do not require to assume, that the provinces are not asking them to assume, and that the provinces themselves are well able to take care of."[34] Ottawa's concern over growing labour unrest, subversive activities, and the ineptitude of provincial police forces, however, provided the Mounties with an opportunity to greatly expand their "market share" and, ultimately, to become heavily involved in provincial and municipal policing. MPs failed several times to abolish the RCMP in 1922 and 1923. Needless to say, had the RCMP been phased out, the landscape of Canadian policing would be far different than it is today.

It is also likely that criticism of the Mounties was, at least in part, politically motivated, an outgrowth of the conflicts that often arose between the Mounties and municipal police forces. These conflicts often led to situations where members of different forces arrested each other. To illustrate one community's attitude toward the Mounties, an editorial in the *Regina Leader* charged that "many a scalawag and scoundrel, many an idle loafer, many a brainless young blood, has worn its uniform and fed at its trough."[35]

The RCMP in the Remote North

A unique feature of Canadian police work is that RCMP officers are posted to small Aboriginal and Inuit communities in Yukon, the Northwest Territories, and Nunavut. The role of the police in these regions, both today and in the past, remains largely unexplored by Canadian police scholars. This topic is examined in Chapter 8. An example is provided by the role of the RCMP in the early days of the Yukon Territory, including the years of the gold rush in the Klondike in the late 1800s.

Prior to 1894, with the exception of the occasional surveyor, there were no government or law officials in Yukon. Order was maintained by the miners through a mechanism known as the "miner's meetings": "Criminal cases were swiftly and, in the beginning, fairly dealt with."[36] With the discovery of gold in 1896 and the gold rush in 1897, the pressure from the large trading companies, the concern that the Americans were intending to occupy the area (Alaska had been purchased in 1867), the increasing liquor traffic, and a desire on the part of the federal government to collect "levies" from the miners, all combined to prompt the federal government to send a small force of NWMP officers to Yukon. Subsequently, small detachments were established at points on the Yukon River where gold was being mined, as well as at entry points into the territory. In the words of one historian, the NWMP "became the chief means by which the federal government eventually established its law, its economic and cultural policies, and its welfare system over the North."[37] The police officers spent a considerable portion of their time on civil tasks, including acting as magistrates and justices of the peace, postal service workers, land agents, coroners, and elections officers.[38]

When RCMP officers were first posted to eastern Arctic communities in the 1920s and 1930s (in what is now Nunavut), most Inuit in this region were living on the land, moving camps with the seasons and with the wild game that were their sustenance. RCMP officers sent there carried out little "real" police work; many had no occasion to arrest anyone during their entire tour of duty. Instead, they played a multifaceted role in the communities (e.g., they operated the post office).

Even in later years, most RCMP officers were poorly equipped to live and work in the eastern Arctic and relied heavily on the Inuit for their survival. One member recalled: "There was nothing in the manual about how to use a dog sled. I learned from the [Inuit] Special Constable. He did all the travelling with me."[39] Another member recalled a time when the Inuit Special Constable guided him through a blinding whiteout (snowstorm): "I went along like a puppy dog. He ran the show. And it was the same thing when we got to the camps."[40] RCMP officers were outsiders and were closely scrutinized by the community. Officers spent much of their time visiting the hunting and fishing camps of Inuit who were living on the land.

The RCMP and Political Dissent: The Historical Record

On a number of occasions in the early 1900s, the federal government used the Mounted Police to quell labour unrest and to counter what it perceived as the growing influence of left-wing activists.[41] On some occasions, this was due to the reluctance of municipal police forces to involve themselves in political demonstrations. In 1886, the commissioner of the Mounted Police wrote, in reference to a railway strike the previous year: "I sent a detachment of police to points threatened . . . I instructed the men in charge of the detachment to use the very severest measures to prevent cessation of the work of construction."[42] This involvement continued into the 1900s.

Strike action by workers seeking higher wages and employment were common throughout the Prairie provinces.

In June 1919, the RCMP was brought in to break the Winnipeg General Strike after the Winnipeg city police refused to take action against the strikers.

The strike was part of the labour unrest that arose after the First World War and was fuelled by the massive unemployment and inflation of the Great Depression, as well as by the success of the Russian Revolution in 1917. The strike was called after negotiations broke down between labour and management in the building and metal trades; workers were demanding the right to bargain collectively as well as improved wages and working conditions. The strike spread across the city until nearly thirty thousand workers had left their jobs. Factories closed, the retail trade was severely affected, and public transit came to a halt. Other public sector employees, including police officers, firefighters, and utilities workers, soon joined the strike in support of the workers and coordinated the provision of essential services. Anxious to prevent the spread of labour unrest to other cities, the federal government intervened.

On June 21, in what came to be known as Bloody Saturday, Mounted Police officers charged into a crowd of protesters, injuring thirty and killing one. Federal troops later occupied the city. Faced with the combined forces of the government and the employers, the strikers returned to work on June 25. It would take another three decades for Canadian workers to gain the right to union recognition and collective bargaining.

Another example is the Estevan Riot (also known as the Black Tuesday Riot), which took place on September 29, 1931. Coal miners in the region had been on strike for better wages and working conditions and had come to Estevan (in southwestern Saskatchewan) to hold a parade to bring attention to their cause. The RCMP intervened, blocking the procession; when the violence was over, three miners had been killed and many others had been wounded and arrested.

In 1935, the RCMP were also used by the federal government, over the objections of the attorney general of Saskatchewan, to stop the On-to-Ottawa Trek, which involved over 400 men who jumped aboard boxcars in Vancouver, heading to Ottawa to confront Prime Minister R.B. Bennett about the poor economy and the lack of jobs. The trekkers made it as far as Regina, where the RCMP intervened to stop the eastward journey of the men, attacking the men with tear gas and clubs. The men were then sent back to British Columbia.[43]

Throughout the 20th century, the RCMP carried out extensive surveillance of politicians, university students, and faculty, and maintained confidential files on hundreds of thousands of Canadians. Covert surveillance on university campuses began during the First World War and continued into the late 1990s.[44] The force was especially interested in left-wing student organizations and faculty during the 1960s, and it used student informants as well as undercover police to gather information. "Subversive" groups targeted for surveillance by the RCMP included those involved in the "counterculture," and this included "hippies" who were identified by their long hair, facial hair among the men, non-conformist clothing, and drug use. In a report prepared in 1969, an RCMP undercover officer wrote: "My experience and conclusion of the drug user is that he is slowly destroying [the] society that we have tried to develop and perfect."[45] The reports of the undercover officers during these times were designed to bolster the case against the legalization of marijuana: "In the case of hippies, RCMP officers wanted to undermine their social appeal, particularly by revealing what the police considered the disturbing implications of the cultural changes that hippies wanted to introduce. . . ."[46] Similarly, the historical record indicates that the RCMP conducted surveillance on the Abortion Caravan, sponsored by the Vancouver Women's Caucus. The caravan travelled from Vancouver to Ottawa to protest the restrictive provisions of the law on abortion. The police were concerned with the group's ties to left-wing organizations.[47]

The reports of the McDonald Commission, completed in 1980–81, documented a broad range of illegal activities and deception on the part of the RCMP during and after the October Crisis in Quebec between 1970 and 1972. This included surreptitious entry, the use of electronic surveillance, illegal opening of mail, and the fact that the RCMP was maintaining files on more than 800,000 individual Canadians. The McDonald Commission report resulted in the passage of Bill C-9, which created the Canadian Security Intelligence Service (CSIS). This civilian agency, which is separate from the RCMP, is responsible for all foreign and domestic intelligence and security.

For an animated debate between then-Commissioner of the RCMP William H. Kelly and historian Lorne Brown on CBC Radio in 1973, see the Media Link "RCMP's Reputation Debated" at the end of this chapter. Then consider Class/Group Discussion 2.1 at the end of this chapter.

Following World War II and during the Cold War—in which the West, including Canada, engaged in an ideological battle with the then-Soviet Union (democracy vs. communism)—the RCMP developed a plan for the mass arrest and internment of individuals who were deemed a threat to the Canadian state. The program, called Operation PROFUNC, was established in the early 1950s and continued until the early 1980s. It targeted "enemies of the state." This program was so secret that Cabinet ministers at the time were unaware of its existence. See the Media Link for the documentary film "Enemies of the State" at the end of this chapter. See also Class/Group Discussion 2.2 at the end of this chapter.

POLICING MORALITY

There are many instances in which the police have been used by governments to police morality. During the late 1950s to the late 1990s, for example, Canadian police services were involved in the extensive surveillance, interrogation, and harassment of gays and lesbians.

Another example of the use of the RCMP by the federal government was during the Cold War (the struggle between the democratic West and the communist Soviet Union) during the 1950s and early 1960s. This included the efforts to purge gays and lesbians from the federal government. This was one of the first instances in modern times that the Canadian government used the notion of "national security" to effectively wage war on its own citizens, in this instance gays and lesbians, and where national security reflected an ideological practice (see Box 2.2).[48] There are clear parallels between these events and those in the early 21st century wherein the requirements of "national security" have resulted in increasing surveillance of citizens and their activities.

The historical record also reveals that police services have been used by governments as an instrument to criminalize homosexuality. This is illustrated in the raids conducted by police on gay bathhouses across Canada in 1981 (see Box 2.3).

Box 2.2

Purging Homosexuals: The RCMP, the Professor, and the Fruit Machine

During the Cold War with the Soviet Union, the Canadian federal government was concerned about Soviet spies infiltrating the federal government, and homosexuals were viewed as a national security risk. It was believed that gays and lesbians posed a security risk since they would be susceptible to being blackmailed by spies into giving up government secrets. The RCMP created files on at least 9,000 persons who were suspected of being homosexual.

Persons who were determined to be gay were fired from their government position. In his article, "'Character Weaknesses' and 'Fruit Machines': Towards an Analysis of the Anti-Homosexual Security Campaign in The Canadian Civil Service," Canadian sociologist Gary Kinsman noted that: "The RCMP was an integral part of both the security regime and security investigations . . . The RCMP set up an investigative unit within the force, called A-3, to hunt down and purge homosexuals within its ranks and with the government more generally" (p. 149).

To assist in detecting gays in government, the RCMP and a psychology professor from Carleton University developed a "homosexual detector" (more commonly referred to as "the fruit machine"). The detector involved showing applicants to the civil service images of nude and semi-nude men and women and filming their response. The fruit machine measured the pupils of the eyes, perspiration, and pulse for supposed erotic responses to gay porn. The assumption was that homosexuals' pupils would respond in a certain way to the male images. The machine was developed but never utilized. Follow the Media Link, "RCMP Uses 'Fruit Machine' to Detect Gays," at the end of this chapter.

For an in-depth study of these and other events, see *The Canadian War on Queers: National Security as Sexual Regulation*, by Gary Kinsman and Patrizia Gentile.

Sources: G.W. Kinsman and P. Gentile. 2009. *The Canadian War on Queers: National Security as Sexual Regulation.* Vancouver: UBC Press; and G. Kinsman. 1995. "'Character weaknesses' and 'fruit machines': Towards an analysis of the anti-homosexual security campaign in the Canadian civil service." *Labour/Le Travail, 35*, pp. 133–161.

POLICE WORK IN THE EARLY 21ST CENTURY

Policing in the early 21st century has a number of attributes. There has been the emergence of increasingly sophisticated forms of criminality, including cybercrime, human trafficking, organized gangs, and various terrorist threats and acts.

Expansion of the Police Role

The role of the police has expanded exponentially beyond law enforcement due to a variety of factors, including legislation and policy, downloading of responsibilities by provincial and municipal governments, and the myriad of demands that are made on police services by the community. Concurrently, police services have

Box 2.3

Operation Soap: The Toronto Bathhouse Raids

Prior to the arrest of over 1,000 protestors at the G8 summit in Toronto (see Box 7.8) the bathhouse raids were the largest mass arrests in Canada. Nearly 200 police officers arrested 286 men in four Toronto bathhouses.

Similar arrests took place in other cities across the country. In Edmonton, police raided the Pisces Health Spa in May 1981. The incident was later the basis for a stage play, *Uncovered*. Interestingly, the notes from one of the undercover police officers written at the time revealed that many of the officers in the Morality Control Unit had refused to participate in the raid, which "was ultimately deemed by their superiors to be 'above and beyond the call of duty'" (Gelinas, p. 7). A former undercover officer recalled: "The first time that my partner and I went in, I had no clue what a gay man looked like or acted like. So we went in over-playing the role and quickly realized that the men that we were meeting in the club were no different from us" (cited in Gelinas, p. 8). For an account of these and other incidents involving the gay community and the police, see *The Canadian War on Queers* (by Kinsman and Gentile) and "The Night They Raided the Pisces Club," by Ben Gelinas; also, refer to the Media Links section at the end of this chapter for links to the radio story, "The Toronto bathhouse raids," and the video, "'No more raids!' Toronto bathhouse raid protests - raw tape."

Sources: B. Gelinas. "The night they raided the Pisces Club." *Edmonton Journal.* December 30, 2010; and G.W. Kinsman and P. Gentile. 2009. *The Canadian War on Queers: National Security as Sexual Regulation.* Vancouver: UBC Press.

Courtesy of the Canadian Lesbian & Gay Archives

Protest following the bathhouse raids in Toronto

become proactive in establishing collaborative relationships with agencies and communities to address issues of crime and disorder.

This includes not only law enforcement but also a variety of initiatives with the community policing model that are designed to improve the quality of life in communities and address the needs of vulnerable and at-risk groups. Community policing is discussed in Chapter 8.

The Pluralization of Policing

Beginning in the early 21st century, police work became increasingly "decoupled" from governments and more closely associated with the private sector.[49] This was reflected in the increasing breadth of activities of private security guards, who began to be involved in surveillance, arrests, and the search of individuals found on private premises, including shopping malls.

The increasing costs of policing have contributed to an increasing diversification of approaches to the delivery of services traditionally performed by sworn police officers. These developments are discussed in Chapter 3.

Tiered policing has been touted as an alternative model for the delivery of police services. This involves a variety of personnel, including sworn police officers, sworn officers with limited powers (i.e., special constables, community constables, private security officers, and community groups and volunteers).[50] Tiered policing is discussed in Chapter 3.

tiered policing
a model of police work involving a mix of traditional sworn police officers with new types of police and private security personnel

Private security firms have been growing exponentially and are now providing services once performed solely by provincial and municipal police services. The public police no longer have a monopoly on the provision of police services, and there is growing concern that the line between private and public policing is becoming blurred. Private security guards, for example, are now involved in surveillance, arrests, and the search of individuals found on private premises, including shopping malls.

There has also been the emergence of **collaborative policing** arrangements, which involve public police and private security officers working together in venues such as sporting arenas. The public police are contracted by the company that operates the venue. The result is a network of surveillance comprising public and private police.

collaborative policing
the cooperation between public and private police

Recall from our earlier discussion that private police forces existed even before the first organized police service was founded, in London in the early 1800s.

Police scholars have referred to the new reality as the **pluralization of policing**.[51]

pluralization of policing
the expansion of policing beyond the public police to include para-police and private security

This transformation of policing is, perhaps, as significant as the creation of the first organized police forces in England in the 1800s.

This trend has been fuelled by a number of factors, including increased public concern about security and safety, the rising costs of public policing, and gaps in police service delivery. As well, there has been a growth in the number of private property spaces where people actually live (e.g., condominiums, gated communities, and the like). There is a concern that policing has become increasingly "decoupled" from governments and more closely associated with the private sector and that there has been an increased focus on security.

The line is also being blurred between the powers and duties of private security officers and those of the public police. This confusion is often heightened by the fact that the uniforms of private police may look very similar to those of the public police, especially to a citizen in distress or under suspicion.

Police scholars have identified a number of benefits and concerns associated with public/private police partnerships and collaboration.

Technology and Policing

Three technological innovations in the 20th century radically altered the delivery of policing services: the telephone, the patrol car, and the two-way radio. These led to fundamental changes in how police services were delivered and were the basis for the professional model of police work (discussed in Chapter 8). Policing became reactive; that is, when a citizen telephoned with a complaint, officers in patrol cars were dispatched to the scene by two-way radio. While this allowed officers to cover a large area, officers became more isolated from the communities they served. The patrol car, rather than the neighbourhood beat, became the "office" of the police officer, and this led to the centralization of police command and control.

Other new technologies, such as centralized dispatch systems and computer terminals in patrol cars, further distanced officers from the community. The computer screen, rather than community residents, often became the primary source of information for officers. No longer could "civilians" interact with and communicate their concerns to local police constables. Instead, all calls were to be made to a centralized telephone number. Calls for assistance were prioritized by dispatchers who were far removed from the neighbourhood and unfamiliar with residents and their concerns.[52]

An ongoing question is whether police services have come to rely too heavily on technology to the exclusion of the human dimension of police work. An example is the introduction of mobile data terminals in patrol cars in the 1980s, computers that provide patrol officers with instant access to a variety of data files, including persons and vehicles. The fear is that officers have become so wedded to accessing information from the in-car computer that they no longer spend time out of the patrol car on a proactive basis, becoming familiar with the communities they police and developing alternative sources of information, including informants. In one First Nations community in Ontario, the Ojibwa word used to describe the police translates roughly into "men with no legs," referring to the fact that officers who patrol the reserve rarely left their cars.

Among the high-technology innovations that were introduced during the late 20th century were new weapons, including conducted energy devices (CED) such as the Taser (discussed in Chapter 8), the use of global positioning systems (GPSs) for patrol cars, sophisticated computer programs for crime analysis and criminal intelligence analysis (discussed in Chapter 9), and DNA analysis for crime investigation (discussed in Chapter 10).

The Rise of the Canadian Warrior Cop? Officer Friendly Becomes GI Joe

On August 9, 2014, a young Black man named Michael Brown was shot to death during an encounter with a white police officer, Darren Wilson, in

Ferguson, Missouri, a suburb of St. Louis. The shooting ignited weeks of protests in the community and across the U.S. The response of the Ferguson Police Department (sworn officer strength: 54) to the protests was highly aggressive and involved the conspicuous display of military weaponry. The incident brought to public attention the increasing militarization of U.S. police services and the rise of the "warrior cop." This militarization includes the deployment of snipers in battle fatigues and the use of an armoured personnel carrier.

Previously, a report by the American Civil Liberties Union, titled "War Comes Home: The Excessive Militarization of American Policing," had concluded that American policing had become "unnecessarily and dangerously militarized" primarily due to U.S. federal government programs that provided military war equipment to local police services. This included armoured personnel carriers and equipment for ERT (Emergency Response Team) and SWAT (Special Weapons Assault Team). In many police services, these teams have become para-military units that have increasingly been used for drug enforcement, which often involves executing a search warrant, and other incidents that were traditionally handled in a less forceful manner. There are concerns that these police services, particularly in smaller towns and cities, have not received adequate training in how to safely and appropriately use the high-tech military equipment they receive. This heightens the risk for community residents, persons involved in encounters with the police, and the officers themselves.

The ACLU study found that "the militarization of American policing is evident in the training that police officers receive, which encourages them to adopt a 'warrior' mentality and think of the people they are supposed to serve as enemies, as well as in the equipment they use, such as battering rams, flashbang grenades, and APCs [armoured personnel carriers],"[53] View the documentary films, "Radley Balko on the Militarization of Police" and "Strossel: Radley Balko Debates Ohio Sheriff 'Rise of the Warrior Cop' The Police State' 8/15/2013," listed in the Media Links the end of this chapter.

There are concerns that the militarization of the police is occurring in Canada as well. The New Glasgow (Nova Scotia) Regional Police Service, which serves the two communities of New Glasgow and Trenton (combined population of 12,178, according to the 2011 Census), received a light armoured vehicle from the Department of National Defence to be used in a variety of situations. In speaking to the acquisition, the chair of the Police Board stated: "The reality is that in this day and age, unpredictable situations can and do happen everywhere, from the smallest towns and villages, to major international cities.[54] The police-reported crime rate in New Glasgow has been declining; from 684 per 10,000 population in 2012 to 581 per 10,000 population in 2013.[55]

In 2010, the Ottawa Police Service spent $340,000 to purchase an armoured vehicle equipped with steel bodywork, machine gun–proof glass, gun ports, and a roof turret.[56] Records indicate that, in addition to armoured vehicles (with the armaments removed), the DND has donated night vision goggles and military apparel to police services (Quan, 2014).[57]

Canadian criminologist Robert Gordon has observed that there has been a "creeping militarization" in Canada, "because policing fashions in the U.S. tend to have a fairly major impact on policing fashions in Canada."[58] A major concern is that rather than making communities safer and more secure, militarization drives a wedge between the police and the community and undermines the original principles of Sir Robert Peel. It remains to be seen whether the terrorist attack on Parliament Hill on October 22, 2014, will accelerate the militarization of the police. See Class/Group Discussions 2.3 and 2.4, both at the end of this chapter.

Summary

The discussion in this chapter has focused on the origins and evolution of policing in Canada. It was noted that while strongly influenced by the English system of policing and the principles of Sir Robert Peel, the policing in this country has a unique history. In the early days, policing was heavily influenced by politics and patronage. Although the RCMP emerged as a national symbol, it was used by the federal government to quell riots and suppress dissent. It and other police services were also involved in policing morality, including purging homosexuals from the government and spying on persons and groups who were deemed to be a threat to order. Policing in the early 21st century is characterized by an expansion of the police role, pluralization, collaborative policing arrangements, and the militarization of policing.

KEY POINTS REVIEW

1. Prior to the Industrial Revolution and the development of capitalism, policing in England was a community responsibility.
2. There was widespread opposition to the creation of the first organized police service in London in the early 1800s.
3. Sir Robert Peel sought to legitimize the new Metropolitan Police in London by setting out a number of principles for policing—principles that continue to guide contemporary police work.
4. Policing in Canada was strongly influenced by the evolution of policing in England. However, a number of major events have shaped the course of Canadian policing from the days of the early settlers to the present.
5. Prior to the formation of organized police forces in Canada, policing was a community responsibility.
6. The early municipal and provincial police and the RCMP had very distinct roles.
7. There was often tension between municipal police forces and the RCMP.
8. There was often a disconnect between the image and reality of the RCMP.
9. A review of the historical record reveals that the police were used by governments to suppress political dissent, conduct surveillance on citizens, and police morality.

10. In the early days, the RCMP played a pivotal role in the remote North.
11. Police work in the early 21st century is characterized by an expansion of the police role and pluralization, including tiered policing, collaborative policing, expanding networks of surveillance, and militarization.

KEY TERM QUESTIONS

1. What was the **hue and cry**, and how did this reflect the arrangements for policing in England prior to the Industrial Revolution and the development of capitalism?
2. Describe the principle underlying the **frankpledge system** and how it operated.
3. What was the importance of the **Statute of Winchester**, passed in England in 1285?
4. What was the importance of the **Justice of the Peace Act**, passed in 1361?
5. What did the **Metropolitan Police Act**, passed in 1829, do, and why is this act important in any study of policing?
6. Who was **Sir Robert Peel**, and what was his contribution to the field of policing?
7. What is **tiered policing** and why has it developed in Canada?
8. Define **collaborative policing** and the **pluralization of policing.** What are their implications for the delivery of policing services?

CRITICAL THINKING EXERCISES

Exercise 2.1. The Resistance to Peel's Police and Peel's Principles of Policing

1. In retrospect, do you think that early Londoners were right to be suspect about the creation of organized police services?
2. Peel's principles were developed in the early 19th century. We are now in the early 21st. century. Needless to say, much has changed during the past 200 years. Consider each of Peel's principles: which ones are still relevant for police services and which ones are less relevant or are irrelevant today?

CLASS/GROUP DISCUSSION EXERCISES

Discussion 2.1. Competing Perspectives on the Role of the RCMP

After listening to the debate in "RCMP's History Debated" (see Media Links, below), discuss the following questions:

1. What is your reaction to the main points made by former RCMP Commissioner Kelly and historian Lorne Brown?
2. What do the points made by each debater suggest about the role of the police generally, and the RCMP more specifically, in Canadian society?

Discussion 2.2. Limits on Police Surveillance?

There is a history in Canada of the police spying on groups that are deemed to be a threat to social order. Many of these groups have not been involved in criminal activity. If you were part of a commission that was tasked with setting guidelines for the police related to surveillance, what would the guidelines be?

Discussion 2.3. Peel's Principles and the Militarization of the Police

Considering Peel's principles of policing, respond to the following observation: "The increased militarization of the police undermines the assertion of a non-oppressive civil force—the façade of social function falling away to many of those on the receiving end of public order policing, revealing the repressive state body beneath."[59]

Discussion 2.4. Canadian Police History

In reading the history of Canadian police work, what surprised/concerned you the most?

MEDIA LINKS

Visit www.nelson.com/canadianpolicework4 for links to these videos and other additional content available with this text.

"RCMP's reputation debated," CBC Digital Archives, 1973, cbc.ca/archives

"North-West Mounted Police in the late 1800s," CBC Digital Archives, 1964, cbc.ca/archives

"Enemies of the State," The Fifth Estate, CBC, October 5, 2010, cbc.ca/fifth

"Scarlet Guardians: RCMP officers in training," CBC Digital Archives, 1958, cbc.ca/archives

"RCMP uses 'fruit machine' to detect gays," CBC Digital Archives, 2005, cbc.ca/archives

"The Toronto bathhouse raids," CBC Digital Archives, 1981, cbc.ca/archives

"'No more raids!' Toronto bathhouse raid protests - raw tape." CBC Digital Archives, 1981, cbc.ca/archives

"Radley Balko on the Militarization of Police," ReasonTV, August 6, 2013, youtube.com

"Strossel: Radley Balko Debates Ohio Sheriff 'Rise of the Warrior Cop' The Police State 8/15/2013," MikeHansonArchives, August 20, 2013, youtube.com

3 Contemporary Canadian Policing

LEARNING OBJECTIVES

After reading this chapter, you should be able to:

- Describe the structure of contemporary policing in Canada
- Describe provincial and municipal police services
- Identify and discuss the unique organizational and operational attributes of the RCMP
- Discuss the use of tiered policing, using the province of Alberta as an example
- Identify and discuss the distinctions between public police and private security services
- Discuss the attributes of police services in the early 21st century, including the adoption of corporate practices, strategic planning, environmental scans, the use of best practices, and the police service as a learning organization
- Discuss the role of police associations and police unions in Canadian policing
- Describe the role of leadership in Canadian policing
- Discuss the issues that surround measuring police performance, including the use of crime rates and clearance rates
- Describe the new measures of police performance that have been developed in recent years

THE STRUCTURE OF CONTEMPORARY CANADIAN POLICING

Public policing in Canada is carried out at four levels: federal, provincial, municipal, and First Nations. In addition, there are private security services and para-police services. The latter are generally staffed by officers with special constable status. These include the Canadian Pacific Railway Police Service and the Canadian National Railway Police Service, which carry out policing roles for their respective organizations, as well as transit police forces, which provide security and protection for property and passengers in major urban centres such as Montreal, Toronto, and Vancouver. The members of the BC Transit Police in the Greater Vancouver region have full peace-officer powers and are the only armed transit police in the country. The railway police have federal peace-officer authority, and in some jurisdictions, they are appointed as special constables. At the federal level, the Canada Border Services Agency began arming officers in 2007.

Five Canadian police services—the RCMP, the Toronto Police Service, the Ontario Provincial Police (OPP), the Sûreté du Québec (SQ), and the Service de police de la Ville de Montréal (SPVM)—account for just over 60 percent of all police officers in Canada.

Canadian police services vary greatly in size and in terms of the areas for which they are responsible. At one end of the scale, there are three-officer RCMP detachments in many remote northern communities; at the other, there are thousands of officers in the urban centres of Toronto and Montreal.

The major urban police services have similar divisions, or sections. These include the following:

- *Operational patrol.* Patrol division, dog or canine unit, identification squad, traffic, reserve/auxiliary.
- *Investigative.* General investigation, major crimes, special crimes (e.g., sexual offences).
- *Support services.* Information, report, or filing; communications centre; victim services; community services/crime prevention.
- *Administrative.* Finance and payroll, property office.
- *Human resources.* Staff development, recruiting, training.
- *Research and planning.* Strategic planning, crime analysis, audit.

Canadian police services, like their counterparts worldwide, have a rank structure that reflects their paramilitary organization. Most police services have a chief constable, one or more deputy chief constables, superintendents, inspectors (often referred to as commissioned officers, although they are not actually commissioned), and non-commissioned officers, including staff sergeants, sergeants, corporals, detectives, and constables.

The Arrangements for Policing

To a foreigner (and to many Canadians), the arrangements for the delivery of police services in Canada can be quite complex and confusing. For example, the London (Ontario) Police, an independent municipal police service, has responsibility for policing within the city boundaries, while the London detachment of the OPP has jurisdiction in the rural areas outside the city. In addition,

Figure 3.1. Policing in the Greater Vancouver Region

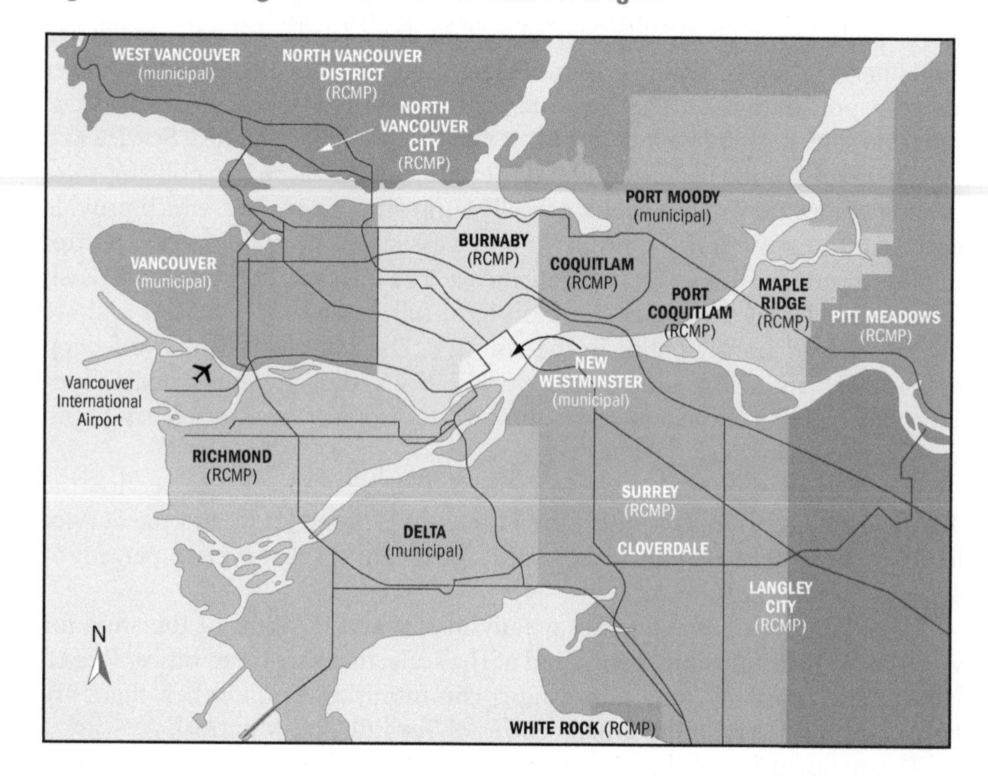

the RCMP has its provincial headquarters in London and operates as a federal police force in the areas policed by the London Police and the OPP.

The picture is especially complex in the Greater Vancouver region, Figure 3.1, which is the last urban region in the country without one dominant police force.

In Ontario and Quebec, there are provincial police forces and municipal police forces, although in Quebec, the Sûreté du Québec (SQ), the provincial police force, is not involved in policing municipalities under contract. The RCMP in these provinces functions only as a federal police force enforcing federal statutes. In contrast to the western regions of the country, the RCMP is not highly visible in Ontario and Quebec. And in a unique twist, the Royal Newfoundland Constabulary—a provincial police force—provides policing services to three areas of Newfoundland and Labrador: St. John's, Mount Pearl, and the surrounding communities referred to as the Northeast Avalon; Corner Brook; and Labrador West, which includes Labrador City, Wabush, and Churchill Falls. The rest of the province is policed under contract by the RCMP.

In Ontario, under the Police Services Act, a given municipality has a number of options in terms of how it provides policing services: (1) establish its own independent municipal police force; (2) amalgamate its police service with one or more other services; (3) share police services with one or more other municipalities; or (4) contract with the OPP for police services.

If the Constitution Act had been followed to the letter, Ontario and Quebec would not be the only two provinces with independent provincial police forces,

RCMP officers would not be involved in municipal policing, and there would be no independent municipal police services.

FEDERAL POLICE: THE ROYAL CANADIAN MOUNTED POLICE

The RCMP is unique among the world's police forces. It has a national headquarters in Ottawa, two regions, and 15 divisions. The headquarters of these divisions are generally located in the provincial and territorial capitals and are under the supervision of a commanding officer. The regions are overseen by a deputy commissioner west and east. The divisions, in turn, are organized into subdivisions, which are themselves organized into detachments. It is at the detachment level that uniformed officers deliver most police services. Specialized services and operational support units are available at the subdivision to support officers at the detachment level.

The RCMP Act (R.S. 1985, c. R-10) provides the framework for the operations of the RCMP. As the federal police force in all provinces and territories, the RCMP enforces most federal statutes, such as the Controlled Drugs and Substances Act and lesser-known statutes such as the Canada Shipping Act and the Canada Student Loans Act. Under the RCMP Act, RCMP officers have the powers of peace officers as well as the powers of customs and excise officers for the entire country. This makes RCMP members unique among Canada's police officers. The federal government covers the costs of the RCMP when it serves as a federal police force. When the RCMP functions as a provincial or municipal police force, policing costs are shared between the federal and provincial/territorial or municipal governments. The split in cost sharing varies among jurisdictions.

contract policing
an arrangement whereby the RCMP and the Ontario Provincial Police provide provincial and municipal policing services

The RCMP, through its National Aboriginal Policing Services Branch, also operates a number of Aboriginal policing programs, including the RCMP First Nations Community Policing Service. This service, which is the main Aboriginal policing initiative of the RCMP, recruits, trains, and posts Aboriginal police officers to First Nations communities. These officers are full-status members of the RCMP with all of the attendant powers and responsibilities. First Nations communities have the right to request the services of Aboriginal members of the RCMP.

Policing Provinces and Municipalities under Contract

Although the RCMP is a federal police force, roughly 60 percent of RCMP personnel are involved in **contract policing**, serving as provincial and municipal police officers under agreements between the RCMP and the provinces/territories (except in Ontario and Quebec, which have their own provincial police forces, and a portion of Newfoundland/Labrador). To provide policing services

© Yvette Cardoza/Alamy

RCMP officer

under contract, the RCMP, through the Government of Canada, negotiates municipal policing agreements with individual municipalities.

The sole exception is in British Columbia, where there is a general policing agreement between the federal and provincial governments for the delivery of contract policing services to specific municipalities. RCMP members employed under these agreements also conduct federal enforcement investigations.

The RCMP's reach extends to the international level: there are RCMP liaison officers in a number of countries in the Asia–Pacific Region, in Europe, and in the Americas. RCMP liaison officers provide a bridge between foreign police forces and their Canadian counterparts; they also assist in cross-national investigations.

Organizational Features of the RCMP

As a national police force, the RCMP has several distinctive organizational characteristics. These include a broad mandate: The RCMP is involved in a broad range of policing activities, including federal policing, contract policing at the provincial and municipal level, and international peacekeeping. One result is that the resources and capacities of the Mounties have been overextended, which has led many observers to question whether the RCMP can effectively carry out all of its current mandates. Most Western countries have created different organizations to carry out specialized policing functions. Figure 3.2 illustrates the range and complexity of the RCMP's policing responsibilities.

RCMP officers (along with their OPP and SQ counterparts) carry out their duties in a variety of environments across the country, from small coastal villages in Newfoundland and British Columbia, to Aboriginal and Inuit communities in the North, to large suburban communities. The challenges of doing police work in remote and northern communities are discussed in Chapter 6.

Nationwide Recruiting and Centralized Training

As a national police force, the RCMP recruits officers from across the country and trains them at a central facility in Regina, Saskatchewan, known as the Training Academy.

Transfer Policy

Traditionally, and quite unlike their municipal counterparts, RCMP officers were rotated among detachments every two years or so. While the transfer policy provides members with the opportunity to police in a number of different environments in the course of their career, thereby enhancing their skills and expertise, the drawbacks of this policy may include the disruptive impact on the officer's family, officers' lack of familiarity with the communities they are policing, and a lack of continuity in program initiatives and police–community partnerships.

Non-union

Unlike their provincial and municipal counterparts, RCMP officers have historically been prohibited by legislation from forming a union. The members'

Figure 3.2. The Broad Mandate of the RCMP

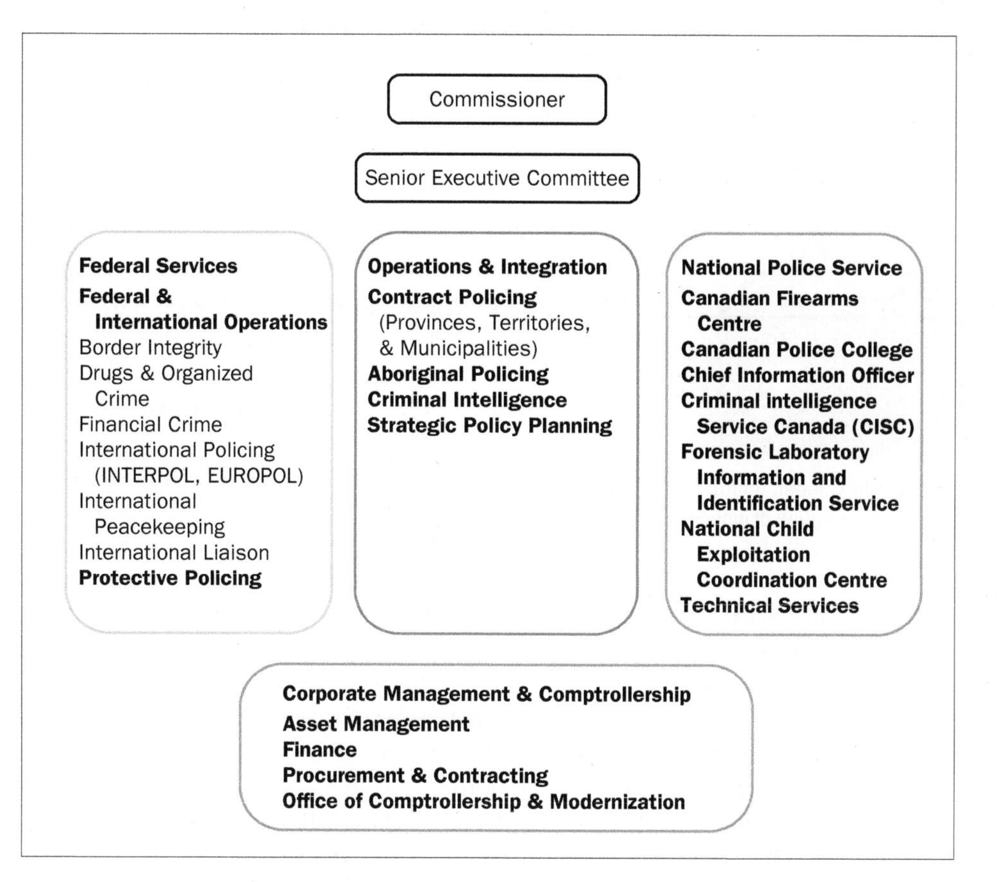

Source: C. Murphy and P. McKenna, "Rethinking Police Governance, Culture, and Management," p. 33. (Ottawa: Public Safety Canada, 2007), http://publicsafety.gc.ca/rcmp-grc/_fl/eng/rthnk-plc-eng.pdf. Reprinted by permission of Christopher Murphy.

interests have been represented through the **Division Staff Relations Representative (DivRep) Program.** This program provides officers with a channel for expressing their concerns on a wide range of employment issues.

Division Staff Relations Representative (DivRep) Program
in lieu of a union, a program that provides RCMP officers with a way to express their concerns to management

The Mounted Police Professional Association of Canada, comprised of sworn and civilian members of the RCMP, represents the professional and employment concerns of its membership.[1] It is not a union, and RCMP officers have no right to strike. In a landmark case in 2015, the Supreme Court of Canada ruled that the law barring RCMP officers from forming a union was unconstitutional and that officers had the right to collectively bargain (*Mounted Police Association of Ontario v. Canada (Attorney General)*, 2015 SCC 1). The federal government was given one year to rewrite the laws that govern the RCMP. This decision will have a far-reaching impact on the operations of the RCMP.

The arrangement whereby the RCMP provides municipal police services under contract has come under increasing scrutiny amidst concerns about governance and accountability. While independent municipal police services are subject to local police boards and municipal councils, in those municipalities which the RCMP polices under contract, there are no police boards and the local mayor and council have no mandate to oversee their work. Some observers thus argue

Provincial police forces, such as the Sûreté du Québec (pictured here) and the OPP, are responsible for the administration of justice.

that the RCMP is "in" but not "of" the communities they police, and that it is often difficult to ensure that RCMP detachments are responsive to the community's priorities and requirements.

PROVINCIAL POLICE

The provincial/territorial governments are responsible for the administration of justice. To this end, they oversee police services, prosecute offences, staff courthouses with judges, and operate programs for adult and young offenders as well as correctional facilities for offenders who receive sentences totalling less than two years. Police services generally fall under the purview of provincial ministries of justice or attorneys general.

There are currently three provincial police forces in Canada: the Ontario Provincial Police, the Sûreté du Québec, and the Royal Newfoundland Constabulary (RNC). As noted earlier, the RNC polices only the communities of Corner Brook, Churchill Falls, Labrador City, St. John's, and a few other smaller neighbouring communities. The rest of the province, including the highways, is policed by the RCMP. There are no independent municipal police forces in Newfoundland.

Provincial police forces police rural areas and areas outside municipalities. They enforce provincial laws as well as the Criminal Code. Some municipalities in Ontario are policed under contract by the OPP. Except in Ontario and Quebec and certain parts of Newfoundland and Labrador, the RCMP provides provincial policing under contract with provincial governments. When the RCMP acts as a provincial police force, it has full jurisdiction over the Criminal Code as well as provincial laws. Similar to the RCMP, provincial police officers may be rotated between detachments.

In Ontario, the OPP provides policing services to communities that do not have municipal police services; polices waterways, trails, and roadways; maintains the province's ViCLAS (Violent Crime Linkages Analysis System) and the provincial Sex Offender Registry; and provides policing services to a number of First Nations communities that have not exercised the option to have a First Nations police service.

REGIONAL POLICE SERVICES

Especially in the eastern regions of the country, regional police services are a key feature of Canadian policing. Most of these services have been formed through the amalgamation of several independent police departments into one large organization. Regional police services have been a feature of policing in Ontario for many years. Today, a number of regional police services, including the Peel Regional Police (the largest regional police force in Canada) and the Halton Regional Police, provide policing services to more than half of Ontarians. In Quebec, the Service de police de la Ville de Montréal (SPVM) provides policing services to the City of Montreal and several surrounding municipalities.

Proponents of regional policing contend that it is more effective at providing a full range of policing services to communities and is less expensive than having a number of independent municipal departments. Critics of regional policing argue that a regional police service is too centralized and does not offer the opportunity for effective community policing. The trend toward regionalization will continue to be driven by fiscal considerations and by the growing need for police services to maintain interoperability.

MUNICIPAL POLICE

As the name suggests, municipal police services have jurisdiction within a city's boundaries. Municipal police officers constitute two-thirds of the police personnel in the country and enforce the Criminal Code, provincial statutes, municipal bylaws, and certain federal statutes such as the Controlled Drugs and Substances Act. Most police work is carried out by services operating at this level.

Municipalities can provide police services in one of three ways: (1) by creating their own independent police service; (2) by joining with another municipality's existing police force, which often means becoming involved with a regional police force; or (3) by contracting with a provincial police force—the OPP in Ontario and the RCMP in the rest of Canada except Quebec, where there is no provision under provincial law for the Sûreté du Québec to contract out municipal policing services.

Municipalities with their own policing services generally assume most of the policing costs, sometimes with assistance from the provincial government. A notable trend in Ontario has been the decline in the number of independent municipal police services and a concurrent increase in contracting with the OPP to provide those services.

FIRST NATIONS POLICE

Aboriginal peoples have become increasingly involved in the administration of justice, especially in the area of policing. This is perhaps appropriate, given the conflicts that have arisen between the police and Aboriginal peoples both today and in the past. Autonomous Aboriginal police forces build on a history of Aboriginal peacekeeping that preceded European settlement.

Within the framework of the federal **First Nations Policing Policy**, the federal government, provincial and territorial governments, and First Nations communities can negotiate agreements for police services that best meet the needs of First Nations communities. These communities can choose to develop an autonomous reserve-based police force or to use First Nations officers from the RCMP (the OPP in Ontario). Funding for Aboriginal police forces is split between the province and the federal government.

First Nations Policing Policy
a framework that allows First Nations to negotiate a policing arrangement suitable to their needs

Today, there are autonomous Aboriginal police services in all of the provinces except Prince Edward Island and Newfoundland and Labrador, although there are none in the territories. Among the larger Aboriginal police forces that are involved in policing multiple reserve communities are the Ontario First Nations Constable Program, the Six Nations Tribal Police, and the Nishnawbe-Aski Police Service in Ontario; the Amerindian Police in Quebec; and the

Aboriginal police forces exist in almost all provinces now, administering justice within a framework that meets the needs of their communities.

Dakota-Ojibway Police Service in Manitoba. There are smaller Aboriginal police forces in Alberta and British Columbia.

Aboriginal police officers generally have full powers to enforce the Criminal Code, federal and provincial statutes, and band bylaws on reserve lands—and in some circumstances, off reserve as well (see *R. v. DeCorte*, 2005, 1 S.C.R. 133). There are also band constables, appointed under provisions of the Indian Act, who are responsible for enforcing band bylaws. Band constables are not fully sworn police officers, and their powers are limited.

First Nations police services experience challenges in a number of areas, including recruitment and training, and meeting the demands for service in communities, many of which are afflicted with poverty and high levels of violent crime. There is also often a lack of qualified on-reserve police candidates and few pre-employment training and upgrading programs to prepare potential First Nations recruits for careers in policing. Table 3.1 sets out the police services by jurisdiction. See Critical Thinking Exercise 3.1 at the end of this chapter.

SPECIAL CONSTABLES

Provincial police acts generally provide for the appointment of special constables, who are granted powers similar to those of a police officer, to be used in special settings and circumstances, including campus police services. In Ontario, the duties of OPP special constables have been expanded to include providing assistance for security in courtrooms, DNA sample collection, and prison guard duties. This expansion of duties is part of the trend toward tiered policing.

In addition to public police officers and private security officers, there are officers who are most appropriately categorized as **para-police**. These officers are not fully accredited peace officers. Generally, though, they are sworn as special constables, which gives them the power to make arrests if there are reasonable and probable grounds to do so.

Courtesy of Winnipeg Police Service.

Winnipeg police cadets

Para-police officers are involved in policing airports, university campuses, and national and provincial parks, and in protecting railway property. These officers are generally not armed, but they may carry handcuffs and pepper spray and wear body armour. The RCMP operates a program of community program officers (CPOs), unarmed civilian members that do not wear a uniform and focus on liaising with the community; additionally, a Community Constable (CC) program is composed of uniformed, armed officers who provide tactical support for RCMP officers but who are not first responders. Other police services have personnel variously called cadets (Winnipeg Police Service) and community safety personnel (Vancouver Police Department) who are unarmed and play a support role in their respective police services.

para-police
unarmed officers who generally have special constable status

TIERED PUBLIC POLICING IN ALBERTA

In Chapter 1, it was noted that the late 20th/early 21st centuries have witnessed a rise in the costs of policing and the search for alternative models of public policing. The development of tiered public policing is most notable in the province of Alberta. RCMP officers serve as federal, provincial, and in many communities, municipal police officers under contract. There are also eight independent municipal police services, the largest of which are Calgary and Edmonton. In addition, the province has created the Public Security Peace Officer Program, which operates under the provincial Peace Officer Act. These officers enforce provincial statutes. Community peace officers, level 1, respond to non-urgent calls, including theft under $5,000 and mischief under $5,000; have the authority to arrest and release; and can investigate and submit reports on non-injury motor vehicle collisions. Level 2 community peace officers are primarily involved in administrative roles. Although unarmed, community peace officers have the power to arrest and to use reasonable force when necessary.

The province has also expanded the role of sheriffs beyond their traditional role as officers of the court, ensuring order in the court and transporting prisoners. Sheriffs in Alberta manage counter-terrorism security information; provide protection to provincial executives, including the Premier; staff the Fugitive Apprehension Sheriff Support Team (FASST); conduct traffic enforcement; and operate the Sheriffs Investigative Support Unit (SISU), which provides investigative support to police services. Whether the tiered model of policing in Alberta will serve as a model for other jurisdictions remains to be seen.

TABLE 3.1
Police Services by Jurisdiction

	Provincial	Municipal	Aboriginal
Alberta	RCMP contract	RCMP contract; municipal police services	Yes
British Columbia	RCMP contract	Municipal police services; RCMP contract	Yes
Manitoba	RCMP contract	Municipal police services; RCMP contract	Yes
Newfoundland	RCMP contract	Royal Newfoundland Constabulary polices several communities, including St. John's; no independent municipal police services	No
New Brunswick	RCMP contract	Municipal police services; RCMP contract	Yes
Northwest Territories	RCMP contract	RCMP contract	No
Nova Scotia	RCMP contract	Municipal police services; RCMP contract	Yes
Nunavut	RCMP contract	RCMP contract	No
Ontario	Ontario Provincial Police	Provincial municipal police services; OPP contract	Yes
Prince Edward Island	RCMP contract	Municipal police services; RCMP contract	No
Quebec	Sûreté du Québec	Municipal police services	Yes
Saskatchewan	RCMP contract	Municipal police services; RCMP contract	Yes
Yukon	RCMP contract	RCMP contract	No

There has also been an expansion of the bylaw enforcement capacity in municipalities. The City of Edmonton, for example, has community standards peace officers who provide an immediate response to bylaw issues (e.g., construction noise), and uniformed transit peace officers who focus on order maintenance and the prevention of disorder on the city's transit system.

UNIVERSITY AND CAMPUS POLICE SERVICES

Another type of police force are university police services. In Ontario, these services are commonly referred to as "campus community police," as in the University of Windsor Campus Community Police and the University of Toronto Campus Community Police. These police services are staffed by special constables appointed under the Ontario Police Services Act, and their officers have full police officer powers on university property. The University of Alberta Campus Security Service is also staffed by officers with special constable status. Other universities are patrolled by contract security officers under the supervision of campus-based supervisors.

A number of factors influence the effectiveness of university police services, even where the officers have special constable status. These include the view commonly held by local police that university officers are glorified security guards, and the reluctance of local police to respond in support of university police, owing to the perception that university-related issues and incidents are mundane and not a priority. This may result in a "gap" between the expectations of the university community and the level of interest and response from local police services.

POLICE PEACEKEEPING

RCMP officers, along with their provincial and municipal counterparts, are involved in a variety of international peacekeeping activities. This has included Sierra Leone, Afghanistan, Sudan, and Haiti. The officers function mainly as technical advisers and instruct local police forces in new policing strategies.

There has been considerable debate around the effectiveness of these deployments, with some observers arguing that the impact of the officers is minimal and that the missions are mounted in order to "show the flag"—that is, to raise the profile of the Canadian government overseas. Among the difficulties that have been identified are the lack of pre-deployment training for officers being sent on peacekeeping missions and the fact that Canadian officers are often part of a multinational force of police officers, among whom there is wide disparity in both skills and level of professionalism.[2] The deployment of police officers overseas is one example where police officers may be being used for political purposes.

PRIVATE SECURITY SERVICES

It was noted in Chapter 2 that private security services have become a feature of the Canadian policing landscape and are now providing services previously performed by provincial and municipal police services. Private security officers outnumber public police officers by four to one.

There are two main types of private security: (1) security firms that sell their services to businesses, industries, private residences, and neighbourhoods; and (2), companies that employ their own in-house security officers. Across Canada, a number of communities have hired private security firms to provide twenty-four-hour security patrols.

The activities of private security officers include mobile and foot patrol, property protection, medical/emergency response, arrest (using citizen's arrest powers), criminal investigations, crime prevention consulting, security surveillance, and personal protection. In some venues, such as sporting events and concerts, private security officers and police officers may work in collaboration.

The expansion of the activities of private security firms into areas traditionally serviced by public police organizations has often resulted in uncertainty about the powers and authority of private security officers. Of particular concern is the transformation of private security officers into para-police through the extension of their activities beyond loss prevention and the protection of property to encompass order maintenance and enforcement.[3] Other observers have expressed the concern that although public police are accountable to oversight commissions and—in the case of municipal and provincial police forces—to elected community officials, no similar systems of governance are in place for private security officers.[4]

Generally, private security personnel have no more legal authority than ordinary citizens to enforce the law or protect property. However, private security officers can arrest and detain people who commit crimes on private property. Recent court cases suggest that private security personnel must adhere to the provisions in the Charter of Rights and Freedoms only when making an arrest.

There are a number of important distinctions to be made between public police and private security officers:

- Private security officers work for private companies whose raison d'être is profit. Public police officers, in contrast, work for the public and are generally not involved in issues related to economic profit.
- Public police are controlled and held accountable through various public, government-sponsored agencies and organizations.
- Private security services are not required to adhere to provincial police acts or to the policing standards that supplement police act legislation.
- There is no onus on private security services to engage in community-based policing. Private security forces are, in essence, an extension of company management and are concerned primarily with protecting the owner's investment.
- Public police are armed and have the authority to use deadly force, enforce the law, maintain order, and provide a wide range of non-enforcement services to the general public.

See Class/Group Discussion 3.1 at the end of this chapter.

THE CHANGING POLICE SERVICE

Historically, little attention was given to the organizational features of police services. Most attention was on the activities of the officers. The emergence of community policing in the 1980s shifted attention to how police services were structured and how resources were deployed. This focus has continued in the early 21st century, with efforts to identify the attributes of "good" police services and the organizational capacities that are required for the police to be effective and efficient. These include being professional, accountable, and transparent, and having a capacity for self-monitoring.[5]

Police services are increasingly adopting practices found in the private sector, including strategic planning, environmental scans, and the use of best practices. This has been driven in large measure by the fiscal crises of governments, which, in turn, has put more pressure on police services to become accountable, effective, and efficient. More emphasis is being placed on planning, research, and evaluation, as well as the consideration of best practices in other police services and how these might be applied.

Strategic Planning

strategic planning
the identification of police priorities and objectives and associated resource requirements

Strategic planning involves identifying how existing police resources will be allocated, as well as establishing the objectives to be achieved on an annual and/or multiyear time frame.

Strategic plans contain specific goals and objectives as well as performance and outcome measures, and they often identify the officer(s) responsible for assuming a leadership role in achieving the goals and objectives.

Strategic plans, however, often do not include sophisticated measures of police performance and the outcomes of initiatives. Often, for example, strategic plans measure performance by listing the activities that the police service and its officers have been involved in. Activities, however, do not equate with outcomes.

Besides producing an annual report, many police organizations have a multiyear strategic plan in place that sets out priorities and objectives for the organization and the specific initiatives that will be undertaken to achieve them. The requirement that police services engage in strategic planning has been enshrined in policing standards in many jurisdictions.

There is often a considerable "gap" between the strategic planning process and the evaluation of the outcomes of the goals and objectives that are set forth in strategic plans. Police services, along with other public-sector institutions such as social services and education, have been slow to develop measures that would facilitate a quantitative analysis of the extent to which the goals and objectives of the strategic plan have been achieved.

Environmental Scans

Environmental scans are studies designed to identify community, legislative, policy, and other forces in the community (here referred to as "the environment") that will result in demands on the police.

environmental scans
studies designed to identify trends that may impact demands on the police

A typical environmental scan involves gathering information on a number of factors external to the police service, including demographic, social, and economic trends; calls for police service and crime trends; and the impact of legislative and policy changes. Many police services conduct scans annually to ensure a constant flow of information, on the basis of which changes in policies and operational practice can be made. Environmental scans conducted by or for police services generally include an examination of demographic trends, crime trends, youth crime, victimization, traffic, calls for service, the role and impact of technology in policing, police resources, public perceptions of the police, and the impact of legislation and court decisions on the police.

This information is used to guide police policy and operations in the community and, as well, is made available on the police service website to increase public awareness of the key attributes of the community that will affect their quality of life. Conducting environmental scans on a regular basis is a feature of a best practices police service.

The Use of Best Practices

A term frequently heard in the discussion of policing is **best practices**. These are organizational, administrative, and operational strategies that have been proven through evaluation studies to successfully prevent and respond to crime.

best practices
organizational, administrative, and operational strategies that are effective in preventing and responding to crime

An example of a best practice is developing strategies to solicit feedback from the community about the quality of policing services, citizen satisfaction with the police, problems in the community that may require police attention, and the extent of criminal victimization (including the fear of crime).

Another example of a best practice is the shifting and deploying of officers based on an analysis of calls for service in order to maximize the effectiveness and efficiency of available resources. A ten-hour shift for officers has been determined by research studies to be the optimal shift length, and best practices police services deploy officers based on an analysis of demands for service.[6] Conversely, the traditional shift pattern of having officers work two days and two nights with four days off is generally considered not to be an efficient or effective model of deployment, particularly in the absence of an analysis of calls for service, which vary throughout the week and by time of day.

A key capacity of best practices police services is having the capacity to implement evidence-based practice. This means that the police service is able to implement with fidelity, it being noted that: "If you want to replicate a successful program, you have to plan carefully and pay attention to details to accurately reproduce critical program elements that often include specific procedures, personnel qualifications, and client characteristics.[7] Police services must have a number of capacities in order to effectively respond to the demands from the environments in which they carry out their tasks.

The Police Service as a Learning Organization

learning organization
the notion that a police service is constantly seeking improvement, learning from successes as well as from initiatives that did not achieve their intended goals

A key best practice is the notion that the police service should be a **learning organization**—seeking constant improvement—learning from successes as well as from initiatives that did not achieve their stated goals.

This requires the police service to develop the capacity to evaluate its strategies as well as to be receptive to the experiences of other police services. It is a process of continuous improvement. Programs that are not supported by evaluation research as being effective are discontinued (cf., the discussion of the D.A.R.E. program on p. 249).

organizational wisdom
an in-depth understanding of the community and its residents, crime and disorder, and agencies and organizations that can be mobilized to prevent and respond to crime

The concept of the police service as a learning organization also includes the accumulation of **organizational wisdom**, an in-depth understanding of the community and its residents, crime and disorder, and agencies and organizations that can be mobilized to prevent and respond to crime. The policy of transferring RCMP, SQ, and OPP officers who are involved in policing communities under contract may hinder the development of organizational wisdom, which may in turn reduce their effectiveness.

THE ROLE OF POLICE ASSOCIATIONS AND POLICE UNIONS

Another feature of the Canadian policing landscape is police associations (or police unions). Police associations are typically established within the context of provincial labour relations codes, and they operate within that statutory framework. Most non-commissioned officers, from the rank of probationary constable to staff sergeant (except RCMP officers), are members of a police association (e.g., the Winnipeg Police Association). Some associations/unions also represent civilian police personnel, special constables, or other categories of employees that are employed by police services.

Police associations operate independently from the police service, and their employer. The activities of the associations centre on providing representation for officers in grievance proceedings, negotiating the employment contract with senior management and the municipality, providing educational opportunities for officers, and sponsoring research, among others. They are the bargaining agent designated to negotiate and administer collective agreements, which include provisions that cover wages, benefits, and other working conditions.

The Canadian Police Association (CPA) is the national body comprised of the various police associations from across the country (see www.cpa-acp.ca). The CPA represents Canadian police officers and facilitates educational opportunities, sponsors research, and advocates for the membership on national policing issues (see Police Perspective 3.1).

THE ROLE OF POLICE LEADERSHIP

> *I think most police leaders are too focused on today. Too many chiefs want that immediate gratification. I do too. But I have to be strong enough to make sure that the police board understands, and the community understands, that the success won't be today. And, if I don't have the guts to do that, then I probably shouldn't be in the position I'm in. It's like my meetings with the Black community. They don't necessarily care to tell you what you should think, but they do want to know what you think.*
>
> A Canadian chief constable

Police Perspective 3.1

The President of the Canadian Police Association Comments on the Role of Police Associations/Unions in Supporting Officers

Associations and unions assist police members with workers' compensation claims, Employment Standards Act issues, and Police Act matters, particularly in relation to discipline regulations as they exist from province to province across Canada.

One of the key roles undertaken by any association or union representative is to provide support when members face challenges in relation to their employment. These challenges can be disciplinary or may arise from other matters that police officers become involved in from time to time, both professionally or personally. A union or association representative can act as an advocate for a member and in that role facilitate communication between the member and the police service. Police associations/unions focus on the member's interests in the broader public interest and from a perspective more closely rooted in the front line of policing.

Source: Personal communication with author, 2014.

Chief constables and their executive team play a variety of roles in a police service. They set administrative and operational policy, and liaise with the police board and with municipal government. Among the more important responsibilities of chief constables and their executive team are setting the budget, allocating resources, and providing the framework for strategic planning and operations. These officers also have a significant impact on the culture of the organization and can determine whether the police service will adopt best practices, be evidence-driven, and be a learning organization (see Police Perspective 3.2). The discussion of the police occupation in Chapter 5 considers the impact that the police organization can have on the levels of stress that officers experience and their risk of developing post-traumatic stress.

Although all police services are organized hierarchically with chains of command and authority, there is considerable variability with respect to the size of police services, their areas of jurisdiction, and the costs of delivering police services. The police-to-population ratio is the number of officers per 100,000 population. A review of the "police-to-pop" ratios across the country reveals considerable disparity. For example, here are some police-to-population figures for selected communities across Canada: Gatineau, Quebec, 139; Kelowna, British Columbia, 125; and Moncton, New Brunswick, 111.[8]

Caution should be exercised in assuming that a police service with a lower police-to-pop ratio will be more effective: much depends upon how the police service utilizes the officers that it has and whether it is guided by best practices.

Police Perspective 3.2

A Senior Police Leader Comments on the Role of Police Leaders in Fostering the Development of Officers

In recent years, we have been very focused on trying to develop our officers to their full potential: teaching them early on to be successful, however they frame that; providing them with mentors. Our promotion process is built around developing very well-rounded officers. We have quarterly meetings where we talk about succession planning right down to the constable level: "Who are the officers who look like they are going to be high achievers? What are we doing to give them the best chance at success?" At the middle management level, we actually assign people to keep an eye on these officers to make certain they are getting mentorship. This includes supporting them when they are applying for specific positions. We really do pay attention to that. We hire bright, educated people who bring so much to the organization. It's our job that if they are lacking certain skills, we can provide the opportunity for them to develop.

Source: Personal communication with author, 2014.

The increasing concerns with the costs of policing have led to a focus on the cost per officer. This includes the cost of one officer per year, including salaries and benefits, but not including additional payments for overtime. For most police services, the cost per officer is in the $100,000-plus range.

MEASURING POLICE EFFECTIVENESS

A key issue surrounding the operation of police services is how to measure performance. **Performance measurement** can be taken to mean the collective actions taken by a police service to assess the efficiency and effectiveness of its activities and interventions. Performance-based management ". . . essentially uses performance measurement information to manage and improve performance and to demonstrate what has been accomplished."[9]

performance measurement
the collective actions taken by a police service to assess the efficiency and effectiveness of its activities and interventions

Performance measures can improve the delivery of policing services, while simultaneously assisting the police service with the rationalization and justification of costs and expenditures. They are also useful for identifying areas of difficulty in policing, and can be used to assess how well specific policies and strategies are working in practice (see Chapter 9).[10]

Most police services in Canada remain wedded to two traditional measures of police performance that are hold-overs from the professional model of policing: crime rates and clearance rates. Even in those police services that have adopted a community policing approach, the performance assessments of individual police officers are still heavily oriented toward enforcement activities.[11]

Crime Rates

Crime rates are perhaps the most easily attainable, yet potentially the most problematic, publically available measure of police performance. Similar to a profit margin's importance to businesses, crime reduction is seen as the "bottom line" in policing, to be monitored exclusively by crime statistics.[12] Strategic plans of police services generally contain percentage targets for crime reduction, and annual reports highlight achievements in reducing specific types of criminal activity in the community.

There are, however, a number of difficulties associated with crime rates, one of which is that there are many points of "slippage" between actual and official rates of crime. Official statistics are dependent upon accurate recording. Moreover, it is also recognized that there may be a considerable amount of criminal activity that remains undetected and unreported. The initial decision of someone, such as a crime victim or witness, to call the police may have a subsequent effect on the official crime rate. It is known that certain segments of the community, including newcomers, members of visible and cultural minorities, and persons with English or French as a second language may be reluctant to call the police for assistance. This makes it especially important that a police service reflect the diversity of the community that it polices.

Research surveys also reveal that there is chronic under-reporting of many types of crime due to an often accurate perception among the victims of crime that there is little the police can do. If a police service does not have the capacity to engage in best-practice policing and/or if the service is under-resourced, there may be an inability to effectively respond to criminal victimization. This has a ripple effect.

For crime rates, there can be problems of interpretation. For example, does an increase in official crime rates mean the police are ineffective? Or does it mean they are catching more criminals? Another problem with using official crime rates to assess police effectiveness is that the focus is on "crime fighting" to the exclusion of other measures of police performance. In addition, much of what the police are asked to do by governments and communities—and, in some instances, are required by legislation and policy to do—has little to do with crime rates. In most jurisdictions, police officers do not spend most of their time pursuing criminals (although as noted in Chapter 6, they may be responding to incidents that have the *potential* to include a violation of the law). It is also important to note that the police may have little impact on the reason why crime occurs; factors include poverty, social issues, addiction, and family dysfunction.[13]

Clearance Rates

clearance rates
the proportion of the actual incidents known to the police that result in the identification of a suspect, whether or not that suspect is ultimately charged and convicted

Another traditional measure of police performance is the clearance rate. **Clearance rates** are the proportion of the actual incidents known to the police that result in the identification of a suspect, whether or not that suspect is ultimately charged and convicted. Using these measures is problematic on a number of counts.

In British Columbia, police do not legally charge individuals, so the clearance rates do not necessarily only include those cases that Crown Counsel has decided to proceed with. If a suspect has been identified, and the police have enough evidence to recommend charges, then the case is generally considered "cleared." Clearance rates are closely associated with the resources and capacities of a police service, as well as the effectiveness and efficiency of police operations.

Further, not all police officers work in the same types of communities: some communities are more crime-ridden than others. Research in Quebec has found, for example, that police services in small communities are more likely to clear crimes than in large urban areas and in areas with high poverty levels;[14] and police officers do not all engage in the same type of police work: some are involved in patrol, others in investigative units, etc.

In communities where there is a high police-to-population ratio and in which police officers have a high per-officer Criminal Code caseload, officers may not have the time or resources to effectively investigate crime. This may result in lower clearance rates, which may, in turn, undermine the legitimacy of the police in the eyes of community residents, further contributing to underreporting of victimization.

New Measures of Police Performance

Reducing social disorder and providing reassurance to the community are equally important roles of the police, yet these activities are generally not measured. In recent years, a number of new measures of police performance, which capture the multifaceted role of the police, have been developed, including the following:

- Levels of community and victim satisfaction with the police and feelings of safety, as measured by surveys.
- The success of a police service in achieving its stated goals and objectives and fulfilling its mission statement.
- The success of the police in achieving specific performance objectives, including a reduction in the response times for 911 calls and effective target hardening and problem solving with respect to specific types of crime and in identified problem areas in the community.
- The extent to which the police are involved in developing innovative programs to address issues relating to diversity, including in the LGBT community, the visible-minority communities, and Aboriginal communities.
- The degree to which the police are involved in interagency partnerships with social service agencies, non-governmental organizations, and community groups.
- The nature and extent of involvement of community volunteers in various police programs and services. See Class/Group Discussion 3.2 at the end of this chapter.

Summary

The discussion in this chapter has focused on the structure of policing in Canada. Policing is carried out at the federal, provincial, and municipal levels and on First Nations reserves. The RCMP has a broad mandate (some observers say too broad) that includes federal policing and providing provincial and municipal policing under contract. In recent years, tiered policing has emerged in an attempt to control the escalating costs of policing. There has also been an exponential growth of private security services, although there are key differences between the public police and private security officers with respect to training and oversight, among other issues. Leading police services in Canada have a number of attributes, including the use of corporate practices, strategic planning, environmental scans, and best practices. These police services are learning organizations that are focused on continuous improvement. Police associations and police leaders play critical roles in the operation of police services. A number of measures of police performance have been developed beyond the traditional measures of crime rates and clearance rates.

KEY POINTS REVIEW

1. Public policing in Canada is carried out at four levels: federal, provincial, municipal, and First Nations.
2. The RCMP has a number of organizational and operational features that make it unique among the world's police services.

3. Tiered policing has emerged in an attempt to control the escalating costs of policing.
4. Private security officers outnumber public police officers by four to one.
5. There are key distinctions between public police and private police, particularly with respect to training, accountability, and authority.
6. Key features of leading police services include the adoption of corporate practices such as strategic planning, the use of environmental scans and best practices, and being a learning organization.
7. Police associations and police unions advocate on behalf of police officers in areas such as working conditions, wages, and support programs and services.
8. Police leaders play a number of pivotal roles in a police service, including setting the budget, allocating resources, and creating the framework for strategic planning and police operations.
9. The traditional measures of police performance are crime rates and clearance rates.
10. A number of new measures of police performance have been developed, including levels of community and victim satisfaction with the police, the extent to which the police develop and implement innovative programs and strategies, and the degree to which the police are involved in collaborative partnerships with the community, agencies, and organizations.

KEY TERM QUESTIONS

1. What is **contract policing**, and where does it occur in Canada?
2. Describe the RCMP's **Division Staff Relations Representative (DivRep) Program**.
3. What is the federal **First Nations Policing Policy**, and what options are provided to First Nations communities by this policy?
4. Who are the **para-police**?
5. Define and discuss the role of **strategic planning**, **environmental scans**, **best practices**, and the police service as a **learning organization** in Canadian policing.
6. What is meant by the notion of the **organizational wisdom** of a police service?
7. Define **performance measurement** and then discuss its importance in the study of policing.
8. What are **clearance rates** and why might these not be a good measure of police performance?

CRITICAL THINKING EXERCISES

Exercise 3.1. The Effectiveness of Police Services

Across Canada, there are a variety of policing arrangements, including the RCMP, which serves as the provincial police service in many provinces (and the only police service in the three territories); provincial police services; regional police services; municipal police services; and First Nations police services.

Assume that you have been tasked with determining which of these policing arrangements is most "effective." What type of framework would you create to determine the answer to this question? What types of data would you gather? What indicators of "success" would you use?

CLASS/GROUP DISCUSSION EXERCISES

Discussion 3.1. Debating the Role of Private Security Firms

In some regions of the country, neighbourhoods have hired private security firms to provide a patrol presence. Residents contend that the public police do not have the resources to provide sufficient protection to residents, particularly with respect to property crime.

Your Thoughts?

What are the positive and less positive features of private security companies providing patrols under contract to neighbourhoods?

Discussion 3.2. Measuring Police Performance

The discussion in this chapter has highlighted the traditional way in which police performance has been measured. Critics of these measures contend that they do not capture the wide range of activities that police officers are involved in. Place yourself as a member of a municipal panel that has been charged with developing ways to measure the "success" of your police service. What performance measures would you use? What are the strengths and limitations of each performance measure that you have identified?

4 Police Ethics and Accountability

LEARNING OBJECTIVES

After reading this chapter, you should be able to:

- Define and discuss ethics, codes of ethics, and ethical dilemmas
- Describe the reasons why police officers experience ethical dilemmas, and provide examples of ethical dilemmas
- Describe what is meant by "rotten apples," "rotten barrels," and "rotten orchards"
- Identify the types of police misconduct and the behaviour associated with each type
- Describe what is meant by noble cause corruption
- Discuss the role of police governance and police oversight in ensuring police accountability
- Compare and contrast the oversight of the police with other criminal justice personnel
- Compare and contrast the features of the dependent, independent, and interdependent models of public complaints and investigations of the police
- Discuss how tragic events have served to improve police oversight and accountability
- Describe the issues surrounding the effectiveness of oversight and investigations

POLICE ETHICS

Ethics in policing bears directly on issues of reform, control, and the legitimacy of law enforcement institutions in a democratic society.[1]

What Are Ethics?

Ethics have been defined as how behaviour is perceived as right or wrong. The term is often used interchangeably with morals, although ethics is often used in the context of the professions, while morals are described in relation to right or wrong in one's private life.[2] The focus on police ethics is designed to reduce the likelihood that police officers will become involved in unprofessional and illegal behaviour.

ethics
how behaviour is defined as right or wrong

In carrying out their tasks, Canadian police officers are required to adhere to a **code of ethics**. These are contained in the various provincial police acts across the country, in provincial policy documents, and in the manuals of individual police services. Codes of ethics generally contain sections on integrity, ethical decision making, and the requirements that police officers must carry out their duties fairly and impartially, must uphold the rights and freedoms guaranteed in law, must uphold the principles of democracy and the rule of law, and must maintain a high standard of ethics both on and off duty. The British Columbia Police Code of Ethics, for example, contains a statement of the fundamental principles of policing, guiding values (i.e., citizenship, fairness, integrity, and respect), a statement of the primary responsibilities of police officers, and questions that should guide the ethical decision making of officers.[3]

code of ethics
policies that establish standards of behaviour for police officers

Note that these codes of ethics are directed toward individual officers, rather than the police services in which they work. Ensuring that police services behave ethically is a more challenging task.

The need to be concerned about police ethics and professionalism has assumed even greater importance with the judgment of the Supreme Court of Canada in *R. v. McNeil*, 2009, SCC 3, which held that the Crown has a duty to disclose the disciplinary records of officers involved in investigating an accused person. This case arose when it was discovered that the constable investigating a person who was later charged and convicted of various drug-related offences, had himself been criminally charged with a drug-related offence.

Ethical Dilemmas

The wide variety of situations in which police officers find themselves, coupled with the discretion they are given in carrying out their tasks, often creates an **ethical dilemma**. There are situations in which a person has to make a decision or take a course of action in the face of two or more conflicting ethical principles or values.[4]

ethical dilemma
a situation in which a person has to make a decision or take a course of action in the face of two or more conflicting ethical principles or values

An ethical dilemma for a police officer has been described as

1. a situation in which the officer did not know what the right course of action was, or
2. a situation in which the course of action the officer considered right was difficult to do, or
3. a situation in which the wrong course of action was very tempting.[5]

These situations are likely to arise in policing, given the wide variety of encounter situations in which officers become involved, coupled with the discretion and authority that they exercise. Among the questions that are designed to assist police officers in avoiding ethical difficulties are the following: Is the activity or decision consistent with organizational or agency policy and the law? Do the outcomes or consequences generate more harm than good? What are the outcomes or consequences resulting from the activity or decision and whom do they affect? Can the activity or decision be justified legally and ethically?

WRONGDOING IN POLICE WORK

The fact that the police have a high degree of discretion in carrying out their mandate creates the potential that officers will become involved in misconduct and even corruption.[6] The actual extent of police wrongdoing is difficult to determine. Many cases do not come to light; in the case of the RCMP, prior to 2012, there was no record kept of the hundreds of cases of serious misconduct.[7]

Criminologists have ascribed wrongdoing among police to inadequate recruitment and training standards, a lack of accountability and oversight, and an attitude among some police officers that they are able to act with impunity.[8]

Police officers may be held liable for violating the policies and procedures of the police service in which they work and are also liable, civilly and criminally, for their conduct. Canadian courts have established that police officers are held to a higher standard of conduct than ordinary citizens. Sanctions for officers can range from a verbal or written reprimand, forfeiture of pay, suspension from the police service with or without pay, recommendations for counselling, or a directive that the officer resign. Officers may also resign voluntarily at any point prior to or during the misconduct proceedings.

The Police Subculture and Police Wrongdoing

The recruitment, selection, and training of police officers has come a long way from the early days of Canadian policing, when officers were generally selected for their physical prowess rather than their ethical standards (see Chapter 2). Although police services have rigorous admission standards, this does not prevent some police officers from engaging in unprofessional and even illegal conduct while on the job. Police malfeasance may occur at the patrol officer level, in case investigation (including in the use of informants), in the interrogation of crime suspects, and when providing testimony in court. The issues surrounding case investigation are discussed in Chapter 10.

There is little research on the factors that are associated with a police officer becoming involved in misconduct. It has been suggested that the occupational subculture of the police, discussed in Chapter 5, may contribute to, facilitate, and justify police misconduct. As the Canadian police scholars Chris Murphy and Paul McKenna have noted, "The demand for loyalty and solidarity with other police officers serves as a master value that insulates and protects police deviance and makes it difficult to govern officers' behaviour from within but especially from outside the organization."[9] This is often referred to as the "blue wall of silence."

Research studies have found that while most police officers will report what they consider to be serious incidents of misconduct on the part of fellow officers, incidents that are viewed as minor are less likely to be reported. Interestingly, preliminary research has found that civilian police staff are less likely to report police misconduct than sworn officers, particularly in situations where the incident is more serious.[10] This is a particularly significant finding given the increasing role of civilians in police services, and it suggests that there may be a subculture of silence among civilian staff.

Rotten Apples, Rotten Barrels, and Rotten Orchards

Police misconduct by the police may involve individual officers ("**rotten apples**") or groups of officers ("**rotten barrels**"), or it may be ingrained in the organizational culture of the police service ("**rotten orchards**").

rotten apples
individual police officer misconduct

rotten barrels
group misconduct by police officers

rotten orchards
misconduct by a police service

The research suggests that police misconduct in Canada is more of the "rotten apple" and, to a lesser extent, "rotten barrel" variety and that it is not pervasive. A study conducted by the RCMP found 322 incidents of corruption during an eleven-year period from 1995 to 2005, some of them related to organized crime. Many of the cases were attributed to poor supervision and/or life pressures on the officers.[11] Interestingly, the average length of service of the officers at the time of their first corrupt incident was thirteen years.

There is little evidence that there are "rotten orchard" police services in this country. Put another way, police misconduct occurs more often on an individual basis involving individual officers or groups of officers rather than permeating an entire police service. The emphasis in Canada has been nearly exclusively on the misconduct of individual police officers, and there have been few investigations into systemic police corruption in police services or into the organizational conditions that may foster officer misconduct.[12]

There have been exceptions to this, however. The misappropriation of the pension and insurance fund by several senior officers in the RCMP provided the catalyst for the transformation that is now underway in the force. Investigations by parliamentary committees found that there were serious violations of the RCMP's core values and code of conduct, as well as of the Criminal Code, by some senior officers. One committee report concluded: "The RCMP's normally high ethical standards were violated in this case...RCMP senior management allowed an ethical culture to develop which discouraged the disclosure of wrongdoing and did not hold individuals to account for unethical behaviour. This has led to a crisis of confidence amongst the RCMP rank and file."[13]

The general categories of police misconduct in order of increasing severity are as follows: (1) violations of departmental regulations and standards of professional conduct; (2) abuse of discretionary powers and authority; (3) actions, often criminal, that undermine the administration of justice; and (4) commission of a criminal offence (see Table 4.1). Note that an incident of misconduct may involve one or more of these categories; for example, an officer who is charged with the excessive use of force will generally face an internal disciplinary hearing as well. Even if the officer is found not guilty in a court of law, the officer will still face an internal disciplinary hearing that may result in sanctions, including dismissal from the police service.

TABLE 4.1
General Categories of Police Misconduct

Type of Misconduct	Behaviour
Violations of departmental regulations and standards of professional conduct	Discreditable conduct (acting in a disorderly manner that is prejudicial to discipline or likely to discredit the organization, such as two officers involved in a physical altercation with one another), neglect of duty, insubordination, harassment of fellow officers, deceit (instances in which an officer willfully or negligently makes false or misleading oral or written statements, which includes destroying or concealing evidence and altering official documents without authority).
Abuse of discretionary powers and authority	Many of the activities in this category are referred to as "corrupt practice" and include an officer (1) failing to account for money or property that has been received; (2) incurring an obligation or debt that may affect his or her duties; and (3) improperly using his or her position for private advantage. The abuse of authority includes arresting or charging someone without cause, using unnecessary force, or being discourteous or uncivil to a member of the general public.
Actions, often criminal, that undermine the administration of justice	This includes activities such as fabricating evidence, "backfilling" police notebooks, committing perjury in court while under oath (also called "testilying"), and obstructing justice in an attempt to secure a conviction. Many of these actions are referred to as **noble cause corruption**, which is defined as "a mindset or subculture which fosters a belief that the ends justify the means." The mission of the police to make communities and their residents safe is viewed as justifying the violation of regulations and the law, for a higher good—"bending the rules for a greater good." The difficulty of this type of thinking is that it reflects a view that "justice should be dispensed on the street and not in the courtroom." Or for the more cynical, "Never let the truth stand in the way of justice."[14]
Commission of a criminal offence	Police officers may become involved in the commission of criminal offences in conjunction with their policing duties or while off duty. These offences may range in severity from petty crimes, such as disturbing the peace, to more serious offences, such as domestic violence, drug trafficking, manslaughter, or murder.

noble cause corruption
a view by police officers that the ends justify the means (misconduct)

The following scenario demonstrates how noble cause corruption may occur:

> A subject is walking down the street when he turns and takes flight because he observes a police car coming in his direction. The officer engages in a foot pursuit and observes the subject discard an unknown item into the bushes during the pursuit. After capturing the suspect, the officer discovers he is a convicted felon on probation. The officer retrieves a firearm from the bushes but never actually saw what the item was that the subject discarded. If the officer testifies truthfully, the subject may survive his probation violation hearing. If the officer lies at the hearing, and testifies that he saw the subject discard a firearm, his probation will be definitely violated and a dangerous criminal will be off the streets.[15*]

This is the type of dilemma that a police officer may face when there is a temptation to exaggerate the truth. Overzealous officers may rationalize their decisions:

> Several teens are driving around in a stolen motor vehicle, and the officers stop them. The young men jump out and run away, the officers

* From the Public Agency Training Council newsletter. Reprinted by permission of the Public Agency Training Council (PATC).

> chase them, and arrest only two passengers. Unfortunately, for the officers, neither of [the teens arrested] was driving the vehicle. The officers file a report identifying one of the teens as driving the vehicle and the other as possessing contraband found on the floorboard. The officers chalk up felony arrests and call it a productive night.[16*]

Following is an actual case in which a police constable manipulated evidence and lied about it, an example of corrupt practice:

> A constable with expertise in forensics was called to assist in the investigation of a double homicide. Following the investigation, the constable provided the senior investigator on the case with her field notes, which indicated that the rifle that was the murder weapon was found at the scene, unloaded. The exhibit custodian found that the rifle had ammunition in it. A week later, the constable provided field notes from a second notebook, which indicated that she had found ammunition in the rifle during her initial investigation. When questioned by her supervising officer as to the discrepancy between the two sets of field notes, the constable lied and stated that her first set of field notes had been contaminated with blood at the murder scene. The first notebook was then turned over to the exhibit custodian. It had been smeared with red paint, which she later admitted was designed to look like dried blood.[17**]

An example of police officers "testilying" (not telling the truth when giving testimony under oath) occurred in the Commission of Inquiry into the death of Robert Dziekanski at the Vancouver Airport (see Police File 7.1, p. 196). From his inquiry into the incident, retired Justice Thomas Braidwood concluded that the four officers who were involved in the incident with Mr. Dziekanski made "deliberate misrepresentations" to the inquiry regarding the events that culminated in Mr. Dziekanski's death.[18]

A special prosecutor subsequently recommended that charges of perjury be laid against the four officers involved in the incident. Two of the officers were subsequently found guilty of perjury.

Another practice that undermines the administration of justice is "backfilling." Officers have sometimes been caught making additional entries subsequent to those made at the time of the incident or shortly afterwards. This practice may be revealed during the examination of an officer's notes by defence counsel during a trial, at which time entries in addition to those that have been disclosed to the defence are discovered. In one case, for example, a constable pled guilty to discreditable conduct after he met with an on-duty officer and rewrote several prisoner log sheets to cover up an assault on a prisoner.

The practice of backfilling seriously undermines the evidence given at a trial and may preclude an officer from continuing to refer to their notes during a trial. It may also result in a stay of proceedings on the grounds that there was

---

* Martinelli, T.J.. 2006. "Unconstitutional Policing: The Ethical Challenges in Dealing with Noble Cause Corruption," *The Police Chief*, 73(10), 16–22.

** Hutchinson, B. 2009. "What Does the Force Do with a Wayward Mountie?" *National Post*, December 12, http://www.bcpolicecomplaints.org/rcmp_discipline.html; http://www.monctonforums.com/index.php?topic=1369.0

nondisclosure of evidence to defence counsel by the prosecution. The Canadian courts regard a police officer's notes as a reflection of the professionalism and credibility of the police officer. Loss of credibility seriously limits the ability of that officer to bring cases to court. In addition, notes that have been back-filled are unreliable as an investigative tool. These types of cases often result in criminal charges.

Commission of a Criminal Offence

The most severe type of misconduct is when police officers become involved in criminal behaviour. This includes cases in which criminal harassment has occurred in a police service, most often involving a male officer directed toward a female officer. Other examples include a Peel Regional Police officer, sentenced to five years and eight months in federal prison for stealing what he thought were kilos of cocaine as part of an RCMP sting operation, and two Saskatoon Police Department officers convicted of unlawful confinement of an Aboriginal man and each sentenced to eight months in prison. The convictions of the Saskatoon officers were related to the incidents known as the "Starlight Tours." In 2012, a Winnipeg Police Service officer was convicted of several counts of sexual assault and sentenced to sixteen months in prison.

A high-profile case was that of former Montreal organized crime investigator Benoit Roberge, convicted of gangsterism and breach of trust for selling information to the Hells Angels motorcycle gang. Roberge was convicted in April 2014. He committed suicide shortly thereafter. This case is documented in the CBC *Fifth Estate* documentary "Walk the Line." See the Media Link at the end of this chapter.

Rotten Orchards: The New Orleans Police Department

In rare instances, an entire police service may be infected with corruption and criminal activity. The New Orleans Police Department (NOPD) has a long history of documented malfeasance, including crimes committed by police officers in the aftermath of Hurricane Katrina in 2005. The storm, which devastated much of the city, created chaos on a broad scale, and the NOPD was often an additional problem for residents struggling to survive in the storm's aftermath. On numerous occasions, police officers were found to have used excessive force, including shooting a person in the back seven times and attempting to destroy evidence of killings. Several police officers were subsequently convicted for their role in the shooting deaths of several African-Americans. All received lengthy sentences of incarceration (one of which was twenty-five years).[19]

The actions of the NOPD in the aftermath of the storm are captured in a video story entitled "Law & Disorder," available for viewing on the website of the PBS program *Frontline*. See the Media Link at the end of this chapter.

Activities in the Grey Area of Police Work

There are some activities that fall into what is often called the grey area of police work, and individual police officers are required to exercise good judgment in ensuring that their behaviour is not improper. It is often difficult to determine the point where discretion crosses the line and becomes discriminatory or illegal. An example involves officers accepting gifts and gratuities (such as free or discounted restaurant meals) or favourable treatment from the general public or the business community (often referred to as graft). These might be viewed as gestures of goodwill and appreciation rather than as efforts to compromise the integrity of the officer or police service.

The challenges of assessing the behaviour of officers in the grey areas are highlighted in the case presented in Critical Thinking Exercise 4.1 at the end of this chapter.

Off-Duty Activities and Misconduct

One of the grey areas in police ethics and professionalism is that of the off-duty conduct of police officers. That is, to what extent are officers held accountable for their actions and decisions when not in uniform and not on duty. While Canadian courts have held that police officers are held to a higher standard of conduct than ordinary citizens, there is also the recognition that officers have the right to a measure of freedom when they are off duty. The challenge is to maintain a balance of the interests of the police agency and the privacy rights of officers.[20]

Most police services have oath statements in which officers pledge to conduct their private and professional lives in an exemplary manner. And many provincial police acts and individual police services have provisions that address off-duty conduct. Police services also generally have policies regulating extra-duty and off-duty employment. Extra-duty employment is when the police service, for a fee, provides officers who would otherwise be off shift for events (e.g., sporting events, movie set locations). Off-duty employment involves activities that take place in the private sector and are separate from the police service. Most police services either restrict off-duty employment or prohibit it.

The nature of police work requires officers to exercise enforcement authority 24 hours a day, 365 days a year. It would be both unprofessional and unethical for a police officer to ignore this obligation even on days off. For example, an off-duty officer who observes an impaired driver or a shoplifter has a professional obligation to intervene. The level of intervention will vary with the circumstances and gravity of the offence.

At a minimum, the off-duty officer has an obligation to report the incident to the nearest police service. The off-duty officer may sometimes feel that direct intervention is required, which may include arresting the offender. This is provided for in Section 494 of the Criminal Code, which authorizes anyone to make an arrest under certain circumstances, as well as Section 495, which relates more specifically to the powers of arrest of those who identify themselves as police officers.

Several other issues surround work performed by off-duty officers. These include part-time employment, the use of force, and departmental liability. Off-duty officers are required to exercise diligence and attentiveness when away from the workplace. Also, they must conduct their personal lives in a manner that does not jeopardize the integrity of the police service that employs them. Every officer has an obligation to maintain a healthy and balanced lifestyle to ensure that he or she is both mentally and physically able to work effectively while on duty.

Off-duty police officers who intervene in situations where a crime or other situation has occurred over which they would have authority had they been on

Police Perspective 4.1

Ethics and the Off-Duty Officer

An officer who was on his way home from work in his own car, was "cut off" on the highway by another vehicle. He began to flash his headlights at the other vehicle in front of him, indicating that the driver should pull over. When she did not, he followed her until she pulled into the driveway of her home. He pulled into the driveway behind her, and proceeded to write out a traffic ticket for her alleged driving infraction. During this encounter he used very abusive and insulting language. As a result of the other driver's complaint, the officer was disciplined for disreputable conduct.

Source: Marin, R.J. (Chair). 2010. Discussion Paper 7. Off-Duty Conduct. Ottawa: Royal Canadian Mounted Police External Review Committee.

duty are generally considered to have the authority to arrest someone as if they were on duty. Conversely, if an officer abuses his or her authority while off duty, there may be sanctions applied by the department. This occurred in the case profiled in Police Perspective 4.1. In the situation described in that case, the officer had the authority to intervene in an offence that he observed and, in so doing put himself back "on duty," following which he engaged in disreputable conduct.

The provisions regarding off-duty activities are necessarily vague, and incidents are considered on a case-by-case basis. While illegal behaviour by officers who are off duty is unethical, not all unethical behaviour by off-duty officers is illegal. Generally, an officer will be sanctioned by the police service for off-duty behaviour only in those cases where the officer's actions are connected to their position as a police officer. Officers who are accused of off-duty criminal behaviour may be subject to both the criminal court process as well as to the disciplinary process in the police service.

Many complaints filed against the police are found not to be grounded.

REDUCING POLICE WRONGDOING

Equal attention must be given to preventing police wrongdoing. One strategy that has been proposed is ethics testing for police applicants, police recruits, and in-service officers. Police services have placed an increasing emphasis on the ethical integrity of applicants, and concerns over integrity are a primary reason that applicants are unsuccessful in their bid to become police officers. The recruit application process for police services generally involves an ethics and integrity questionnaire, and these topics are also covered in interviews with the prospective applicant.

It should not be presumed that misconduct is limited to patrol officers: In 2014, the former head of the Quebec provincial police was charged with fraud, theft, and breach of trust, along with three other high-ranking police officers in the Sûrete du Québec.[21]

The ethics of police officers have received little attention from police service scholars in Canada. There is some research from other jurisdictions, most notably Australia where inquiries into police corruption have provided the catalyst for ethics testing of officers and for research studies.

Although there are no statistics kept on violations of ethics by Canadian police officers, there is some evidence that the overall ethical integrity of police services and their officers has improved over the decades. This is due in part to a breakdown of the traditional police subculture that placed a premium on maintaining a code of secrecy even to the extent of protecting officers engaged in unethical and criminal behaviour.

THE ROLE OF POLICE LEADERSHIP IN ETHICS AND PROFESSIONALISM

Effective police leadership is required to ensure that a police service carries out its activities in an ethical and professional manner and that officers are held to a high standard of conduct. When individual, or groups of, police officers engage in misconduct, it is often the consequence of weak leadership and an organizational environment that does not have clear lines of accountability and effective supervision in place.

Police leaders can imprint a strong sense of ethics and professionalism in their police services, but this requires ongoing vigilance and continual organizational improvement. Unfortunately, most police services do not provide in-service ethics training, nor do they require officers to complete ethics programs and courses for advancement. As one scholar has noted, "Law enforcement agencies often view ethics instruction as a single training block, when it should be continually re-enforced. [O]ne lone course is unlikely to develop values or to change behaviors"[22]

The comments of a police officer on a forum on police ethics are instructive:

> [It] is incredibly important to have leaders with the moral courage to stand up for the right thing even if it is not popular. This profession draws to it those who are naturally physically courageous. In my opinion it is even harder to be morally courageous in the face of opposition from subordinates, peers, supervisors and the uninformed public. A strong moral leader has so much influence.[23]

A research study conducted on the Philadelphia (Pennsylvania) Police Department found that police officers who perceived the department as fair and just in its managerial practice were less likely to follow a "code of silence" or to believe that noble cause corruption was justified. And there were lower levels of misconduct among those officers who felt that the police service was organizationally "just," that is, that supervisors treated officers fairly, promotions were based on merit, and discipline was meted out fairly.[24]

POLICE ACCOUNTABILITY

A key trend in Canadian police work is a focus on ensuring that the police are accountable. Given the unique powers that police officers have, including the power to use lethal force and the power to deprive citizens of their freedom (see Chapter 7), it is essential that there be in place structures of accountability. It is also important that these structures, and the processes associated with them, be, to the greatest extent, transparent and accessible to citizens in the community. Should the citizenry come to perceive that police officers are not held accountable for their actions, and the structures of governance viewed as distant and impersonal, community confidence and trust in the police will be compromised.

police governance
the structures that guide the policies, strategic direction, and goals of a police service

police oversight
the processes that are in place to receive and respond to citizen complaints about the police

Efforts to hold the police accountable are made through governance and oversight. There is a distinction to be made between **police governance** and **police oversight**. The governance of the police generally refers to the structures that are in place to guide the policies, strategic direction, and goals of a police service. Oversight of the police most commonly refers to the processes that are in place to receive and respond to citizen complaints about the police.[25] At issue is the need to balance the powers that the police have to ensure the safety and security of citizens, while ensuring that these powers are not abused and that citizens' rights are not violated.

The growing complexity of police work and increased emphasis on public approval, transparency, and service have required new accountability structures.[26]

Canadian police services are held accountable through several means:[27*]

- *Political accountability* to governing authorities
- *Legal accountability* to the law through the courts and judiciary
- *Accountability to administrative agencies*, including complaints commissions, human rights commissions, provincial police commissions, auditor generals, and ombudsmen
- *Direct public accountability* through mechanisms such as freedom of information legislation
- *Accountability to the community*, often through community policing committees that play an advisory role
- *Special ad hoc accountability* through processes such as royal commissions, commissions of inquiry, task forces, and inquests

GOVERNANCE OF THE POLICE

> *No other criminal justice professional comes under as much constant and public scrutiny–but no other criminal justice professional wields so much discretion in so many circumstances. The scrutiny is understandable when one realizes that the police are power personified.*[28**]

A primary way in which the police are held accountable is through structures of governance. While it is important that the police be free from political interference, there must be governmental and judicial oversight of police activities.

---

* *In Search of Security: The Future of Policing in Canada by the Law Commission of Canada*, pp. 88–89. http://dsp-psd.pwgsc.gc.ca/Collection/JL2-26-2006E.pdf. Law Reform Commission of Canada, 2006. Reproduced with the permission of the Department of Justice Canada, 2015.

** Pollock, J.M. 2010. *Ethical Dilemmas and Decisions in Criminal Justice*. Belmont, CA: Wadsworth/Cengage Learning.

Governance is challenging: On the one hand, the police require a degree of operational autonomy to effectively and efficiently carry out their mandated tasks. Given the nature of their mandated role, the police need to be free from government interference and influence. It is important that the police not become an instrument for implementing government policy or to support specific political agendas. Historically, this has been unavoidable.

On the other hand, the principles of due process and of a democratic society require that there be mechanisms in place to govern the police, to ensure that police services do not exceed their mandate and compromise the rights of citizens. However, as several observers have noted, the precise nature and extent of the independence required by the police has remained unclear.[29]

Governance models are designed to achieve a number of goals, including maximizing efficiency in the utilization of available resources, achieving performance targets, maintaining specific standards of service, maintaining client (citizen) confidence, and ensuring that complaints about officers or the service provided are fairly considered and responded to.[30]

Figure 4.1 sets out the structures of police governance. Note that there are differences in how federal, provincial, regional, and municipal police services are governed.

The Minister of Public Safety is responsible for oversight of the RCMP within the framework of the RCMP Act, while the provincial police services of the Ontario Provincial Police, the Sûrete du Québec, and the Royal Newfoundland

police acts
the legislative framework for police services

policing standards
provisions that set out how police services are to be maintained and delivered

police boards and police commissions
bodies that provide oversight of police

Figure 4.1. Structures of Police Governance

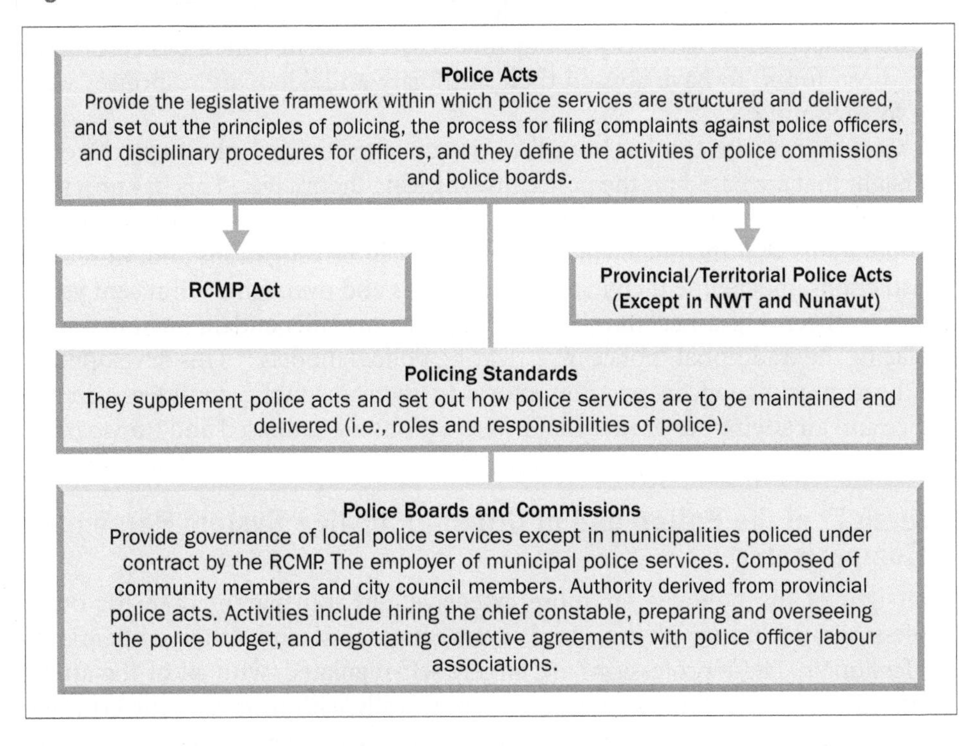

Source: From Griffiths. *Canadian Criminal Justice*, 5E. © 2015 Nelson Education Ltd. Reproduced by permission. www.cengage.com/permissions.

Constabulary are governed by the relevant provincial ministry. Municipal and regional police services, on the other hand, are governed by police commissions or police services boards composed of elected and/or appointed citizens.[31]

A concern is that the structures of oversight have not kept pace with the pluralistic nature of police work in the 21st century. For example, oversight commissions tend to consider the public and private police as separate entities, while, in fact, there is considerable overlap and collaboration in their activities. It has been noted that the regulation of private policing "tends to reflect a business regulation model rather than a model of public service governance."[32]

In recent years, concerns have also been expressed about the absence of structures of governance for the RCMP when they are serving as the contracted provincial police service and in the capacity of a contracted municipal police service. To address this, the federal government in 2014 enacted the Enhancing Royal Canadian Mounted Police Accountability Act. Among its provisions were the creation of the Civilian Review and Complaints Commission for the RCMP (CRCC), a civilian oversight body, which is discussed below (see the section The Oversight of RCMP Officers).

OVERSIGHT OF THE POLICE

Accountability of the police to the public includes the conduct of police officers and how they treat citizens. This, in turn, affects the levels of trust that the public has in the police as well as public perceptions of fairness and the extent to which the public ascribes legitimacy to the police. The legitimacy of the police can be seriously undermined by events in which police officers have been found to have abused their authority and adequate responses were not forthcoming.

Concurrent with this has been the critique of traditional structures of police oversight that are based on the police investigating themselves. This has provided the catalyst for the rise of civilian oversight and the emergence of models of accountability that include civilian involvement in investigations and, in several jurisdictions, independent civilian investigations and oversight.[33] In recent years, there has been a gradual trend toward civilian or independent review bodies replacing the traditional "police investigating police" models.[34] This development has been precipitated, in part, by efforts to increase public confidence in the police and an attempt to ensure that investigations are unbiased and transparent.

Oversight of the Police and of Criminal Justice System Personnel: A Comparison

Oversight of the police is far more extensive and transparent than for other professions, including physicians, lawyers, engineers, and other credentialed professionals. These professions are largely self-regulated, with all of the attendant difficulties that this presents. More specifically with respect to the criminal justice system, the activities and decisions of police officers are subject to more extensive internal and external review than their criminal justice counterparts (see Table 4.2).

TABLE 4.2
The Oversight of Criminal Justice Personnel: A Comparison

Position	Internal and External Oversight
Police officer	Internal and external accountability; civilian oversight; subject to criminal charges and civil suits
Crown counsel	Subject to internal review; no independent oversight; generally immune from prosecution and being required to testify in court
Defence lawyer	Subject to review/sanction by professional association; no independent oversight
Judge	Provincial/territorial judges subject to internal review; federal judges subject to review/sanctioning/dismissal by the Canadian Judicial Council; eight public inquiries into the behaviour of judges from 1971 to 2009; removal rare; no external independent oversight for judges at any level of the court system
Probation officer	Subject to internal review; generally immune from prosecution; no external independent oversight
Parole board member	Subject to internal review; generally immune from prosecution; no external independent oversight
Parole officer	Subject to internal review; generally immune from prosecution; no external independent oversight

To a much greater extent than other agencies, the police must justify their actions and counter the initial impressions and accounts of events that are placed on social media, and they are held accountable to political bodies, including municipal councils, provincial/federal governments, and in some instances, First Nations governments. For other criminal justice agencies, there is no equivalent of the independent, civilian-staffed investigative units with responsibility for police, including Ontario's Special Investigations Unit (SIU), the Alberta Serious Incident Response Team (ASIRT), and British Columbia's Independent Investigations Office (IIO). Rather, these systems generally investigate themselves. In the field of corrections, for example, the federal Office of the Correctional Investigator and the various provincial ombudsmen can only make *recommendations* and have no independent authority to implement changes in correctional policy and practice or to hold corrections personnel responsible for specific actions/inaction.

Police officers can be held accountable for their actions under the Criminal Code, as well as under civil law, provincial statutes, and freedom of information acts. As well, various police boards, complaint commissions, and investigative units both within and outside police services have the authority to oversee and review the actions and decisions of police officers. Governments may also call commissions of inquiry or appoint task forces to inquire into specific incidents involving a police service. A number of these inquiries are discussed throughout the text.

It is argued that the extensive oversight of the police is necessary due to their powers, including the authority to use lethal force. However, other criminal justice personnel make decisions that can have lethal consequences: a parole board releasing a dangerous offender who subsequently causes the death of a person(s) in the community; the decision of a Crown counsel to stay the proceedings against a person charged with a serious criminal offence who subsequently offends in a violent, lethal manner (as happened in the case of the decision of a British Columbia Crown counsel to stay proceedings against Robert Pickton in 1989; Pickton went on to murder dozens of women);[35] the failure of corrections personnel to intervene to prevent a prisoner from committing suicide (as happened in the well-documented case of Ashley Smith);[36] or the failure of a parole officer to adequately supervise a high-risk offender in the community, resulting in harm, including death, to a person(s) in the community. It is not only the police who exercise discretion that can result in serious incidents occurring.

OVERSIGHT OF POLICE SERVICES AND OFFICERS: THE COMPLAINT PROCESS

A key component of police work in a democratic society is that there be an open and transparent process by which citizens can complain about the police and by which serious incidents involving the police are investigated. Structures of police oversight and the procedures for receiving, and investigating, complaints against the police are an integral part of the governance structure. In most police services, the number of compliments received by police services exceed the number of complaints. In 2012, for example, the London (ON) Police Service received 131 "thank you" letters from the public and 101 complaints, most of which were "conduct complaints."[37]

Historically, persons in the community who had complaints about the behaviour of police officers were required to file their grievances with the officer's department, which then conducted an investigation. This was an intimidating process and probably deterred many potential complainants and resulted in investigations that were biased in cases where complaints were filed. Police services have traditionally resisted attempts to establish processes for external review. However, systems for citizens to file complaints against police officers are one way to ensure police accountability and to maintain the public's trust and confidence, as well as to identify systemic problems in police–community relations. In recent years, increasing attention has been given to the investigation of complaints against the police. And the existing structures and processes for responding to complaints have come under increasing scrutiny.

The process by which a person may file a complaint against the police is similar across the country, although there is considerable variation in the structures that are in place to receive and investigate the complaints. Generally speaking, citizens can file a complaint about the conduct of a police officer, the policies of a police service, or the services provided by a police service. Under the Police Act in British Columbia, for example, there are three types of complaints: (1) service or policy complaints, relating to the policies, procedures, and services of a police service; (2) public trust complaints, which are related to alleged misconduct by a police officer; and (3) internal discipline complaints, relating to the officer's conduct in the police service.

The most frequent complaints against police officers involve the conduct of police officers and include allegations of disreputable conduct, abuse of authority, and poor officer attitude.[38] The types of activity in a particular police district may impact the number and types of complaints filed against police officers. High-intensity environments, such as entertainment districts that attract large numbers of younger persons and neighbourhoods with a high percentage of visible minority residents with a history of distrust of and conflict with the police, may produce higher levels of complaints against the police.

All police services have internal policies to which police officers are accountable, internal units to investigate alleged misconduct on the part of officers, and a disciplinary process that includes a variety of sanctions that can be imposed on officers found guilty of misconduct. Officers who work in internal investigation units have a difficult and challenging mandate.

Complaints can also be filed against the conduct of an off-duty police officer, if the conduct compromised the duties of the officer or the reputation of the police service. The time limit is generally six months for filing a complaint, and complaints are usually restricted to the person who was directly affected by the actions of the officer or of the police service.

The sanctions imposed by the police service for these infractions can include having the constable work a fixed number of days without pay and/or a demotion in rank, or dismissal. Often, officers resign prior to being formally dismissed. In some cases, disciplinary action may be delayed to provide the officer with the opportunity to address personal issues that were associated with the misconduct, such as alcohol or drug issues, family issues, or psychological issues. See Class/Group Discussion 4.1 at the end of this chapter.

Informal Resolution of Complaints

All jurisdictions and the RCMP provide for the informal resolution of complaints. This requires the agreement of both the subject officer and the complainant to participate in a session guided by a facilitator.

Most of the complaints filed against police officers are resolved informally, often through some form of mediation. This occurred in the case presented in Box 4.1 in which the officers were alleged to have violated public trust and abused their authority.

Box 4.1

The Coffee Shop Incident

The complainant alleged that he was at a coffee shop and had exited the washroom when he noticed two men staring at him. The complainant ignored them and they allegedly twisted his arm behind his back and placed him under arrest. The complainant resisted and demanded to see identification as the officers were not in uniform. The officers allegedly pulled the complainant outside and punched him. A coffee shop employee enquired as to what was going on when he was told to "back off, they were police officers." The complainant said he was hit until he fell to the ground and was handcuffed. The complainant was taken to jail, then released in the morning with a ticket for public intoxication. The complainant and respondent reached a resolution using the mediation process. The discussions that occurred during the mediation were useful and educational for all parties.

Source: British Columbia. Office of the Police Complaint Commissioner, 2009:19.

The Oversight of RCMP Officers

RCMP External Review Committee
an oversight body of the RCMP that hears appeals from RCMP officers who have been disciplined

Civilian Review and Complaints Commission for the RCMP (CRCC)
an independent civilian body that receives complaints made by citizens against RCMP officers who are policing under contract

Two bodies oversee the conduct of RCMP officers: the **RCMP External Review Committee** and the **Civilian Review and Complaints Commission for the RCMP (CRCC)**.

The former hears appeals from RCMP members who have been disciplined for an infraction of force regulations. The CRCC is an independent federal agency that receives and reviews complaints made by citizens about the conduct of RCMP officers who are policing under contract (that is, who are serving as provincial or municipal police officers; see http://www.crcc-ccetp.gc.ca).

The most common citizen complaints relate to the quality of RCMP investigations, the use of force, search and seizure, the attitude of the officer in an encounter situation, and the quality of service provided. These complaints are initially referred to the RCMP for investigation and disposition. If the complainant is not satisfied with the outcome of the RCMP investigation, the commission may conduct an independent review and recommend appropriate actions to the RCMP commissioner. The CRCC also has the authority to conduct reviews of RCMP activities, including policies, programs, and practices.

Roughly one-tenth of the 2,500 or so complaints that are made against the RCMP each year are reviewed by the commission at the request of complainants. In most cases, the findings of the commission support the RCMP's disposition of the complaint. In many cases, the commission uses alternative dispute resolution (ADR); this process brings together the complainant and the RCMP member(s) as soon as possible after the incident in an attempt to resolve the outstanding issues informally.

MODELS OF PUBLIC COMPLAINTS AGAINST THE POLICE AND INVESTIGATIONS OF POLICE OFFICER MISCONDUCT

There is considerable variation across the country in the models that are used in an attempt to receive and investigate complaints against the police. Generally speaking there are three models of investigations, referred to as (1) the dependent model, (2) the interdependent model, and (3) the independent model (see Figure 4.2). The features of each model are set out in Table 4.3.

The Dependent Model

dependent model (of investigation)
the practice of police investigating themselves

In the **dependent model (of investigation)**, complaints filed against the police and serious incidents are investigated by the police. The police service is given the responsibility to undertake investigations, including criminal investigations, into cases involving other police officers.

There are two subtypes in the dependent model: one involves the police service investigating its own officers (internal); the second subtype involves the investigation being conducted by officers from another police service, either within or outside the particular jurisdiction (external; see Table 4.3).

In certain cases, police services will request that officers from another police service conduct the investigation. The external approach is widely used in an attempt to avoid an investigation being conducted by an officer's peers and colleagues. It is common practice, for example, for the RCMP and other police

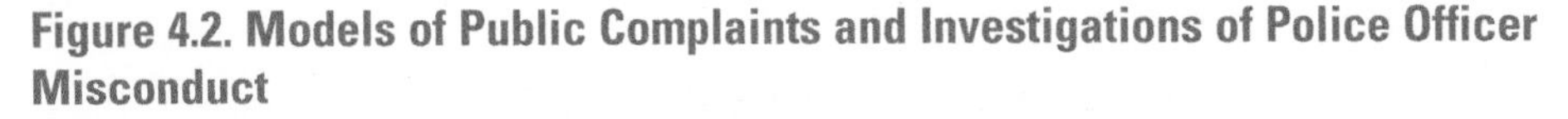

Figure 4.2. Models of Public Complaints and Investigations of Police Officer Misconduct

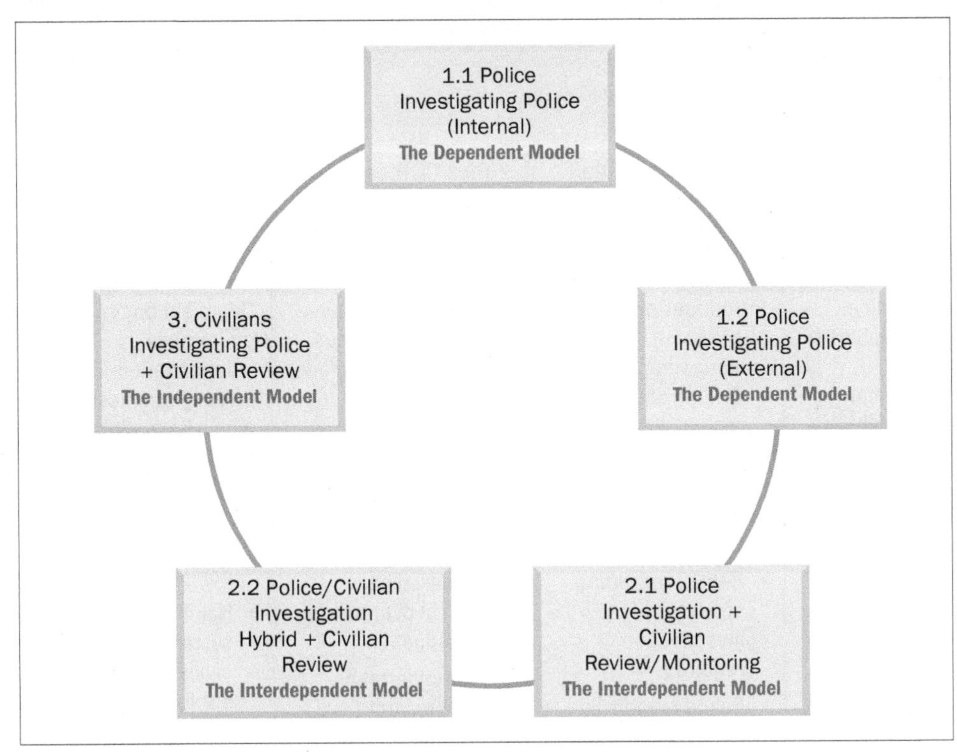

Source: *Police Investigating Police: A Critical Analysis of the Literature,* http://crcc-ccetp.gc.ca/en/police-investigating-police-critical-analysis-literature, Commission for Public Complaints Against the RCMP, 2009. Reproduced with the permission of the Civilian Review and Complaints Commission for the RCMP, 2014.

services to call upon the officers from other police agencies (and other RCMP detachments) to conduct investigations, particularly in more serious cases.

This model of police accountability has come under increasing scrutiny in recent years, and there is a widespread perception among the public and politicians that the police should not investigate themselves. This is due to the poor optics of a police-on-police investigation and questions as to whether the police can conduct a thorough and unbiased investigation on their colleagues. Of concern is the influence of the police culture on investigations, with one police scholar stating: "One of the reasons that the police cannot be trusted to investigate themselves is the way they are socialized. Policemen and women have been shown to spend much of their time socializing with other policemen and women. As a result, they may be insensitive to prevailing social norms and public expectations."[39]

The primary benefit of the dependent model rests in the availability of experienced and legally empowered officers. As well, the availability of resources ensures that the expertise of the investigating body is well established and supported. However, the primary concern with this model is the bias that may be inherent in the police investigating themselves. This, in turn, may lead to allegations of cover-ups, mishandling of investigations, and the police protecting their own. Regardless of whether these concerns have any real basis in any particular case, it is the perception of bias and favouritism that provides the strongest support for movement away from the dependent model.

TABLE 4.3
Models of Investigations of Police

1. Dependent Model		2. Interdependent Model		3. Independent Model
1.1 Police Investigating Police	**1.2 Police Investigating Another Police Force**	**2.1 Police Investigation and Civilian Review/ Monitoring**	**2.2 Police/Civilian Investigation and Civilian Review**	**3. Civilian Investigation and Review**
Represents police investigating police criminal investigations: • Police fully responsible for the investigation and administration of public complaints • No civilian involvement in a criminal investigation • Oversight body recognizes complaints regarding service, internal discipline or public trust • Oversight body may be an appellate authority	Represents police investigating another police force: • Involves formal arrangements (memoranda of agreement) in place with another police force to handle investigation of police officers in cases of death or serious bodily harm • Unlegislated process • In place only in select provinces in Canada	Introduces civilian observation to investigation • Civilian observer responsible to monitor criminal investigation (not direct or oversee investigation) • Regular reporting on status of investigation required • Police responsible for investigation, adjudication, and administration of public complaints	Oversight body may choose from various options, which include: a) may supervise/ manage parts of police criminal investigation (beyond monitor/oversee) conducted by police b) may assume control over police investigation c) may undertake independent criminal investigation • Oversight body can refer investigation to police force • Police can be involved in some form of collaboration, cooperation, or coordination of the actual investigation of public complaints with oversight body	Oversight body undertakes independent criminal investigation for cases within its mandate • Police are excluded or removed from process of investigating public complaints • Hallmark of this system is that civilian personnel are fully responsible for investigation • Nil ability to refer investigation to police

Source: *Police Investigating Police: Final Public Report,* http://www.cpc-cpp.gc.ca/prr/rep/rev/chair-pre/pipR/pip-finR-eng/pdf, Commission for Public Complaints against the RCMP, 2009. Reproduced with the permission of the Civilian Review and Complaints Commission for the RCMP, 2014.

There are a number of advantages to the dependent model, including the presence of investigative expertise in the police service and a knowledge of policing. On the other hand, the optics of the police investigating themselves may undermine the legitimacy of the police, and investigators may be (or be perceived to be) sympathetic to fellow officers.

interdependent model (of investigation)
a procedure for complaint investigation with varying degrees of civilian involvement

The Interdependent Model

In the **interdependent model (of investigation)**, there are varying degrees of civilian involvement in the process. The two subtypes of the interdependent model are (1) civilian observation only and (2) civilian–police hybrid investigation (see Table 4.3).

The first subtype of the interdependent model limits the civilian involvement in the investigation phases of a complaint, which continue to be conducted by police officers. The civilian contribution involves oversight after the investigation is complete, to ensure that the investigative process adhered to policy. In the hybrid subtype of the interdependent model, however, there is considerably more civilian involvement. Typically, civilians work closely with police officers to investigate a complaint. The hybrid model, therefore, extends civilian involvement beyond an oversight role to one of active participation in the investigation.

A number of criticisms have been directed toward the interdependent model, chief among them being that there is no true "independent" review of the police.[40] Generally, the investigation is conducted by police officers, and in most cases, the civilian reviewers cannot conduct independent investigations or hearings, subpoena witnesses, or retrieve documents.[41]

The Independent Model

In the **independent model (of investigation)**, there is an exclusive reliance on civilians to conduct all phases of the investigation, including investigating complaints and incidents and making recommendations (see Table 4.3).

independent model (of investigation)
a complaint procedure in which civilians conduct all phases of the investigation

Although this model often includes retired police officers who are well versed and experienced in such investigations, they no longer possess their original police powers. Conversely, the model may also be run exclusively with civilians who have no prior connections to, or experience with, policing. This model is considered highly objective and impartial, as the police play no role in the investigation. On the other hand, there may be challenges in securing police cooperation in the investigation, and the investigators may be viewed as not having the requisite expertise to conduct a throughout and impartial investigation.

THE ROLE OF POLICE COMMISSIONS

All of the provinces have police commissions or public complaints commissions that are involved in providing oversight of police services in their respective jurisdictions. These bodies hear appeals from officers who have been sanctioned by internal disciplinary hearings, initiate investigations and inquiries into how police services are being delivered, and receive complaints from the general public. For links to the oversight agencies in Canada, go to http://www.oiprd.on.ca and search for "oversight organizations."

ESTABLISHING MECHANISMS TO ENSURE COMMUNITY INPUT INTO POLICING

In recent years, there have been a number of initiatives across Canada to provide community input and oversight of the police. In Alberta, for example, communities policed by the RCMP under contract have the option to establish a policing committee. The activities of the policing committees in Alberta include overseeing the agreement between the city and the Government of Canada for the employment of the RCMP; providing key feedback to the RCMP concerning policing, as well as to city bylaw enforcement strategies and activities; cooperating and liaising with key groups in creating programs that are pursuing initiatives to improve public safety; reviewing and advising city council on the annual protective services goals and priorities; and assisting the officer in charge in resolving public complaints.[42] Similar provisions for the establishment of policing committees exist in the province of Ontario. Note, however, that community policing committees are not mandatory and that there is no legal requirement that the police consult with policing committees.

INCREASING POLICE OVERSIGHT: THE LEGACY OF TRAGEDIES

There have been a number of critical incidents in recent years that have resulted in significant reforms to police oversight across the country. In Yukon, the death of an Aboriginal man, Raymond Silverfox, in a police cell prompted numerous reforms, including the creation of a Yukon Police Council. This is the first of its kind in an RCMP-policed jurisdiction.[43] (See the discussion of the death of Raymond Silverfox in Chapter 8.) On October 14, 2007, Robert Dziekanski, a Polish immigrant who had arrived at Vancouver International Airport, became involved in an incident with four RCMP officers. In the ensuing encounter, he was Tasered by the officers and subsequently died. This case is discussed further in Chapter 7. The recommendations of the final report of a Commission of Inquiry looking into the Dziekanski case led to the creation in 2012 of an Independent Investigations Office (IIO) in British Columbia, a civilian-directed and -staffed agency that investigates police incidents involving serious harm or any alleged Criminal Code violation by a police officer in the province (see http://www.iiobc.ca).

In Manitoba, the death of Crystal Taman prompted significant reforms for police oversight (see Box 4.2).

Box 4.2

The Death of Crystal Taman

At 7:00 a.m. on February 25, 2005, Crystal Taman was driving to work. While stopped at a red light, her vehicle was rear-ended by a pickup truck driven by an off-duty police officer, Derek Harvey-Zenk, who was returning home from an all-night party with his colleagues from the Winnipeg Police Service.

The provincial government appointed a special prosecutor for the case. Harvey-Zenk was charged with impaired driving causing death, refusing a breathalyzer test, dangerous operation of a motor vehicle causing death, and criminal negligence causing death. Two years later, however, the charges were pled down to dangerous driving causing death (a lesser charge than criminal negligence causing death) and the other charges were dropped. At sentencing, Harvey-Zenk received a conditional sentence of two years less a day, to be served at his home. He also resigned his position in the Winnipeg Police Service.

The controversy surrounding the case, and specifically concerns that Harvey-Zenk received preferential treatment as a police officer, prompted the Manitoba government to appoint a Commission of Inquiry. The inquiry, headed by a retired Ontario provincial court judge, examined the response and decisions of the chief and several officers in the East St. Paul Police Service, as well as the investigation conducted by the Winnipeg Police Service Professional Standards Unit, which was requested by the East St. Paul Police Service to conduct an investigation.

The inquiry found that the then-Chief of the East St. Paul Police Service, Harry Bakema, who had previously worked with Harvey-Zenk in the Winnipeg Police Service, botched the investigation, falsified his field notes, and gave false evidence at the inquiry.

A key recommendation of the inquiry was that the provincial government create an independent oversight agency to investigate alleged criminal acts of police officers. Subsequent to the inquiry, the provincial government enacted a new Police Services Act that created the Manitoba Police Commission, civilian-led boards with the power to hire and fire police chiefs for major municipal police services, and a directive to the police commission to establish an Independent Investigation Unit that will investigate serious incidents involving the police, including the police use of lethal force. The provincial government also settled a civil suit that had been filed by the Taman family. The East St. Paul Police Service was disbanded and replaced by an RCMP detachment.

Following an external investigation by the RCMP, in late 2010, the former chief was subsequently charged with perjury, criminal breach of trust, and obstruction of justice. In 2013, he was found not guilty on all charges.

Sources: Hon. R. Salhany (Commissioner). (2008). *Taman Inquiry into the Investigation and Prosecution of Derek Harvey-Zink*. Winnipeg: Ministry of Attorney General, retrieved from http://www.tamaninquiry.ca; and D. Pritchard. (2013, November 1). "Ex-Police Chief Harry Bakema Found Not Guilty in East St. Paul Crash Aftermath." *Winnipeg Sun*, retrieved from http://www.winnipegsun.com/2013/11/01/ex-police-chief-bakema-awaits-legal-fate.

THE ADEQUACY OF THE POLICE COMPLAINT/INVESTIGATION PROCESSES

There are a number of ongoing concerns about the adequacy of the police complaint and investigation process. Serious flaws have been found in the way in which the RCMP investigates its officers for alleged misconduct. In one study, it was found that in 25 percent of the cases, the investigator knew the officer who was under investigation; in one-third of the cases, the primary investigator was at the same or lower rank than the officer being investigated; and in 60 percent of the cases, only one investigator was assigned to the case. The report also found that there were no uniform standards for conducting investigations and that there was considerable variation in the qualifications of the officers conducting the investigations.[44]

Aboriginals and the Complaint Process

A number of inquiries have raised the question as to whether existing police complaint processes meet the needs of First Nations peoples and that First Nations may not be aware of the process for filing a complaint against the police and/or do not have faith in the complaint process.[45] The various complaints commissions receive very few complaints. This either means that there are few difficulties that arise between the police and Aboriginals, or (the more likely scenario) for a variety of reasons, that Aboriginal people do not exercise their right to complain about the police.

A review of policing in Yukon found that many residents had little understanding of, or faith in, the complaints process. Some residents expressed the fear that there would be retaliation if they filed a complaint. In the words of one resident:

> I wouldn't make a complaint even if I knew how to do it. I would fear what they would do to me when they found out I made a complaint and they would find out. This is a small town and there is no way to keep it from them.[46]

To better serve the interests of First Nations and Metis people in Saskatchewan, the Federation of Saskatchewan Indian Nations operates a Special Investigations Unit composed of First Nations staff with policing and justice-related experience.

THE EFFECTIVENESS OF OVERSIGHT AND INVESTIGATIONS

Despite increased attention on the need to provide oversight of the police and to ensure that investigations of the police are transparent, thorough, and unbiased, there is little research on the effectiveness of the various models that have been developed. The extent to which police boards and commissions, commissions of inquiry, task forces, and other investigations into police conduct have improved the accountability of the police cannot be determined.

The term "toothless wonder" for example, has been used to describe the Ontario SIU. The Work of the SIU has been hindered by a lack of resources and limited legal authority.[47] Oversight agencies often find themselves at the centre of controversy. This occurred in the shooting death of Greg Matters, profiled in Box 4.3.

In the absence of research studies, it is not possible to determine the validity of the advantages and disadvantages that have been identified for each of the three models for public complaints and investigation discussed above. For example, while there is an emerging consensus that the traditional model of police investigating police is inadequate, the means by which effective civilian investigation and oversight can be implemented, while ensuring the involvement and cooperation of the police, have yet to be determined.[48] See Critical Thinking Exercise 4.2 at the end of this chapter.

Box 4.3

The Shooting of Greg Matters

The British Columbia Independent Investigations Office (IIO) found itself at the centre of controversy in the shooting death of Greg Matters, a 40-year-old Canadian military veteran who had served in Bosnia and was being treated for post-traumatic stress disorder. Mr. Matters was shot on September 10, 2012, by a member of an RCMP Emergency Response Team who went to the Matters' residence to assist on a warrant for his arrest. A thirty-hour standoff ensued, during which Mr. Matters threatened an RCMP officer with a hatchet.

The final IIO report into the incident was issued in April 2013. It concluded that no criminal charges should be filed against the RCMP officers who were involved in the incident. The report stated that Mr. Matters had been shot by a member of an RCMP Emergency Response Team "with two bullets to the chest" after allegedly threatening an ERT member with a hatchet.

A pathologist's report submitted to the coroner's inquest into the incident concluded that Mr. Matters had been shot twice in the back. Despite this, the director of the IIO indicated in a supplementary report in June 2014 that there was no new evidence that a criminal offence had been committed by the RCMP officer, and that the investigation would not be reopened. According to the IIO director, the RCMP officer who fired the shots was protecting the life of another officer. Therefore, in his view, the direction of the shots was not an issue. However, several weeks later, the director of the IIO announced the appointment of a civilian monitor to reopen the investigation. It was also revealed that the RCMP flew a helicopter over the scene at low altitude, likely triggering Mr. Matters's post-traumatic stress disorder.

The report of the civilian monitor was released in November 2014; it found no fault with the IIO's investigative process in the case, although the integrity of the investigation was compromised somewhat by the decision of the IIO director to assign two officers to the case in violation of the province's Police Act. Both officers had worked for a police service within the previous five years.

See the documentary film on the case, "In the War Zone," in the Media Links at the end of this chapter.

Sources: S. Cooper. (2014, June 18). "Review of Matters case not closed yet." *Vancouver Province*, retrieved from http://www.bcpolicecomplaints.org/greg_matters_bc_iio_independent_investigations_office_review.html; and M. Nielsen and C. Evelyn. (2014, November 18). "Lawyer clears IIO in Matters investigation," *The Prince George Citizen*, retrieved from http://www.princegeorgecitizen.com/news/local-news/lawyer-clears-iio-in-matters-investigation-1.1590161.

Summary

This chapter has examined ethics and accountability in policing. Due to the nature of their work, police officers are often presented with ethical dilemmas. The decisions they make may lead to various forms of misconduct and wrongdoing. In contrast to their criminal justice counterparts, police officers are subjected to many layers of accountability. Each of the models of public complaints and investigations of the police have advantages and disadvantages. In recent years, there has been an increase in civilian oversight of the police. In several jurisdictions, this has been prompted by tragic events and their aftermath. It was also noted that there is a paucity of research on the effectiveness of the various structures and models of police oversight and investigation.

KEY POINTS REVIEW

1. Given the unique powers and authority of the police, it is essential that there be structures of accountability and governance.
2. The discretion and authority vested in police officers, and the wide variety of encounter situations in which they become involved, result in officers experiencing ethical dilemmas.
3. Codes of ethics establish standards of behaviour for police officers to ensure that they carry out their tasks ethically, with integrity, and within the parameters of the law.
4. There are a number of types of police misconduct, ranging from violations of departmental regulations and standards of professional conduct to the commission of a criminal offence.
5. Research studies suggest that, in Canada, police misconduct is more the rotten apple rather than the rotten barrel or rotten orchard variety.
6. Much police misconduct occurs in the "grey area" of policing where the lines are blurred between the proper use of discretion and unethical or illegal behaviour.
7. Police officers are held to a high standard of conduct even when they are not on duty.
8. Police acts, policing standards, and police boards and commissions are designed to provide governance and accountability of the police.
9. The oversight of the police is far more extensive and transparent than for other professions in the criminal justice system.
10. Police officers can be held accountable for their actions under the Criminal Code and through a variety of other oversight and review processes and agencies.
11. Although it is important that the police be independent of political interference and have a degree of operational autonomy, there must be structures in place to ensure that they do not exceed their mandate and infringe on the rights of citizens.
12. It is important in a democratic society that there be an open and transparent process by which citizens can complain about the police and, in this process, by which complaints are investigated. Most of the complaints against police officers that are founded are resolved informally, often through mediation between the officer(s) involved and the citizen.
13. A number of high-profile tragedies have provided the catalyst for reforming the police complaint and investigative process.

14. There is little research on the effectiveness of the various models of police oversight and investigation, and what findings do exist suggest that these models are often challenged to meet their mandate.
15. The police subculture may contribute to, facilitate, and justify police misconduct.
16. Police leadership plays a significant role in ensuring ethics and professionalism in the police service.

KEY TERM QUESTIONS

1. Define and discuss **ethics**, **codes of ethics**, and **ethical dilemmas** and their role in police work.
2. What is meant by **rotten apples**, **rotten barrels**, and **rotten orchards**?
3. What is **noble cause corruption** and how does it occur?
4. Compare and contrast **police governance** and **police oversight**.
5. What role do **police acts**, **policing standards**, **police boards**, and **police commissions** play in the governance of the police?
6. Describe the role of the **RCMP External Review Committee** and the **Civilian Review and Complaints Commission for the RCMP (CRCC)** in the oversight of the RCMP.
7. Describe the **dependent**, **interdependent**, and **independent models** of police complaints and investigation, the subtypes that exist within each model, and the advantages and disadvantages of each model.

CRITICAL THINKING EXERCISES

Critical Thinking Exercise 4.1. The Case of the Off-Duty Date

Two patrol constables in an urban police service are called to the scene of a domestic dispute. On arrival, they determine that the woman has been physically assaulted by her boyfriend, who is subsequently arrested and charged under the Criminal Code. Several days after the incident, one of the officers involved in the incident, who is on his day off, sees the other officer, who is also on his day off, in a city park with the female victim of the assault. The officer and the female victim are walking hand in hand. In the view of the other officer, they are obviously on a "date." A month later, the boyfriend appears in court and the two officers are called to give evidence under oath about the incident.

Your Thoughts?

1. Is there anything wrong with the officer dating the crime victim?
2. What action, if any, should be taken by the officer who observed his colleague with the woman in the park?
3. Should either or both of the officers be precluded from giving evidence in the court case? Explain.

Critical Thinking Exercise 4.2. How Effective Are Police Oversight Agencies?

> An independent and effective complaints system is of fundamental importance for the operation of a democratic and accountable police service.... Independent and effective determination of complaints enhances public trust and confidence in the police and ensures that there is no impunity for misconduct or ill-treatment (Filsted and Gottschalk, 2011).

The discussion in this chapter has identified a number of models for police oversight, each of which has advantages and disadvantages. A challenge that has been identified by police scholars is how to measure the effectiveness of police oversight agencies and the extent to which these agencies have developed best practices based on their performance outcomes. One measure of effectiveness might be a decrease in the number of complaints filed against the police in a particular jurisdiction, indicating a reduction in police misconduct. However, a decrease could, alternatively, be interpreted as a lack of trust on the part of citizens in the oversight agency, resulting in fewer complaints being filed. Similarly, there are often no procedures in place to monitor the impact of an intervention by a police complaints agency on the subsequent attitudes and behaviours of the subject officer.

Among the suggestions have been offered by police scholars for assessing the effectiveness of police oversight agencies are the following:

1. The quantity and quality of received complaints: a higher level of relevant complaints indicates improved process performance
2. Complaints completion process and time: complaints are handled in a professional and timely manner.
3. Conviction rate from complaints charges: more convictions relative to prosecutions indicates improved results performance.
4. Learning and advice for police agencies: the oversight agency communicates information back to the police service on the cases handled, which, in turn, is used by the agency.
5. Confidence in the police oversight agency: a higher level of confidence among the public and the police indicates improved process and result performance.

Source: C. Filsted and P. Gottschalk. (2011). "Performance Evaluation of Police Oversight Agencies." *Policing & Society*, 21(1), 96–109.

Your Thoughts?

1. In your opinion, which of the measures set out above (if any) could be used to evaluate the effectiveness of police oversight agencies?
2. What are the strengths and weaknesses of the proposed measures?
3. What criteria would you use of assess the effectiveness of police oversight agencies? And what are the strengths and weaknesses of each of the criteria that you have identified?

CLASS/GROUP DISCUSSION EXERCISES

Class/Group Discussion 4.1. Officer Misconduct and Discipline: Case Studies

Following are several cases involving misconduct by police officers and the discipline that was imposed.

Recall from earlier in this chapter that the sanctions imposed by the police service for misconduct can include having the constable work a fixed number of days without pay and/or a demotion in rank, or discharge/dismissal/resignation. Disciplinary action may be delayed to provide the officer with the opportunity to address personal issues that were associated with the misconduct, such as alcohol or drug issues, family issues, or psychological issues.

Case 1: The Smackdown.

While off duty in a small northern community, a police constable drove around in his police cruiser looking for an eleven-year-old boy who had alleged assaulted his nine-year-old stepson. The constable was accompanied by his wife, stepson, and their baby. When the boy was located, the constable's wife exited from the cruiser and invited her son to punch the eleven-year-old. The son hit the eleven-year-old several times, leaving the boy bloodied. The constable then drove away without offering any assistance to the boy. The constable's wife subsequently pled guilty to assault.

Source: B. Hutchinson, "What Does the Force Do with a Wayward Mountie?" *National Post*, December 12, 2009, A9.

Your Thoughts?

1. Should the constable be charged with assault?
2. If not, what penalty, if any, should he receive?

Case 2: Incident at McDonald's.

An off-duty constable entered the drive-thru lane at a McDonald's and became involved in a confrontation with three youths who were on foot and placing an order in front of him. The constable left his vehicle, grabbed a young woman, and punched her in the face. Bleeding profusely and with fractured teeth, she fell to the ground. The constable left the scene. He was charged with common assault and pled guilty.

Source: B. Hutchinson. (2009, December 12). "The Mounting Mountie Misconduct." *National Post*, p. A9. Reprinted at and retrieved from http://www.bcpolicecomplaints.org/rcmp_offences.html.

Your Thoughts?

What penalty, if any, should be imposed by the sentencing judge? Why? What penalty, if any, should be imposed by his police service? Why?

Case 3: The Case of the Wrong-Way Officer.

After having a few beers with a colleague while off duty, the police inspector drove his car into a lane reserved for transit buses. He was stopped by a municipal transit officer at which point he flashed his badge and told the transit officer that he was on duty. The transit officer allowed the police officer to drive away but pulled him over again when he noted that the officer's vehicle was swerving. The local municipal police were called, and following a breathalyzer test, the police inspector received a twelve-hour roadside suspension.

This same officer had seven previous incidents of disgraceful conduct, related to inappropriate sexual relations with a female officer who was taking one of his training courses. Despite attempting to disrupt the investigation, he was suspended for fifty-five days, docked twenty-five days' pay, and prohibited from teaching future training courses.

Source: B. Hutchinson. (2009, December 12). "The Mounting Mountie Misconduct." *National Post*, p. A9. Reprinted at and retrieved from http://www.bcpolicecomplaints.org/rcmp_offences.html.

Your Thoughts?

1. Was the discipline imposed appropriate?
2. As a member of the disciplinary board, what penalty, if any, would you impose on the officer? Why?

Case 4. The Constable, His Wife, and the Hells Angels.

Crossing the border from Manitoba into the U.S., a police constable's wife was stopped and questioned by U.S. border authorities. During the interview, she told the agents that she had former business dealings with a member of the Hells Angels and continued to visit him in prison. The U.S. authorities contacted the RCMP, which conducted an internal investigation. This revealed that the constable had viewed 185 documents relating to his wife and the Hells Angel in the RCMP's national data bank over a period of several months. Interviewed by RCMP investigators, the constable admitted that he made the data checks, but denied sharing the information with the Hells Angels, although he did admit to sharing some of the information with his wife.

Source: G. Dimmock. (2011, May 30). "Mountie Disciplined for Sharing Crime Data," *Vancouver Sun*, p. B3.

Your Thoughts?

What penalty, if any, would you impose as a member of the disciplinary board?

The Actual Decisions for Class/Group Discussion 4.1.

Case 1: The constable was not charged with assault, but an adjudication board imposed a sanction of loss of four days' wages. He was allowed to continue on active duty.

Case 2: The constable received a suspended sentence and one year on probation. The police adjudication board docked him ten days' pay and he returned to active duty.

Case 3: The disciplinary board imposed a sanction of loss of five days' wages and he returned to active duty.

Case 4: The investigation resulted in the constable being docked eight days' pay.

MEDIA LINKS

Visit www.nelson.com/canadianpolicework4 for links to these videos and other additional content available with this text.

"Walk the Line," *The Fifth Estate*, CBC, January 24, 2014, cbc.ca/fifth

"Law & Disorder," *Frontline*, PBS, August 25, 2010, pbs.org/frontline

"In the War Zone," W5, CTV, October 5, 2013, ctvnews.ca/w5

5 The Police Occupation

LEARNING OBJECTIVES

After reading this chapter, you should be able to:

- Identify and discuss the basic and preferred qualifications for police officers
- Discuss the importance of recruiting diversity
- Describe the recruit selection process
- Discuss the competition for previously experienced officers (PEOs)
- Discuss the models of recruit training
- Describe the socialization of police recruits into the role of police officer
- Discuss operational field training
- Discuss the issues surrounding being a police officer, including the working personality of police, the police culture, and the types of police officers
- Discuss the challenges of police work, including the various sources of stress experienced by officers
- Describe the consequences of stress, including post-traumatic stress disorder and the challenges of addressing the difficulties experienced by officers

The occupation of policing is unique. Police work presents challenges, risks, and rewards, and it requires special knowledge, skills, and abilities.

BECOMING A POLICE OFFICER

The basic reasons why people choose to become a police officer, most commonly the opportunity to help people, job security, and the prestige of the profession, have remained fairly constant over the years.[1] However, there has been a continued decline in the numbers of youth who are interested in a career in policing and in the perceived levels of support from their family and friends for becoming a police officer. In 2010, only 3 percent of youth surveyed nationwide indicated that policing was their primary choice for a career, although only 10 percent of those surveyed felt that a person's race could affect their chances of becoming a police officer.[2] See Police Perspective 5.1.

Competition among applicants to police services is highly competitive at every stage of recruiting. Many of those accepted have completed some post-secondary education and many have undergraduate degrees. Most police recruits are mature individuals with a variety of life skills and have had a variety of life experiences that include travel, volunteer work, and/or full-time employment. An applicant must be prepared to have every aspect of their life (good, bad, and ugly) examined, including, in some instances, open sources such as Facebook.[3] See Class/Group Discussion 5.1 at the end of this chapter.

Basic Qualifications

Recall from the discussion in Chapter 2 that, historically, there were minimal qualifications for becoming a police officer. Physical stature was the primary consideration in the early days of Canadian policing. Women were generally

Police Perspective 5.1

A Police Leader Speaks about Becoming a Police Officer

In many cases, people don't know what to expect when they become a police officer. Their ideas come from TV shows. The types of persons we are hiring have to have volunteer experience and life experiences, but I don't think people have a full handle on what policing is until they get out there and do the job.

Dealing with people in crisis, mentally ill, drug addicted; intoxicated; persons who are not committing any crimes but are causing disruption.

Source: Personal communication with author, 2012.

excluded from operational police work until the 1970s, and even during this time, physical guidelines generally limited women to civilian positions in police services. The RCMP has a number of restrictions that were biased against women and other candidates. Follow the Media Link, "RCMP Recruits in 1957," at the end of this chapter to listen to an interview conducted with the commissioner of the RCMP by CBC Radio in 1957.

basic qualifications
the minimum requirements for candidates applying for employment in policing

Those who are considering a career in policing must have certain **basic qualifications**, often referred to as core competencies. These include Canadian citizenship (some police services will accept landed immigrants), being physically fit and able to complete a rigorous physical abilities test, having at least a Grade 12 education, integrity and honesty, and good judgment. It is on the issue of integrity that many applicants to police services "wash out." This includes providing incomplete and/or inaccurate information to police recruiting officers.

Preferred Qualifications

preferred qualifications
requirements that increase the competitiveness of applicants seeking employment in policing

Police agencies also seek out candidates with **preferred qualifications**. These include knowledge of a second language or culture, an important skill set in policing a diverse society, and volunteer experience, which may include volunteering at a community police station, serving as an auxiliary or reserve in a police service, and coaching youth sports. Some post-secondary work is also important. Perhaps one of the most important attributes of a prospective candidate is work/life experience, which may include international travel and/or living abroad, work involving extensive contact with the public, and positive references from past employers.

Arguably, candidates with broader life experience are more likely to cope well with the stresses inherent in police work. They are also more likely to empathize with the troubled individuals they encounter. Applicants who are still living at home with meals and laundry service provided will generally be at a competitive disadvantage, and their applications may be put on hold until life experience has been gained in the "outside" world. This is one explanation why the average age of police recruits in many police services is in the late 20s. In the Toronto Police Service, for example, the average age of recruits hired over the past ten years was about 28 years; 31 percent were over the age of 30. In contrast, in 1995, the average age of recruits for the TPS was about 22 years.[4]

The extent to which preferred qualifications may be a deciding factor in an applicant being hired by a police service will depend upon a variety of factors, including the overall applicant pool, the number of positions to be filled, and the specific police service. Police services attempt to hire applicants who are a good "fit" with the organization, and this may result in some applicants being successful with one police service and not with another. Note well that persons interested in a career in policing may have to be flexible in terms of which police services they apply to: due to fiscal restraint, police services in one province may not have many positions, while in another province, police services may be hiring. Candidates who are willing to relocate may have a greater likelihood of securing a position.

Police services generally require candidates to have a number of competencies. *Essential* competencies are those that a recruit must possess before becoming a police officer; they include self-confidence, communication skills, adaptability and flexibility, the ability to think analytically, and the ability to exercise self-control. *Developmental* competencies are those that can be acquired through training; they include assertiveness, a community orientation, and the ability to network and collaborate in gathering information and solving problems.

For an example of the application process for a municipal police service, see the website of the Edmonton Police Service. It includes a link for applicants that sets out various steps in the application process and also provides information and resources for prospective applicants, including an Employability Assessment that can be completed online (http://www.joineps.ca/ApplicationProcess/NewApplicants.aspx). See also the webpage, How do I become a Toronto Police officer? at http://www.torontopolice.on.ca/careers/uni_become_officer.php.

Some criticism has been directed toward police services for emphasizing the more enforcement and militaristic aspects of policing in order to attract recruits. See Class/Group Discussion 5.2 at the end of this chapter.

Pre-employment Education Programs

Quebec's provincial police act requires that all applicants first complete a three-year college program and obtain a diploma awarded by the École nationale de police du Québec, or meet standards of equivalence to this program. This program of study includes general academic courses as well as instruction in criminology, policing, and law. After this, candidates must complete the basic Patrol Officer Training Program.

In Ontario, Police Foundations is a pre-employment training program offered by a number of community colleges. It includes courses in criminology and psychology as well as in more specific areas of police work, such as criminal law, rules of evidence, forensic investigation, case investigation, and conflict resolution. On completing the two-year course, students receive a Foundations Training Certificate and then write a provincial exam. Applicants who pass the exam are eligible for employment by any police service in Ontario, although graduation from the program is not a requirement for applicants to police services in Ontario nor does it guarantee employment with a police service. Over the past thirty years, an average of 30 percent of the graduates of the Police Foundations program have found employment in policing.

Recruiting Diversity

Recall from Chapter 2 (Box 2.1, p. 29) that one of Peel's principles is that "police should maintain a relationship with the public that is based on the fact that the police are the public and the public are the police."

Besides seeking applicants with preferred qualifications, police services seek to attract qualified applicants who reflect the diversity of the communities they will be serving. Police services are making efforts to increase the numbers of women, visible minority, Aboriginal, and LGBT officers. This often involves targeting specific communities and holding "outreach" recruiting sessions.

The proactive approach by Canadian police services to increase the diversity of their recruit classes appears to be paying off. Although the majority of recruits are still Caucasian males, the trend is reflected in the makeup of a recent recruit class in the Toronto Police Service:

Women: 20%
Visible minorities: 33%
Post-secondary: 64%
Police/military experience: 18%
Second language: 62%
Third language: 21%

The languages represented in the recruit class included Albanian, American Sign Language, Arabic, Armenian, Cantonese, Croatian, Czech, Dutch, Farsi, French, German, Greek, Gujarati, Hindi, Hungarian, Italian, Japanese, Korean, Malayalam, Mandarin, Pidgin, Polish, Portuguese, Punjabi, Romanian, Russian, Slovakian, Spanish, Tagalog, Tamil, Urdu, and Yoruba.[5] However, there is still much work to be done. See recent figures on the composition of the Toronto Police Service by uniform rank in Table 5.1.

Successful recruitment efforts have also contributed to the increased proportion of women recruits graduating from the RCMP Training Academy ("Depot" Division). The proportion of women at the Training Academy over the last five years has increased by 8 percent while graduation has increased by 4 percent.[6]

In 2014, the RCMP announced a goal of sending as many women as men to the Training Academy in Regina.[7] This has raised the spectre that police services may be directed to establish hiring quotas, an issue that has been surrounded by considerable controversy. See Class/Group Discussion 5.3 at the end of this chapter.

TABLE 5.1
Composition Profile by Uniform Rank, 2010, Toronto Police Service

Senior officers	Racial minorities: 12% Aboriginal: 0% Females: 14%
Staff sergeants and sergeants	Racial minorities: 12% Aboriginal: 0.6% Females: 17%
Constables	Racial minorities: 20% Aboriginal: 1% Females: 18%

Source: Adapted from Toronto Police Service. 2011. *Planning for the Future...Scanning the Toronto Environment*, p. 207. Toronto.

Recruiting Programs to Increase Diversity

Many police services have developed initiatives to attract qualified visible minority and Aboriginal recruits. The Ontario Provincial Police (OPP) operates a number of programs, including the following:

- *PEACE* (Police Ethnic and Cultural Exchange), which encourages students from visible and cultural minorities to participate in a police-sponsored summer employment program.
- *Asian Experience,* a program in which potential recruits of Asian background spend several days interacting with in-service members.
- *OPPBound,* a multiday program in which potential minority recruits and women participate in a variety of activities with in-service members.

In addition, the OPP has produced recruiting brochures and pamphlets in a variety of languages, including Cree, Farsi, Hindi, and Pashto, among others.[8]

Owing to a long history of suspicion and distrust, police services have faced challenges in attracting Aboriginal recruits. The RCMP has perhaps been the most successful at this, having expanded its efforts to recruit Aboriginal members, who then become involved in policing Aboriginal communities. Two programs are of note:

- *Aboriginal Cadet Development Program (ACDP),* directed at Aboriginal people who are interested in a policing career with the RCMP but who do not meet the basic entry requirements. This program is designed to help them overcome identified deficiencies. Those who enroll in the program are assessed at the Training Academy in Regina and then returned to a detachment in their home area. They are provided with financial support and given two years to meet the RCMP's basic entry requirements. If they do so, they enter the RCMP Training Academy in Regina.
- *Aboriginal Pre-Cadet Training Program (APTP).* This is a summer program for Aboriginal youth that includes three weeks at the Training Academy in Regina and eight weeks working under the supervision of an RCMP member in a detachment near their home. The AYTP is not a pre-employment training program, but it does provide an opportunity for Aboriginal youth to become familiar with the role and activities of the RCMP.

The Saskatoon Police Service (SPS) worked in partnership with several groups in the province to establish the Saskatchewan Police Aboriginal Recruiting Committee (SPARC). The objective of this initiative is to increase the number of Aboriginal applicants and officers in the SPS. The twenty-eight-week Aboriginal Policing Preparation program at Saskatchewan Polytechnic has also contributed to the number of Aboriginal applicants. The number of Aboriginal officers in the SPS increased from 4 to 5 percent in the year 2000 and to 11 percent in 2014.[9]

It is increasingly recognized that police services should reflect the diversity of the communities they serve, but this is easier said than done. The official record reveals some encouraging developments, but it also reflects the difficulties police services have had in recruiting women and minorities. The reasons why are complex, but they surely include the following: the failure of police services to devote the necessary resources to attracting women and minorities; the negative perceptions of the police held by many visible minorities, based on experiences with the police in their country of origin and in Canada; and the view that policing is not an honourable profession (see Police Perspective 5.2).

Lesbian, Gay, Bisexual, and Transgender (LGBT) Recruiting

Historically, there was an extreme reluctance on the part of LGBT persons to apply for police services, due to mistrust of the police, caution about revealing their sexual orientation, and a concern that some police officers would refuse to work with an openly gay or lesbian police officer on the street. The acceptance of gays and lesbians by police services has been facilitated by human rights legislation and the increasing number of outreach initiatives to the LGBT community taken by police services. Police services often place recruiting ads in gay lifestyle publications, post on social media, and appear at LGBT events. The Ontario Association of Chiefs of Police has produced a resource document that sets out best practices for recruiting and retaining LGBT police personnel.[10] It is suggested that police services proactively recruit from the LGBT community and, once officers are hired, to work to create an inclusive work environment.

Police Perspective 5.2

A Police Leader Speaks about Recruiting Diversity

As a police leader, it's about creating an environment in which people from various groups feel comfortable in applying. It's about embracing that 15-year-old for when they're 25. If you wait for them to come through the door, first of all they may come, but they may not be the right candidate. So we have a Youth in Policing initiative program that just finished its fourth summer. This year we had forty-five kids, all coming from high-risk communities: two Caucasian girls, four Caucasian boys, and the rest were Koreans, Chinese, Somalis, Congolese. A lot of those kids had never been to a police building before. And every kid had to come with one, or both, parents for a four-hour session before they could join. And the reason I want their parents there is that I can guarantee you that they haven't been to our offices either. And to try to get them to understand that it is this important for us as much as it is for the kids. And at the end of the year, the wrap-up is spectacular. We bring them all back at Christmas for a luncheon with me. We keep them engaged for one more time. Get them through that stage of exposure to gang activity and, hopefully, see some of them as recruits. We have our first recruit from four years ago now. She was 17, now she's 21, and she's just applied and she'll go into a spring recruit class.

Source: Personal communication with author, 2012.

LGBT police officers may view their sexual orientation as an occupational asset in assisting the police service to develop stronger relationships with the community.[11] In Canada, the presence of openly LGBT officers in police services is becoming normalized and a non-issue. This reflects a general trend in Western police services. See the website for Serving with Pride, an organization in Ontario of LGBT police officers, special constables, civilian members of police services, and others who support equality and diversity (servingwithpride.ca).

The Recruit Selection Process

Those applicants who have the basic qualifications as well as some preferred qualifications must still complete a number of further steps before being accepted as recruits. Selection processes vary somewhat among police services, but most involve some or all of the following steps:

- *Initial application.* Interested applicants submit a resumé and complete an application form that includes sections on education, employment history, key life events, and volunteer experience.
- *Entrance examination.* Typically, applicants must complete a written, timed examination. Most examinations include a variety of questions covering spelling, grammar, reading comprehension, and general arithmetic and may also include a number of scenarios for which the applicant is required to select a course of action and/or recall specific items of information. These exercises are designed to provide the police agency with preliminary insights into the character, personality, and judgment of the candidate.
- *Psychological testing.* This is designed to determine the applicant's suitability for a career in policing and involves a number of psychological measures. Applicants may also be required to have an interview with a psychologist.
- *Polygraph testing.* In some provinces and for the RCMP, candidates are subjected to a polygraph test, although such tests are not used in Ontario and are in limited use in Quebec.

Courtesy of Edmonton Police Service.

A recruiting poster from the Edmonton Police Service

- *Intake interview.* Most police agencies require that the applicant be interviewed early on by a recruiting officer. The questions range from general queries about personal history, attitudes, and behaviour to specific questions about drug use and personal integrity.
- *Pre-entry physical testing.* Depending on the agency, the applicant will be required to pass a test of physical abilities (see the earlier section on Basic Qualifications). If they excel, so much the better for the applicant.
- *Peer interview.* Some police agencies require the applicant to participate in a peer interview. Typically, several officers from the police service question the applicant on his or her suitability for policing.

If all of these stages are successfully completed, the applicant's documentation is forwarded to an executive officer or review committee. All of the selection process results and documents are then reviewed to determine whether the applicant should be hired. At this crucial stage, the applicant is compared against other suitable candidates.

In Ontario, the Constable Selection System (CSS) is used by most police services to assess recruits. This system was designed to eliminate multiple applications to police services across the province, which typically resulted in multiple assessments of the same applicant. It is also is meant to standardize the assessment criteria and to make selections less arbitrary. For an example, check out the website for the Thunder Bay (Ontario) Police Service (http://www.thunderbaypolice.ca/careers). For detailed information on the Ontario Constable Selection System, see http://www.oacp.on.ca/programs-courses/constable-selection-system.

While recruiting standards are very similar across the country, the weight given to specific items of information does change. Even a decade ago, a candidate's use of marijuana would likely result in disqualification. This may no longer be the case; rather, a primary concern may be the recency of drug use (e.g., candidates who use drugs the morning prior to the interview to calm their nerves will not make it to the next round). An important consideration is that candidates must be honest and open about their lives, the decisions they have made, and what lessons were learned from poor decisions.

It is estimated that 90 percent of applicants to police services across the country are unsuccessful, although the rates of successful applicants appear to vary by police service, even within the same province. At any one point in time, some police services may be aggressively hiring, while others may take applications but not be hiring, generally due to budgetary restrictions. As noted, ethical and integrity issues are two common reasons why applicants are washed out of the process. As the former director of a police training academy told your author, "It's all about integrity and ethical standards."

RECRUIT TRAINING

Police recruit training programs are intense, multifaceted, and classroom based. While training for newly hired probation and parole officers has a significant online component, all police training occurs on a face-to-face basis. This approach is much more amenable to providing recruits with scenario-based training that will assist them once deployed into the field. On average, police recruit training is much longer than for other criminal justice practitioners: in British Columbia, municipal police recruits undergo a block training regimen that covers thirty-five weeks. In contrast, the training for probation officers in British Columbia is approximately seventeen weeks, and much of the course material is delivered online.

Notably absent are intensive training programs for other criminal justice practitioners, including Crown counsel and members of parole boards. Concerns have been expressed, for example, that persons need have no special expertise to be appointed as a provincial or federal parole board member, and the training that is provided is much shorter in length and is often delivered online.[12]

One current and one former police academy instructor offered their views on the changing profile of police recruits and on police training (see Police Perspective 5.3).

Police Perspective 5.3

A Patrol Sergeant and a Former Police Academy Instructor Comments on the New Generation of Police Recruits

It's changed significantly in many respects since I was a recruit. In other ways, it's come full circle. When I started twenty years ago, I was 21 years old. There was nobody who was twenty-seven or older. A two-year diploma was above average; many had only high school. I was a Caucasian male and that was a majority of the recruits—very few females. In my class of thirty, there were four females. There is more diversity in today's recruit classes. They are more reflective of the population. There are still challenges in recruiting diversity.

There has been a move to bring more mature recruits; it is common to see 30-year-old recruits; some are in their 40s—second career. The view is that mature recruits are more stable, have their family life together; they have a long track record that can be checked. You can't check on a 21-year-old. The problem is that 45-year-olds don't like working night shifts; they don't want to go out and take calls at three o'clock in the morning. They are more susceptible to injury. A lot of those more-mature recruits don't want to work in patrol any more. They often have a sense of entitlement because they are older. There are challenges in hiring older recruits, along with the benefits.

The new generation of officers is much more broad in their interests. They will give you full hours but then want their own lives, their own friendship networks. Back when I was hired, it was much more of a thin blue line; officers would socialize together. There is a sense that this is a job that I do and on my days off, I'm going to live my own life.

Source: Personal communication with author, 2012.

Police Training Facilities and Programs

Box 5.1 provides a listing of police training facilities in Canada.

Basic recruit training varies in both length and structure. The Ontario Police College program is eight weeks; that of the Saskatchewan Police College is seventeen. RCMP recruits receive twenty-two weeks of training in Regina, followed by a similar length of time at a training detachment.

The larger police services in Ontario supplement the training offered at Aylmer by providing recruits with several further weeks of in-house training. In-service training is provided by the OPP at a training facility in Orillia, and by the Toronto Police Service (TPS) at Charles O. Bick College. TPS recruits (referred to as "cadets-in-training") are required to complete several stages of training. In Quebec, the training program at the École nationale de police has introduced a psychological test (M-Pulse) designed to assess the suitability of cadets for police work. The test measures a variety of personality attributes, from poor interpersonal skills, to racist or sexist attitudes, to the likelihood that the cadet would use excessive force. As one police observer in the province stated, "You can have a very bright wacko who can run 8 km in nothing flat—but there's no assessment of his suitability [to become an officer]."[13]

Box 5.1

Police Training Facilities in Canada

Province	Training Facility
British Columbia	Justice Institute of British Columbia, Police Academy
Alberta	Edmonton Police Service and Chief Crowfoot Learning Centre, Calgary Police Service
Saskatchewan	Saskatchewan Police College, University of Regina; RCMP Training Academy, Regina
Manitoba	Winnipeg Police Service Training
Ontario	Ontario Police College, Aylmer; Ontario Provincial Police Academy, Orillia; Charles O. Bick Police College, Toronto Police Service
Quebec	École nationale de police du Québec, Nicolet
Nova Scotia	Atlantic Police Academy, Holland College, Charlottetown
Prince Edward Island	Atlantic Police Academy, Holland College, Charlottetown
New Brunswick	Atlantic Police Academy, Holland College, Charlottetown
Newfoundland and Labrador	Police Officers Training Program, Memorial University
Yukon, Northwest Territories, Nunavut	RCMP Training Academy, Regina

British Columbia's Police Academy, where all municipal police recruits in that province are trained, has a unique program based on several training blocks (see Box 5.2).

There is considerable variation across the country in terms of how new recruits are trained. Generally, though, recruit training programs focus on three areas: physical training, academics, and skills. An underlying theme throughout the training and promotion processes in police services is **competency-based training**, which focuses on the acquisition of specific, measurable skills and knowledge that can be transferred to the operational level. This sort of training includes legal studies, the use of force, and various skill sets.

competency-based training
recruit training that focuses on the acquisition of specific skills and knowledge

At all training centres, police officers in Canada generally receive instruction in legal studies, investigation and patrol, community relations, use of force and firearms training, traffic studies, driver training, and physical training. Most police services require the trainee to assume the costs of training, including accommodation and room and board for residential training programs.

Box 5.2

Recruitment and Training in British Columbia: A Unique Approach

The recruitment and training of municipal police officers in British Columbia has several unique features.

All prospective recruits are required to pass a review at the Assessment Centre located at the Justice Institute Police Academy. Candidates are tested in five exercises: (1) a group discussion, (2) an oral communication situation, (3) a fact-finding, decision-making scenario, (4) a writing exercise, and (5) a background interview. Among the attributes measured in each of these exercises are decision making, decisiveness, flexibility, initiative, integrity, interpersonal tolerance and sensitivity, observation skills, oral and written communication skills, personal impact, practical intelligence, problem confrontation, stress tolerance, and the ability to learn. Recruits are assessed by a team of officers from the various independent municipal police services.

Once hired by a municipal police service, recruits are trained at the Justice Institute of British Columbia Police Academy. The training consists of three blocks, during which classroom learning alternates with field experience.

- Block I (13 weeks) at the Police Academy. Emphasis on police skills, including driver training, firearms, arrest and control, investigation and patrol techniques, legal studies, and physical fitness.
- Block II (13–17 weeks) at the recruit's home police department. Field training under the guidance of a field trainer provides an opportunity for the recruit to apply Block I knowledge in an operational setting.
- Block III (8 weeks) at the Police Academy. Additional knowledge and skills development.

After completion of Block III, the recruit graduates as a qualified municipal constable and returns to their home police service.

Source: Courtesy Justice Institute of British Columbia.

Training programs are designed to introduce recruits to "real life" situations they may encounter on the street. The Ontario Police College, for example, has a replica drug lab, which it uses to train both recruits and in-service officers in how to identify, investigate, and safely dismantle illegal drug operations. In Regina, the RCMP has two modern houses and a "detachment" on the grounds of the academy. The houses are used for various scenarios, including those involving domestic violence; the detachment is used to train recruits in

Don Healy/LEADER POST. Reprinted by permission.

Police recruits in training

Police Perspective 5.4

A Police Academy Instructor Speaks about Training Recruits to Make "Split Second" Decisions

We do hands-on training and simulation drills—reality-based training, stress inoculation. We put them through a variety of investigative and patrol scenarios. The recruits are being conditioned to act appropriately in encounter situations. We condition the recruits through simulations and scenarios. These are based on real-life situations that occurred on the street. We always tell them nothing is a routine. Always expect the unexpected. Once you get into that sleepy-comfortable zone, that's when things are going to happen.

Source: Personal communication with author, 2013.

the various tasks and activities that arise at the operational level. Similarly, the Quebec Police Institute has a "virtual police station."

Police Perspective 5.4 offers more from a police academy instructor about training recruits.

The RCMP Pre-employment Training Model

In contrast to their provincial and municipal counterparts, RCMP cadets are not employees of the RCMP. Rather, a cadet is classified as a *potential* member of the RCMP, on a temporary contract while at the Training Academy in Regina. This makes it far easier for the academy to release trainees who do not meet the Mounties' requirements. Only a cadet who completes the entire cadet training program, and who reaches all of its standards, will be offered an employment contract with the RCMP. The recruit then completes a six-month field training period in an RCMP detachment. In essence, then, a cadet must successfully complete six months of difficult and demanding work before being sworn in as a regular RCMP officer.

Because cadets are not considered members of the RCMP, they are not governed by the RCMP Act, nor are they represented by the DivRep system. The academy has focus groups to ensure that cadets are able to voice their concerns to senior management when a conflict arises. Cadets may also appeal any decision made regarding their evaluation or their dismissal from the academy. This appeal can go all the way to the Federal Court of Canada.

The training that RCMP recruits receive at the Training Academy is generic and designed to provide them with a core foundation of policing knowledge and skills. Only on graduation are RCMP recruits hired as members of the RCMP; they are then sent to a field training detachment. On completing six months of field training, they may be posted anywhere in Canada as federal officer or as a provincial or municipal police officer working under the RCMP contracts. In contrast, police officers in independent municipal and provincial police services across Canada are often trained at a location in the community or within the province, are hired by their respective departments before entering the training academy, and know which municipality they will be policing after they graduate—probably for their entire policing career.

Read about the experiences of one RCMP recruit at the Training Academy in Police Perspective 5.5. See also Critical Thinking Exercise 5.1 at the end of this chapter.

Cross-Cultural and Diversity Training

Training is essential to addressing racism and cultural insensitivity among police officers. Police services generally include cross-cultural and diversity training as part of the curriculum for new recruits. However, it is questionable whether this training is sufficient to prepare officers for the diversity in the communities they will be policing. Cultural awareness training often comprises only a small portion of the overall training program, and there is often not time to consider specific groups. For example, course materials on First Nations, Métis, and Inuit peoples and visible and cultural minorities are often combined. There is often

Police Perspective 5.5

An RCMP Recruit's First Week at the Training Academy

It was a very intimidating place. You are very much standing out while everyone else is walking around knowing exactly what they are doing and fitting in. I was intimidated when I first got there. I was very surprised about how open everybody was. There wasn't a competition between 'I'm in a senior troop and you are a new guy." Everyone was very helpful. I remember walking down the street trying to find my dorm, and there were a half-dozen people who offered to help. It was very humbling given the amount of history there.

The first week was spent getting you adjusted to your environment and what to expect. And then things ramped up very quickly. We had a full troop of thirty-two members. My troop was fantastic; we got along quite well. We helped each other out and picked up the slack where we could.

Most everyone felt that they were where they should be. Most people who are in the RCMP want to be in the RCMP—diverse backgrounds, guys with degrees in chemical engineering, recent high school graduates. Everyone had their own strengths. No one adjusted poorly. You adjusted as well as your weakest person. We were all in the same boat.

For me, time management was one of my biggest things. I'm a lot more organized now than I was. You wake up at 5:30 or 5:45 Monday to Friday; your breakfast is at 6:15. You've got classes all day. You have to go to the firing range; you have to polish your boots, iron your things. It really comes down to you don't really have time to do anything. You have to learn that you can only do so much, that you can't say yes to everything. For me, it was learning to be efficient with my time.

Source: RCMP constable, personal communication with author, 2013.

no opportunity for officers posted to Aboriginal and Inuit communities to learn about the culture and traditions of the people they will be policing. Officers continue to be posted to First Nations, Métis, and Inuit communities with minimal knowledge of the culture and history of the people they serve, and the officers often do not have the language skills to communicate with elderly residents who may not speak English or French.

COMPETITION FOR PREVIOUSLY EXPERIENCED OFFICERS (PEOs)

previously experienced officers (PEOs)
in-service police officers who are interested in leaving their current police service

The need for qualified recruits has spawned increased competition among municipal and provincial police forces and the RCMP for **previously experienced officers (PEOs)**, who, for a variety of personal and/or professional reasons, may be amenable to leaving their current police service. A number of police services have special recruiting teams that target PEOs, and it is not unusual for the police services to "raid" officers from one another. Most of the larger police services have a specific section on their websites devoted to attracting in-service officers.

The increasing mobility of PEOs presents a number of challenges. Police services must find ways not only to attract but also to retain personnel. It can no longer be assumed that a police officer will spend an entire career with the same department, and there is unprecedented movement of officers between police services, including the RCMP. In Ontario, officers may move between municipal police services as well as between the OPP and municipal police services.

Police services must carefully examine the performance records of PEOs to ensure that they are not "problem" officers who are being pushed out of their existing police service.[14] This task is made more difficult by the reluctance of police personnel to provide negative references for a colleague applying to another police service.

IN-SERVICE TRAINING

The training provided to police officers as their careers progress is variously referred to as **in-service training**, refresher training, requalification training, advanced training, or career development training. Usually, it is conducted by individual police agencies or by provincial training centres. A key issue regarding this type of training is whether it should be mandatory or optional. Some police services require officers to complete a specified number of training hours or an in-service training course; others offer in-service training as an option. As well, police services require officers to qualify on an ongoing basis in the use of firearms, control techniques, batons, oleoresin capsicum (OC, or pepper spray), and Tasers. The trend in Canadian police services is toward integrating in-service training with career development; in other words, officers are required to achieve certain educational and training competencies in order to apply for advancement.

in-service training
training courses for serving police officers

The Canadian Police College (CPC) in Ottawa is funded by the federal government and administered by the RCMP. The education and training programs it offers are national in scope and are designed to provide municipal and provincial police officers, as well as RCMP officers, with upgrading and development programs, research and information, and advice.

The specialized training courses at the CPC are typically two to three weeks in duration and cover a variety of subject areas, including advanced collision analysis, clandestine laboratories investigation, electronic search and seizure, senior police administration, strategic intelligence analysis, and so on.

FROM THE ACADEMY TO THE STREET: SOCIALIZATION INTO THE ROLE OF POLICE OFFICER

Becoming a police officer involves two distinct socialization processes: formal and informal. Formal socialization is accomplished through the selection process and police training programs. These programs provide new recruits with a vast amount of information on a myriad of subjects relating to policing. Informal socialization occurs when recruits interact with older, more experienced officers and with their peers on the job.

Impact of the Police Academy

Besides providing knowledge and skills, training academies provide a mechanism for socializing new recruits into the occupation of policing. Far too little attention has been paid by police scholars to the experiences of police recruits in training programs as they are transformed into police constables, and to how these experiences shape their attitudes, expectations, and behaviour. This process of "socialization" into the police occupation may have an impact on the recruit's self-image, values, perceptions, and behaviour. The recruit's level of education has been found to have no effect on success in the academy or as a police officer, which raises a number of questions relating to the issue of how to predict the performance of recruits. A challenge is to develop measures to assess the validity of the criteria used to select and train police recruits, and to measure the effectiveness of police officers during their careers.[15]

Most police recruits are motivated, at least initially, by a desire to help people and serve the community. The training experience can have a strong impact on this, however. Research studies have found that, for many recruits, the police academy experience makes them more cynical, more suspicious of people, and generally, more vigilant.[16] The extent to which recruits exhibit these attitudinal and behavioural traits, however, depends to some extent on the personalities and values of the individual. There are also attributes of the police academy that do not fit well with the principles of community policing, including a hierarchical, paramilitary structure that encourages an "us vs. them" mentality, deference to authority, and the development of strong bonds and in-group loyalty among recruits. The extent to which these features of the police academy experience have hindered the implementation of community policing initiatives has yet to be researched in Canada.[17]

Despite the critical role that recruit training plays in policing careers, very little is known about how new recruits feel about the training they receive and the relevance and impact of academy training once recruits are assigned to operational patrol. As the former director of a police training academy stated, "Some outstanding book-smart recruits struggle on the street, and others struggle in the academy but do well on the street. Until you actually get the new officer out on the street, it's difficult to tell how they are going do to, how they are going to interact and handle encounter situations."[18]

The Field Training Experience

operational field training
instructing the recruit on how to apply principles from the training academy in the community

During this second component of the training/learning process, known as **operational field training**, the recruit learns to apply the basic principles taught at the training centre. Under the guidance and assistance of a senior officer, the recruit is exposed to a wide variety of general police work. During this critical phase, the specially trained senior officer (often referred to as the field trainer or mentor) makes sure that the recruit is able to meet the demands and challenges of police work.

The length and structure of field training varies among police services. For example, Vancouver police recruits spend up to seventeen weeks under the supervision of a field training officer (FTO), whereas new RCMP officers work with a field coach for twenty-four weeks after graduating from the RCMP Training Academy and being sworn in as peace officers. And while municipal police recruits in British Columbia complete their field training during Block II, prior to returning to the police academy for Block III, new RCMP officers receive their field training *after* completing the program at the training academy.

Police services are paying increasing attention to ensuring continuity between the training a recruit receives in the academy and the supervision provided once the new recruit is involved in operational policing. FTOs play a significant role in the training process and have a strong influence on the attitude and policing style that the new recruit develops. A key objective of the FTO is to enhance the skills and knowledge the recruit has gained at the academy in a way that lessens the "disconnect" that has historically existed between the training academy and the street. This will reduce the likelihood that the new officer will become cynical and discard the skill sets and attitudes learned in recruit training.

Commenting on the issues of the academy versus on-the-street work, a patrol sergeant stated: "It's a balance of both. You have to ensure that individuals have the right skill set and the knowledge to do the work. Equally important is that officers spend a significant amount of time in patrol to learn by doing: learning investigative skills and how to handle difficult people; developing those skills on the job; doing the actual work."[19]

There is some evidence, though, that in certain instances, field training may negate the recruit's positive attitudes toward various aspects of policing, including community policing and problem solving.[20] Given the role of FTOs in moulding the attitudes and perceptions of new recruits, it is important for police services to select FTOs carefully and to monitor their approach to that role.[21] New recruits need to be matched with competent and motivated trainers who represent the best skill sets the organization has to offer.

BEING A POLICE OFFICER

Having completed academy and field training, the new officer becomes a member of the police service and begins adopting and adjusting to the attitudes and behaviour that distinguish the occupation of police work. Research on the police occupation has generated a list of key attitudes, perceptions, and behaviours of police officers. Many of these are components of what Jerome Skolnick labelled the **working personality of police officers**—a set of attitudes and behaviours that develop out of the unique role police officers play and the duties they are asked to perform.[22]

working personality of police officers
a set of attitudinal and behavioural attributes of police officers

blue-light syndrome
an attitudinal set that emphasizes the high risk and action component of police work

code of silence
officers protecting one another from outside scrutiny and criticism

The Working Personality of Police Officers

Components of the working personality include the following:

- A preoccupation with danger, an excessive suspicion of people and activities, and a protective cynicism
- The practice of a **code of silence** to protect fellow officers
- Strong in-group solidarity (the "blue wall" or "code of silence") with other police officers
- Attitudes that emphasize the high risk/action component of police work, often referred to as the **blue-light syndrome**

hypervigilance
elevated alertness about potential dangers in the environment

- **Hypervigilance**, which includes physiological arousal, elevated levels of alertness, attentiveness to details of the environment, and interpretation of seemingly neutral aspects of the environment as potentially dangerous

Reconsidering the Working Personality of Police Officers

It has been forty-plus years since Skolnick proposed the existence of an occupational culture of police and identified the components of the working personality of police officers. Throughout that time, the validity of his arguments has been strongly debated. One question is whether the police personality is a result of nature or nurture. Put another way, do people who apply to become police officers already have many of the above-noted personality traits, or do these traits develop as a result of police work? A possible answer is that it depends: on the personality of the individual officer, their response to training, and the police service itself.

A second question revolves around the extent to which police officers' isolation, in-group solidarity, and traditional distrust and suspicion of the general public are being undermined by emerging trends in policing. These trends include community-based policing, the decentralization of traditional command-and-control structures, the empowerment of patrol officers, the development of partnerships between police and communities, and the changing face of police recruits.

A third issue that Skolnick did not address is the impact of the specific operational environment on the police personality. The discussion in Chapter 6 will reveal that patrol officers carry out their tasks in a variety of environments, ranging from small towns and rural areas to large urban areas. Police officers who work in OPP, RCMP, or Sûrete du Québec (SQ) detachments in small, rural, or remote communities have little choice but to interact with community residents; those who work in large cities *can* choose not to do so. The size of the community does not guarantee positive police–community interactions: relations between the police and Aboriginal persons in rural and remote areas of the country have often been afflicted by mutual suspicion and distrust. This is discussed in Chapter 8.

Fourth, there may well be at least two distinct cultures within police services: one is occupied by senior managers, who are focused on a much broader range of issues than are street-level police and case investigators, who comprise the second culture. Police managers are often judged according to their success at convincing patrol officers to support the organization's goals and incorporate the objectives of senior managers into daily patrol practice.

Police scholars generally agree that the traditional police culture has been transformed in recent decades. This is owing to a variety of factors, including the changing environments in which police carry out their mandate; the requirements of community policing, which brings officers in closer and more frequent contact with the community; and the increasing gender and ethnic diversity within police services. Notwithstanding all this, researchers continue to find elements of a police culture characterized by an "us versus them" mentality, suspicion and distrust of certain segments of the community, and strong in-group loyalties.[23]

There are remnants of the traditional police culture, especially in terms of the view that police officers are "different" from other people. Also, police services are still structured on a paramilitary model wherein the primary mission is "to serve and protect" the community from the less desirable elements in society. There does appear to be an overarching identity among police officers, one which states: "A cop is a cop is a cop. Some are better than others, some are worse. But we are all made out of the same stuff."[24] In short, some of the elements of police culture appear to have transformed while others remain intact.[25]

That said, every patrol officer has their own style of policing, and not every officer exhibits the characteristics of the working personality and in the extent to which the attitudes and behaviour of officers reflect the tenets of the police culture. The nature and influence of the police culture varies with the organizational, operational, legal, political, and social context of the police service at hand.

From a review of the literature, one police scholar concluded:

> Police personality, as a distinct entity, does exist. It exists as a result of the confluence of a specific baseline set of desirable personality traits and occupational socialization. It is also a function of, and is strongly characterized by, a police culture, created by the needs of officers to maintain personal safety and enhance their professional capabilities.[26]

What is evident is that there will be variability in the extent to which any one police officer exhibits the traits of the working personality.

Positive and Negative Features of the Police Culture

The police culture has many positive features. Given the unpredictability of the encounter situations in which officers become involved and the potential for violence, it is crucial for officers to trust one another and develop camaraderie. In-group solidarity helps individual officers cope with the more stressful aspects of police work and is also a source of support.

There are a number of potentially negative consequences of the police culture, however, including police alienation from the general public and other agencies and organizations; police officer alienation from management; resistance to organizational and operational change; unethical and unprofessional behaviour (discussed in Chapter 4); and biased policing and racial profiling (examined in Chapter 6). The police culture may also hinder officers seeking assistance for difficulties they are facing on the job.

To summarize, while it may not be possible to quantify the existence of a distinct police personality, and while a considerable mythology surrounds police work, many police officers believe there *is* a working personality of police that sets them apart as an occupational group. Ironically, this belief may in itself make the working personality of police a reality. The occupational perspectives of police officers and their working personality may have a significant impact on operational patrol work and decision making in encounter situations on the street and in case investigations. See Critical Thinking Exercise 5.2 at the end of this chapter.

How Dangerous Is Police Work?

In reality, police officers consistently face a lower fatality rate than those employed in mining, construction, commercial fishing, and forestry. Police officers, however, may face a higher risk of being assaulted and of having non-lethal violence used against them. This includes being bitten by people with infectious diseases and being exposed to toxic environments. And it is important to remember that the *potential* for violence and death is always present in police work. Officers become preoccupied with danger largely because of the unpredictability of the people and events they encounter. Even routine activities, such as traffic stops, hold the potential for violence.

The Occupational Outlook and Career Aspirations of Police Officers

Many attempts have been made to develop typologies of police officers in order to determine the differences in how they view their careers. Most classifications are based on officers' occupational outlook and career aspirations. The research suggests that not all police officers share the same orientation and career aspirations.[27]

At least five "types" of police officers have been identified, based on their key interests and career orientations:[28]

- *Self-investors.* Family life, job stability, security
- *Careerists.* Promotion, prestige, achieving a management position
- *Specialists.* Professional growth, acquisition of new skills, challenging positions
- *Social activist.* Social and institutional change, helping others
- *Enforcers.* Gathering evidence, apprehending criminals, solving crimes, obtaining convictions

Attached to each type are a number of assumptions relating to how officers exercise discretion and carry out police work. It is generally thought that an officer's operational style remains constant across various policing environments and encounter incidents. Research into police activities and decision making, however, suggests that this assumption may be simplistic and that typologies may in fact obscure many factors that influence the behaviour of police officers. There is some evidence that the attitudes, behaviour, and career orientation of an officer may change in the course of their training and career. A police recruit may enter the training academy with a certain attitude set and exit training with modified views. Similarly, a rookie officer may begin their career as a social activist or an enforcer but then may have a different orientation in later years, having developed more realistic expectations of what they can accomplish or experiencing a certain level of burnout. A major challenge for officers as they move through their career is to avoid cynicism.

The attitudes of patrol officers may also vary with the particular area being policed and the types of encounters in which they become involved. For example, increasing levels of crime and disorder in patrol districts may heighten the cynicism of patrol officers if they see few results from their efforts, and they thus become pessimistic about improving the community's quality of life. Officers patrolling districts where there is less crime and disorder may experience less frustration and cynicism. Similarly, patrol officers who do not have access to up-to-date information on chronic offenders and crime hot spots in their areas may become frustrated with the inability to apprehend offenders and improve the quality of life in the community.

THE CHALLENGES OF POLICE WORK

> *"I have to say that I would not want my kids to do this job anymore, as it is just too tough on the body, the brain, relationships, and overall wellbeing."*[29]

Although police work can be satisfying and challenging, it can also be stressful. The effects of stress experienced by police officers range from minor annoyances (which can be managed) to alcohol or drug addiction, depression, and suicide.[30]

> This is a generation of officers who see themselves as sheepdogs, caught in the unforgiving position of herding the unwilling and standing guard against their aggressors. For them, admitting weakness means risking advancement in their career, potentially falling off a community pedestal and planting seeds of doubt in the minds of their colleagues about whether they can do the job. Things are changing, but it's a slow process with much more work ahead.[31*]

A sample of officers ($N = 225$) in the U.S. who were surveyed five months after leaving the training academy identified a number of stressors on the job. The highest rated items were "danger on the streets" (49 percent), followed by work schedule (40 percent), report writing (37 percent) and the challenges of maintaining a work/life balance (35 percent).[32]

Several common sources of stress for police officers are discussed below.

An RCMP officer rests his head at a roadblock after the fatal shooting of RCMP officers in Moncton, 2014.

---

*Yogaretnam, S. 2014. "Walking the Thin Blue Line: How Stigma is Silencing Police Officers," *Ottawa Citizen*, October 10.

The Police Role and Mandate

The nature of the police occupation itself can wear on officers, one Canadian police detective noted: "We're the fixers. We come in and no matter what's going on, we're expected to be on an even keel, we're supposed to have all the answers. As an officer, you don't feel that you can say out loud, 'Hey, I don't feel great.'"[33]

Recall from the discussion in Chapter 1 that the police must carry out their enforcement duties while at the same time exercising their discretion and authority so as not to infringe on the Charter rights of those with whom they come into contact. This may be a source of stress for officers, particularly when politicians and the general public have unrealistic expectations of the police. As well, strikes, protests, and other disturbances (such as those associated with Aboriginal land claims) can place police officers in the midst of chaos and indecision by politicians and may result in actions by the police that are later found to have been racist and discriminatory. The police are also often required to enforce unpopular laws; and when they do, as the most visible and accessible component of the political system, they find themselves targets of public wrath.

The Criminal Justice System

In Chapter 1, it was noted that police work in the early 21st century is significantly impacted by court decisions and legislation. These are two major factors in the increased workload. As one officer stated:

> An example is an impaired driver, which we used to process within two hours in 1985. And now a regular case will take an officer off the road for literally an entire shift and more. There are so many forms, intoxilyzer docs, MTO notices, videos, and just time-consuming form-typing on the computers, that sometimes supervisors cringe when too many are arrested at once, because there is no one left on the road to answer the other calls . . . (the stabbings and shootings and robberies, domestics, . . .).[34*]

From their investigation of work/life balance among Canadian police officers, Linda Duxbury and Christopher Higgins reported that the officers in their study experienced increasing demands and that the work had become more complex: "The sheer volume of the work (assigned files, phone calls, walk ins, e-mails) is overwhelming and the stress is exacerbated by other people's sense of urgency, unrealistic deadlines, pressures to do a high quality job, the increased complexity of the cases, and a culture that makes it unacceptable to say no."[35]

Police personnel are often required to inject themselves into situations that others are fleeing. They are exposed to extreme violence, individual suffering, and death. Because of the realities that surround police work, officers may become desensitized to life in general. Much of police work involves long

* From K. Egan, 2014. "What price policing? The aftershock of Kal Ghadban's tragic end," *Ottawa Citizen*, 30 September, http://ottawacitizen.com/opinion/columnists/egan-what-price-policing-the-aftershock-of-kal-ghadbans-tragic-end. Material reprinted with the express permission of *Ottawa Citizen*, a division of Postmedia Network Inc.

periods of monotony punctuated with bursts of extreme excitement, often referred to as the "startle effect."

Many situations demand a quick response by officers, and this jolts them both mentally and physically. For example, an officer may be sitting peacefully in a restaurant having coffee at 3 a.m. only to be dispatched suddenly to a man-with-a-gun call. The officer goes from a calm, relaxed situation to a life-and-death situation within seconds. Officers who are assigned to high-intensity special units, such as Emergency Response Teams and strike forces, may find themselves in high-stress situations for hours or days at a time.

Traumatic events such as homicides, suicides, the deaths of children, and multi-victim accidents can also take a toll on officers. Another source of trauma is involvement in a shooting incident (see Chapter 7). Exposure to incidents like these may lead officers to develop post-traumatic stress syndrome, which is characterized by flashbacks, depression, and loss of sleep. See the comments of one officer about the demands of the job in Police Perspective 5.6.

Paperwork may also cause stress. Officers often spend hours recording events that took only a few minutes to transpire. For example, an officer who detains an impaired driver after a failed breathalyzer test may spend many hours processing the individual and completing the necessary paperwork, even though it took only a few minutes to detect and arrest the offender. Legislation and Supreme Court decisions have placed a greater onus on police officers to provide extensive documentation on cases.

The Community

The community may be a source of stress for police officers. Officers assigned to environments with high levels of crime and social disorder may encounter interpersonal conflicts and threats of violence on a daily basis. Patrol officers may find themselves working in communities where residents neither trust nor support the police.

Police Perspective 5.6

A Patrol Officer Comments on the Demands of the Job

During my ten years on the job, I have done and seen things that most people wouldn't see in their lifetime. I gave CPR to a 3-week-old baby, knowing that the baby was dead for hours; pulled people out of cars crushed to the point of no recognition; helped a grandma with groceries in a store parking lot; and chased people through most backyards in this city without owners even knowing it. All in all, you never know what you get on a busy night.

Source: From K. Egan, 2014. "What price policing? The aftershock of Kal Ghadban's tragic end," *Ottawa Citizen*, 30 September, http://ottawacitizen.com/opinion/columnists/egan-what-price-policing-the-aftershock-of-kal-ghadbans-tragic-end. Material reprinted with the express permission of *Ottawa Citizen*, a division of Postmedia Network Inc.

Communities often have unrealistic, and conflicting, expectations of what the police can accomplish with respect to preventing and responding to crime and social disorder. These expectations may also be a source of stress for police officers. In some communities, there may be tense relations between the media and the police, and between the police and advocacy groups. Many Canadian communities are multicultural, and most police officers assigned to strongly ethnic patrol areas do not speak the language or know the culture of the local residents.

Police officers posted to northern and remote communities may experience high stress levels because of the challenging environments in which they work. Remote and rural communities often have much higher rates of crime—especially violent crime—than urban centres. Policing in these high-demand environments, where backup may not be readily available, can take a toll on officers and result in high levels of stress.[36] In recognition of this, officers are generally posted to these isolated locations for no more than two or three years. Policing in northern and remote communities is discussed in Chapter 8.

Being a Woman Police Officer

Women police officers may experience higher levels of stress than their male counterparts.[37] This is due to experiences of sexual harassment as well as (along with minority officers) more subtle forms of discrimination. Research studies have shown that women who work in male-dominated professions (such as policing, the military, and firefighting) are more likely than women in other professions to be harassed.[38]

Harassment, particularly of female police officers, is an issue that has received increasing attention. A national survey of RCMP officers found that 19 percent of the respondents indicated that they had been harassed on the job by a superior, supervisor, or co-worker during the previous year (although there was no gender breakdown indicated).[39] View the documentary film "Behind the Line," which presents the stories of four RCMP women officers who were subjected to sexual harassment and allegedly assaulted by the same superior officer (see the Media Link at the end of this chapter). The RCMP is working to alter the organizational climate so as to eliminate the conditions that contribute to the harassment of women officers.[40]

Research has found that female police officers believe that less serious forms of police sexual misconduct are quite prevalent due in large measure to the police culture and the difficulties of changing this culture. This includes making vehicle stops in order to meet the driver or occupants, and flirting with female citizens. Efforts to address harassment in the police service may have limited effectiveness. As one female officer stated:

> Things haven't changed much. It's business as usual. We have a sexual harassment policy, everybody got training, the chief did a big song-and-dance about how this stuff [sexual harassment] was a thing of the past, but it didn't change things much. The same guys who acted like jerks before are still jerks today.[41*]

* Maher, T.M. 2010. "Police Sexual Misconduct: Female Police Officers' Views Regarding Its Nature and Extent," *Women & Criminal Justice*, 20(3), 263–82.

As of mid-2015, a class action harassment suit brought by nearly 300 women who are current or former RCMP officers was working its way through the courts. The suit alleges that the women experience/experienced gender-based discrimination and harassment, including name-calling, sexist pranks, and verbal propositions for sexual favours.[42] The issue of harassment is also at the centre of some cases that are brought forth for disciplinary hearings.

Female officers may experience stress in trying to combine being a police officer with being a mother. An exploratory study of the experience of female officers ($N = 6$) attempting to combine motherhood with policing found that the women perceived a need to prove themselves again in the force. One officer stated: "And I always feel like I'm having to prove myself all over again to that person, or to that group of people, or to that team. Even though my work and my past should speak for itself, like everybody else."[43] This study also found that motherhood isolated these officers from their co-workers and led to changes in their career and personal priorities; at the same time, these women sensed that their career choices and opportunities had become more restricted. All of the officers in the study found themselves struggling to redefine themselves and to reconcile their role as an officer with that of a mother.

The Police Service

A variety of stressors arise from the police service itself. Departmental policies, a lack of resources, conflict with peers, and unsupportive or ineffective management may increase the stress levels of officers. This has led some observers to contend that the police organization is a greater source of stress than police operations.[44]

Among the findings of an annual RCMP employee survey were that 50 percent of the officers surveyed indicated they did not feel that their senior leaders were competent to carry out their responsibilities, although just over 70 percent indicated that there were clear goals and objectives for their job and just over 60 percent responded that they would strongly recommend their job to someone who was interested in a career with the RCMP. Of concern is that nearly 50 percent of the respondents stated that they did not feel that actions would be taken on the results of the survey. This suggests that, with respect to this survey and the RCMP, there is considerable work to be done in improving the organizational climate and dynamics.[45] A perceived lack of career opportunities has been associated with officers leaving police work. Also, officers may find the traditional paramilitary structure of their police service a source of frustration.

Another source of stress for officers is inadequate resources to respond to the community's demands for service. This may result in patrol shifts being short-staffed and investigative units being backlogged with cases. Whether senior managers are able to secure the necessary officers, as well as equipment for those officers, and how they deploy the available resources (i.e., efficiently or not), has an impact on the stress levels of rank-and-file officers. Officers who begin their shift with a lengthy roll of "calls waiting" and who spend their entire shift responding to calls with little time for proactive policing may become frustrated and disillusioned.

There may also be an organizational climate in the police service that fosters conflict among officers. A review by the Commission for Public Complaints Against the RCMP of more than 700 harassment complaints filed between 2005 and 2011 found that 90 percent of the complaints related to "bullying," including psychological abuse and belittling and demeaning behaviour; 6 percent concerned "discrimination" associated with ethnicity, a disability, or some other factor; and 4 percent of the complaints related to sexual harassment.[46] The Commission also found that in some provinces, male members of the RCMP accounted for an equal share of the complaints against the RCMP.

These findings suggest that workplace conflicts in the RCMP extend beyond sexual harassment. Among the recommendations of the report were that the RCMP develop a timely and transparent process for responding to complaints (some were found to have taken up to four years to investigate and complete), develop a mandatory training program for harassment investigators, and send employees for training on issues related to harassment in the workplace. Of some concern were the findings from an internal survey ($N = 426$) conducted in one RCMP Division, which found that women officers did not trust the RCMP to deal appropriately with complaints of harassment.[47]

Research studies in the U.S. have found that officers working in smaller police services experience higher levels of stress than their colleagues in larger police services.[48]

Shift Work and Tired Cop Syndrome

tired cop syndrome
a jet-lag state of police officers, primarily due to shift work

Concern is growing about **tired cop syndrome,** a jet-lag state that may place officers at a greater risk of accidents and poor decision making. Shift work is a major contributor to officer fatigue, and it is often identified by officers as a major impediment to high-level performance.[49]

The impact of shift work on the health and well-being of workers is well documented. Prolonged exposure to night shifts results in an individual who is sleep deprived and prone to poor performance, accidents, and health problems. Research studies indicate that shift workers suffer accumulating sleep deficits. Furthermore, night-shift workers in general perform at a lower level than their day-shift counterparts, are involved in more on-the-job accidents, and are less alert. Shift work increases the risk of cardiovascular disease, gastrointestinal disorders, miscarriage, preterm birth, and menstrual problems. It also increases feelings of irritation and strain, and a general feeling of malaise.[50] A study ($N = 3,232$) published in 2014 found that shift work was associated with chronic impairment of cognition due to psychological stress.[51]

All of these factors may have a significant impact on the exercise of discretion and decision making by police officers. There is a substantial body of research evidence that indicates that the officers who are impaired by sleep deprivation and fatigue may be unable to consider the consequences of their decisions and may have difficulty de-escalating situations that require the use of soft policing skills.[52]

Despite this, many police services continue to shift officers in a two-days/two-nights/four-off pattern. In addition, officers must also make court appearances, which may result in an officer being at the court all day and then working a night shift. It has been suggested that police services modify shift schedules so as to have longer shift intervals and/or keep officers in the same shift for several months at a time. While administratively convenient, there is concern that this type of shift schedule takes a toll on officers. Many officers seek "day job" and specialty unit positions in the police service in an attempt to escape from uniform patrol shifts. Promotions often allow officers to move out of uniformed patrol and into specialty units.

To reduce the jet-lag and tired cop syndrome, some police services have modified the traditional shifting pattern. In Toronto, for example, officers work seven "day" shifts, followed by six days off; six "evening" shifts, then five days off; and seven "night" shifts, then three days off.

Police officers posted in rural and remote community may be at particular risk of tired cop syndrome. In the absence of systems of support and in communities with high rates of crime and disorder, officers may find themselves working long hours without relief and are never really "off shift." Officers may go for weeks or months without a day off.

Being an Aboriginal, Visible/Cultural, or LGBT Officer

An understudied area of Canadian policing are the experiences of Aboriginal persons, persons from visible/cultural minority communities, and LGBT persons who become police officers. The challenges they experience may be significant. One Aboriginal police officer stated to your author, "Some people would view you as a traitor. I've had that from my own family." A retired Aboriginal officer, Ernie Louttit, recalled that when he joined the Saskatoon Police Service in 1987, "I was the third Native officer, and there was an old boys' club. And they didn't want to work with women; they didn't want to work with natives." He also recalled a backlash against him from the Aboriginal community: "It was both ways, so a lot of Native people would call me an 'apple'—like I was red on the outside and white on the inside—and I was betraying my own people by being a police officer."[53] (See his book, *Indian Ernie: Perspectives on Policing and Leadership,* published in 2013.) Recall from earlier in the discussion that the Saskatoon police has increased its numbers of Aboriginal officers significantly over the past decade.

Similarly, for LGBT officers, the police service must respect the privacy of their personal lives and the extent to which they feel comfortable disclosing their status, both within the police service and in the community.[54]

A high-profile case was that of Baltej Dhillon, now an RCMP staff sergeant, a Sikh who immigrated with his mother to Canada from Malaysia during his high school years. While completing a criminal justice program at a local community college, he became interested in becoming an officer in the RCMP. After submitting his application, he was told by the RCMP that he would be accepted to go to the Training Academy, but that he would have to remove his turban.

As recently as 1990, RCMP policy did not allow officers to wear the Sikh turban, and there was considerable controversy surrounding the decision of the then-RCMP commissioner to support a change in policy, which was done by the federal government. Opponents of allowing police constables to wear the turban had argued that it would forever alter the national icon's image of the Stetson-wearing Mountie. A CBC News clip, produced in 1990 and available online, presents the story; see the Media Link at the end of this chapter.

Police Work and the Police Family

Police work has often been referred to as anti-family. It has the potential to generate family stress and crises, yet little research has been done on this topic. Sources of stress on the police family include always being on duty, particularly for officers in rural and remote communities who must be available twenty-four hours a day, even during their days off; the ever-present potential for callouts; and the transfer policy in the OPP, SQ, and RCMP, wherein police families may be periodically moved.

A national survey of RCMP officers found that nearly 30 percent of the officers did not feel that they were able to balance their personal, family, and work needs.[55] Another study of work/life balance and employee well-being among a large sample (N = 4,500) of Canadian police officers found that nearly three-quarters of the officers worked more than forty-five hours per week, and one-third had to work evenings and weekends at home to complete their work. This high workload placed the officers at "high risk with respect to work-life conflict, stress, depressed mood, absenteeism and poorer physical health."[56] A study of 233 officers at all ranks and civilians in the criminal investigation services unit in the Ottawa Police Service reported high levels of overload in their work roles (52 percent), high stress levels (47 percent), and high levels of depressed mood and at a high risk of burnout (33 percent).[57]

Most officers develop strategies for coping with the stressors they encounter on the job. One Indo-Canadian officer stated to your author: "I meditate every day, do yoga, go to the gym."

THE CONSEQUENCES OF STRESS: POST-TRAUMATIC STRESS DISORDER (PTSD) AND SUICIDE

These stressors may place officers at risk of mental health disorders and alcohol and/or drug abuse.[58] Research in the U.S. has found that stressful law enforcement duties are associated with a high risk of sudden cardiac death among officers.[59]

Constant exposure to stressors may also lead to burnout, a general term used to describe physical, emotional, and mental exhaustion.[60] The costs of this burnout are high: for the officer, the officer's family, the police service, and the community. These include the fiscal impact of psychological injuries suffered by officers: during the time period from 2006 to 2012, the Ontario Provincial Police paid out a total of $3.5 million in compensation to 100 officers who had filed claims for operational stress injuries associated with traumatic workplace incidents.[61] There is also research to suggest that high stress levels may affect officer performance and make officers more susceptible to misconduct.[62]

Post-traumatic Stress Disorder

Of increasing concern is the prevalence of **post-traumatic stress disorder (PTSD)** among police officers. Officers who are involved in critical incidents, such as a shooting, or who are exposed to extreme violence, individual suffering, and death may develop PTSD, an extreme form of critical incident stress that includes nightmares, hypervigilance, intrusive thoughts, and other forms of psychological distress.[63] One U.S. study found that among a cohort of police officers ($N = 100$), there was a 35 percent rate of post-traumatic stress.[64] There does appear to be variability among officers as to their susceptibility to PTSD: resilience, satisfaction with life, and gratitude have been found to mitigate the symptoms of PTSD.[65]

post-traumatic stress disorder (PTSD)
an extreme form of critical incident stress that includes nightmares, hypervigilance, intrusive thoughts, and other forms of psychological distress

Traumatic events such as homicides, suicides, the deaths of children, and multi-victim accidents can take a toll on officers and lead to burnout and, in some instances, suicide.[66] These experiences may be compounded by shift work, which results in officers working all hours of the day and night with a significant impact on sleep patterns. A study ($N = 4{,}957$) of a sample of U.S. and Canadian police officers found that just over 40 percent of the officers suffered from at least one sleep disorder.[67] There is also some evidence to suggest that the working environment in a police service may affect the extent and severity of PTSD among officers. Inadequate resources, a lack of support, and conflict among officers may contribute to officers being at risk of PTSD.[68] For one officer's experience with PTSD, see the Media Link, "Peter's Story," at the end of this chapter.

As mentioned in the preceding section, there is research to suggest that high stress levels may make officers more susceptible to misconduct, and as well, constant exposure to stressors may also lead to burnout, a general term used to describe physical, emotional, and mental exhaustion. A report of the Ombudsman of Ontario called the provincial government to task for failing to develop adequate services to address "occupational stress injuries."[69] As well, it is important to determine the incidence of PTSD among officers, much of which may go undiagnosed and untreated.[70]

See Box 5.3 for the experience of one police officer.

Suicide

If left unaddressed and in severe cases, PTSD can result in officer suicide, although there are other causes as well. In the first six months of 2014, there were twenty-six suicides by Canadian first-responders—a group that includes firefighters, paramedics, and police officers. From late April to October 2014, there were twelve confirmed suicides among active Canadian police officers. The absence of a national database of police suicides in Canada precludes an examination of the factors that may be associated with police officers taking their life, including rank and length of career, personal history, age, gender, ethnicity, and exposure to critical events, among others.

Box 5.3

Officer "Carl"

Officer Carl has spent more than 20 years in policing, mostly with the OPP. He has worked in different areas and been exposed to multiple traumatic scenarios. He was threatened with knives and guns and had a young girl die in his arms. A colleague was killed, another was almost beaten to death on the job, while a third committed suicide after he retired. After years of getting by, of being "a good cop," Officer Carl's world began to crumble under the accumulated weight of stress.

He became depressed, had panic and insomnia attacks, and began to isolate himself from others. Knowing the stigma attached to mental illness within the police culture, he tried to suppress his symptoms. But it became increasingly harder to hide. In his words: "Imagine being in a job where if they take your gun away, you're done. Or if someone even thinks they should take away your gun you're done. You can't tell them. You have to take it and just hang on to it as long as you can. I thought I could get through the rest of my career. I really did. I tried like hell. I tried, I cried, I worried about it, I stressed over it. Life was hell for me at home. . . . There were all those thoughts of 'I just can't do it anymore.'"

One day at work, the dam broke. With his wife's assistance, Officer Carl sought medical help, and was diagnosed with post-traumatic stress disorder. Like other officers we spoke with, Officer Carl felt isolated—"off on an island"—while on leave. He received [Workplace Safety and Insurance Board] benefits until he was fit to return to accommodated work.

Officer Carl had difficulty with the process of returning to work, finding it frustrating and inflexible. He tried to get on with the job of being a good cop, but his condition deteriorated and his symptoms reappeared. He went on another medical leave and is now back at work on modified duties. Officer Carl believes the OPP could assist its members suffering from operational stress injuries by providing a list of private psychologists, making periodic psychological assessments available for all members, and creating an appeal process for members who disagree with the return-to-work process. He also believes there should be enhanced mandatory operational stress injuries training for all members, involving peers who have recovered from such injuries, and that the Employee Assistance Program Coordinator's position should be full-time. He thinks the OPP should keep statistics on operational stress injuries and suicides, and suggested that it also strike a committee to address operational stress injuries, particularly return-to-work issues.

Source: From Ombudsman Ontario, 2012 (October). *In the Line of Duty*, pp. 18-19, http://www.ombudsman.on.ca/Ombudsman/files/c4/c43aef71-b2ac-4008-ac89-124f56d8dd75.pdf. Reprinted with permission of the Office of the Ombudsman of Ontario

Research studies in the U.S. have generally found that police officers do not have higher rates of suicide than the general population and that policing does not rank among the top professions at risk of suicide. The highest rates are among physicians, dentists, finance workers, and lawyers.[71] However, most studies compare the suicide rates of white males. When gender is considered, a different picture emerges: Caucasian women police officers in the U.S. have a suicide rate 2.03 times that of non-police, Caucasian women.[72] For Black male police officers, policing is the riskiest of all of the professions. Much more research remains to be done in Canada to understand not only the factors that contribute to police officer suicides but also the levels of risk for different groups of officers.

Research in the U.S. has found that the incidence of police family homicide-suicides were much higher than for the general population. The perpetrator in the majority of the homicides was a male police officer, and the victim was a spouse or female acquaintance.[73] A particular problem among police officers is homicide-suicides, which are most common among higher ranks of officers. Antoon Leenaars and colleagues have written a report and "psychological autopsy" of a homicide-suicide involving a retired police superintendent and an acting inspector in the London (Ontario) Police Service.[74]

PROGRAMS AND INTERVENTIONS FOR OFFICERS EXPERIENCING OPERATIONAL STRESS

Most police services have employee assistance plans, and some have wellness coordinators who provide support and assistance to officers who are experiencing difficulties on the job or in their personal and family lives. A number of police boards have supported the adoption of the National Standard for Psychological Health and Safety in the Workplace, developed by the Canadian Standards Association. These are voluntary guideline standards that organizations can use to create safe and healthy environments for employees (for more information, search for "National Standard" at the Mental Health Commission of Canada website at mentalhealthcommission.ca).

The Calgary Police Service has been at the forefront of addressing mental and physical health issues among its officers, adopting the Road to Mental Readiness (R2MR) program from the Canadian military. This program is operated in collaboration with Alberta Health Services, the Department of National Defence, and the Mental Health Commission of Canada. It is designed to provide officers with an understanding of mental health issues, how to remain healthy, and how to assist other officers in doing so as well.[75]

Of concern is that many police officers experiencing PTSD do not seek professional assistance. The traditional cultural values of the police occupation, including the tenet to "man up" in the face of adversity and to not disclose personal problems for fear of being viewed as "weak," mitigate against officers seeking assistance.[76] The OPP ombudsman study found that the stigma surrounding operational stress injuries was still acute and that officers who were suffering from these challenges were often isolated and not supported by management.[77] Many police services have also been slow to develop a strategic plan to address mental and physical health issues among officers. An inquiry into the OPP, for example, found that the information and training provided to officers was "ad hoc and not coordinated" and that there was no overall strategic plan to address the issues of operational stress in the service.[78]

Summary

The discussion in this chapter has centred on the police occupation. The issues surrounding recruiting and training police officers were discussed, and it was revealed that Canadian police services are taking proactive measures to increase the numbers of women, Aboriginal, visible/cultural minority, and LGBT recruits. The recruiting process is comprehensive and competitive, although there is concern that it may not prepare officers for the challenges they will face on the job. The culture of the police provides the relationships of trust that are required in responding to high-risk incidents; on the other hand, the police culture may condone or protect officers engaged in unethical behaviour and may contribute to the reluctance of officers to seek assistance for problems they are facing on the job. Police officers face numerous challenges and stressors, which may significantly impact their professional and personal lives. In recent years, there has been a heightened awareness of the need to provide services for officers who are afflicted with post-traumatic stress disorder and officers who may be at risk of suicide.

KEY POINTS REVIEW

1. There are both basic qualifications (core competencies) and preferred qualifications for individuals considering a career in a Canadian police service.
2. Canadian police services are making efforts to increase their diversity.
3. The recruit selection process has many stages and includes interviews, a medical examination, various tests, a background investigation, a polygraph examination (except in Ontario and most of Quebec), and other assessments.
4. There are a number of models of police recruit training in Canada.
5. There is competition among police services for previously experienced officers (PEOs).
6. Police recruits undergo a process of socialization into the role of police officer as they move from the academy to the street.
7. During operational field training, the recruit learns to apply the basic principles taught at the police training academy under the guidance of a field training officer (FTO).
8. Among the facets of the police occupation are the working personality of the police, the culture of the police, and the various occupational outlooks and career orientations of individual police officers.
9. The challenges of police work include role conflict, the decisions of other components of the criminal justice system, the demands of police work, the often unrealistic and conflicting demands of the community, conflicts with peers and supervisors, and shift work.

10. The stress experienced by police officers can affect their personal and professional lives, in some instances lead to post-traumatic stress syndrome, and place officers at risk of suicide.

KEY TERM QUESTIONS

1. Identify and describe the **basic qualifications** (core competencies) required of prospective police recruits and the **preferred qualifications** that may be advantageous in applying to a police service.
2. What is meant by **competency-based training**?
3. Why are **previously experienced officers (PEOs)** important in any discussion of police recruiting, and what are the issues surrounding the efforts of police services to attract these officers?
4. What types of **in-service training** are available to police officers?
5. Discuss the importance of **operational field training** and the role of field training officers (FTOs).
6. What is the **working personality of police officers**? Why is this concept important in any study of police work, and what does the research say about the extent to which it exists in police work today?
7. Define and discuss the importance of the following for discussions about police culture: (a) the **code of silence**, (b) the **blue-light syndrome**, and (c) **hypervigilance.**
8. What is **tired cop syndrome** and how might it affect police work?
9. Discuss **post-traumatic stress disorder (PTSD)** among police officers, its causes, and the challenges that are encountered in addressing it.

CRITICAL THINKING EXERCISES

Critical Thinking Exercise 5.1. A Comparison of Police Training Models

Consider the RCMP training model as opposed to the training model for municipal and provincial police services. What are the strengths and limitations of these models? What changes, if any, would you make?

Critical Thinking Exercise 5.2. The Positive and Less Positive Features of the Police Culture

The discussion in this chapter has revealed that the police culture has a number of positive features, but also some negative consequences. How is this dilemma to be resolved?

Research studies indicate that police officers are often reluctant to seek help when they are experiencing high levels of stress and even in those instances in which they are afflicted by PTSD. In your view, should it be mandatory for officers who exhibit signs of severe stress or PTSD to seek treatment?

CLASS/GROUP DISCUSSIONS

Class/Group Discussion 5.1. Should Police Services Have the Right to Ask Applicants for Access to Their Facebook Page?

"Applicants should expect to be asked for their Facebook account. Students should pay attention to what's on their Facebook page. The recruiting officers will go into the applicant's Facebook page and observe what's going on there. It's primarily to determine who their friends are, if there are any ethical or integrity issues, and what their level of emotional maturity is. Even after you become a police officer, there is an expectation that the officer will give attention to what's on their Facebook page" (personal communication with a former director of a Canadian police training academy, 2013).

Across North America, an increasingly larger number of employers are requesting that potential employees provide access to their Facebook page or other social media postings as part of the application process. Proponents of this strategy argue that applicants should be open and transparent about their activities, while critics argue that it constitutes an invasion of privacy.

Your Thoughts?

1. What is your position on this issue?
2. If you applied to a police service and access to your Facebook page was requested as part of the application process, would you provide it?
3. Is there anything currently on your Facebook page that might affect your application to a police service?

Class/Group Discussion 5.2. A Recruiting Video for the Royal Newfoundland Constabulary: Over the Top?

In 2014, the Royal Newfoundland Constabulary (RNC) unveiled a new video designed to attract recruits to the police service. Titled "Diverse. Capable. Proud. This is Today's RNC," the video was criticized in the media for being a "marketing disaster" and for undermining the excellent work that the RNC has done in recruiting diversity to the service. In the words of one media observer, the improvements in employment equity are "completely lost in the thunderous screaming and symphonic gun-waving. If there is diversity on this force, it's deeply obscured beneath body armour and assault weapons" (Rollman, p. 1). There are concerns that the scenes in the video of officers with assault rifles dressed in military-style uniforms highlight only a small part of the police role and one that most officers are rarely involved in (CBC News, p. 2).

In defending the video, the RNC chief constable stated that the video was designed to get the attention of young persons who live in a social media–dominated world and wasn't the only message that the RNC sent out to potential recruits.

View the video on youtube.com and consider the following questions:

1. Do you feel that the RNC recruiting video is "over the top"?
2. In your view, are the criticisms of the video justified?
3. If you are/were interested in a career in policing, would this video strengthen or lessen your interest? Why?

Then view the parody of the RNC video, produced by an artist and activist in St. John's. Search for "RNC Tourism Video" at youtube.com. What is your response to this video?

Sources: CBC News. (2014, October 21). "RNC chief defends hard-hitting recruitment video", retrieved from http://www.cbc.ca/news/canada/newfoundland-labrador/rnc-chief-defends-hard-hitting-recruitment-video-1.2807330; H. Rollman. (2014, October 21). "The RNC recruitment ad: Pretty film, marketing disaster." TheIndependent.ca, retrieved from http://theindependent.ca/2014/10/21/the-rnc-recruitment-ad-pretty-film-marketing-disaster/

Class/Group Discussion 5.3. Should There Be Hiring Quotas for Police Services?

The RCMP is one police service that has set benchmarks for hiring women, visible minorities, and Aboriginals. It has been suggested that quotas be established to ensure that these benchmarks are met. Opponents of quotas contend that setting quotas would result in lowering standards for police recruits.

Your Thoughts?

What is your position on the issue of hiring quotas in policing?

MEDIA LINKS

Visit www.nelson.com/canadianpolicework4 for links to these videos and other additional content available with this text.

"RCMP recruits in 1957," CBC Digital Archives, May 2, 1957, cbc.ca/archives

"1990: Sikh Mounties permitted to wear turbans," CBC Digital Archives, March 15, 1990, cbc.ca/archives

"Behind the Line," *The Fifth Estate*, CBC, December 9, 2011, cbc.ca/fifth

"Peter's Story," Royal Canadian Mounted Police, December 10, 2014, youtube.com

6 Patrol and General Duty Policing

LEARNING OBJECTIVES

After reading this chapter, you should be able to:

- Understand the nature of patrol and the areas of patrol work
- Discuss the role of dispatchers and communications officers in managing calls for service
- Discuss the issues surrounding the deployment of mobile patrol units, including staffing, patrol unit utilization, patrol unit response times, and patrol officer skill sets
- Identify and discuss the key concepts that are useful in understanding the decision making of patrol officers
- Discuss the use of mediation and conflict resolution skills by patrol officers
- Consider the impact of social media on the decision making of patrol officers
- Describe how patrol officers perceive and respond to persons and events
- Identify the factors influencing the decision making of patrol officers and provide examples
- Discuss the unique challenges faced by officers in policing northern and remote communities
- Describe the issues that surround police encounters with persons with mental illness and multi-needs populations and the efforts that are being made to address these issues
- Discuss the issues that surround policing visible/cultural/religious minorities
- Describe the role of body-worn cameras in monitoring the decision making of the police

Early in this text it was noted that a key attribute of police work (and one that distinguishes it from the work of other criminal justice personnel) is that it is carried out in the community rather than the safe confines of an office. The street is the domain of patrol officers, and there is no way for them to avoid the weather, the long nights, or people and their problems. These realities force officers to become intimately familiar with their working environment and to develop skill in assessing situations, exercising discretion, and making effective decisions. Uniformed patrol officers are often referred to as the "eyes, ears, arms, and legs" of police services.

THE STREET AS "THE OFFICE"

Being on the front line of the criminal justice system, the police have more contact with the general public than do other criminal justice personnel. Police officers are the only criminal justice personnel who are available in large numbers 24/7/365. EMS and fire/rescue are available to be dispatched, while police officers are constantly deployed. And there are incidents in which EMS and fire will not become involved without the assistance of the police, such as an incident involving a mentally ill person.

The police are often the agency of first and last resort. Whereas many police activities are highly visible, other professionals in the criminal justice system (e.g., judges, probation officers, and correctional officers) operate in relative obscurity. Criminal court judges, for example, make decisions within the safe confines of a courthouse and have the luxury of considering the case facts and carefully weighing the interests of the community, the victim, and the offender before issuing a judgment.

Although judges' decisions may be controversial, they are in large measure immune from the scrutiny (including social media) that police officers receive in carrying out their day-to-day tasks. Similarly, in contrast to the police, the decisions made by probation and parole officers with respect to the management of offenders in the community have low visibility, even in instances where serious harm has resulted from these decisions.

It is patrol officers who respond to the primary calls for service that the public makes to police services, and it is citizen requests that generate the most police contacts with the public. As the most visible representatives of the criminal justice system, they are—more than most other criminal justice personnel—subject to attacks on their judgment and decision making. It is they who are most often blamed for the failings of the criminal justice system generally. And they are often the first to be held accountable by politicians, the public, the courts, and even their own supervisors when difficulties arise.

Patrol Work

Five duties of police officers are recognized under common law and are at the core of police work: (1) to prevent crime, (2) to protect life and property, (3) to preserve the peace, (4) to apprehend offenders, and (5) to enforce laws. Patrol officers are involved in a wide range of situations, including responding to incidents involving law enforcement, order maintenance, and service; conducting investigations; making arrests; executing warrants; and attending court. In actuality, patrol officers are not equally involved in all of these activities. Much depends on the specific environment in which officers are carrying out their duties—for

Perry Mah, Edmonton Sun

Edmonton police patrol officers issuing a ticket.

example, whether it is a high-crime inner-city neighbourhood or an affluent wealthy suburban community. Other factors include the resources the police service has at its disposal and the amount of time officers have to engage in proactive, preventive policing (as opposed to responding to calls for service). Generally speaking, the prevention and apprehension components of the officer's duties are secondary to maintaining order and providing service.

Depending on the level of calls for service, patrol officers may have an opportunity to engage in problem-solving policing, address problem premises, and engage in a wide range of proactive policing activities, including conducting street checks of individuals of interest. Note that not all of the activities of patrol officers are captured in "dispatched" calls for service. On a daily basis, patrol officers are involved in many interactions and situations with community residents that do not result in any formal action being taken. This includes situations in which officers use their discretion to defuse conflicts and resolve disputes. It also includes cultivating "sources" (informants)—that is, people in the patrol area who can provide them with information on crimes that have been committed, or are going to be committed, and the names of people involved in criminal activities. It also includes participating in various community policing initiatives.

Patrol work can be highly diversified, though much depends on the size of the department. Officers in smaller police services tend to be responsible for a broader spectrum of duties, while larger departments have specialized units to provide various services. This is particularly the case in policing remote northern communities. Larger police services provide a buffer and a "safety in numbers" environment for patrol officers; they also have more extensive support services for patrol officers, including victim services, traffic sections, canine units, and so on. Also, patrol work takes place in a wide variety of task environments, which determine the volumes and types of calls to which officers are asked to respond.

Patrol officers are also a valuable source of information for the police service. A considerable amount of information is gathered by officers in encounters with community residents and from others, including informants (see Chapter 10). Officers often have an in-depth understanding of the neighbourhoods and districts they police. It is important that there be a process by which this information can be included in the analyses conducted as part of intelligence-led policing (see Chapter 9).[1]

The types of activity that patrol officers are involved in are determined largely by calls to the police from the general public. Generally speaking, responding to high-priority crime calls represents only about 20 percent of patrol officers' duties. This has provided the opportunity to explore a variety of alternative service-delivery models, such as community constables, discussed in Chapter 3. However, research on the nature of calls for service suggests the need to consider whether calls for service have the *potential* to require enforcement (see Police File 6.1).

Table 6.1 indicates the ten most frequent calls for service for the Waterloo Regional Police Service.

TABLE 6.1
Ten Most Common Citizen Calls for Service to Police Communications

2013 Top Ten Calls	Frequency	New Call Every...
1. Bylaw complaint	8,769	60 minutes
2. Compassionate to locate	6,905	1 hour 16 minutes
3. Domestic dispute	5,805	1 hour 31 minutes
4. Motor vehicle collision–property damage	5,097	1 hour 43 minutes
5. Theft under $5,000	4,968	1 hour 46 minutes
6. Alarm	4,058	2 hours 10 minutes
7. Unwanted person	3,973	2 hours 12 minutes
8. Driving complaint	3,760	2 hours 20 minutes
9. Administrative/routine detail	3,500	2 hours 30 minutes
10. Injured/sick person	3,334	2 hours 38 minutes

Source: Courtesy Waterloo Regional Police

Police File 6.1

The Risks of Crime: Findings from a U.K. Study

An analysis of 4.7 million recorded incidents in six police services in the U.K. found that a high percentage of the incidents to which police officers respond included either a crime having been committed or the risk of a crime being committed. In contrast to the widely held view that only about 20 percent of police officers' time is spent on crime, the study found that if responding to incidents where there was a *risk* of crime, the rate was at least 80 percent.

Additional findings of the study included the following:

1. An overwhelming portion of police officers' time was spent on crime or stopping things that the public felt was dangerous or wrong or should cease immediately.
2. In 28 percent of the 4.7 million recorded incidents, a crime had actually taken place, and in 17 percent of the 4.7 million incidents, some form of ASB (anti-social behaviour) had occurred.
3. In the bulk of the remaining incidents (a further 55 percent), there was the *potential* for crime

that the police could not discount without a closer examination of the circumstances.

4. In almost 90 percent of incidents recorded in the six police services, there was a crime or the potential for a crime to happen. Across the 36 shifts observed, officers spent about 80 percent of their time on activity that related directly or indirectly to crime.

Overall, the significance of this study was that the preventive and enforcement role of police officers may consume most of their time. The specific breakdown of the various roles of the police will depend upon a variety of factors, including the nature of the community being policed, the extent to which there has been downloading onto the police, community demands on the police, and the nature and extent of crime and disorder in the community, among other factors. These findings also suggest that there may be limitations in the extent to which policing functions can be assumed by private security officers and other para-police in a tiered policing arrangement (see Chapter 3).

Source: Her Majesty's Inspectorate of Constabulary. (2012). *Taking Time for Crime: A Study of How Police Officers Prevent Crime in the Field*. London: Author. Retrieved from http://www.justiceinspectorates.gov.uk/hmic/media/taking-time-for-crime.pdf

The new recruit soon learns that a large part of police work is routine and administrative—in John van Maanen's words, "the proverbial clerk in a patrol car."[2] For most patrol officers, this work is insufficient to maintain their interest and enthusiasm. In the view of one police officer: "It's monotonous at times. Pushing a police car is pretty boring, until something happens. You can make it as exciting as you want to—you can stop every car that ever drove through your area. Or you can choose to do nothing. For the most part, it's fairly monotonous."[3]

The modern patrol vehicle is virtually an office on wheels. Police services have equipped their vehicles with laptop computers, cellphones, and radios. Mobile display terminals (MDTs) allow police officers to communicate with other patrol officers, to access drivers' records, and to run criminal information checks on people through the **Canadian Police Information Centre (CPIC)**. This is a computerized information system that contains information on vehicles, individuals, marine equipment, criminal records, dental characteristics, prison inmates, and wandering persons.

Canadian Police Information Centre (CPIC)
the centralized, computer-based information system used by police services

Some observers have expressed concern that police services are becoming too dependent on technology. Officers may come to rely too heavily on computer-generated information, to the exclusion of "human" intelligence gathered by developing contacts in the community. Patrol officers may not have—or take—the opportunity to engage in proactive activities outside their patrol vehicles. In one Ojibway community in Ontario, the Aboriginal word for the police translates to "men with no legs," the subtext being that the officers who patrol the community never leave their patrol cars.

STRATEGIES FOR MANAGING CALLS FOR SERVICE

As the only public safety agency open 24/7, police services receive hundreds or—in some locales—even thousands of requests for service every day.

The public's requests for service and the policing tasks mandated by the law and government policy far outstrip available police resources.

Dispatchers and Communications Officers: The Gatekeepers

The greater part of police work is assigned to patrol officers by dispatchers or communications officers.

Dispatchers and communications officers (COs) receive the initial request for service, gather basic information from the caller (including name, address, and type of situation), prioritize the call, and allocate available patrol resources. To ensure they are gathering the information necessary to properly interpret and prioritize calls, they apply the **W system**, which includes the following types of questions:

W system
the approach used by police dispatchers to determine key facts about a call

WHERE: Where did this happen? Where are you now? Where is the suspect?

WHAT: What is happening? What is the problem? What do you need?

WHEN: Is this happening now? How long ago? When did he/she leave?

WHO: Who is calling? Who is the suspect? Who else is involved? Who told you this?

WHY: Why did you wait to call? Why is he threatening you? Why do you think that?

WEAPONS: Are there any weapons? What are they? Does he carry weapons?

The dispatcher uses all of this information to determine the call's priority (see below) and then forwards it to the patrol officers. It is important that officers obtain as much information as they can about the situation. Much of this information is provided by the dispatcher while the officers are en route to the scene. An increasing number of calls to police are made from cellphones, which causes some problems as, unlike land lines, it is not possible to pinpoint the exact location of the caller.

Dispatchers must "get it right." On some occasions, failure to do so has resulted in serious injury and even death.

Call Priority Categories

Police services prioritize calls for service in basically the same way across the country. Priority 1 are emergency calls that require immediate police attention and include life-threatening situations that can lead to death or grievous bodily harm. Priority 2 calls are serious but are not life threatening and include break and enter (B&E) in progress. Priority 3 and Priority 4 calls are routine and less serious, including "cold" B&Es. Note that not all calls to the police result in the dispatch of a patrol unit (see Figure 6.1).

Figure 6.1. Total and Dispatched Calls for Service, Toronto Police Service, 2001–2010

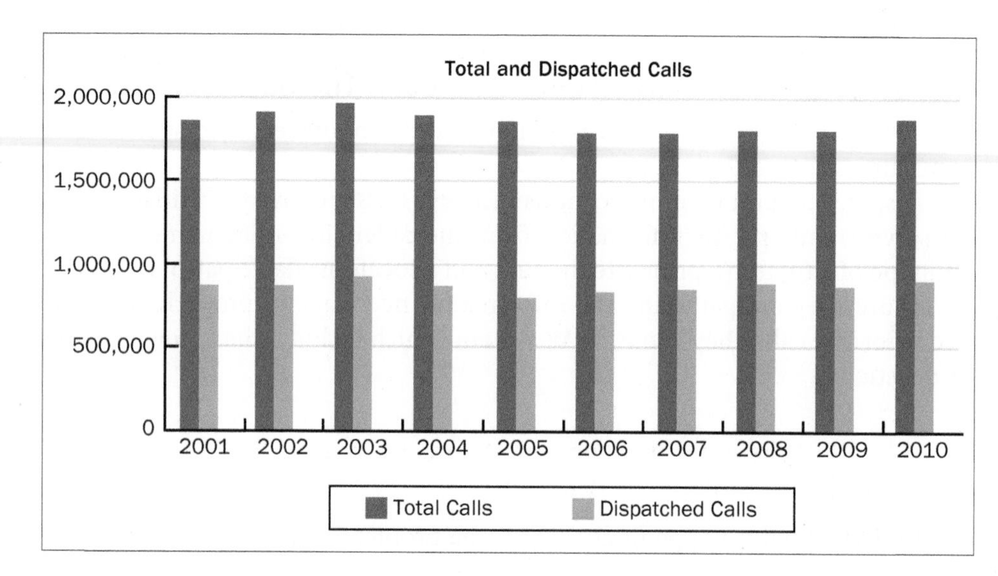

Source: From Toronto Police Service, 2011. *Planning for the Future*, p. 171, http://www.torontopolice.on.ca/publications/files/reports/2011envscan.pdf. Reprinted with permission.

Police File 6.2 presents an incident to which patrol units responded that would be classified as "assist general public."

Police File 6.2

A Call for Assistance

Patrol officers in a major urban centre are dispatched to an apartment occupied by a man, a woman, and a newborn. A call had been made to the police by the midwife of the woman, who had been called by the husband, who felt that his wife was depressed and possibly suicidal. A supervising sergeant, two male constables, and one female constable respond to the call. The husband admits the sergeant and the female constable to the premises, wherein a lengthy discussion ensues about the situation. A key issue that emerges from the discussion is that the mother is emotionally exhausted and, as well, is experiencing stress due to an inability to breast-feed her baby. Her usual source of breast milk in such situations is closed for the weekend, and she is opposed to feeding the baby commercially sold formula. The sergeant places a call to a patrol unit staffed by a police constable and a social worker, who attend the scene. The sergeant and the three constables depart the premises. After a long discussion with the social worker, the woman agrees to feed her baby formula until breast milk can be obtained. The social worker speaks further with the couple about the other issues in their life and relationship.

Calls for service to police organizations are managed both at the organizational level and at the street level. Police services have developed response strategies aimed at reducing organizational costs, ensuring operational effectiveness and efficiency, and providing an adequate level of service. **Call shedding** is a practice that acknowledges that police services can no longer respond to all calls for service, and that other organizations and agencies in the community must help them.

call shedding
a strategy to discard or divert calls for service to match available police resources

When the volume of calls to the dispatch centre exceeds the number of available patrol units, **call stacking** occurs, and the calls are placed in a queue until a unit becomes available. Most calls in a queue at any given point in time are in the Priority 3 and Priority 4 categories; during heavy demand times, though, Priority 2 calls may be awaiting dispatch as well. An excessive volume of calls can have a negative impact on response times to Priority 1, 9-1-1 calls for service.

call stacking
prioritizing calls for service

Differential police response (**DPR**) strategies attempt to differentiate among requests for police service in terms of the optimal forms of police response. DPR strategies are a key way for police services to allocate their resources so as not to be overwhelmed by less serious calls for service. Calls are scanned by police personnel, who determine whether the call is a request for information or a referral, or if it requires police attendance. Guidelines mandate whether police attendance at the scene is necessary.

differential police response (DPR)
categorizing calls for service based on the response required, such as patrol car or no patrol car

DPR strategies enable a broader range of response options than traditional practice, which is to dispatch a patrol officer as quickly as possible. Response alternatives include delayed response by patrol officers to some types of calls, dispatch of civilian personnel instead of sworn officers, taking reports of some crimes by telephone, or asking complainants to walk in or mail in their reports. Many services have telephone response teams that handle many complaints and follow-ups over the telephone, including cases involving minor property damage complaints.

The Computer-Aided Dispatch (CAD) System

The CAD system is used by communications personnel in emergency services and policing to record calls for service and to monitor the response of units in the field. This system contains a variety of information on the incident, including the identity of the caller, the location of the incident, the time at which the call was received and dispatched, and the identity of the officers and how they were at the scene, among other details. The CAD system provides an important database for police services when they analyze demands for and responses to service.

THE DEPLOYMENT OF PATROL UNITS

To improve its effectiveness and efficiency, police services are paying increasing attention to patrol deployment, with particular emphasis on officer workload (time spent on reactive and proactive activities); the response to calls for service, including response times; and the number of arrests.

The challenge for police services is to link patrol resources with call workloads and to maintain consistent levels of service that will allow for proactive policing activities as well as responses to calls for service. In most jurisdictions, demands for police service are not spread equally throughout the week; there are "peak" periods, most often Friday and Saturday nights.

Patrol Shifts

How a police service allocates its patrol resources can have a strong impact on the effectiveness and efficiency of police work. A key factor here is how patrol officers' shifts are arranged. Any shifting model must consider service delivery issues and issues relating to the quality of life of patrol officers. In an ideal world, the shift system used by a police service would match as closely as possible the demands for service, thus ensuring an adequate number of available patrol units. This ideal is tempered, however, by the provisions of labour agreements as well as by the importance of considering quality-of-life issues for patrol officers. Recall from Chapter 5 that shift work can be a major source of stress for police officers.

Patrol officers across Canada work a variety of shift lengths, ranging from eight to twelve hours. With the exception of the RCMP, which is not unionized, shift hours are generally established through collective bargaining between the police union and the municipality. Research studies have found that ten-hour shifts are optimal for maintaining the work/life balance for officers.[4]

One- and Two-Officer Patrol Units

In some police services, patrol car staffing falls under the collective agreement between management and the police officers' association or union. In Vancouver, for example, the collective agreement stipulates that 60 percent of patrol units will have two officers and 40 percent will have one officer; in Toronto, the collective agreement requires that after dark, police must work in two-officer cars. In other police services, such as the Durham Regional Police, patrol car staffing is not part of the collective agreement and is decided by management. The RCMP rarely deploys two-officer patrol units, not even in British Columbia, where the Mounties are involved in policing large urban communities.

There is a debate in academic and policing circles as to whether patrol officers are most efficiently deployed in one- or two-officer patrol units. Many front-line patrol officers contend that one-officer units compromise officer safety. Also, many of them prefer to work in pairs and believe that doing so improves both performance and morale. Many police managers, on the other hand, contend that officers who work in single-patrol units are more efficient, make more arrests, complete more reports, and receive fewer citizen complaints. There is also the issue, not researched, as to how the personalities of officers who work in two-officer units may affect their performance. Distractions, misunderstandings, and disagreements may occur during long shifts in the patrol car. It is also possible that mixed-gender patrol cars may produce dynamics that affect officer performance, although this topic has not been researched.

Studies attempting to correlate the staffing of patrol units with officer efficiency, productivity, attitudes, perceptions, and safety have produced few conclusive results. American studies suggest that one-officer patrol units are safer and more efficient than two-officer units, and figures from Statistics Canada indicate that more officers in two-officer patrol cars were killed than in one-officer cars.[5] An exhaustive study of patrol deployment in the Vancouver Police Department found that response times to Priority 1 calls were longer for one-officer units than for two-officer units during both the day (21 percent longer) and the night (35 percent longer); furthermore, two-officer units were more likely to proactively enforce warrants and court orders, conduct street checks (routine checks where officers speak with known criminals or suspicious persons), generate intelligence information, arrest individuals, locate stolen vehicles, conduct licensed premise checks, and investigate suspicious circumstances (including suspicious persons and vehicles).[6]

Patrol Unit Utilization

A key issue in police services is how patrol units are utilized. **Allocated patrol time** (also referred to as reactive policing) is the amount of time that uniformed patrol officers spend responding to calls for service from the general public. In many police services, patrol officers have little time for non-reactive policing, and it is not unusual for them to begin their shifts with twenty or thirty calls for service in the queue. **Unallocated patrol time** (also referred to as *proactive patrol*) is the amount of time uniformed officers have that is not committed to responding to calls for service. The best-practice standard is for patrol officers to have at least 30 percent of their time unallocated so that they can engage in proactive and problem-solving activities. Note also that most police services do not approximate this standard.

allocated patrol time
the amount of time that patrol officers spend responding to calls from the general public

unallocated patrol time
the amount of time that patrol officers have that is not committed to responding to calls for service

The Edmonton Police Service, for example, had a 2013 target that 25 percent of patrol officers' time should be for "directed" activities; however, the average directed time during that year was 15.2 percent.[7]

A field study of patrol officer activity of RCMP officers in Surrey, British Columbia ($N = 441$ ride-alongs), found that the primary activities of patrol officers fell into several categories and consumed different portions of patrol officers' time during shifts:[8]

1. **Investigative**. Taking statements, searching for evidence, doing surveillance, and report writing/updating (35.7 percent)
2. **Protecting**. Patrolling, guarding a scene, and responding to calls for service (30.1 percent)
3. **Preparation.** (9.8 percent)
4. **Maintenance.** (7.8 percent)
5. **Suspect**. Searching for suspect, detaining/arresting suspect, and booking/interviewing suspect (6.9 percent)
6. **Talking to another officer.** (5.9 percent)
7. **Assistance**. Assisting another police agency and non-police agencies, training other police (2.9 percent)
8. **Court**. Discussing with prosecutor, attending pre-trial matters, preparing disclosure, and attending trials (0.6 percent)

The various activities, and the amount of a patrol officer's time they take, will vary between different "task" environments (see The Task Environment section below), although, interestingly, there was little variation between the patrol districts in the Surrey study.

Figure 6.2 provides a breakdown of proactive/reactive/administrative duties for police officers in the Waterloo Regional Police Service.

Patrol officers who spend more than half their time responding to calls for service may experience higher levels of stress. Also, they are unable to engage in crime prevention initiatives and problem solving, and they may not conduct proper on-scene investigations. In the words of one patrol officer: "I feel like I don't have time to fully address the complainant's issues; there is pressure to wrap up the incident as soon as possible and move on to the next call."[9] (personal communication) Within a community policing model, it is important that officers have time to engage in problem solving; to develop relationships with agencies, community groups, and residents; to utilize proactive enforcement strategies, including problem-solving policing; and to participate in various crime prevention and response initiatives (see Chapter 9). Such initiatives include hot-spot policing, problem-oriented policing, conducting street checks, cultivating informants, and addressing issues of street disorder.

Police services vary greatly in terms of the amount of reactive and proactive time that uniformed patrol officers have. Key factors include the level of demand for policing services, how efficiently patrol resources are deployed, and the availability of patrol resources.

When patrol units spend most of their time doing reactive policing, a question needs to be asked: Is the police service under-resourced, or is it deploying

Figure 6.2. Duties of Patrol Officers in the Waterloo Regional Police Service, 2009

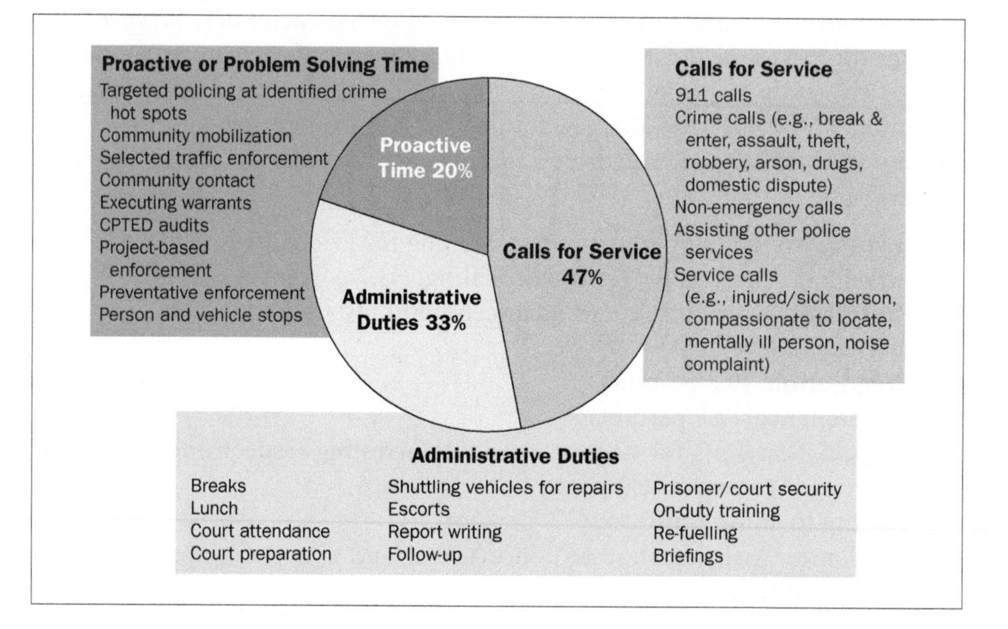

Source: Courtesy Waterloo Regional Police.

its patrol resources inefficiently? This question has been studied in an effort to ensure that patrol units are deployed as effectively as possible. When that is the case, police services have a strong argument to take to municipal councils when lobbying for additional patrol positions.

Patrol Car Response Times

A key element in the police response to calls for service is the amount of time that elapses between when the call is received at the communications centre and when a dispatched unit arrives at the scene (see Figure 6.3).

Note that *response time* is generally broken down into dispatch delay and travel time, whereas *service time* refers to the travel time and the time the units remain at the scene. There is some evidence to suggest that the time that officers remain on scene for Priority 1 calls has increased in recent years, due to a variety of factors, including the seriousness and complexity of the calls, legislated procedures that must be followed, and the training and experience of officers in handling calls.[10]

The best-practice response time for Priority 1 calls is generally considered to be seven minutes, which includes a two-minute average dispatch time and a five-minute travel time to the scene. In most urban police services, however, the response time to Priority 1 calls is much longer. In Toronto in 2009, for example, the average response time for Priority 1 calls was just over ten minutes.

There is no conclusive evidence that crime levels are affected by the response times of police patrol units to Priority 1 calls. However, rapid response to Priority 1 calls does strengthen the ability of the police to protect victims

Figure 6.3. Response Timelines

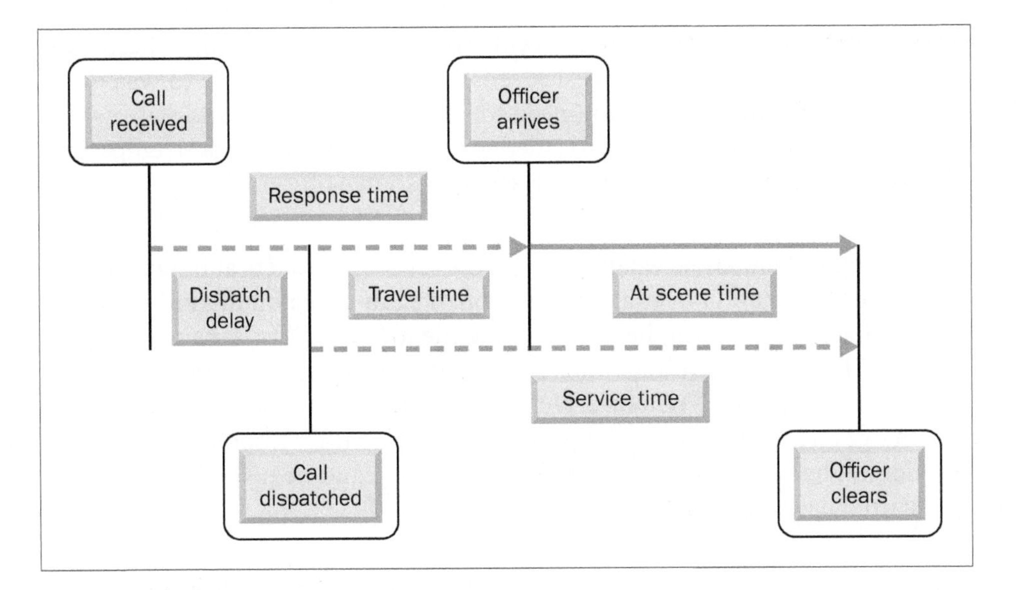

Source: Shreveport Police Department. Reprinted with permission.

and complainants, to arrest offenders, and to preserve and gather evidence. As well, a short response time to a Priority 1 call may increase the likelihood that suspects, victims, witnesses, and complainants will still be at the scene. Also, community residents *expect* the police to respond promptly to calls for service, especially those involving life-threatening situations. A failure of the police to do so may reduce levels of public support for the police and undermine their legitimacy in the community.

In many urban police services, the response times to Priority 1 calls has been increasing. The Edmonton Police Service had a 2013 target of responding to Priority 1 calls in less than seven minutes 80 percent of the time, but were only able to meet this target 69.7 percent of the time.[11]

Similarly, the response times to Code 1 (emergency) calls in the London (Ontario) Police Service increased nearly 14 percent from 2009 to 2012, from 4 minutes 51 seconds, to 5 minutes 31 seconds.[12] These increases in response times may be due to a number of factors, including ineffective deployment and shifting of patrol units and the increasingly complex nature of the Priority 1 calls that are attended. The time that a patrol unit spends on scene is also important as it may contribute to slower response times to other calls that are in the queue.

Patrol Officer Skill Sets

Given the highly interactive nature of patrol work, officers must develop skill sets that facilitate information gathering, conflict resolution, and the provision of service to community residents. This requires that officers be good listeners, be able to process large amounts of information quickly, and make definitive decisions. These are the so-called **soft skills** of police work.

soft skills
patrol officer skills sets centred on information collection, communication, and conflict resolution

An important skill for patrol officers is good judgment. Officers must be firm and authoritative yet able to show empathy and compassion. Officers must also avoid becoming cynical. Recall from Chapter 5 that a core element of the working personality of the police is cynicism. In the words of one officer: "You become cynical and develop this sick sense of humour. You have to watch out, because it grows around you. You need to be able to identify it and step away."[13] Patrol officers must not become so jaded that they lose the capacity to empathize. This is reflected in the comments of a school resource officer:

> I thought, "You know what? Screw it. I don't pull numbers at bingo. You broke the law and I'm gonna charge you." I came down on this kid. Then this hard-ass kid (who had been telling me to "f–off," "fuck the school") says, "I just don't care anymore." All of a sudden, my spider senses kicked in and I thought, "Whoops! He doesn't care about whether there are charges. He doesn't care about getting kicked out of school. What else doesn't he care about?" I poured on the caring and he just lost it—just started bawling. I had turned it around.[14*]

*McDonald, J.M. 2006. *Gold Medal Policing: Mental Readiness and Performance Excellence*. New York: Sloan Associate Press.

STREET WORK: PATROL OFFICER DISCRETION AND DECISION MAKING

> *"It's always easy to armchair QB these after the fact, but at the time when the officers are making the decisions on scene, it's just not so easy to think of every possible scenario."*[15]

discretion
the power or right to decide or act according to one's own judgement

A predominant feature of policing is the exercise of **discretion**. Discretion can be defined as "the power or right to decide or act according to one's own judgement."[16] The exercise of discretion comes into play long before the officer actually arrives at the scene. How does a citizen decide to report an incident to the police? How is the call prioritized by the dispatcher? How much latitude do individual patrol officers have in determining the order in which they attend calls?

Properly applied, discretion enables police officers to be effective in their work, although it is important that officers be held accountable for the misuse of their discretion. There is often a fine line between discretion and discrimination. The effective use of discretion often develops as the officer gains on-the-job experience. Many of the landmark decisions of the Supreme Court of Canada concern decisions and actions taken by police officers in carrying out their tasks.

Although there is no specific legislation that addresses the use of discretion by police officers, the Criminal Code apparently encourages officers to exercise it in the course of their duties. The Code states, for example, that a police officer *may* make an arrest in circumstances where there are reasonable and probable grounds to believe that an offence has been committed. Properly applied, discretion enables police officers to be effective in their work, although it is important that officers be held accountable for the misuse of their discretion.

Officers may decide whether to make an arrest where, by law, an arrest may be warranted. Note also that police officers are more likely not to arrest than they are to arrest in encounter situations. Among the non-arrest options are threats, warnings, mediation, separating the parties, or simply doing nothing. An important part of the patrol officer's job is problem solving.

The policing literature reflects considerable diversity of opinion regarding the exercise of discretion by police officers and the extent to which such powers should be structured and controlled. Opinions vary as to how much discretion police officers actually have and whether they are exercising their discretion in a fair and equitable manner.

In his classic treatise on police discretion, written decades ago, Kenneth Culp Davis argued that, while police discretion should not (and cannot) be eliminated, it needs to be structured, confined, and controlled. As well, the police should acknowledge that it is impossible to enforce the law in full at all times.[17] The reality is that the police engage in selective enforcement, which necessarily involves the exercise of discretion. Police officers must have the discretion to tailor their decision making to the requirements of a given encounter or case. This raises a question: How are we as a community to define the parameters within which discretion is to be exercised? It may well be that police officers are most effective when they do not exercise their full enforcement powers, but instead use discretion to mediate situations and to resolve conflicts at hand in an informal manner. There is often an ethical component to the exercise of discretion by police officers.

Research suggests that a variety of considerations may come into play, including whether making an arrest will make a difference in the long run, the organizational priorities of the police service, and for practical reasons, the amount of time and paperwork that an arrest would require. An example is an officer issuing a 24-hour roadside suspension for an impaired driver, rather than undertaking the multi-hour process required to formally arrest a person for DUI.[18] This is why caution must be exercised in measuring the success of anti-drinking and driving initiatives by the police: the rates of arrest for DUI may drop, but there may be a corresponding increase in the numbers of 24-hour roadside suspensions that involve less paperwork and are less time-consuming.

Obviously, as the level of seriousness of the call increases, the amount of police discretion decreases. In many incidents, particularly those of a minor nature, the officer may encounter ethical dilemmas due to the situation. This might include having to decide whether to arrest an alleged shoplifter who is poor and/or elderly. In these types of situations, the officer may have to weigh the demands of the business owner that the person be arrested, with the moral issue of arresting a person who is no threat to the community and who stole out of necessity or due to a mental disability.

Other dilemmas surround incidents where there is no clear violation of the law. This requires the officer to find a solution and to problem solve. Family and interpersonal disputes present these types of dilemmas: "Typically, boyfriends want girlfriends removed, girlfriends want boyfriends removed, parents want children removed, and husbands want wives removed, or vice versa, and the police officers called to the scene must apply the law to what is essentially a family dispute."[19]

Court decisions, legislation, and the operational policies of police services have constrained the discretion exercised by patrol officers. Patrol officers' discretion is constrained as well by legislation and policy. One example is the zero tolerance policies toward domestic violence and spousal assault that have been adopted by provincial governments across Canada. These policies require police officers to take action in cases where there is evidence that a spouse has been psychologically or physically harmed.

The actions of patrol officers may also be subject to review by supervisors. Except in smaller police services, a senior supervisor is always on duty, either on patrol or at the station. These officers are responsible for overseeing the activities of patrol officers during their shift. When serious events occur, the senior supervisor will always be on scene to direct the response and coordinate the investigation.

selective (or situational) enforcement
discretionary enforcement due to the inability of police officers to enforce all of the laws at all times

Because it is impossible for officers to enforce all laws all the time, they practise **selective (or situational) enforcement**, which in turn requires them to exercise discretion. They base their actions on a number of factors, including safety and the seriousness of the incident/offence. The call load of the officer(s) may also affect how much time the officers at the scene have to consider various options in an encounter situation.

Officers should also be aware of factors that might be influencing their decisions. They must take pains to remain objective and free of bias. They should make every attempt to de-escalate situations and to avoid conflict or a physical confrontation. Verbal skills rather than force should be used to encourage the subject to comply with the officer's request.

Officers are required to balance the requirements of the law and values.[20] In many encounter situations, officers have considerable discretion to weigh these factors. These decisions often get made in the "grey areas" of police work—situations in which the officer could enforce the law and take formal action but where there are intervening variables that may be addressed that will result in an informal resolution of the incident. See the Critical Thinking Exercise 6.1 at the end of this chapter.

It is important to emphasize that every action a police officer takes may ultimately be scrutinized by the courts or the public, or both. Controversies that erupt over decisions made by police officers are often a consequence of how officers exercised discretion in specific encounters and whether they abused their discretionary power or violated the rights of suspects.

For example, a police officer who lets an impaired driver park his car instead of arresting him may be responsible for any subsequent behaviour on the part of that driver. If the impaired individual returns to his vehicle, drives away, and causes an accident in which an innocent person is killed, that officer will likely be called on to justify the decision not to arrest the driver. In other instances, the public may have been watching—and in more and more incidents, recording—the actions of the officer with a cell phone camera.

Patrol officers may sometimes deliberately avoid involving themselves in problematic situations. This has been referred to as FIDO, an acronym for "F*** it, drive on." Perhaps the officer concludes that, rather than becoming involved in an incident that may lead to a citizen complaint (or in an incident that often recurs), it is best to pass on by, pretend not to have witnessed it, and let someone else deal with it. However, this response isolates officers from the communities they police; furthermore, abdicating police authority can be as inappropriate as abusing that authority. The FIDO phenomenon may have become more prevalent with the increased visibility of the police, discussed in Chapter 1. Officers realize that they are always "on camera."

In this context, it may be a challenge to supervise patrol officers (see Police Perspective 6.1).

Patrol Officer Use of Mediation and Conflict Resolution

Patrol officers make an arrest in only a small percentage of encounters.[21] What, then, do they do the rest of the time? Police scholars have paid surprisingly little attention to how patrol officers mediate and resolve conflicts, although officers may utilize a number of methods other than making an arrest:

- *Avoidance.* Taking no action, doing nothing, or telling the disputants to "take a walk" and clear out of the area.
- *Referring the conflict to other agencies for resolution.* Accessing agencies or services with the expertise to address the problem at hand, including neighbourhood dispute resolution groups, landlord–tenant dispute resolution boards, and other community or government services.

Police Perspective 6.1

A Patrol Staff Sergeant Speaks about the Challenges of Supervising Patrol Officers

The biggest challenge in supervising patrol officers is ensuring that there is a high level of compliance with various accountability requirements, making certain that members are taking required training courses, and making certain that they are writing reports that will withstand scrutiny from Crown counsel. The supervising sergeant also tries to make certain that patrol officers feel there is value in their work. A small number of officers will tend to occupy most of a supervisor's time with their various problems. This includes absenteeism from work, personality conflicts, etc. Front-line supervisors can have a significant impact on the job satisfaction of patrol officers.

The expectations on patrol officers have become much more onerous in recent years. Officers are scrutinized externally more than ever, with social media and various oversight bodies, including the internal professional standards section, the police complaints commission, and in serious incidents, civilian investigation bodies. They are constantly being videotaped. They have to be mindful that everything they do could be second-guessed by somebody. This may make officers hesitant to act for fear of scrutiny down the road. The view may be, 'I'd rather not get involved in that situation.' We don't want members not acting for fear of what may happen later.

Sources: Personal communication, a patrol staff sergeant with author, 2012.

- *Intimidation and coercion.* Threatening to arrest the disputants if hostilities do not cease.
- *Mediation.* Acting as a neutral third party in an attempt to address the interests of the disputing parties. This requires the disputants (minimum of two) to participate in the process and is most appropriate for disputes that are one-time incidents and that do not have a history of underlying issues.[22]
- *Restorative justice approaches.* Conducting or participating as a member of a sentencing circle, family group or community conference, or other restorative justice program designed to resolve conflict or respond to criminal behaviour or youth offending. Police participation in restorative justice practices is discussed in Chapter 9.

During an encounter, patrol officers often employ subtle techniques to help defuse the conflict. These include taking a period of time to check identification and record information on the incident; providing an opportunity for the disputants to calm down and thus de-escalate the conflict; and speaking individually with each party.

As patrol officers become more experienced, they develop strategies for resolving conflicts and disputes informally. These strategies are influenced by the officer's personal style of policing, including the way he or she exercises discretion, and their "verbal judo" skills. When community policing is adopted, patrol officers are more likely to become involved in identifying solutions to problems instead of merely reacting to them with formal interventions.

The Impact of Social Media

A key feature of the police is their visibility. This has been increased with the emergence and widespread use of social media. Police are aware that their actions in encounter situations will most likely be recorded by bystanders and that portions may be posted on YouTube and other websites, often before the officer completes the paperwork. This is most common in encounters where force is used. While this increased visibility may serve as a check on police officers' misuse of discretion and, in some cases, the excessive use of force, it can also result in officers avoiding certain encounters or being hesitant to make certain decisions or to use justifiable levels of force. One concern is that bystanders may not understand the total context of the police officer's interaction with the person of interest (see Police Perspective 6.2).

A high-profile encounter situation that was recorded and posted on YouTube in 2013 (and which, as of 2015, had received over 2 million "hits") illustrates a number of issues surrounding bystander recording of police actions. See Class/Group Discussion 6.1, "An Encounter and an Explanation," at the end of this chapter.

Police Perspective 6.2

A Patrol Officer Speaks about Bystanders Recording Encounter Situations

"Usually people will be like 'Oh, police brutality' or stuff like that or 'let him go, let him go,' 'take the cuffs off he didn't do anything wrong.' Rarely is it 'way to go cops for grabbing that guy!' It's usually the down side ... But you know people are often unaware of the totality of what the circumstances are. They just see that we've put some guy in handcuffs and now it's 'why are you doing that,' 'let him go.' It depends on the circumstances but generally speaking it's usually the jackass kind of statements that are prominent ... You can't stop what people are saying ... What you have to do is just be calm and professional and manage the situation. You have to accept the fact that they are going to say those comments and that it's being recorded."

Source: B. Muir. (2014). *Community surveillance of police–citizen encounters: Canadian police officers in YouTube* (Unpublished honours thesis). School of Criminology, Simon Fraser University, Burnaby, BC, pp. 57–58.

Police Perceptions of Persons and Events

Patrol officers bring to their work a cognitive lens through which they determine the levels of trouble and danger (or the potential for these) that people and situations present. This lens affects how officers exercise discretion, as well as the specific actions they take in encounter situations. To respond to incidents efficiently, they use a conceptual shorthand consisting of typifications and recipes for action.

typification
how patrol officers depict or categorize the people and situations they encounter

recipes for action
the actions taken and decisions made by patrol officers in various types of encounter situations

Typifications are constructs or formulations of events based on the officer's experience; they denote what is typical or common about people and events they routinely encounter. **Recipes for action** are the actions normally taken and decisions normally made by police in certain situations. As we'll see, the action taken and the way discretion is exercised can depend, at least in part, on the individual officer.

Most officers divide situations into those requiring "real" police work and those that are "bulls***."[23] Real police work includes situations where officers may need to "use the tools of the trade."[24] In the view of more traditional officers, most requests from the public are not real police work. "Not real" includes neighbourhood disputes, minor traffic accidents, and noisy parties. Note here that community policing, by definition, involves many "not real" service and order maintenance activities.

Police officers, using typifications and recipes for action, tailor their decision making to the particular neighbourhood and population being policed. While on patrol, they use a variety of visual *cues* to determine whether a person is out of place or an activity is unusual for the area. A poorly dressed individual or an older vehicle in an upscale neighbourhood, for example, would attract the attention of patrol officers; so would a well-dressed individual loitering on skid row. Also, police may ignore deviant (even illegal) behaviour in one neighbourhood where it is common, yet respond aggressively to it in a neighbourhood where it is rare. Many officers try to learn as much as possible about the area they are policing, and much of their information comes from community residents rather than car-computer databases. These officers understand the importance of face-to-face contact in police work.

symbolic assailants
individuals encountered by patrol officers who display mannerisms and behaviours that suggest the potential for violence

Patrol officers are especially wary of **symbolic assailants**, that is, "persons who use gestures, language and attire that the policeman has come to recognize as a prelude to violence."[25] A primary cue that officers use in determining the potential for violence is the demeanour of the subject. Officers are continually scanning an encounter situation for verbal and nonverbal cues to determine the level of risk posed by the person(s) of interest.

Assessments of people and situations and the subsequent risk assessments are important elements of street-level police work. When officers err in their assessments, they risk exercising discretion inappropriately and placing themselves or others present at risk. Furthermore, all police encounters—even those that officers typify as routine—are potentially violent. Risk is always present, and officers must be prepared at all times to use deadly force. As one patrol officer commented: "My thought process is that if you're prepared for the worst, then everything is going to be so much easier to handle."[26]

A major challenge for patrol officers is to avoid complacency. One officer stated: "In policing, complacency is dangerous. It also depends upon the people you are dealing with. If you're dealing with a drug addicted person, for example, repetition will happen. But even if you deal with them on a daily basis, never assume everything's going to be fine. You never know."[27]

A defining attribute of police (and patrol work) is the uncertainty that surrounds many encounters and the *potential* for serious injury and death. One police scholar has described this uncertainty and its impact on patrol officers as follows:

> Although patrol work is mostly trivial and non-criminal, it is nonetheless fraught with uncertainty. Officers can never forget that at any moment the boredom of a long shift can be shattered by a call that can be harrowing, traumatic, dangerous or life-threatening. The dilemma for patrol officers is that they must prepare for war even though they are rarely called upon to fight. To relax invites risk; to be constantly on guard invites over-reaction.[28*]

In 2005, four RCMP officers were murdered in the rural Alberta community of Rochfort Bridge, near Mayerthorpe, northwest of Edmonton. The officers had been assigned to maintain security on a farm property where stolen goods had been discovered. See Media Link "Four RCMP Officers Killed in Mayerthorpe, Alberta" at the end of this chapter.

Statistics on the deaths of Canadian police officers indicate that, during the nearly 50-year period between 1961 and 2009, officers were most often murdered while investigating robberies and in incidents involving domestic disputes. In recent years, however, more officer homicides have occurred during traffic stops of suspicious vehicles/persons and during traffic violation stops.[29]

The Task Environment

The **task environment** is composed of the organizational context and the community and areas in which police officers carry out their activities (see Figure 6.4). Across Canada, there is a variety of policing environments, from major urban areas to suburban communities to rural, northern, and remote communities (see photos below). As well, the particular attributes of a given neighbourhood or community—including its socio-economic features and the composition of its population (i.e., age, diversity)—determine in large measure the types of incidents that occur there, the demands that are made on the police, the types of encounter situations that arise, the relationships that develop between the police and the community, and the ability of the police to respond to the community's needs. A study of patrol deployment in the Hamilton (Ontario) Police Service found differences in the frequency and types of calls for service across the various policing divisions in the city and between the different beats within the divisions.[30]

task environment
the organizational context and the community and areas in which police officers carry out their activities

Policing districts or divisions within the same municipality may place different demands on patrol officers: one area may have a high concentration of newcomers; another afflicted by gang activity. For an insightful look at the Aboriginal gang issue in Winnipeg, for example, see the Media Link, "Warriors Off the Res: Aboriginal Gangs in Winnipeg," as well as Critical Thinking

*Bayley, D.H. 2005. "What Do the Police Do?" In T. Newman, ed. *Policing: Key Readings*. Portland: Willan Publishing. 141–49.

Figure 6.4. Factors Influencing the Decision Making of Police Officers

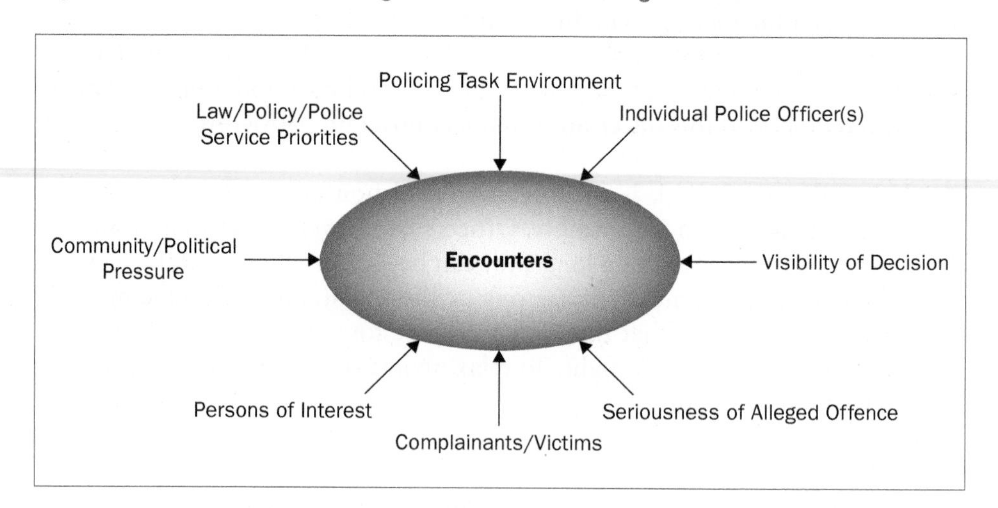

Source: From Griffiths. *Canadian Criminal Justice*, 5E. © 2015 Nelson Education Ltd. Reproduced by permission. www.cengage.com/permissions.

Exercise 6.2, "Hobbema, Alberta: A Challenging Task Environment," both at the end of this chapter.

Crime Severity Index (CSI)
the method used in Canada to denote the levels of violent and property crime and to measure the effectiveness of a police service

A key difference among communities is the nature and extent of crime. The **Crime Severity Index (CSI)** is the method used in Canada to denote the levels of violent and property crime and to measure the effectiveness of a police service.

The CSI uses weights that assign higher values to more serious crimes and lower values to less serious high-volume crimes, based on actual sentences handed down by the courts in all provinces and territories. The CSI includes all Criminal Code violations, including traffic and drug violations, as well as all federal statutes. Each index has been standardized at 100 for the base year of 2006. A jurisdiction with a higher proportion of more serious crimes will have a higher CSI value, while a jurisdiction with a higher proportion of less serious crimes will have a lower CSI value. The CSI is not available for police services with populations of less than 1,000. Data for police services with populations less than 5,000 should be used with caution.

There is considerable variability in the CSI scores for communities. Following are the CSI scores for selected municipalities in 2012: Saint John, New Brunswick, 67.12; Quebec City, Quebec, 47.79; and Kelowna, British Columbia, 104.05.[31] There are a number of factors that may contribute to a high CSI score, including a lack of resources in the police service and/or a failure to use resources effectively and efficiently.

The Canadian criminologist Rick Ruddell has drawn attention to the unique challenges of "boomtown" policing—providing police services in communities that have experienced rapid growth due to resource extraction. This results in a large influx of outsiders who may shuttle in and out of the community; a lack of adequate infrastructure, including housing, social services, and education; and high rates of crime and disorder.[32] Large numbers of workers, most of whom are from other regions of the country, with money to spend may lead to increased incidents of alcohol and drug use, bar fights, domestic violence, and impaired driving. This may stretch police resources.

THE CANADIAN PRESS/Jonathan Hayward

Vancouver's Downtown Eastside: a challenging policing environment

© Brett Gundlock/Corbis

Fort McMurray, Alberta: a "boomtown" policing environment

However, it is important that research studies be conducted to determine the nature and extent of crime in any boomtown community. A study of crime in the Regional Municipality of Wood Buffalo (which includes Ft. McMurray, the centre of oil sands production in Canada), conducted by criminologist Neil Boyd, found that the violent and property crime rates were lower than the national averages and decreasing.[33] This finding contradicted media reports that the region was overrun by crime.

Each community presents its own challenges, and police services must ensure that their organizational priorities and operations are tailored to the needs and demands for service.

Police services and officers need to develop operational strategies that are appropriate to the environment at hand. These strategies may be especially difficult to devise for cultural and ethnic communities because of language and cultural barriers.

Couch/Wikipedia

Akulivik, Northern Quebec: a remote, northern policing environment

Research studies have found that patrol practice may vary between different districts or precincts in the same police service. Similar situations may be handled differently, depending upon the officers who are assigned to the area, the style and orientation of supervising officers, and cultural and community expectations, among other considerations.[34]

Patrol officers develop an intimate knowledge of the "flora and fauna" of the areas they police: "Like tour guides in the museum of human frailty, they can point to houses where they are repeatedly called to mediate family disputes, upmarket apartment complexes where young swingers frequently hold noisy parties, troublesome 'biker' bars where drugs are sold, business premises patrolled by a vicious dog, street corners where drug dealers collect, car parks often hit by thieves, warehouses with poor alarm systems and places where police officers have been shot and wounded."[35] Part of the skill set of patrol officers is knowing not only what is going on in their territory but also who may be involved in criminal activity and who may be vulnerable to victimization.

From the perspective of many officers, a "busy" area is one with a relatively high diversity of calls; they view these areas as the most interesting to work in. In busy areas, the police are exposed to a greater number of calls involving violence, high-risk incidents, and serious crimes. Skills such as conducting interrogations, preparing search warrants, cultivating informants, and carrying out surveillance are more likely to be used in busy districts.

The Encounter: Factors Affecting Police Decision Making and Outcomes

Researchers have attempted to identify the factors that create the dynamic of the encounter as well as its outcome. Attention has focused on the following: the officer; the suspect, if one is present; the complainant/victim; and the occurrence.

The Officer

Chapter 5 examined the career orientations of police officers. The particular background and orientation that a police officer brings to his or her work may influence how discretion is exercised, as well as the decisions made in encounter situations. It is interesting to note that American researchers have found no relationship between the level of education of police officers and the probability of arrest or the likelihood of conducting a search during an encounter with a person of interest.[36]

Research studies have found that the behaviour of police officers in encounter situations is a primary determinant of attitudes toward the police and of public confidence in the police. Citizens who felt they were treated with respect by an officer report higher levels of trust and confidence in the police.[37] Conversely, citizens who perceive that they have unsatisfactory contact with the police may have less favourable opinions of the police (see also Chapter 8).[38]

There is also some evidence to suggest that the less respectful police officers are toward suspects and community residents, the less likely these people are to comply with the law and with any requests the officers make.[39] The behaviour of the officers can sometimes escalate an incident and place them at risk of assault.

Similarly, the ethnicity and/or gender of the officer seem to have no direct influence on outcomes in routine police–citizen encounters in the United States. Female officers do not appear to have differential views of community policing or community residents and neighbourhoods.[40] The absence of field studies precludes a determination of whether the same is true in Canada. It is unknown, for example, whether First Nations police officers make decisions differently than their non-Aboriginal colleagues in policing First Nations communities.

Officers tend to distinguish between the general public, who are to be protected, and (in police parlance) "scroats" or "scum," who are to receive police attention. Police researchers have tried to find links between police action and a suspect's alleged offence and his or her attributes (e.g., ethnicity, age, relationship to the victim, demeanour). Suspects who are young, a member of a visible minority, and from a lower socio-economic background may be more likely to be typified as requiring police intervention. The demeanour of both the officer and the suspect may also influence the outcome of an encounter. The demeanour of each may change during the encounter and determine the outcome and the decisions that are made by the officer.[41]

There are few empirical studies of whether Canadian police officers *systematically* discriminate against certain groups and persons on the basis of their ethnicity, religious beliefs, age, gender, or other attributes. However, the high arrest rates of Aboriginal people in many parts of the country, and the ongoing conflicts between visible minorities and the police in some urban areas, warrant close examination. Of particular concern is whether police officers engage in racial profiling (discussed below in the section The Police and Visible/Cultural/Religious Minorities: The Issues of Biased Policing and Racial Profiling).

The Complainant/Victim

Complainants themselves do much to determine the actions that officers take during encounters. The extent to which officers provide assistance and act on the complainant's wishes may depend on the attributes and actions of the complainant and the officer's assessment of his or her credibility. Complainants who are uncooperative, aggressive, and known to the police from past encounters may receive less assistance than those deemed sincere and "respectable." Also, officers may be less likely to consider the preferences of complainants who are perceived as having contributed to their own victimization. Of course, in certain encounters—for example, those involving domestic assault—the officers must act even if it means going against the preferences of the complainant/victim.

In carrying out their mandate, police officers must consider the needs of crime victims. This includes providing information on how to access resources such as counselling, as well as providing feedback on the progress of the case investigation. Many police services operate victim services units; others have entered into collaborative arrangements with community agencies and organizations to provide victim assistance. Victim assistance programs are staffed mainly by volunteers, who provide information to crime victims on the progress of case investigations, facilitate the return of property to victims, and refer victims to other services in the community.

Efforts have been made to develop services for *groups* of victims, such as the elderly, Aboriginal people, and battered and sexually abused women and children. "Safe" houses have been created, as well as sexual assault centres and various crisis intervention services. The latter include twenty-four-hour hotlines, counselling, and information on community resources.

A key objective of these programs is to ensure that secondary victimization does not occur—that is, that the crime victim has his or her needs addressed by the police and other criminal justice personnel. Special challenges are presented by incidents involving LGBT victims.

The Occurrence

The seriousness of the alleged offence, the presence of weapons or violence, the circumstances surrounding the event, the individuals involved—all of these may affect officers' actions. Also, the task environment in which the occurrence takes place may affect the actions taken by police. For example, two individuals fighting in a skid row area may merely be separated and sent on their respective ways, while a similar incident in a higher income neighbourhood, where such an occurrence is rare and out of character, may result in a more formal police response, especially if one of the combatants is not from the area.

POLICING IN NORTHERN AND REMOTE COMMUNITIES

An understudied and less visible component of Canadian police work is policing in northern and remote communities, which includes the northern regions of the provinces and the territories of Yukon, Northwest Territories, and Nunavut. Policing in northern communities presents officers with numerous challenges on both a professional and personal level. It tests their resourcefulness, their mental and physical stamina, their adaptability and resilience, as well as their policing skills. For many officers, these challenges are a primary reason they sought out a northern posting.

Police officers may be the only permanent representative of the criminal justice system and may perform a number of other duties as well. This includes RCMP members acting as Crown counsel in some rural and remote communities, a practice that has raised concerns particularly with respect to the requirements of disclosure.[42] The support structures and services found in larger communities are absent in northern and remote communities.

Northern jurisdictions consistently report the highest rates of crime and violence in Canada, rates that exceed those of high-crime cities in the United States. In 2013, the Crime Severity Index scores for Yukon (165.7), Northwest Territories (314.4), and Nunavut (281.9) were significantly higher than for other jurisdictions (e.g., Nova Scotia, 69.8; Ontario, 52.5; Alberta 83.7).[43] Crime in Northwest Territories and Nunavut is about four times the national average; in Yukon, about twice the national average.[44]

high-visibility/high-consequence policing
police work in the North that places officers under constant scrutiny and the high impact of their decisions

Given the small size of communities in the North, the role of the police assumes even more significance than in urban areas. Policing in the North is **high-visibility/high-consequence policing**. It's high visibility in the sense that members are operating in small detachments in communities that generally have under 500 residents. And it's high consequence in the sense that the dynamics that develop between the member and the community have a significant impact on the member, his or her family, community residents, crime victims, and offenders (see Police Perspective 6.3).

One RCMP constable commented on the difference between being one of many officers in a large detachment and being posted to a small detachment in Nunavut. He pointed out that in remote communities, officers are on call twenty-four hours a day: "Here, you only have one life, one identity. There is never a hanging up of the hat."[45]

The officers in northern communities perform a much more multifaceted role than their counterparts in the southern, more urban regions of the country. One officer posted to Nunavut commented:

> Our mandate is to do just about anything that needs doing in the town and that includes everybody else's job. I've done everything—filling out

Police Perspective 6.3

An RCMP Constable Speaks about Policing in a Yukon Community

There are a number of skill sets that you develop when you police in the North that you may not have developed policing in a larger community down south—when you are a member of the community and everyone knows you, and you're dealing with deep-rooted problems that go way back. Here, when I go to a call, you know the family and their history. Unlike down south, I can't just arrest them and put them in jail. You have to be aware that you can cause more damage by just following policy. We take a lot more time to do things. These are neighbours we are dealing with. It's not anonymous policing. You will see these people again—in the store, at a hockey game. I use a lot of discretion; I may drive an impaired person home. I've had situations where a person I gave a break to has come to my assistance. You can't treat people like a hard-ass. You'll see them at the post office. You can't just put a number to them. They are your neighbours.

Source: Personal communication with author, 2013.

income tax returns, being involved in funerals or hunting with the elders, or fixing the hamlet truck or doing plumbing repairs at the teachers' houses. It's part-time policeman, part-time maintenance man ...[46*]

The challenges encountered by police officers in northern communities also provide support for a fundamental principle of community and remote policing, which is the de-structuring of centralized "command and control" hierarchies and the empowerment of line-level officers to work with communities to address problems of crime and disorder and to establish, and sustain, trust. It presents unique opportunities for officers to become involved with the community (see Police Perspective 6.4).

Officers who have policed in the North have identified a number of attributes that are required to be effective in delivering policing services. These include maturity, common sense, and self-reliance. As one officer stated: "You have got to be easygoing. You can't let things bother you; you have to be capable of working alone and dealing with a certain amount of stress."[47] Policing in northern communities also places stress on the police officer's family, which may be affected by the isolation and officers going for days, or months, without a day off.

Police officers in these communities may be at a high risk. In 2010, the four members of the RCMP detachment in Cape Dorset were removed from the community and placed on stress leave (termed an "advanced health intervention" by their commander), following a month in which there were two

*Griffiths, C.T., G. Saville, D.S. Wood, and E. Zellerer. 1995. *Crime and Justice Among Inuit in the Baffin Region, N.W.T, Canada.* Burnaby: Criminology Research Centre, Simon Fraser University.

Police Perspective 6.4

An RCMP Commanding Officer in the Canadian North Speaks about the Role of the Police in Northern Communities

Law enforcement is only one component of police officers in northern communities. The other components are building community capacity, building trust, and building the legitimacy of the police. The officers need to be involved in community activities and understand what the priorities of the community are. In the North, it is important to maintain a dialogue with the communities, to understand what their priorities are; the challenge is to assist in building community capacities, while providing assistance and not "owning" the initiatives.

It is a matter of building relationships. The officers have personal relationships in the community that one doesn't have in larger urban areas. There are high community expectations of officers and high demands on the officer's time: "Come to our pot luck (and bring a dish)." "Come to the hockey game." A key issue is stress and fatigue of officers.

Source: Personal communication with author, March 2014.

homicides in the community of twelve hundred persons and a shooting spree by two teenagers that resulted in bullets lodging in an RCMP residence and a wound to one of the young men.[48]

ENCOUNTERS WITH PERSONS WITH MENTAL ILLNESS (PwMI)

The deinstitutionalization of mental health patients in the 1960s and 1970s resulted in a growing number of persons with mental illness (PwMI) requiring care and treatment in the community. The concept of deinstitutionalization was primarily accepted on the premise that psychiatric units and community care facilities would be developed in all major communities in the lower mainland.[49] However, this did not generally occur, with the result that many PwMI became homeless and destitute and without the necessary supports to manage their issues. The challenges have become even greater in cases of persons who are severely addicted and mentally ill (SAMI) and have complex treatment needs that cannot be met by community-based programs and services.

These conditions have resulted in patrol officers encountering more and more people with mental illness. Whatever the common image of police activities, officers are as likely to be called to a mental illness crisis as to a robbery. Due in part to the downloading discussed in Chapter 1, wherein there is a paucity of resources for PwMI, police officers have become de facto community mental health workers and are the first responders to the mentally ill on the streets and in neighbourhoods. In many jurisdictions, 25 to 30 percent of calls for service involve a mental health component. Some individuals have hundreds of contacts with the police annually.[50] This has a significant impact on police resources. A review of police encounters with PwMI in Toronto conducted by former Supreme Court of Canada Justice Frank Iacobucci found that there had been a failure of the provincial mental health system to provide adequate community-based treatment resources. In his view, the police alone could not effectively address the needs of PwMI and that a robust response was required by the provincial mental health system and other agencies.[51]

Police officers may spend significant amounts of time waiting with PwMI to be admitted to hospitals. A study in Edmonton found that during a three-month period in 2013, officers spent fifteen hundred hours in hospitals, costing the police service approximately $100,000 and taking them away from patrol duties. Fifty-four percent of the hours were related to PwMI.[52]

Patrol officers often determine whether the PwMI will be put into the criminal justice system or diverted to the mental health system. However, officers face numerous difficulties in dealing with mentally ill persons on the street, including a lack of referral resources and the fact that many of the persons with mental illness cannot be apprehended under mental health acts, as they do not meet the criteria of being a danger to themselves or others.

Concerns have been raised that the police inappropriately use arrest to resolve encounters with mentally disordered people; this is most commonly referred to as the "criminalization" of the mentally ill. Research studies, however, have not supported this assertion.[53] Rather, Canadian police officers generally demonstrate high levels of benevolence and empathy toward mentally ill people, as well as a strong interest in linking them with appropriate services.[54] It also does not appear that PwMI are subject to any higher levels of use of force by patrol officers than are mentally stable suspects.[55]

Box 6.1 profiles several cases that illustrate the demands that are placed on one municipal police service by persons in crisis.

Initiatives to Address the Issues of PwMI

Over the past decade, police agencies have been developing specialized approaches for managing encounters with mentally ill people.[56] Most major police services ensure that officers receive crisis intervention training (CIT) where they learn about mental illness and various strategies for managing encounters with PwMI. Positive outcomes have been reported by police services that have adopted the CIT model, including lower rates of arrest of PwMI.[57] The Edmonton Police Service has developed a training program to improve interaction and communication between PwMI and the police. The training has resulted in less use of force with PwMI.[58] See the Media Link, "Edmonton police using less force with mentally ill after University of Alberta course," at the end of this chapter.

Police services also embed officers in multi-agency response teams that focus on PwMI to reduce their likelihood of being in crisis and having contact with the justice system. Mobile crisis teams—patrol units staffed by a police officer and a nurse, social worker, or mental health professional—are a common feature in many municipalities. There are also mental health liaison officers who provide a point of contact between the police service and medical and social

Box 6.1

Calls to a Police Service Regarding Chronic/Repeat Persons with Mental Health Concerns

Case 1: Suicidal Female
A chronically suicidal female generated over forty-eight police files in 2014 alone, nineteen of which occurred between April 10 and May 14, 2014. Police have apprehended this female twelve times under Section 28 of the Mental Health Act.

This female suffers from full-spectrum FASD (fetal alcohol spectrum disorder), addiction issues, and borderline personality disorder.

Case 2: Elderly Male with Dementia
An elderly male suffering from dementia has made over 154 unfounded calls to police over the past two years.

Although each call is deemed unfounded, police must attend every time a report is called in.

Case 3: Mother Concerned for Her Son
A mother concerned for her son called the police to help with her son who is currently living with her. The male has no previous mental health diagnosis.

Upon police review, this male has generated over 233 calls for service since 2006. Police attended his home with a psychiatrist, and the male was certified and taken to hospital.

Case 4: Homeless Man with Psychotic Disorder
A 30-year-old homeless man with a psychotic disorder has generated 2,048 calls for service between 2005 and 2014, 507 of which occurred in the city. The calls refer to a range of actions by the male, including acting bizarrely, talking to himself, aggressively panhandling, sleeping in business alcoves, or being found in women's washrooms.

Source: Materials provided to author from a municipal police service.

services in the community and who may assist in managing the case files of at-risk persons.[59]

Studies have shown that in those jurisdictions with a specialized response, there are lower rates of inappropriate use of arrest of mentally ill people.[60] A study of an integrated mobile crisis service in Halifax involving clinicians and police officers found that there were improved response times despite an increase in the use of this service by patients, families, and service partners, and an increase in the use of follow-up services by patients, as compared to a control group.[61]

In Red Deer, Alberta, the Red Deer Police and Crisis Team (PACT) is a collaborative partnership between the police and the Red Deer Primary Care Network to provide a front-line response to persons who are experiencing a mental health crisis. The team is composed of an RCMP officer and a registered psychiatric nurse who conduct street-level interventions and make referrals to the appropriate resources. See the Media Link, "Police and Crisis Team (PACT)," at the end of this chapter.

An evaluation of the PACT program found that it reduced hospital admissions, improved collaboration among the police and agencies in the community, and diverted PwMI from court appearances and incarceration to community-based resources (see Police Perspective 6.5).[62]

Police Perspective 6.5

A Police Leader Speaks to the Challenges of Policing Multi-Needs Populations

The police have extensive contact with multi-needs populations, which include persons who are challenged with mental health issues, homelessness, addiction, poverty, and FASD (fetal alcohol spectrum disorder). These persons come to the attention of the police since we are the front-line workers for any problem. The fire and rescue service and emergency medical service have very defined roles. The police deal with everything else.

Today, we have a lot better communication and coordination with other agencies, including mental health services and health agencies. In our police service, we have a joint program designed to help people who have a lot of contact with the police. We have a constable who focuses on persons who are homeless. She liaises with a variety of agencies, including the housing authority and social services. It's also important to remember that these special needs populations are also often at risk of becoming the victims of crime.

Source: Personal communication with author, August 2014.

THE POLICE AND VISIBLE/CULTURAL/RELIGIOUS MINORITIES: THE ISSUES OF BIASED POLICING AND RACIAL PROFILING

Two issues have been flashpoints between the police and visible-minority communities: bias-free policing and racial profiling. **Bias-free policing** requires police officers to make decisions "based on reasonable suspicion or probable grounds rather than stereotypes about race, religion, ethnicity, gender or other prohibited grounds."[63] Bias-free policing relates to the equitable treatment of *all* people of diversity. Since the terrorist attacks on the World Trade Center in New York in 2001, the disruption of planned attacks in the U.S. and Canada, and the killing of two Canadian soldiers by extremists, there are concerns that people who appear to be Muslim and/or of Middle Eastern origin may be singled out for discriminatory treatment by security personnel at airports, by customs officers, and by the police. There have, for example, been complaints from Muslim airline passengers that they are more often singled out for interviews and secondary inspections when arriving at Canadian airports. In 2013, the Canada Agricultural Review Board found that an Arab Muslim passenger had been singled out because of his race at a Montreal airport and overturned a fine that had been imposed for illegally importing meat.

bias-free policing
the requirement that police officers make decisions on the basis of reasonable suspicion and probable grounds rather than stereotypes

Racial profiling, in contrast, is most commonly associated with visible minorities and Aboriginals. **Racial profiling** has been defined in a number of ways. The definition used significantly affects the focus of research studies as well as how the findings of those studies are interpreted; it also affects determinations regarding whether a police service engages in racial profiling. American police researchers Lorie Fridell and colleagues suggest that racial profiling occurs

racial profiling
police targeting of members of a particular racial group on the basis of the supposed criminal propensity of the entire group

"when law enforcement inappropriately considers race or ethnicity in deciding with whom and how to intervene in an enforcement capacity."[64] This definition leaves open the possibility that police officers may at times "appropriately" consider race or ethnicity when deciding when, with whom, and how to intervene in situations. In *R. v. Brown*, 2003, O.J. No. 1251, the Ontario Court of Appeal defined racial profiling as involving "the targeting of individual members of a particular racial group, on the basis of the supposed criminal propensity of the entire group."

Profiling can lead to racial discrimination, which may manifest itself overtly, subconsciously, or systemically. Canadians often hold stereotypical views of visible minorities that are not conscious.

overpoliciing

a disproportionate police focus on a racialized population or neighbourhood

pretext policing

police stops or searches for a minor reason that lead to more intrusive intervention

Two police practices that are associated with racial profiling are overpolicing and pretext policing. **Overpolicing** occurs when the police focus disproportionately on a racialized population or neighbourhood, while pretext policing is wherein "the ostensibly detain or investigate an individual for one reason when, in reality, there is a secondary purpose or ulterior reason to the interaction."[65]

Pretext policing is most commonly associated with police stops or searches and may occur for a minor reason, such as a traffic violation, which then leads to a more intrusive intervention, such as a vehicle search. Overpolicing often results in a disproportionate contact of visible minority or Aboriginal persons with the police and results in not only distrust of the police but also the development of stereotypes by police officers that the particular group is prone to criminality.[66]

© Robert McDougall/Urban Alliance on Race Relations

Breaking down racial stereotypes

A project focusing on youth in the Jane-Finch community in Toronto gathered the perceptions of young persons ($N = 50$). One youth commented on the negative stereotypes that are often held of young Black men:

> People automatically see you as a black young person and they feel that you being black, you would never amount to nothing. Especially coming from the Jane-Finch community, automatically number one what they think is that you being black, you're never going to be nothing good. But that's not always true.[67*]

Most police services have operational policies that explicitly prohibit racial profiling by their officers. The OPP policy, for example, states: "Illegal profiling is not permitted and shall not be tolerated in any respect. Illegal profiling means taking law-enforcement actions, such as stopping/questioning/searching/detaining/arresting a person, based solely on the person's race, sex, ancestry, age, sexual orientation, family status, place of origin, marital status, disability, creed, colour, citizenship, ethnic origin,

*Assets Coming Together Youth Project. 2010. *Jane-Finch Youth Speak Out: Turf, Violence, Well-Being.* Toronto: York University.

[and/or] same-sex partnership status."[68] Research has found, however, that the extent to which policies on racial profiling are implemented and effective depends in large measure on the police organization itself and the strength of its leadership.[69]

Racial Profiling versus Criminal Profiling

One issue is whether police actions are based on racial profiling or criminal profiling, and whether actions by a police officer that may be interpreted as racial profiling may also be considered as good police work. (See Critical Thinking Exercise 6.3 at the end of this chapter.) Courts and tribunals have determined that in some cases, the behaviour of individual police officers was racist and discriminatory.

MONITORING POLICE DECISION MAKING: THE USE OF BODY-WORN CAMERAS

The use of cameras worn by patrol officers has emerged as a major development in early 21st-century policing. Body-worn cameras (BWCs) are designed to record police officer interactions in encounter situations—providing a recording of events. BWCs are able to capture some of what the police officer is seeing, doing, and saying during an encounter. Among the potential benefits of BWCs is increasing the transparency of police operations and the accountability of police officers; providing accurate evidence of police–citizen encounters, which can reduce complaints against the police (and associated civil suits) and reduce false accusations; and providing a more complete recording of police–citizen encounters than those recorded on officer's court notebook.[70] BWCs can also provide a more complete record of an encounter situation than smartphones used by bystanders. In this way, BWCs may serve to counter the selective recordings by citizens.

There are, however, a number of issues surrounding the deployment of BWCs, including privacy issues for the officer and the general public and concerns that an omnipresent camera will discourage officers from engaging in certain encounter situations and affect, in a negative manner, how they exercise discretion. There are also concerns that the presence of BWCs will be an invasion of citizens' privacy, make victims/witnesses/suspects reluctant to speak with the police, diminish the value of an officer's word in court, and undermine public confidence in the police. As well, this technology does not record how the officer perceives what they are seeing and how this information is being cognitively processed.[71] See the Media Links, "Police Body Camera HD 1080P Police Body Worn Video Camera Wolfcom 3rd Eye" and "Police Officer's Body Worn Video Camera Catches Taxi Driver's Dangerous Driving in Bath," at the end of this chapter.

A pilot project on equipping Edmonton Police Service officers with BWCs, conducted between 2011 and 2014, produced a number of preliminary findings that are instructive.[72] Among the findings were that there was strong public support for the use of BWCs; officers in the study felt that the use of BWCs reduced the threat of assaults against officers and produced good evidence; officers often forgot to activate the camera; and there were concerns that the camera did not capture the entire context of the encounter. The study identified a number of costs associated with equipping officers with BWCs, including hardware purchases, uniform adaptations, video storage, and training, among other costs. The researchers concluded that hard evidence is still lacking as to the benefits of BWCs.

For the results of an evaluation of body-worn cameras in the Phoenix Police Department, see the PowerPoint presentation by Charles Katz and colleagues.[73] See also Class/Group Discussion 6.2 at the end of this chapter.

Summary

The discussion in this chapter has centred on patrol and general duty policing. Patrol officers are the eyes, ears, arms, and legs of police services and are involved in a number of activities on a 24/7 basis. Police services have protocol for managing calls for service, and dispatchers and communications officers play a key role in allocating patrol resources. It is important that patrol units be deployed efficiently and that officers have the opportunity to engage in proactive police work as well as responding to calls. Patrol officers exercise discretion in encounter situations, resulting in situational enforcement. There are a myriad of factors that may influence the decision making of patrol officers, including attributes of the person of interest, the victim/complainant, and the alleged offence. Policing northern and remote communities and responding to incidents involving persons with mental illness are particularly demanding on officers. Although body-worn cameras are being touted as a way to increase the accountability of the police and to monitor the decision making of officers, the research to date as to their cost/benefits is inconclusive.

KEY POINTS REVIEW

1. The five duties of patrol officers recognized under common law are to prevent crime, protect life and property, preserve the peace, apprehend offenders, and enforce laws.
2. The types of activity that patrol officers are involved in are determined largely by calls to the police from the general public.
3. Police services utilize a variety of strategies for managing calls for service, including practising call shedding, prioritizing calls, and employing differential response strategies.
4. Police services are paying increasing attention to patrol deployment, including officer workloads and the performance of patrol units.
5. Patrol officers have considerable discretion in carrying out their tasks.
6. Police officers bring to their work a cognitive lens through which they determine levels of trouble and danger—or the potential for trouble and danger—that people and situations present.
7. There are a variety of factors that influence the decision making of patrol officers in encounter situations.
8. Police officers carry out their tasks in a variety of policing environments.

9. It is often said that police officers have a "sixth sense" about people and situations.
10. Aboriginal peoples residing in urban centres face unique challenges that may result in high levels of contact with the police.
11. Police officers are experiencing more and more encounters with the mentally ill, and police services have developed initiatives to more effectively respond to this population.
12. Two issues that have been flashpoints between the police and visible/cultural/religious minorities are bias-free policing and racial profiling.
13. Racial profiling can lead to racial discrimination, which may manifest itself overtly, subconsciously, or systemically.
14. Two police practices that are associated with racial profiling are overpolicing and pretext policing.
15. Policing in the Canadian North presents police officers with unique challenges and opportunities.
16. Body-worn cameras are being considered as a way to monitor the decision making of patrol officers.

KEY TERM QUESTIONS

1. What is the **Canadian Police Information Centre (CPIC)**?
2. Describe the **W system** as used by police dispatchers and communication officers.
3. What is meant by **call shedding**, **call stacking**, and **differential police response (DPR)**?
4. Define **allocated patrol time** and **unallocated patrol time**, and note why these two concepts are important in any discussion of police mobile unit utilization.
5. What is meant by the **soft skills** of police work?
6. Define **discretion** and then describe how the practice of **selective (or situational) enforcement** is related to the police exercise of discretion?
7. What are **typifications** and **recipes for action**, and how do these two concepts help us understand the decision making of patrol officers?
8. What are **symbolic assailants**, and how does this concept assist in an understanding of police decision making?
9. What is the **task environment** of patrol officers and how might it affect their decision making?
10. What is the **Crime Severity Index (CSI)** and why is it important in any discussion of patrol officers?
11. Why is police work in northern and remote communities often referred to as **high-visibility/high-consequence policing**?
12. What is meant by **bias-free policing** and how is this notion related to **racial profiling**?
13. Define **overpolicing** and **pretext policing** and note how they are related to the activities and decision making of patrol officers.

CRITICAL THINKING EXERCISES

Critical Thinking Exercise 6.1. The Impaired Stockbroker, the Restaurant Manager, and the Patrol Sergeant

A patrol sergeant and two patrol officers are dispatched to a bar-restaurant in a trendy area of a Canadian city. The manager has summoned the police to deal with an unruly patron who has gone on a rampage in the men's washroom and caused an estimated $1,500 worth of damage. The manager identifies the culprit, and the officers discreetly handcuff him and remove him from the premises. Outside, the officers discuss the situation with the slightly impaired patron and the manager, all the while being constantly interrupted by the patron's girlfriend, who promises to take him home if they release him. The restaurant manager indicates that while he does not wish to have the patron arrested, he does want the damages covered.

Your Thoughts?

What are the possible courses of action that the patrol sergeant could take? What are the pros and cons of each possible course of action? What would you do if you were the patrol sergeant? The actual decision of the patrol sergeant is present at the end of this chapter (p. 177).

Critical Thinking Exercise 6.2. Hobbema, Alberta: A Challenging Task Environment

The attributes of a particular community will determine the nature and extent of crime and social disorder and the demands that are placed on a police service. If the community is highly troubled, this presents challenges for both the community and the police. View the videos "Hobbema: Short Documentary" (https://www.youtube.com/watch?v=Koz-6B1E5RE) and "Hobbema, Alberta" (https://www.youtube.com/watch?v=xuCloy-17iU). Then consider (1) how the dynamics in this community may challenge for residents and the police, and (2) what measures might be taken to address these challenges.

Critical Thinking Exercise 6.3. Racial Profiling versus Criminal Profiling

Part of the difficulty in determining whether a police service and its officers engage in racial profiling is distinguishing between racial profiling and criminal profiling. As discussed in Chapter 5, a defining attribute of the police culture is suspiciousness of people and circumstances. While critics of the police argue that racial profiling is endemic to police work, police officers contend that they profile criminals, with particular attention to "signals and 'unusual fits.'"[74] This is the process of *typification* discussed earlier.

Officers in the Hamilton Police Service offered the following perspectives on racial profiling, criminal profiling, and the importance of the context in which a person is identified for a police stop. In speaking of one particularly high-crime area with a high Black population, an officer stated:

> [I]f that's where the crime is, I'm going to be pulling over people who do crime. It's like going fishing. You go where the fish are if you're going to catch fish. If you're going to catch criminals, you end up having to do that..."[75]

A visible-minority police officer offered an additional perspective:

> When we're out on the street, we rely on our instincts. We are trained investigators in the sense that we need to do profiling. And what kind of profiling is that? Criminal profiling. It has nothing to do with racial profiling...We profile criminals.[76]

The importance of placing profiling within the larger context of police work was noted by another minority police officer:

> It's a very difficult job and the nature of the job forces you to stereotype and discriminate. When I'm driving my cruiser at 2 o'clock in the morning, and I see...[one of the interviewers] in a shirt and tie driving a Mercedes, I think nothing of it. But if I was to see a black 20-year-old, guess what? He's getting pulled over.[77]

Your Thoughts?

1. What is your reaction to the perspectives of the officers interviewed in the Hamilton Police Service?
2. What methods would you use to determine whether a police officer, or a police service, was engaged in racial profiling?

The Case of the Smuggled Pork Rolls: Racial Profiling or a Good Decision?

Keeping in mind the comments of the officers in the Hamilton Police Service in the preceding Critical Thinking Exercise, consider the following case.

In November 2012, a woman returning to Ottawa from a trip to China indicated on her customs declaration card that she was not bringing any meat or meat products back into Canada. In the officers' experience, travellers from China often bring back agricultural products, and sensing that the woman was nervous, he referred her to secondary inspection. During the secondary inspection, the woman was found to have a number of "assorted pork products" from China in her luggage. She was fined, but appealed her case to the Canada Agricultural Review Tribunal. At the tribunal, it was argued that she had forgotten to eat the products prior to landing in Canada and was feeling sick and confused upon arrival.

The Decision of the Canadian Agricultural Review Tribunal

In 2013, the tribunal ruled that she had been the victim of racial profiling by the customs officer and dismissed the fine. The basis of this decision was that she had been unfairly targeted as a Chinese person. The federal government appealed that ruling to the Federal Court of Appeal.

The Decision of the Federal Court of Appeal

In 2014, the Federal Court of Appeal overturned the decision of the agricultural tribunal, stating that the decision of the customs officer to detain the woman was made on the basis of her demeanour during the initial interviews and his professional experience. In presenting the decision of the court, one of the judges stated:

> "Officers on the front line, such as the officer herein, cannot be expected to leave their experience—acquired usually after many years of observing people from different countries entering Canada—at home. . . . The officer simply asserted in his statement that in his experience it was not uncommon for Chinese persons to bring agricultural products with them upon returning from China. The officer's hunch, based on his experience and his observance of the respondent's demeanour, was confirmed by the secondary examination."

This decision means that federal customs officers can use their experience in making decisions about which persons to stop and search.

Your Thoughts?

1. What is your opinion about the decision of the Federal Court of Appeal in this case?
2. Do you think that the decision in this case has implications for discussions of racial profiling in policing?
3. Should the findings of the federal court in this case be applied to police officers as well? Why? Why not?

Source: Duffy, A. (2014, October 14). Appeal court overturns racial profiling case involving customs officer. *Ottawa Citizen.* Retrieved from http://ottawacitizen.com/news/local-news/appeal-court-overturns-racial-profiling-case-involving-customs-officer

CLASS/GROUP DISCUSSION EXERCISES

Class/Group Discussion 6.1. An Encounter and an Explanation

View the video "Honest Cops" on YouTube (https://www.youtube.com/watch?v=f23CPcTdY2M) and then consider the following:

1. What was your reaction to the encounter and what transpired?
2. Do you feel that the police officer "owed" an explanation to the bystanders?

3. What precedent, if any, is set by this encounter?
4. Should there be limits on recording the actions of police officers?

Class/Group Discussion 6.2. Body-Worn Cameras (BWCs)

Should all police officers be equipped with BWCs? What arguments in support of them—and what concerns—do you find most persuasive?

MEDIA LINKS

Visit www.nelson.com/canadianpolicework4 for links to these videos and other additional content available with this text.

"Four RCMP officers killed in Mayerthorpe, Alberta," CBC Digital Archives, March 4, 2005, cbc.ca/archives

"Warriors Off the Res: Aboriginal Gangs in Winnipeg," VICE News, July 10, 2014, youtube.com

"Edmonton police using less force with mentally ill after University of Alberta course," by Pamela Roth, *Edmonton Sun*, March 18, 2013, edmontonsun.com

"Police and Crisis Team (PACT)," Red Deer (Alberta) Primary Care Network, 2013, reddeerpcn.com/pact

"Police Body Camera HD 1080P Police Body Worn Video Camera Wolfcom 3rd Eye," Wolfcom Enterprises, August 6, 2011, youtube.com

"Police Officer's Body Worn Video Camera Catches Taxi Driver's Dangerous Driving in Bath," British Transport Police, October 9, 2013, youtube.com

Answer to Critical Thinking Exercise 6.1

In this case, the patrol sergeant had the legal grounds to arrest the patron, although the restaurant manager indicated that he did not want formal action taken. The decision of the patrol sergeant was to have private restitution made to the restaurant. It was determined that the patron had not yet paid for dinner. With the girlfriend's consent, the patron's credit card was produced and given over to the manager, who added the damage ($3,500) to the patron's dinner bill. The charge slip was signed by the patron, who was released and departed with his girlfriend.

Your Thoughts?

What was your decision in this case? What is your view of the action taken by the patrol sergeant?

7 Police Powers and the Use of Force

LEARNING OBJECTIVES

After reading this chapter, you should be able to:

- Discuss the impact of the Charter of Rights and Freedoms on police powers
- Describe the powers of the police with respect to detention and arrest, search and seizure, entrapment, and interrogation
- Discuss the legal provisions for the police use of force
- Describe the National Use of Force Model
- Identify the five levels of resistance that individuals may present to a police officer
- Identify and discuss the levels of force intervention and the associated progressive use-of-force response levels available to police officers
- Discuss the issues surrounding the use of less-lethal force options
- Identify and discuss the correlates of the police use of force
- Discuss the issues surrounding the use of force and persons with mental illness
- Describe how social media may affect the police use of force
- Discuss police powers and the use of force in public and political protests
- Define and discuss the phenomenon of victim-precipitated homicide ("suicide by cop")

In the opening pages of the text, it was noted that there will always be tension between the need to maintain order and to ensure the rights of citizens. This tension is evident in the discussion of the powers of the police. A key question is: How can Canadian society balance the rights of citizens with the police's authority to ensure order and to pursue criminal offenders? This question has assumed even greater significance in the wake of the terrorist attacks that resulted in the death of a Canadian soldier in Quebec and another on October 23, 2014, at the War Memorial in Ottawa by a sole assailant who subsequently attacked Parliament. Partially in response to these attacks, the federal government passed Bill C-51 (short title, Anti-terrorism Act, 2015). This legislation expanded the powers of police and enforcement agencies. The legislation encountered considerable opposition, including from the Canadian public. A poll conducted in March 2015 ($N = 1{,}239$) found that 56 percent of those who were aware of the legislation disapproved of it, while 23 percent approved. Opposition to Bill C-51 was strongest among Canadians aged 18 to 34. Only a month earlier, a similar poll revealed that 82 percent of Canadians surveyed supported the legislation.[1]

A number of observers have pointed out that the police already have significant powers to combat terrorism. The federal privacy commissioner and his provincial counterparts cautioned that additional legislation was not required and that police and national security agencies had sufficient powers to combat the threat of terrorism. The privacy commissioner also called on the federal government to bring an evidence-based approach to any discussion of additional powers for police and security agencies.[2]

In the post-9/11 era, law enforcement and security agencies have increased the electronic surveillance of Canadians. This includes wiretaps and warrantless requests by agencies to telecommunications companies such as Rogers and Bell Media for subscriber information. In 2011, for example, there were eighteen thousand reported wiretaps/intercepts of conversations on various communication platforms, including wireless, and 1.2 million requests made to telecom companies for information.[3]

One of the difficulties is that persons who have contact with the police may not know what powers the police have and also may not know their individual rights. This may be particularly problematic for persons newly arrived in Canada, but it may also be the case for many Canadian citizens, including the elderly or persons with a mental health disability.

Note that the following discussion does not present a detailed examination of police powers. Space limitations aside, it is assumed that students have access to more in-depth materials in other courses. Readers with an interest in police powers are encouraged to monitor Supreme Court of Canada (SCC) decisions, which can be accessed at http://scc.lexum.org. The cases presented in this chapter should be considered only as illustrative of the types of issues that arise surrounding police powers.

Another equally important feature of the police role is the authority to use force, including lethal force, and this is also considered in the following discussion.

THE CHARTER AND POLICE POWERS

As noted in Chapter 1, Canadian police officers derive their authority from the Criminal Code and various provincial statutes. The Criminal Code provides the authority to arrest (Section 495), to use force (Section 25), to search (with a warrant; Section 487), and to obtain DNA samples (Section 487.05), among others.

The Canadian Charter of Rights and Freedoms has had a significant impact in defining the powers of the police. Section 7 of the Charter states: "Everyone has the right to life, liberty and security of the person and the right not to be deprived thereof except in accordance with the principles of fundamental justice." The Charter has entrenched the constitutional rights of those accused of crimes, who have the right to challenge the actions of the police if those rights have been violated. Charter rights, combined with pre-existing legal rules, provide legal safeguards against the unlimited use of police power.

The specific powers of Canadian police are constantly evolving as a result of court decisions and changes in law. Court decisions have held that the police cannot use certain investigative techniques (e.g., electronic surveillance) without prior judicial authorization, and if the police gather evidence illegally, that evidence may be excluded from a trial if its use would bring the administration of justice into disrepute. All relevant information gathered during a case investigation must be disclosed to the defence attorney. In addition, severe restrictions have been placed on the investigative strategy of placing an undercover officer in a jail cell to elicit evidence from a criminal suspect. And the SCC has ruled that law enforcement and security agencies must secure a warrant prior to accessing information on persons through telecom providers. The SCC has also placed limits on the use of the so-called "Mr. Big" stings, wherein suspects are placed in a position where they "confess" to having committed a crime or crimes (*R. v. Hart,* 2014, SCC 52). This controversial technique is discussed in Chapter 10.

In another landmark case, the SCC ruled that the police must obtain a search warrant before asking telecom and Internet providers for details that would identify their customers (*R. v. Spencer*, 2014, SCC 43). The decision called into question the constitutionality of federal legislation that allowed this information to be obtained without a warrant. The SCC held that requests for companies to hand over customer information amounts to a search and therefore requires a warrant. This decision will place limits on federal legislation that allowed law enforcement agencies to conduct "online spying."[4] This is another illustration of the uneasy balance between protecting citizens from potential harm and the requirement that citizens' rights be respected.

On the flipside, as a result of judicial decisions, police officers now have the authority to use a warrant to obtain DNA from a suspect, by force if necessary; to obtain a variety of warrants to intercept private audio and video communications; to run "reverse stings" (e.g., sell drugs as part of an undercover operation and then seize both the money and the drugs); and to obtain foot, palm, and teeth impressions from a suspect.

The SCC has also

- ruled in favour of the police practice of using thermal-imaging technology deployed via aircraft to detect high levels of "heat" from homes, a key indicator of marijuana grow-ops (*R. v. Tessling*, 2004, SCC 67);
- reaffirmed the principle that the police can continue to question a suspect at length, even if the suspect repeatedly tries to invoke his right to silence (*R. v. Singh*, 2007, SCC 48); and
- held that the Charter does not require the presence, upon request, of defence counsel during a custodial interrogation (*R v. McCrimmon*, 2010, SCC 36; *R. v. Sinclair*, 2010, SCC 35).

Historically, Canadians have been willing to trust that the police would "do the right thing" in exercising their powers, and were prepared to give the police more powers to detect and arrest criminals, even if this meant that the civil rights of some individuals would be violated. In recent years, however, due to a number of high-profile incidents and the increased visibility of the police, these views seem to be shifting.

The Power to Detain and Arrest

When most people think of police powers, they think automatically of arrest. Over the years, considerable confusion has surrounded the process of arrest. Many citizens do not know when the police have the right to make an arrest, nor do they know what their rights are in an arrest situation.

arrest warrant
a document that permits a police officer to arrest a specific person for a specified reason

information
a written statement sworn by an informant alleging that a person has committed a specific criminal offence

The power to arrest is provided by the Criminal Code and other federal statutes, as well as by provincial legislation such as motor vehicle statutes. An arrest can be made to prevent a crime from being committed, to terminate a breach of the peace, or to compel an accused person to attend trial.

A formal "arrest" triggers certain requirements on the part of the police, such as to advise the suspect of the reason for the arrest, the right to counsel, the right to remain silent, and so on. That said, most persons are released shortly thereafter on an appearance notice, an undertaking to appear, or a summons to appear in court at a future date. These notices are issued because the person meets the "public interest" requirements of the Bail Reform Act: the seriousness of the offence is noted; identity is established; there is no concern of a continuation of the offence, of a failure to appear in court, or for destruction of evidence. A criminal suspect who is placed into custody will generally be released as soon as possible, on the authority of the arresting officer, the officer in charge of the police lockup, or a justice of the peace (JP).

If an arrest is warranted, and if there is time to do so, a police officer can seek an **arrest warrant** by swearing an **information** in front of a JP. If the JP agrees that there are "reasonable grounds to believe

ac/Photo by Andy Clark, REUTERS

Windsor police make an arrest.

that it is necessary in the public interest," a warrant will be issued directing the local police to arrest the person. Accessing a JP can pose difficulties in rural areas. Several provinces (including British Columbia, Ontario, Manitoba, and Alberta) have developed "telewarrant" programs that provide twenty-four-hour access to JPs. Police officers can apply for and receive warrants by fax or telephone instead of having to appear in person before a JP.

Sometimes the police must act quickly and thus have no time to secure a warrant from a JP. Police officers can arrest a suspect *without* an arrest warrant in the following circumstances:

- They have caught a person in the act of committing an offence.
- They believe, on reasonable grounds, that a person has committed an indictable offence (a more serious offence, such as sexual assault or robbery).
- They believe, on reasonable grounds, that a person is about to commit an indictable offence.

Two additional conditions apply to making an arrest. First, the officer must not make an arrest if he or she has "no reasonable grounds" to believe that the person will fail to appear in court. Second, the officer must believe on "reasonable grounds" that an arrest is "necessary in the public interest." This is defined specifically as the need to

- establish the identity of the person;
- secure or preserve evidence of or relating to the offence; *and/or*
- prevent the continuation or repetition of the offence or the commission of another offence.

However, provisions in the Anti-Terrorism Act give the police the power of preventative arrest. This allows them to arrest persons without a warrant on "reasonable suspicion" (rather than the standard "reasonable grounds") if it is believed that the arrest will prevent a terrorist activity. The person need not have committed any crime and can be detained for up to seventy-two hours.

In practice, arrests are usually made only in the case of indictable offences. For minor crimes (summary conviction offences), an arrest is legal only if the police find someone actually committing the offence or if there is an outstanding arrest warrant or *warrant of committal* (a document issued by a judge directing prison authorities to accept a person into custody upon his or her sentencing, a *bench warrant* for failure to appear at a court process, or a document issued by a parole board to revoke an offender's conditional release).

In some circumstances, an arrest can be unlawful. To make an arrest without a warrant, the officer must have "reasonable grounds" (formerly, "reasonable and probable grounds") to believe that a person has committed an offence. An officer who makes an arrest without reasonable grounds risks being sued civilly for assault or false imprisonment. Moreover, a person who resists an unlawful arrest is not guilty of resisting a police officer in the execution of his or her duty. To make a *lawful* arrest, "a police officer should identify himself or herself, tell the suspect that he or she is being arrested, inform the suspect of the reason for the arrest or show the suspect the warrant if there is one, and, where feasible, touch the suspect on the shoulder as a physical indication of the confinement."[6]

What is the difference between arrest and detention? An officer can detain a person without arrest. The Supreme Court of Canada has held that a detention occurs when a police officer "assumes control over the movement of a person by a demand or direction that may have significant legal consequence and that prevents or impedes access to [legal] counsel" (*R. v. Schmautz*, 1990, 1 S.C.R. 398). In contrast, the primary purpose of an arrest is to compel an accused to appear at trial.

Whether the person has been arrested or detained, an important threshold in the criminal process has been crossed. According to Section 10 of the Charter, anyone who has been arrested or detained has the right to be informed promptly of the reason for the arrest or detention. That person also has the right to retain and instruct counsel without delay, and furthermore, must be told about that right without delay. However, the suspect can choose to exercise that right or not. Also, a suspect who is interviewed by Canadian police officers in the United States must be informed of the right to counsel (*R. v. Cook*, 1998, 2 S.C.R. 597). The Charter-based warning read by police officers in independent municipal police services in British Columbia is reproduced in Box 7.1. The wording of

Box 7.1

Communicating Charter Rights upon Detention or Arrest

Sec. 10(a) I am arresting/detaining you for ———— (State reason for arrest/detention, including the offence and provide known information about the offence, including date and place.)

Sec. 10(b) It is my duty to inform you that you have the right to retain and instruct counsel in private without delay. You may call any lawyer you want.

There is a 24-hour telephone service available which provides a legal aid duty lawyer who can give you legal advice in private. This advice is given without charge and the lawyer can explain the legal aid plan to you.

If you wish to contact a legal aid lawyer I can provide you with a telephone number.

Do you understand?

Do you want to call a lawyer?

Supplementary Charter Warning: (If an arrested or detained person initially indicated that he or she wished to contact legal counsel and then subsequently indicates that he or she no longer wishes to exercise the right to counsel, read the following additional charter warning.)

You have the right to a reasonable opportunity to contact counsel. I am not obliged to take a statement from you or ask you to participate in any process which could provide incriminating evidence until you are certain about whether you want to exercise this right.

Do you understand?

What do you wish to do?

Secondary Warning: (Name), you are detained with respect to (reason for detainment). If you have spoken to any police officer (including myself) with respect to this matter, who has offered to you any hope of advantage or suggested any fear of prejudice should you speak or refuse to speak with me (us) at this time, it is my duty to warn you that no such offer or suggestion can be of any effect and must not influence you or make you feel compelled to say anything to me (us) for any reason, but anything you do say may be used in evidence.

Written Statement Caution: I have been advised by (investigating officer) that I am not obliged to say anything, but anything I do say may be given in evidence. I understand the meaning of the foregoing and I choose to make the following statement.

Approved Screening Device (ASD) Demand: In accordance with the provisions of the Criminal Code, I hereby demand that you provide a sample of your breath, forthwith, suitable for analysis using an approved screening device.

Breath Demand: I have reasonable and probable grounds to believe that you are committing, or within the preceding three hours have, as a result of the consumption of alcohol, committed an offence under Section 253 of the Criminal Code, and I hereby demand that you provide now, or as soon as is practicable, such samples of your breath as are necessary to enable a proper analysis to be made to determine the concentration, if any, of alcohol in your blood and to accompany me for the purpose of enabling such samples to be taken.

Blood Demand: I have reasonable and probable grounds to believe that you are committing, or within the preceding three hours have, as a result of the consumption of alcohol, committed an offence under Section 253 of the Criminal Code, and I hereby demand that you provide now, or as soon as is practicable, such samples of your blood as are necessary to enable a proper analysis to be made to determine the concentration, if any, of alcohol in your blood.

Samples of your blood will be taken by, or under the direction of, a qualified medical practitioner who is satisfied that the taking of those samples will not endanger you or your health.

MVA Section 90.3—12-Hour Licence Suspension: I have reasonable and probable grounds to believe

1. you have alcohol in your body

   or

2. you have failed or refused to comply with the demand to provide a sample of your breath that is necessary to enable a proper analysis of your breath to be made by means of an approved screening device.

I therefore direct you to surrender your driver's licence. Your licence to drive is now suspended for a period of 12 hours from this time and date.

If you produce, to a peace officer having charge of this matter, a certificate of a medical practitioner signed after this suspension is issued stating that your blood alcohol level does not exceed 3 milligrams of alcohol in 100 millilitres of blood at the time the certificate was signed, the suspension is terminated.

MVA Section 215—24-Hour Roadside Prohibition: I have reasonable and probable grounds to believe that your ability to drive a motor vehicle is affected by alcohol (or by drug), and I therefore direct you to surrender your driver's licence.

You are now prohibited from driving a motor vehicle for a period of 24 hours from this time and date.

(for alcohol) However, if you do not accept this prohibition, you have a right to either request a breath test or obtain a certificate from a medical practitioner. In the event that your blood alcohol level is shown not to exceed 50 milligrams of alcohol in 100 millilitres of blood by the test or certificate, this prohibition from driving is terminated.

(for drug) However, if you do not accept this prohibition, you have a right to attempt to satisfy a peace officer having charge of this matter that your ability to drive a motor vehicle is not affected by a drug other than alcohol, and if the peace officer is so satisfied this prohibition from driving is terminated.

OFFICIAL WARNING: You are not obliged to say anything, but anything you do say may be given in evidence.

Source: *Vancouver Police Department, Regulations and Procedures Manual*, http://vancouver.ca/police/assets/pdf/manuals/vpd-manual-regulations-procedures.pdf.

this communication of Charter rights may vary from police service to police service depending on the jurisdiction.

Suspects have a right to retain counsel but do not have an absolute right to have that counsel paid for by the state. Moreover, Section 10 of the Charter does not impose a duty on provincial governments to provide free legal representation to everyone who cannot afford it. In many provinces, free preliminary legal advice is available through a toll-free number on a twenty-four-hour basis. When an arrested or detained person does not have or know a lawyer, police must inform that person of this number and hold off on further questioning to give the suspect an opportunity to access this advice. After that, however, to get free legal representation, the suspect must qualify for legal aid. Failure to advise a person in a timely manner of the right to counsel upon arrest is an infringement of his or her Charter rights. In addition, the Supreme Court of Canada has held that a person's Charter rights are violated when the police (1) refuse to hold off and continue to question an arrested person despite repeated statements that he or she will say nothing without consulting a lawyer; (2) belittle the person's lawyer with the express goal or intent of undermining the person's relationship with that lawyer; *or* (3) pressure the person to accept a "deal" without first affording the person the option to consult with a lawyer.

Search and Seizure

The power of the police to search people and places and to seize evidence also illustrates the fine balance that must be maintained between crime control and due process. Historically, under the common law, the manner in which evidence was gathered did not affect its admissibility in a criminal trial. That all changed with the Charter, Section 8 of which protects all citizens against "unreasonable" search or seizure. Evidence obtained during an illegal search may be excluded from trial if, as indicated in Section 24 of the Charter, its use would bring the justice system into disrepute.

The Supreme Court of Canada has held in *R. v. S.A.B.*, 2003, SCC 60, that for a search to be reasonable, (a) it must be authorized by law, (b) the law itself must be reasonable, and (c) the manner in which the search was carried out must be reasonable. This is illustrated in the case of *R. v. Mann*, 2004, SCC 52, presented in Critical Thinking Exercise 7.1 at the end of this chapter.

There is considerable room for interpretation by the courts as to what constitutes an unreasonable search in any particular case and when admission of evidence would bring the administration of justice into disrepute. Since the passage of the Charter in 1982, there have been hundreds of court cases and numerous books and legal articles dealing with this issue; the same three-plus decades have seen an ongoing debate about what constitutes a reasonable search. As a result, conditions and requirements have emerged regarding prior authorization for a search. Generally, a **search warrant** must be issued. The Supreme Court of Canada has decided that warrants are required in the following situations:

search warrant
a document that permits the police to search a specific location and take items that might be evidence of a crime

- where there is to be secret recording of conversations by state agents;
- in cases involving video surveillance;
- for perimeter searches of residential premises; *and*
- before the installation of tracking devices to monitor people's movements.

Search warrants are generally issued by JPs. Before a warrant can be issued, an information must be sworn under oath before a JP to convince him or her that there are reasonable and probable grounds that there is, in a building or place, (1) evidence relating to an act in violation of the Criminal Code or other federal statute, (2) evidence that might exist in relation to such a violation, or (3) evidence intended to be used to commit an offence against a person for which an individual may be arrested without a warrant.

The following scenario illustrates the principle of reasonable and probable grounds. Your neighbours feel that you match the description of a crime suspect in a bank robbery re-enacted on a televised *Crime Stoppers* program. They telephone the police and anonymously provide your name and address. Can this tip be used to establish reasonable and probable grounds for a search of your home? The answer is no. Although a possible starting point for a police investigation, anonymous tips do not provide reasonable and probable grounds. A concern in establishing reasonable and probable grounds is the source of the information, the credibility of which is likely to be questioned if it is anonymous.

A search without a warrant will generally be illegal, except in two types of situations:

1. While arresting a person, the officer may search the person and the immediate surroundings for self-protection (that is, to seize weapons), to prevent the destruction of evidence (for example, to stop the person from swallowing drugs), or for means of escape.
2. In an emergency situation where an officer believes that an offence is being, or is likely to be, committed or that someone in the premises is in danger of injury, a premise may be entered. In *R. v. Godoy*, 1999, 1 S.C.R. 311, for example, the Supreme Court of Canada held that the forced entry of police officers into a residence from which a disconnected 911 call had been made, and the subsequent arrest of a suspect who had physically abused his common-law partner, was justifiable.

The passage in 2001 of Bill C-36, the Anti-Terrorism Act, expanded the authority of the police to search property associated with terrorist groups and/or activity. One of the more significant decisions on searches was made by the Supreme Court in *R. v. Feeney*, 1997, 3 S.C.R. 1008 (see Box 7.2).

Box 7.2

R. v. Feeney

As part of a murder investigation, the police knocked on the door of the accused's home. Receiving no answer, they entered the home, woke the accused, and arrested him after seeing blood on his shirt. The officers informed the accused of his right to counsel, but not of the immediate right to counsel, and seized evidence from his home that was subsequently used to obtain a search warrant to retrieve additional evidence.

At trial, the accused was convicted of second degree murder. His appeal was unanimously dismissed by the B.C. Court of Appeal. The issue for the Supreme Court was whether the police had violated the accused's right under the Charter to be free from unreasonable search or seizure and his right, upon being arrested, to have access to legal counsel without delay and—either being so—what evidence, if any, should be excluded under Section 24(2) of the Criminal Code. From an examination of the facts in the case, the Court concluded that the legal requirements for a warrantless arrest following a forced entry into a person's private premises had not been met. More specifically, the arresting officer had not believed he had reasonable grounds to arrest prior to the forcible entry.

The Court held that in order to protect the privacy rights of Canadians under the Charter of Rights and Freedoms, the police must obtain a search warrant before entering a dwelling to arrest or apprehend a suspect. In response to this decision, Parliament amended the Criminal Code to require that as a general rule, peace officers must obtain a warrant prior to entering a dwelling to apprehend or arrest someone, but police may enter dwellings and arrest or apprehend without a warrant in those circumstances where entry is required to prevent bodily harm or death or to prevent the loss or destruction of evidence in the case.

In another case, *R. v. A.M.*, 2008 SCC 19, the Supreme Court of Canada held that the use of police drug-sniffer dogs to conduct random searches for drugs in schools and other public places violated the rights of citizens under the Charter not to be subject to unreasonable search and seizure. The principal of an Ontario high school had issued a standing invitation for the police to bring sniffer dogs into the school to enforce the school's zero tolerance policy for drugs and alcohol.

During the search, the drug dog zeroed in on a student's backpack, which was found to contain ten bags of marijuana, ten magic mushrooms, and various types of drug paraphernalia. The student, A.M., was charged with criminal offences. However, Ontario youth courts subsequently cleared the youth, deciding that his Charter rights had been violated. The primary issue for the SCC was whether the use of the sniffer dog was an unreasonable invasion of privacy that amounted to unreasonable search and seizure under the Charter. (The Charter states that everyone has the right to be secure against unreasonable search or seizure.) In its decision, the Supreme Court of Canada held that the sniffer dog's activities constituted as "search" under the provisions of the

Charter and that the dog's search of the backpack as part of a general "sniff search" violated the student's Charter rights.[7] However, in 2013, the court held that a drug-sniffer dog could be used in a case where the police officer had reasonable suspicion that the suspect was involved in a drug-related offence (*R. v. MacKenzie*, 2013, SCC 50).

This decision expanded the situations in which the police could use dogs to search premises, in this case a vehicle that had been stopped for erratic driving. Critics lambasted the decision, one law professor stating that the ruling "has the effect of giving an enormous amount of deference to the instincts and subjective views of police officers, at the expense of some of the liberties we assumed were in place since the Charter [of Rights and Freedoms] came" into effect in 1982.[8] Writing for the majority, one of the justices stated that every police move should not be "placed under a scanning electron-microscope."[9]

While the Feeney case and the *R. v. A.M.* cases constrained police practice with respect to searches, the Supreme Court of Canada appeared to expand police powers of search in the case of Wendell Clayton and Troy Farmer (*R. v. Clayton*, 2007, SCC 32 (see Box 7.3).

Ultimately, it is the courts that decide whether a search warrant has been properly obtained and executed or whether a warrantless search was legal.

A recent decision of the SCC highlighted how the powers of the police need to be clearly defined in the age of the Internet and cellphones (see Box 7.4). In late 2013, the federal government introduced legislation that would expand police powers that would allow the police to take steps to prevent Internet and

Box 7.3

A 911 Call, Police Roadblock, and Search

A caller to 911 stated that several young men outside a Toronto-area strip club were brandishing weapons. The police responded and set up a roadblock, stopping vehicles leaving the club. Wendell Clayton and Troy Farmer, who were in a vehicle not specified by the 911 caller, were stopped and searched by police officers, who found a pair of loaded, semi-automatic handguns in their vehicle. In 2005, the Ontario Court of Appeal, in acquitting the two accused, had ruled that the gun evidence should be excluded as it was obtained by the use of a blockade, which was unlawful since there was no evidence that anyone was in danger, and the police did not limit their search to vehicles described by the 911 caller.

In a 9-0 ruling, however, the Supreme Court of Canada overturned the decision of the Ontario Court of Appeal, deciding that the search was justified. In the decision, one justice wrote that stopping any vehicles that were leaving the parking lot of the club was an "eminently reasonable response," particularly in light of the seriousness of gun-related crime.

Box 7.4

The Search of a Computer

In an investigation of a suspected marijuana grow-op, the police obtained a warrant to search the home of Thanh Long Vu for evidence of the theft of electricity, and documentation identifying the owners and/or occupants of the residence. Entering the residence, the police found marijuana, two computers, and a cellular phone. The police searched the computers as part of their investigation to determine who lived in the home. Vu was subsequently charged with production of marijuana, possession of marijuana for the purpose of trafficking, and theft of electricity.

At trial, Vu's defence lawyer argued that the search of the computers violated his Section 8 Charter rights ("everyone has the right to be secure against unreasonable search or seizure"). The trial judge agreed, noting that the search warrant did not mention access to computers as a source of information regarding the identity of the owners/occupants of the residence, and therefore did not allow a search of the computers. The judge excluded most of the evidence found in the computers and acquitted Mr. Vu of the drug charges. The B.C. Court of Appeal subsequently set aside the acquittals and ordered a new trial. Mr. Vu appealed to the SCC.

The SCC dismissed Mr. Vu's appeal. In its decision, the Court reiterated the importance of the police obtaining prior authorization before a state incursion occurs to ensure that the privacy rights of the individuals are balanced against the interests of the state. In the words of one justice, "It is difficult to imagine a more intrusive invasion of privacy than the search of a personal or home computer."[10] If, as part of a search, the police find computers that may hold important information for the investigation, they must obtain a separate search warrant. The Court found that, although the evidence in this case was illegally obtained, it should be admitted at trial since it did not bring the administration of justice into disrepute, the violation was not serious, and "the state of the law with respect to computer searches was uncertain when the police carried out their investigation…" (*R. v. Vu*, 2013, SCC 60).

cellular phone companies from removing potentially incriminating evidence before a warrant was secured.

The Vu case illustrates the complexities that surround privacy and police access to computers and cellphones and the emerging case law in this area. In 2013, the SCC held that the police are required to have a special wiretap warrant in order to access a suspect's text messages from their wireless provider (*R. v. TELUS*, 2013, SCC 16). However, in 2014, the SCC held that the police could conduct a warrantless search of a suspect's cellphone as part of an immediate investigation (*R. v. Fearon*, 2014, SCC 77). In this case, the officer found a cellphone on the suspect when he was arrested and quickly examined texts and photographs. One of the messages on the cellphone stated, "We did it" and there was also a photo of a handgun. In upholding the suspect's conviction, the SCC held that this type of warrantless search must be limited to a specific purpose and to recent e-mails, text messages, and photos.

Entrapment: An Abuse of Police Powers

Entrapment means just what it sounds like: a person ends up committing an offence that he or she would not otherwise have committed, largely because of pressure or cunning on the part of the police, who are most often operating in an undercover role. The following are controversial examples of this practice:

- An expensive car is left with the keys in the ignition, observed by concealed officers waiting to arrest anyone who steals it.
- A police officer poses as a young girl while trolling websites frequented by pedophiles.
- An undercover officer poses as an intoxicated subway passenger, wearing expensive jewellery and a Rolex watch. Anyone who mugs him is arrested.

Proactive techniques of this kind can be an effective and cost-efficient use of personnel. There is, however, a line between catching those habitually involved in law breaking and creating "situational" criminals—that situations could be created where typically law-abiding people are enticed into criminal activity.

The courts have determined that the line is crossed when a person is persistently harassed into committing an offence that he or she would not have committed had it not been for the actions of the police. People cannot be targeted at random. Rather, there must be a reasonable suspicion that the person is already engaged in criminal activity. For example, in the prostitution example above, the actions of the police do not constitute entrapment because this reasonable suspicion exists.

An SCC case involving the issue of entrapment is presented in Box 7.5.

Canadian courts have generally not allowed the defence of entrapment, which requires there to have been a clear abuse of process.

THE USE OF FORCE

Police should use physical force only to the extent necessary to ensure compliance with the law or to restore order only after persuasion, advice and warnings are insufficient.

—Sir Robert Peel

The authority to use force, including lethal force, is a defining feature of the police role in society. Discussions of the police use of force, however, are hindered by the absence of any national statistics. This makes it difficult to determine the frequency and types of force used in police services. Also, because most civil suits involving alleged misuse of force by police officers are settled out of court, there is no cumulative body of knowledge about the factors that precipitated that use, nor about the appropriateness of such force under the circumstances. Research and statistical information from the United States indicate that the use of force is rare, as is the improper use of force. The use of force also rarely involves weapons and typically occurs at the lower end of the force spectrum, involving grabbing, pushing, or shoving.

Box 7.5

The Reluctant Drug Trafficker

The defendant was charged with drug trafficking and, at the close of his defence, brought an application for a stay of proceedings on the basis of entrapment. His testimony indicated that he had persistently refused the approaches of a police informer over the course of six months, and that he was only persuaded to sell him drugs because of the informer's persistence, his use of threats, and the inducement of a large amount of money. He also testified that he had previously been addicted to drugs, but that he had given up his use of narcotics. The application for a stay of proceedings was refused, and he was convicted of drug trafficking. The Court of Appeal dismissed an appeal from that conviction.

The central issue for the Supreme Court of Canada was whether the defendant had been entrapped into committing the offence of drug trafficking. The Court held that the police in this case were not interrupting an ongoing criminal enterprise; the offence was clearly brought about by their conduct and would not have occurred without their involvement. The Court stated that the persistence of the police requests and the equally persistent refusals, and the length of time needed to secure the defendant's participation in the offence, indicate that the police had tried to make the appellant take up his former lifestyle and had gone further than merely providing him with the opportunity.

For the Court, the most important determining factor was that defendant had been threatened and had been told to get his act together when he did not provide the requested drugs. This conduct was unacceptable and went beyond providing the appellant with an opportunity. The Court found that the average person in the appellant's position might also have committed the offence, if only to finally satisfy this threatening informer and end all further contact. The Court ruled that the trial judge should have entered a stay of proceedings.

Source: *R. v. Mack*, 1988, 2 S.C.R. 903.

The Legal Provisions for Use of Force

The use of force, including lethal force, is governed by both law and policy. The legal justification for the use of force is found in the Criminal Code and in case law. Further support is found in provincial laws such as police acts and in firearm regulations.

The "justification" sections for the use of force are contained in Sections 25 to 33 of the Criminal Code. These sections in effect exempt otherwise criminal actions from criminal liability. Sections 26, 27, and 37 contain equally important provisions pertaining to a police officer's use of force. Court decisions, in both criminal and civil cases, have further shaped the powers and obligations of police officers when utilizing force. In *R. v. Nasogalauk*, 2010, SCC 6, for example, the SCC reiterated: "While police officers may have to resort to force in order to complete an arrest or to prevent an offender from escaping their custody, the allowable degree of force is constrained by the principles of proportionality, necessity, and reasonableness."

Police Acts and Standards

Besides the Criminal Code, provincial laws such as police acts and standards govern and regulate the use of force by police officers. These provisions generally specify that lethal force can be used only to protect against the loss of life or serious bodily harm. The Ontario Police Standards Relating to Police Use of Force also contain provisions for investigating and preparing a report in every instance in which a police officer discharges his or her weapon, regardless of whether a person was killed or injured by the discharge.

The Force Options Model

force options model
provides police officers with a working model that sets out the course of action to be taken in use-of-force situations

The **force options model** for the use of force by police is the foundation of most police training in Canada; it provides police administrators and judicial review personnel with an objective framework for analyzing use-of-force situations. The force options model serves as a guideline, and all police personnel are provided with a working model that clearly outlines the course of action to take in use-of-force situations. It also allows police officers to explain, in an accepted format, how and why force was applied at the time of the altercation. The National Use of Force Model is based on the National Use of Force Framework and reflects the various components of the process by which police officers assess a situation and determine the proper response in order to protect themselves and the general public. The model is presented in Figure 7.1 and Box 7.6.

Demonstrated Threat

demonstrated threat
the level of potential danger posed by a person confronted by police officers, generally in the form of weapons or levels of resistance

Individuals confronted by the police present various levels of potential danger, often called the **demonstrated threat**. These levels typically correspond to the presence of weapons and levels of resistance. With respect to weapons, both the type of weapon and the manner in which it is carried can influence an officer's perception of potential danger. The dangers associated with levels of resistance can change quickly during any incident, and police officers must be alert to all possibilities.

There are five levels of resistance of individuals and related behaviour:

1. **Cooperative.** There is no resistance. The person responds positively to verbal requests and commands. The person willingly complies.
2. **Non-cooperative.** There is little or no physical resistance. The person does not comply to the officer's request, showing verbal defiance and little or no physical response.
3. **Resistant.** The person demonstrates resistance to control by the police officer through behaviours such as pulling away, pushing away, or running away.
4. **Combative.** The person attempts or threatens to apply force to anyone, for example, by punching, kicking, or clenching fists with the intent to hurt or resist.
5. **Showing the potential to cause grievous bodily harm or death.** The person acts in a manner that the police officer has reason to believe could

Box 7.6

The National Use-of-Force Model

The officer continuously assesses the situation and selects the most reasonable option relative to those circumstances as perceived at that point in time.

There are a number of components in the model, beginning with the inner circle and moving outward:

- The *situation*, which requires the officer to continually assess, plan, and act.
- The *behaviour of the subject*, which can range from cooperative to passive resistant, active resistant, assaultive, and presenting serious bodily harm or death to the officer.
- The officer's *perception* and *tactical considerations*, which are interrelated and interact with the situation and behaviour of the subject and affect how the officer perceives and assesses the situation.

Figure 7.1. National Use-of-Force Framework

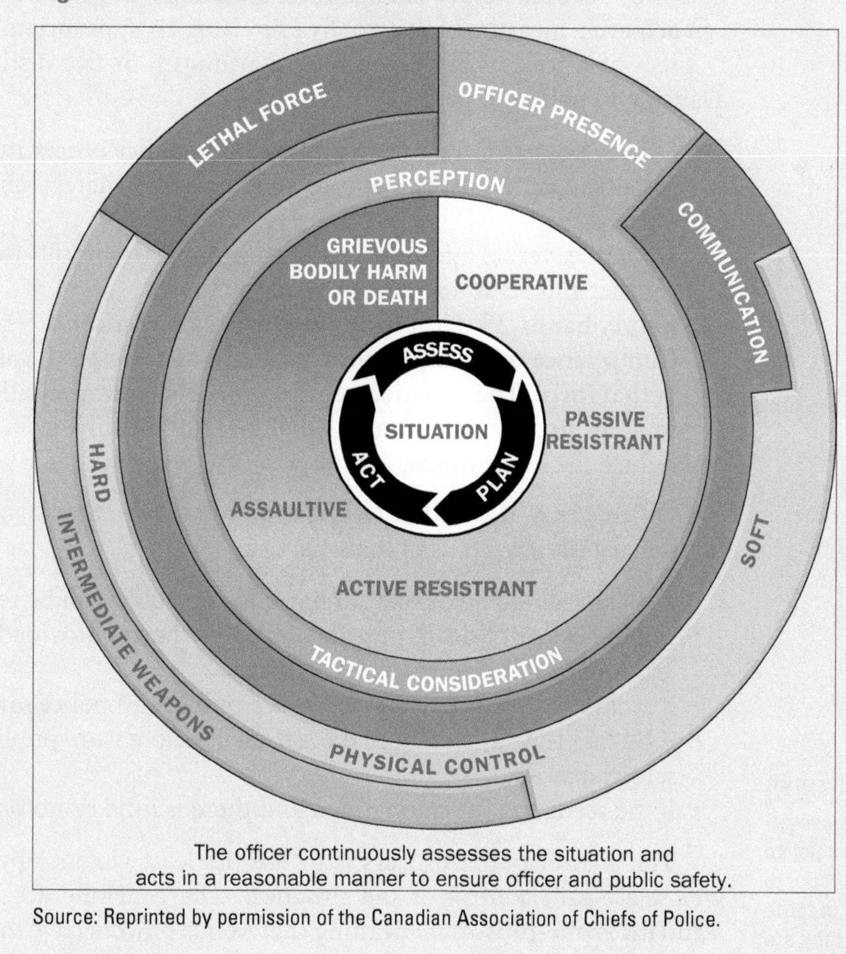

Source: Reprinted by permission of the Canadian Association of Chiefs of Police.

- The officer's *use-of-force options*, which range from officer presence, to communication skills, to the use of soft and hard physical compliance techniques, the use of intermediate weapons, and lethal force. The use-of-force model requires that the officer constantly reassess the situation in order to ensure that the appropriate level of force is being used.

result in grievous bodily harm or death to the public or to the police, for example, using a knife, a firearm, or a baseball bat.

Levels of Force Intervention

The use of force is intended to gain control and compliance, for example, during an arrest or while breaking up an altercation. Although police officers often have no control over the types of encounter situations they become involved in, they can achieve a measure of control by exercising an appropriate level of response. Degrees of force can be placed on a continuum of five distinct force options available to police officers:

1. **Officer presence.** The mere presence of a police officer may alter the behaviour of the participants at an altercation, thereby enabling control of the situation.
2. **Dialogue.** Verbal and non-verbal communication skills may resolve the conflict and result in voluntary compliance.
3. **Empty hands.** Physical force is used to gain control.
4. **Compliance tools.** Equipment or weapons are used to gain control.
5. **Lethal force.** The situation requires complete incapacitation of the subject in order to gain control, and lethal force is the only option available to reduce the lethal threat.

Officers may also decide to tactically reposition; that is, officers can decide to disengage at any point in the situation:

- if the likelihood and extent of harm to the public can be reduced by leaving;
- if there is fear of death or grievous bodily harm, provided it does not expose others to injury or lethal force;
- if seeking assistance will help ensure public and police safety;
- if buying time and gaining distance will help ensure public and police safety; *and/or*
- if the scene has been contained and there is little or no potential for harm.

one-plus-one
the generally accepted use-of-force standard that says police officers have the authority to use one higher level of force than that with which they are confronted

The goal of police officers is to use the least violent option available that will safely gain control of the situation. The generally accepted use-of-force standard is **one-plus-one**, meaning that police officers have the authority to use one higher level of force than that which they are confronted.

There may also be situations in which patrol officers are underarmed; that is, they do not have sufficient firepower to respond to the threat that they are confronted with. This was the case in a critical incident that occurred in Moncton, New Brunswick, on June 4, 2014, resulting in the death of three RCMP officers. An independent review of the incident found that the shooter, Justin Bourque, had a tactical advantage over the responding RCMP officers. He was armed with semi-automatic weapons, while the officers were equipped with pistols. The report also found that the officers were poorly trained in critical incident response techniques, there were communication breakdowns, and there was a lack of a coordinated plan to respond to the threat.[11] In 2015, the Public Prosecution Service of Canada recommended that the RCMP be prosecuted for violating the occupational health and safety provisions of the Canada Labour Code. It is charged that the RCMP did not equip, train, and supervise the officers who were killed in the incident. View the documentary film "Under Fire" listed in the Media Links at the end of the chapter.

Less-Lethal Force Options

A **less-lethal (or lower lethality) force option** is one that is *highly unlikely* to cause death or serious injury to an individual when *properly applied* by a police officer. However, it is possible that death or serious injury may occur, hence the term *less lethal* rather than *less than lethal*. The possibility of serious harm is especially great if the force option is improperly applied by the police officer. In these instances, the less-lethal options may contribute to or even cause serious injury or death.

less-lethal (or lower lethality) force option
a control technique that is highly unlikely to cause death or serious injury

Ideally, a less-lethal weapon will incapacitate the perceived threat to the officer while inflicting only minor injuries to the attacker. However, situations do arise that result in serious physical harm, or death, to the person who is the target of a less-lethal weapon.

The Taser: A Less-Lethal or Lethal Weapon?

Conducted energy devices (CEDs, or more commonly referred to as Tasers) were adopted by Canadian police services as a force option in the late 1990s. The Taser "gun" fires two metal darts, which are attached to wires and enter the subject's skin, generating an electric shock of up to 50,000 volts. The expanded use of the Taser by police services is credited with reducing the number of deaths as a result of the police use of lethal force and, as well, the number of officers injured while carrying out their duties. In 2013, the Ontario government expanded the use of Tasers, allowing individual police services to equip their officers should they choose to do so.[12]

The use of the Taser has been the subject of considerable controversy and has been associated with a number of high-profile incidents, including the death of Robert Dziekanski at Vancouver International Airport in 2008 (see Police File 7.1). There have also been citizen protests.

One issue is the deaths of persons who are in a state of "excited delirium" as a result of mental illness and/or drug use or other challenges. In this state, the person may be incoherent, violent, and non-compliant. The use of electric shocks on such a person can cause a heart attack.

Police File 7.1

The Death of Robert Dziekanski

The most high-profile incident involving the police use of Tasers to date was the death of Robert Dziekanski at Vancouver International Airport. At 2:50 p.m. on October 13, 2007, Mr. Dziekanski, an immigrant from Poland, arrived at the airport following a long flight from his home country. He was fatigued from the flight and spoke no English. For reasons that have still not been adequately explained, Mr. Dziekanski spent nearly 12 hours wandering around the international arrivals area without securing the assistance that would have led him to his waiting mother. At 1:20 a.m., he became agitated and confused, his situation made more difficult due to his limited English. The airport operations centre received calls that a man was acting strangely, and security personnel and RCMP officers were called. Four RCMP officers arrived on the scene. Within minutes, Mr. Dziekanski had been tasered and restrained on the floor by the officers. Shortly thereafter, he died. An autopsy revealed that there were no drugs or alcohol in Dziekanski's system.

The encounter was captured on a cellphone camera by a passenger in the terminal (the video is available on YouTube). The RCMP originally stated that Dziekanski had been Tasered twice, although the video indicated that he had been Tasered a total of five times. This was an excellent example of the consequences of the increased visibility of the police.

The provincial government subsequently launched a public inquiry headed by a retired judge, Thomas Braidwood. The inquiry was in two parts: the first part focused on the police use of Tasers. The second phase of the inquiry examined the circumstances surrounding the death of Mr. Dziekanski. On numerous occasions during the hearing, the four RCMP officers involved in the incident, and their superior officers, provided conflicting testimony. Among the findings of the inquiry were that the responding officers did not make any meaningful attempt to de-escalate the situation; the use of the Taser against Mr. Dziekanski was premature and inappropriate; and the four officers involved in the incident gave conflicting testimony to the inquiry that was not credible. The officers were subsequently charged with perjury for lying to the commission and two of the officers were subsequently convicted of this charge.

Sources: T.R. Braidwood (Commissioner), "WHY? The Robert Dziekanski Tragedy," *Braidwood Commission on the Death of Robert Dziekanski*. Victoria: Attorney General of British Columbia, 2010, http://www.braidwoodinquiry.ca/report/P2Report.php.

There are a few police services that prohibit the use of Tasers on children, pregnant women, and the elderly, although there have been instances in which Canadian police officers have tasered children as young as 11 years old and elderly persons, one of whom was in a hospital bed. There are concerns that CEDs may be more likely to be used on some suspects rather than others (e.g., visible minorities, persons in poverty), although this remains to be explored in Canada. A U.S. research study found that, all things being equal, Hispanic suspects were twice as likely as Whites to be tasered.[13] There is evidence that with the introduction of Tasers, officers came to over-rely on the device to resolve situations, rather than using verbal communication and hands-on applications.[14] The inappropriate use of CEDs may increase public distrust of the police and reduce public confidence in the police.[15]

Following several critical incidents, however, including the death of Robert Dziekanski at Vancouver International Airport, it appears that Taser use is on the decline. In British Columbia, for example, Taser use declined by 87 percent in the five years following Mr. Dziekanski's death (the period 2007 to 2012).[16] The use of Tasers by RCMP officers has also declined during this time.[17] While the controversy surrounding Tasers has resulted in the development of much-needed guidelines, it may also have made officers reluctant to use Tasers even in instances in which they are justified in doing so and in cases that might save a person's life.

Community members protest police use of Tasers.

The Frequency of Police Use of Force

Research on the use of force by several Canadian police services has found that the police used force in 0.7 percent of encounters with the public. Force was more likely to be used in cases where the person was violent and/or under the influence of drugs or alcohol.[18] A study conducted by the Calgary Police Service found that the use of force by police was rare, occurring in only 0.07 percent of encounters with the public and in only 1.5 percent of incidents involving an arrest. Nearly 90 percent of the cases in which force was used involved a person who was under the influence of alcohol and/or drugs.[19]

There has been little research conducted on the use of force by detectives and officers in other specialty, plainclothes units, despite evidence that these officers may use higher levels of force than uniformed patrol officers.[20]

Correlates of Police Use of Force

A number of factors are associated with the police use of force—including lethal force—in encounter situations. These include the level of crime and violence in a community, the dynamics that develop in the encounter situation, (e.g., the actions of the person of interest/suspect), and the attributes of the individual police officer.

The Attributes of the Police Officer

As the average age of police officers increases, their use of force tends to decrease: younger officers and those with fewer years of police experience are much more likely to use force (including lethal force) in an encounter situation.[21] This finding has particular implications in contemporary police services, because increasing numbers of officers have fewer than five years' experience. There is also some evidence to suggest that officers with a university education use force less in encounter situations, perhaps due to an ability to consider more options to resolve the incident.[22]

Research studies suggest that women police officers are not reluctant to use coercive force. There is evidence to suggest that a small number of officers in police services may be disproportionately involved in use-of-force incidents and may be more likely to use excessive force. These "problem officers" are more likely to be younger and to have fewer years of experience on the job.[23]

The Actions and Intentions of the Subject/Suspect

The discussion in Chapter 6 noted that the attributes of the person of interest/suspect are a primary determinant of how officers will exercise discretion and make decisions in encounter situations. These attributes also play a role in police use-of-force decision making. When force is used, it is the subject's own actions, such as threats, that most often provoke the officers.[24] The violence that occurs between a police officer and a suspect is often a continuation of violence that the suspect was involved in before the officers arrived on the scene.[25] Also, several research studies have found that the amount of coercive force used by officers is determined largely by the behaviour of the citizens they encounter, and this plays a much more significant role than non-behavioural attributes such as ethnicity. Further, the amount of force used by officers can be reduced through training courses.[26]

Force is more likely to be used on persons who are uncooperative and antagonistic toward the police. On the other hand, there is no evidence that police officers use excessive force in situations involving persons with a mental illness (PwMI), although several high-profile incidents in which PwMI were shot by police have resulted in considerable public outcry and an increased focus on the use of force with mentally ill persons.

Residents in Toronto's black community *perceive* that the police are more likely to use physical force against them than against other citizens. This perception is supported by a review of cases handled by the Ontario Special Investigations Unit (SIU) (see Chapter 4), which found that Blacks and Aboriginals were over-represented in SIU investigations and in cases in which it was subsequently determined that a civilian death or serious injury had been caused directly by police actions.[27]

A use-of-force instructor at a Canadian police training academy identified a typology of persons that are encountered and the challenges that each "type" present to police officers. This is presented in Police Perspective 7.1.

The quotation below from a police use-of-force instructor includes examples of the threat cues that officers are taught to look for and come to notice experientially:

> You know if you're going to a domestic or an assault in progress, absolutely you're looking for clothing, you're looking for unusual weightiness in the clothing that could signal a weapon. Where are buddy's hands? What's their level of sobriety or state of mind, or willingness to listen or resist? All of those things we train officers to look for.[28*]

*Murphy, J.J. 2014."Beyond a Split-Second: An Exploratory Study of Police Use of Force and Use of Force Training in Canada." Unpublished MA Thesis. Burnaby, BC: School of Criminology, Simon Fraser University. Reprinted by permission of Josh Murphy.

Police Perspective 7.1

A Police Use-of-Force Instructor Discusses the Encounter

A police use-of-force instructor offered the following about the types of persons that officers encounter and how they may influence their decisions regarding the use of force:

> We have three types of people when it comes to policing. Cooperative, uncooperative, and dangerous. Persons may be pretending to be cooperative and they're actually dangerous. So, we have difficult people that we deal with a lot and we have nice people that we deal with a lot and then we have that third group that appear to be nice but they might actually be dangerous. We're okay with the guy being difficult right off the bat, we know who they are. When we break those groups down demographically they're exactly the same. That's what we're training our officers to recognize. Don't underestimate your adversary based upon something and never take someone at face value. It's everything combined in messaging and behaviour.

Source: Murphy, J.J. 2014."Beyond a Split-Second: An Exploratory Study of Police Use of Force and Use of Force Training in Canada." Unpublished MA Thesis. Burnaby, BC: School of Criminology, Simon Fraser University. Reprinted by permission of Josh Murphy.

Officers often speak of a "sixth sense" that warns them of danger and risk. Risk is heightened when a person appears to be cooperative but may pose a high danger. A use-of-force instructor described the importance of patrol officers picking up "cues" from persons in encounter situations. This is particularly important in situations involving persons whom he described as "deceitful"; that is, they appear to be compliant with the officer, but may have other intentions:

> We will really pick up on what we call the sixth sense, the gut feeling that something's not right with this dude and it's kind of freaking me out. Subconsciously, the brain has picked up on some of those threat cues and just hasn't registered consciously yet, but it's close. It's just about to happen. When we say, 'Police, don't move,' and they say, 'Hey, no problem boss, you got me,' and he or she starts to walk backwards with their hands in the air or walk towards you with their hands in the air, those should be bells because we said, 'Police, don't move'...maybe the subject was looking over their shoulder, looking for escape routes, looking for weapons of opportunity, looking for other cops. And it's those little ones that are extremely hazardous if you don't pick 'em up.[29*]

* Murphy, J.J. 2014."Beyond a Split-Second: An Exploratory Study of Police Use of Force and Use of Force Training in Canada." Unpublished MA Thesis. Burnaby, BC: School of Criminology, Simon Fraser University. Reprinted by permission of Josh Murphy.

The Area Being Policed

There is some evidence from the U.S. to suggest that officers who police in high-crime areas are more likely to use force and more willing to accept the unnecessary use of force by fellow officers in that area.[30]

The Inappropriate Use of Force

Every year in Canada there are incidents, some of a higher profile than others, in which police officers misuse force. The use of force in excess of what is necessary can leave the officer criminally or civilly liable for assault or, in rare cases, murder. In 2012, for example, a Toronto police officer was charged with second-degree murder for the death of a suspect during a police drug raid. The officer's weapon discharged during an altercation with the suspect. At the end of a preliminary hearing, the presiding judge determined that there was not sufficient evidence to proceed and ordered a discharge. The Crown appealed and another judge ruled that the shooting was "totally accidental." In October 2013, the Crown filed an appeal. In early 2014, the Ontario Court of Appeal dismissed the Crown appeal, and the officer was exonerated.

In 2013, the police officer who shot Sammy Yatim on a Toronto streetcar (see Box 7.7, p. 202) was charged with second-degree murder, and trial was pending as of 2015. This charge will require the Crown to prove that the officer intended to kill Yatim.

The historical record indicates that in Ontario, 22 officers have been criminally charged in relation to 19 deaths during the time period 1993 to 2013. While there were convictions for impaired driving–related deaths, dangerous driving, and criminal negligence causing death, all of the officers charged with manslaughter and murder were acquitted. It appears that juries are very reluctant to convict police officers who are charged with manslaughter or murder.[31]

In one case, a First Nations man in Terrace, British Columbia, Robert Wright received permanent brain damage in an incident in a police cell at the hands of RCMP officers. The incident resulted in him being in a coma for ten days and requiring brain surgery. He had been arrested for suspected impaired driving.[32] The incident was captured by the video surveillance camera in the cell. See the Media Link, "Violent Takedown by Police Caught on Surveillance Camera in Prison Cell Video in Terrace," at the end of this chapter.

The case was investigated by officers from a municipal police service who recommended that charges be laid against at least one of the officers. However, Crown counsel declined to approve the charges (in British Columbia, Crown counsel must approve all charges). Mr. Wright subsequently filed a civil suit against the province and the officer who assaulted him. The statement of claim was amended to include the allegation that the officer's excessive use of force was exacerbated by the officer's use of steroids. The case was proceeding through the courts as of 2015. See Class/Group Discussion 7.1 at the end of this chapter.

The Use of Force and Persons with Mental Illness (PwMI)

In Chapter 6, it was noted that police officers frequently have encounters with persons with mental illness (PwMI). The increasing number of encounters between police officers and PwMI have led to a number of high-profile incidents involving the use of lethal force. It is important to note that, despite these tragedies, in the overwhelming number of cases, police officers successfully resolve incidents involving PwMI. And it does not appear that PwMI are subject to any higher levels of force than those without mental illnesses.[33]

An Ontario coroner jury inquest into the deaths of three PwMI persons in encounters with Toronto police officers ruled the deaths as homicides. The means that the deaths occurred by another person's actions but there are no criminal implications. The officers involved in the shootings were cleared of wrongdoing by the Ontario SIU (see Chapter 4). Among the 74 recommendations issued by the jury were that there be increased training for dealing with PwMI and that officers should consider the mental state of the person as well as their behaviour in deciding on force options.[34]

For accounts of the impact of the death of a mentally ill relative in an encounter with the police, and video footage of the three deaths, see the Media Links at the end of this chapter: "When Police Kill: The Story of Five Families"; "SIU Called in After Man Shot Dead by Police Outside Scarborough Bank"; "Inquest Hears 911 Call that Preceded Police Shooting"; "Reyal Jardine-Douglas Sat Quietly Before Officer Boarded Bus"; "Sylvia Klibingaitis Told 911 Operator 'I'm Pure Evil'"; and "Police Shootings Inquest: Video Shows Knife-Wielding Woman Chase Officer."

Another high-profile case was that of Sammy Yatim, an emotionally disturbed young man who was shot by a police officer (see Box 7.7).

Social Media and Police Use of Force

In Chapter 1, it was noted that the widespread use of social media has increased the visibility of the police. Although this can contribute to the increased accountability of the police, it may also be impacting the justified use of force by police officers. As one police academy instructor stated: "You will find that police officers are more reluctant to put hands on people when they should be putting hands on people. They don't want to be judged by the media. And that's where the danger lies. This puts them and their partner in a critical situation." This has required that police academy programs train new recruits to follow their training in encounter situations regardless of the presence of cameras.

This "hesitancy factor" in the use of force is revealed in the recollection of a critical incident by a patrol sergeant involving one of his patrol officers:

> There was a robbery of a jewellery store in [an upscale mall]. Shots were fired by the two perpetrators, both of whom were 17 years of age. One of the robbers ran out of the back of the mall and was confronted by a junior police constable. The robber raised his firearm and attempted to fire at the officer, but the gun jammed. The officer pulled out her weapon, but didn't fire. She could have been killed. That hesitation could have cost her life. There seems to be an element of fear in many junior officers to use force.[35]

Box 7.7

The Shooting Death of Sammy Yatim

On July 27, 2013, Toronto Police responded to a call about a disruptive passenger on a streetcar. The man had wielded a knife and ordered everyone off of the streetcar. Witnesses would later say that he appeared to be unstable. Police officers surrounded the streetcar. Sammy Yatim, an 18-year-old with a history of mental illness, was subsequently shot nine times by Constable James Forcillo, a six-year member of the Toronto Police Service. A total of twenty-two police officers were present at the scene. Yatim was then Tasered prior to being taken to hospital where he was pronounced dead. The Ontario Special Investigations Unit assumed control of the investigation. Constable Forcillo was subsequently charged with second-degree murder and attempted murder. The case is expected to go to trial during 2015. See the Media Links at the end of the chapter: "Enhanced Video of Shooting of Sammy Yatim by Toronto Police" and "Watch: Former Police Officer Analyzes Streetcar Shooting Video."

© Rene Johnston/ZUMA Press/Corbis

Sammy Yatim's family leads a rally to protest his shooting death.

The shooting sparked outrage in the community and a review of police use-of-force practice. This incident prompted an external review of police use of force in the Toronto Police Service, with a specific focus on police encounters with the mentally ill. It also accelerated the debate over equipping police officers with body-worn cameras (BWCs).

Source: K.B. Carlson. (2013, August 19). Toronto police officer charged in Sammy Yatim shooting to turn himself in Tuesday. *The Globe and Mail.* Retrieved from http://www.theglobeandmail.com/news/toronto/ontario-police-watchdog-lays-second-degree-murder-charge-in-sammy-yatim-shooting/article13837354/

In some instances, patrol officers will make an effort to explain their actions following a situation that was witnessed and likely recorded by bystanders. As one patrol officer stated:

> I always make an effort to go to the public after a situation and explain, 'This is what happened, and this is why I did this.' A lot of times when you take the time to go to bystanders after and you explain what's happened, they understand and they change their perspective.

Talking to the public can absolutely help situations, even if sometimes people don't want to hear it. It diffuses the public's concerns."[36*]

This occurred in a case known as "Honest Cops." See Class/Group Discussion 7.2 at the end of this chapter.

Police Legitimacy and the Use of Force

In Chapter 1, the legitimacy of the police was identified as a key concept in the study of police work. High-profile incidents in which the police are perceived to have used excessive force, or in which subsequent investigations have determined that excessive force was used, can undermine the legitimacy of the police. The increased visibility of the police has increased public access to use-of-force incidents. With the pervasiveness of cellphone cameras, use-of-force incidents may be posted on Internet sites such as YouTube during or shortly after they occur.

One factor that has likely contributed to the precipitous drop in the public approval ratings of the police from the 80 percent range to 54 percent in 2010, are high-profile incidents involving the police use of force, including the death of Robert Dziekanski at Vancouver International Airport and the encounters between the police and citizens at the G20 summit in Toronto during the summer of 2010. Community members who feel that the police use force improperly may have less confidence in the police and may not cooperative with the police.[37]

The misuse of force can result in a community protesting against the police. See the Media Link "Protesting Police Brutality in Montreal," at the end of this chapter. This occurred in 2010 in Kelowna, British Columbia, following an incident (captured on video) in which an RCMP officer kicked in the head a suspect who was following a command to drop to the ground. The video, taken by a witness, shows the suspect on his hands and knees when the officer kicks him. The officer was subsequently charged with two counts of assault causing bodily harm in relation to that and a previous incident. In 2013, the officer pled guilty to the charge and was given a suspended sentence, plus 18 months of probation, a fine, and community service hours. He resigned from the RCMP. See the Media Links, "Kelowna RCMP Police Brutality" and "Justice For Buddy – Kelowna Police Brutality Update – May 2013" at the end of this chapter.

Police Powers and the Use of Force during Public Protests

In Chapter 1, it was noted that the police are often involved in policing protests, and in Chapter 4, it was noted that police officers may be required to respond to political protests and high-profile incidents that can place the police under scrutiny for the use of force in public disturbances and protests. Critics have argued that, increasingly, protests have been associated with criminality, giving the police license to violate rights and use force legitimately.[38]

---

*Muir, B. 2014. "Community Surveillance of Police-Citizen Encounters: Canadian Police Officers in YouTube," Unpublished Honour's Thesis. Burnaby, BC: School of Criminology, Simon Fraser University.

How police discretion is used and how the various police roles are prioritized will have an impact on the policing of political protests. Strict adherence to enforcing the law at a protest, for example, might involve mass arrests for minor offences. Such mass arrests will inevitably impact on police resources and might undermine the police service's capacity to undertake other police functions. Mass arrests might be perceived as provocative by an otherwise peaceful crowd, escalating conflict and leading to breaches of the peace that might threaten life and property.

A hard or uncompromising attitude to protests prioritizes enforcing the law regardless of the consequences for keeping the peace, whereas a more conciliatory style of policing a political protest generally prioritizes keeping the peace. When keeping the peace is prioritized, police will generally make arrests in a protest situation only when the offences are serious and, on balance, the risk to life and property in not making the arrest outweighs the risk to life and property associated with making the arrest. In democratic states, policing should comply with the law, be accountable and respect human rights.

In 2013, an Ontario judge criticized the Ontario Provincial Police for refusing to enforce his judicial order to dismantle an Aboriginal blockade of a rail line. The judge stated, "We seem to be drifting into dangerous waters...when courts cannot predict with any certainly whether police agencies will assist in enforcing court injunctions against demonstrators who will not voluntarily cease unlawful activities."[39]

The approach that police take to a particular protest or protest movement is likely to have a profound impact on the way the activists and the cause they represent are publicly perceived, as well as the practical outcomes of the protest and the welfare of individuals involved. One of the fundamental differences between liberal democracies and more totalitarian societies is that liberal democracies are more tolerant of dissent and protests. Totalitarian regimes, on the other hand, treat all dissent and protest as criminal. In totalitarian or authoritarian states, the police display a consistently repressive and frequently violent approach toward dissent and protests.

The actions of Toronto Police Service officers in responding to protestors during the G20 summit in 2010 highlighted issues related to police powers and excessive force (see Box 7.8).

Deadly Encounters: The Police Use of Lethal Force

Canadian police rarely use lethal force—only ten times a year, on average. In comparison, roughly three hundred Americans are shot and killed by the police every year. The circumstances in which American and Canadian officers use lethal force are similar; however, American police are involved more often in situations where the perceived threat to officer safety is high.[40]

Fatal shootings by police fall into three categories: (1) a serious criminal offence is being committed; (2) the shooting was a mistake; and (3) the victim precipitated the shooting. In the majority of police shootings that resulted in fatalities, the deceased had just committed a serious criminal offence.

victim-precipitated homicides
incidents in which the victim acts in a manner calculated to provoke the use of deadly force on the part of the police

Some incidents are **victim-precipitated homicides** (also known as "suicide by cop"), which often involve despondent individuals who are suffering from suicidal tendencies, mental illness, or extreme substance abuse; they then act in a manner calculated to force police to use lethal force.[41]

Box 7.8

The G20 Protest in Toronto, 2010

During the summer of 2010, world leaders gathered in Toronto for the G20 summit to discuss a variety of global issues. This was followed by a meeting of the G8 nations outside of the city. These summits ignited large protest demonstrations that resulted in Toronto police arresting over a thousand persons, the largest mass arrest in Canadian history.

Following the incident, the Office of the Independent Police Review Directors (OIPRD) received over 400 complaints against the police from citizens, including persons who were not involved in the protests but were, nevertheless, stopped and searched by police officers. The complaints included allegations of excessive use of force and unlawful arrest and unlawful detention.

An inquiry into police actions during the protests, conducted by the Ontario ombudsman, focused on the enactment of a regulation under the Public Works Protection Act that designated a large area not protected by a security fence as "public works," expanding the powers of the police to arbitrarily arrest and detain persons. Many of those persons who were stopped, questioned, and searched by the police were not involved in the protests and, like the protestors, were unaware of the regulation. Many people were arrested who were in the vicinity of the security fence. The report concluded that this regulation, which was designed to control the protestors, infringed on individual freedoms and "was likely unconstitutional" (Marin, p. 5).

A protester stands in front of a group of riot police during protests over the G20 summit in downtown Toronto, June 2010.

For one perspective on the police and the G20 protests, view the documentary films "Under Occupation: Toronto G20 Operation"; "EXPOSED G20: Toronto Police Provocateurs in Video and Photos"; and "G20 Re-Exposed: Toronto Inquiry Now," listed in the Media Links at the end of this chapter.

Source: A. Marin. (2010). *Investigation into the Ministry of Community Safety and Correctional Services' conduct in relation to Ontario Regulation 233/10 under the Public Works Protection Act: "Caught in the act."* Toronto: Ombudsman of Ontario. Retrieved from http://www.ombudsman.on.ca/Files/sitemedia/Documents/Investigations/SORT%20Investigations/g20final1-en.pdf

The Lethal Force Incident

In most cases, the officers involved in a shooting responded to the perceived threat in an automatic manner, based on their training in dealing with life-threatening situations. In most cases as well, the encounter developed into a lethally violent situation within seconds. In one study, Canadian criminologist Rick Parent interviewed police officers and offenders who had been involved in incidents where suspects had shot at the police. These case studies provide unique insights into the perspectives of each party to the incident. One such case is presented in Police File 7.2.

Critical Incident Stress and the Police Shooting

The risks associated with using force are high: for the individual police officer, injury or even death are possible consequences of every confrontation. Besides the physical risks, police who use force may be subject to internal discipline as well as civil or even criminal liability for their actions (or inactions). Add to this the stress and mental anguish that often accompany a physical confrontation.

critical incident stress
the physiological, psychological, physical, and emotional rections that may occur in an individual who has been involved in a traumatic incident (e.g., patrol officers involved in a fatal shooting)

Police officers involved in a fatal shooting may experience physical and psychological reactions associated with **critical incident stress**. The physical effects include loss of appetite, changes in sleeping pattern, and a marked decrease in sex drive. The psychological effects include depression, guilt, nightmares, flashbacks, fear, and a heightened sense of danger. Police officers involved in shooting incidents that did *not* result in the death of an individual may also experience critical incident stress. Recall the discussion of occupational stresses and PTSD in Chapter 5.

Police services have developed debriefing programs for officers involved in shooting incidents and other traumatic events. These programs may involve mental health professionals and approaches that are designed to assist the officers to address post-traumatic stress reactions. The effectiveness of these

Police File 7.2

In Their Own Words: A Police Officer and a Suspect Describe a Police Shooting Incident

Background to the Incident

In a western Canadian city during the summer, at about 8:00 p.m., two uniformed police officers on bike patrol noticed two suspicious individuals near a small shopping area. While the officers were checking the two individuals, one male suddenly ran away. One of the officers immediately began a foot chase. The officer caught up to the fleeing individual, who produced a handgun. Shooting over his shoulder, the subject again began to run from the officer. Firing six rounds as he ran down the street, near a crowded sidewalk, the suspect gained distance from the officer.

The suspect then disappeared around the corner into the courtyard of an apartment complex. Suddenly, the pursuing officer found himself looking down the barrel of a 25-calibre semi-automatic handgun. The suspect, less than three feet away, aimed the gun at the officer's head and pulled the trigger, clicking on an empty chamber. Fortunately, the gun was out of bullets. Unaware of this, the pursuing officer and his partner both discharged their firearms, wounding the suspect.

Police later found two balaclavas and a knife in a nearby vehicle that was being operated by the suspects. It was believed that the two suspects had intended to commit a robbery when they were checked by the bicycle patrol. In explaining how the incident unfolded, the pursuing officer stated:

> My partner and myself were on bicycle patrol ... The weather was nice; there was a beautiful sunset. We had ridden up to a strip mall where a Mac's Milk was located [in the eastern part of the city]. As we are riding, we see these two suspicious guys hanging around the strip mall so we ride up to these two guys. We begin to check them and run their names [to see if there are any outstanding warrants]. I am dealing with this guy's friend and I checked his name. I knew something was off as he didn't have any ID and his information didn't match. I knew he was lying, something wasn't right. So I asked him his zodiac sign and he didn't know it.
>
> We were three to four feet away from them, checking their names, when this guy burst off and ran across the street. I ran after him and caught up with him. I was able to reach out and give him one shot in the side of the face. He then started to reach towards his waist and I saw him grab something. He started yelling "Stay back! Stay back!" while swearing at me. He then started shooting over his shoulder, with his handgun, as he began to run away. I could see all the pedestrians on the street so I decided to hold fire. People are just scattering as this is happening.
>
> I then yelled out to my partner, "Where did he go? Where did he go?" I thought he went inside this apartment complex. I thought he was in the courtyard of the complex. However, as I came around the corner, I could see this peripheral silver object pointed towards my head. I fired a couple of shots and my partner fired a few shots. That's when we then heard him crying "I'm hit! I'm hit!" I think he also got hit from fragments from our rounds. Then, after he was on the ground, he gave us his real name and said he was an escapee from prison.
>
> The first time I fired my gun was when he was tucked behind the brick wall of the apartment building. Even though it was dry [i.e., there were no bullets in the chamber], he had the gun pointed at my head. To take flight from a police officer is one thing, but to try to kill a police officer is another thing!
>
> When it went to trial, he received a fourteen-year sentence. I've never ever talked to him about what happened that night or seen him since the trial.

In reflecting on the incident, the officer stated:

> After we fired the rounds, I felt a rush through my body and I started having the shakes. Then I was crying right away. Off and on again I began crying. I called my wife right away and talked to her.
>
> I like what I'm doing now. However, from the time that that incident happened until now I could leave the job ... for anything. As a result of this incident, policing is now the fourth or fifth thing in my life. I've

prioritized my life, and policing is a lot lower than it was before this incident happened. To have someone dry fire at your head ... it's a terrible experience.

I wish it had never happened. Sure I got a Chief Constable's award, and later I was honoured at our Honours night, but ... those things really don't mean anything. I wish I had never checked him, I wish that we had just carried on and never seen him. It's just not worth it.

The biggest thing I've learned from this is the priorities in your life. I have a wife and two kids and right after that night, policing dropped right down in my priorities of life. If I could find a comparable job right now that paid the same amount of money, I'd be gone.

The Offender's Perspective

During the interview, the inmate spoke calmly and mechanically about the incident. Ten years earlier, he had been convicted of armed robbery in Halifax. The Nova Scotia courts had imposed a lifetime ban on the possession of firearms by the subject. At the time of the police shooting, the subject was considered "unlawfully at large" from a work release program at a minimum-security prison on the West Coast. He talked about the shooting incident that had resulted in his imprisonment:

I went to the ___ Hotel and bought a .25 calibre handgun. I bought the gun for fifty dollars, a .25 calibre with six rounds. I was flipping it. Bought the gun thirty hours before the incident, and I had plans to sell it for three hundred dollars. I wasn't on any cocaine that night, just drinking Coca-Cola at the pub.

I could have shot the f--ker [police officer] in the head but I didn't—I could have killed him. I didn't want to hurt nobody—I never have hurt anyone in my life. What happened is that I was in the area of ___ and ___ when these two guys [police officers] on bikes see buddy and me and decide to check us.

One cop asks for identification and gets him, my buddy, to call a friend, to verify who we are. I'm out on a work release but packing this handgun on my right side. Then this cop says that he is gonna detain me until he finds out who I am. He checked my name and my buddy's name but it didn't come through. While we were waiting, we started a good conversation with the white guy cop, talking about the pussy in the area.

Suddenly, I ran, I took off running. This cop wants to play supercop, he begins chasing me, and I threw a plastic bottle of pop at him to break his stride. However, he caught me and punched me in the right side of the face. That's when I could have shot him but I didn't.

We both fell down and when I got back up I pulled the gun out ... He was about ten feet away. I aimed it over to the right and said "Stay away, I don't want to hurt anyone." I then took off running again. As I was running, I fired my gun over my shoulder (at the police officer). I also fired the gun from behind a car. I didn't want to hit the cop. I just wanted to scare him so I could get the fuck away.

Once he came around the corner he started firing his gun—"I'm hit, I'm hit!" I went down. When he fired his gun, it went into slow motion—I saw the muzzle face. The whole thing took only ten seconds, max, but it seemed like ten minutes. I was hit, I felt a burning. As I hit the ground I threw my handgun away.

In reflecting on the incident, the inmate stated:

> I'm glad I never shot him. I just wanted to scare him. I was hoping he would have hit the ground and waited for cover. Then I could have run off and ditched my gun. Instead he comes after me—who would believe a cop would run after a guy who's shooting at him!
>
> As a result of the incident I got twelve years for attempted murder and two years for possession of a handgun. It was a stupid incident, ten minutes either way and it would never have happened. It was the first time that I'd been shot at or had shot at someone.

Source: R.B. Parent, "Aspects of Police Use of Deadly Force In North America—The Phenomenon of Victim-Precipitated Homicide," PhD diss., School of Criminology, Simon Fraser University, Burnaby, 2004. Reprinted by permission of Rick Parent.

interventions has been questioned, and there is research evidence to suggest that these programs have no long-term preventative effect on either the post-traumatic stress symptoms or long-term physical health. And for some officers, the debriefings may exacerbate the symptoms.[42]

Police officers involved in shooting incidents may be more resilient than once thought. One study found that few officers suffered long-term negative effects following a shooting incident. Also, the attitudes of officers after the incident were strongly influenced by the personality of the officer, and the attitudes of family, friends, and police investigators.[43] The level of organizational support received and support of family were major factors in the levels of stress experienced.[44] Research on the responses to traumatic events by paramedics and firefighters suggests that individual personality traits play a significant role in how officers respond to, and are affected by, a shooting incident.[45]

Summary

This chapter has discussed police powers and the use of force. It highlights, once again, the challenges that the police face in ensuring public safety while protecting the rights of citizens. The Charter of Rights and Freedoms and court cases have played a significant role in defining the powers of the police, although the parameters of police powers are continually being defined. The powers of the police with respect to detention and arrest and search and seizure were discussed, and several of the more significant court cases in these areas were presented. Entrapment, an abuse of police powers, was examined, and it was noted that for this to be successfully used as a defence, Canadian courts require there to have been a clear abuse of process. The legal provisions for the use of force were discussed, as were the components of the National Use of

Force model. The Taser is a less-lethal force option that has been surrounded by controversy. It was also noted that police officers rarely use force, and there are specific factors related to the levels of force used in encounter situations. Special attention was given to the use of force with persons with mental illness and also to how the inappropriate use of force can undermine the legitimacy of the police. Public and political protests present challenges to the police to ensure that the appropriate levels of force are used. The chapter concluded with an examination of police use of lethal force, highlighted by the perspectives of a police officer and a suspect who were involved in a lethal force incident.

KEY POINTS REVIEW

1. There are tensions between the power and authority of the police and their legal mandate to maintain order, and the values and processes that exist in a democratic society.
2. The Canadian Charter of Rights and Freedoms and court decisions have had a significant impact on the legal powers of the police.
3. Among the key powers of the police are the ones to arrest and detain, to search and seize, and to use force.
4. Entrapment involves an abuse of police powers but is rarely accepted as a defence by Canadian courts.
5. The use of force, including lethal force, is governed by both law and policy.
6. The National Use of Force Model provides the framework for training police officers and provides an objective framework for analyzing use-of-force situations.
7. Five distinct force options are available to police officers.
8. The Taser is a less-lethal force option that has been surrounded by controversy.
9. Police officers rarely use force, and there are a number of factors that are associated with the use of force.
10. The inappropriate use of force can undermine the legitimacy of the police.
11. There are concerns surrounding the use of force by police officers in encounters with mentally ill persons, although these encounters most often end peacefully.
12. Incidents in which lethal force is used can result in critical incident stress for the officers involved.

KEY TERM QUESTIONS

1. What role do an **arrest warrant** and the laying of an **information** play in the police powers of arrest?
2. In what situations is a **search warrant** required, and in what circumstances can a search be conducted without a search warrant?
3. Briefly describe the **force options model**.

4. Discuss what is meant by **demonstrated threat**, and note the five levels of resistance to the police that may be presented by individuals.
5. What is the **one-plus-one** use-of-force standard in policing?
6. What is a **less-lethal (or lower lethality) force option**, and what types of less-lethal compliance tools are available to police?
7. Define and describe the phenomenon of **victim-precipitated homicides** ("suicide by cop").
8. Describe the impacts of **critical incident stress** on police officers.

CRITICAL THINKING EXERCISES

Critical Thinking Exercise 7.1. *R. v. Mann.* A Case of Detainment, Search, and Seizure

As two police officers approached the scene of a reported break and enter, they observed M, who matched the description of the suspect, walking casually along the sidewalk. They stopped him. M identified himself and complied with a pat-down search of his person for concealed weapons. During the search, one officer felt a soft object in M's pocket. He reached into the pocket and found a small plastic bag containing marijuana. He also found a number of small plastic baggies in another pocket. M was arrested and charged with possession of marijuana for the purpose of trafficking.

At trial, the judge found that the search of M's pocket contravened Section 8 of the Canadian Charter of Rights and Freedoms in that, while the police officer was justified in his search of M for security reasons, there was no basis to infer that it was reasonable to look inside M's pocket for security reasons. The evidence was excluded under Section 24(2) of the Charter, as its admission would interfere with the fairness of the trial, and the accused was acquitted. The Court of Appeal, however, set aside the acquittal and ordered a new trial, finding that the detention and the pat-down were authorized by law and were reasonable in the circumstances.

The Supreme Court of Canada subsequently decided that the appeal should be allowed and the acquittal restored. The Court found that the police officers had reasonable grounds to detain M for investigative purposes and to conduct a protective search, but no reasonable basis for reaching into M's pocket. This more intrusive part of the search was an unreasonable violation of M's reasonable expectation of privacy in respect of the contents of his pockets.

Your Thoughts?

1. Do you agree with the decision of the Supreme Court in this case? Explain.
2. Does this decision place too many restrictions on the powers of the police? Explain.
3. What if the officers had found a handgun rather than marijuana?

Source: *R. v. Mann*, 2004, 3 SCR 59.

CLASS/GROUP DISCUSSION EXERCISES

Class/Group Discussion 7.1. The Robert Wright Case: Should the Officer Have Been Charged with Assault?

Read the media reports on the case involving the assault of Robert Wright by RCMP officers in Terrace, B.C., and watch the video (see the Media Link below titled "Violent Takedown by Police Caught on Prison Cell Video in Terrace"). Then discuss the following:

1. Do you think that the actions taken toward Mr. Wright constituted an assault as defined in the Criminal Code, Section 265, which states "(1) A person commits an assault when (*a*) without the consent of another person, he applies force intentionally to that other person, directly or indirectly)"?
2. Should the Crown have followed the recommendations of the investigation by the municipal police officers?

Class/Group Discussion 7.2. A Police Officer Explains

View the video "Honest Cops" on YouTube (https://www.youtube.com/watch?v=wxRbYm8eF28) and then address the following:

1. Describe the dynamic of this situation.
2. Discuss the actions of the bystanders.
3. Discuss the actions of the police officers during and following the incident.
4. Do you think that the officer explaining his behaviour sets a bad precedent?

MEDIA LINKS

Visit www.nelson.com/canadianpolicework4 for links to these videos and other additional content available with this text.

"Under Fire: Were Moncton RCMP officers ready for the call?" Global News, March 26, 2015, globalnews.ca

"Violent takedown by police caught on prison cell video in Terrace," by Tiffany Crawford, *The Vancouver Sun*, October 4, 2014, vancouversun.com

"When police kill: The story of five families," *Toronto Star*, October 14, 2013, thestar.com

"SIU called in after man shot dead by police outside Scarborough bank," 680 News, April 26, 2013, 680news.com

"Inquest hears 911 call that preceded fatal police shooting," CBC News, October 21, 2013, cbcnews.ca

"Reyal Jardine-Douglas sat quietly before officer boarded bus," CBC News, October 22, 2013, cbcnews.ca

“Sylvia Klibingaitis told 911 operator ‘I’m pure evil,’” CBC News, October 30, 2013, cbcnews.ca

“Police shootings inquest: Video shows knife-wielding woman chase officer,” by Laura Kane, *Toronto Star*, November 1, 2013, thestar.com

“Enhanced video - Shooting of Sammy Yatim by Toronto Police,” TheEditPlayer, July 28, 2013, youtube.com

“Watch: Former police officer analyzes streetcar shooting video,” by James Armstrong, Global News, July 30, 2013, globalnews.ca

“Protesting Police Brutality in Montreal,” VICE Media, n.d., vice.com

“Kelowna RCMP Police Brutality,” David Barkes, January 7, 2011, youtube.com

“Justice For Buddy – Kelowna Police Brutality Update – May 2013,” Radio Free Canada, May 3, 2013, youtube.com

“Under Occupation: Toronto G20 Operation,” LibertyDefender84, December 13, 2010, youtube.com

“EXPOSED! G20 Toronto Police Agent Provocateurs in Video and Photos,” DoctorEsperanza, June 29, 2010, youtube.com

“G20 RE-EXPOSED: Toronto Inquiry Now,” SupportLocalScene, January 27, 2011, youtube.com

8 Policing in the Community

LEARNING OBJECTIVES

After reading this chapter, you should be able to:

- **Discuss the principles and effectiveness of the professional model of police work**
- **Define and discuss the principles of community policing and community-based strategic policing**
- **Compare and contrast the professional model of police work and community-based strategic policing**
- **Describe the core elements of community-based strategic policing**
- **Describe how increasing concerns with security and risk may be undermining community policing**
- **Describe several key concepts in the discussion of the police and the community**
- **Describe public attitudes, images, and expectations of the police**
- **Discuss the impact of community policing on the community**
- **Describe the issues surrounding policing diverse communities**
- **Discuss the rhetoric and the reality of implementing community-based strategic policing**

THE PROFESSIONAL MODEL OF POLICING

Even after the creation of formal police services in Canada, policing remained closely tied to communities; police officers patrolled communities on foot and were responsible for a variety of tasks. With the introduction of mobile patrol cars and radio communications systems in the 1920s and 1930s, a **professional model of policing** emerged that was based on the three Rs: random patrol, rapid response, and reactive investigation.

professional model of policing
a model of police work that is reactive, incident-driven, and centred on random patrol

The central premise of random patrol, also known as the *watch system*, is that the mere presence and visibility of patrol cars serves as a deterrent to crime and at the same time makes citizens feel safer. During a typical shift, patrol officers respond to calls and spend the rest of their time patrolling randomly, waiting for the next call for service. In this model of policing, any information that is gathered by the police is limited to specific situations and does not include an analysis of the problems that precipitate crime and social disorder. Little attention is given to proactive police interventions designed to prevent crime and to address the underlying causes of crime in communities. In this model of policing, there is no, or limited, use of analytics to inform police policy and operations.

In the early 1970s, questions were being raised about the effectiveness of random mobile patrol in preventing and reducing crime. In a landmark study known as the **Kansas City Preventive Patrol Experiment**, fifteen areas of that city were divided into three groups: (1) reactive beats, in which police did not engage in preventative patrol and officers were instructed to respond only to calls for service; (2) control beats, in which routine preventative patrol was maintained at the usual level of one car per beat; and (3) proactive beats, in which routine preventative patrol was intensified to two or three times the usual levels.[1]

Kansas City Preventive Patrol Experiment
a study of the effectiveness of random mobile patrol, which found no impact on reported crime, victimization, fear of crime, or citizen satisfaction with the police

The results of the experiment suggested that neither doubling patrol coverage nor eliminating it has any significant impact on reported crime, actual victimizations, fear of crime, or citizen satisfaction with the police. As well, random preventative patrol does not help reduce crime and disorder, nor does it facilitate the development of partnerships with the community.

This lack of impact is due in part to the fact that many of the incidents to which the police respond are only symptoms of larger problems in the community. In fact, it is *how* police resources are allocated and deployed that makes a difference. If the police respond only when they are called and deal only with the incident at hand, the reasons *why* the incident occurred in the first place remain unaddressed, and this increases the likelihood that similar incidents will happen again. As well, in this model of policing, there is little, if any, collaboration with the community or with other agencies.

Research studies have found that, with the exception of specific targeted strategies, levels of crime are generally unaffected by increases in the number of patrol cars, quicker response times by patrol officers, or the number of arrests made by patrol officers. Police File 8.1 sets out some key findings with respect to the effectiveness of the professional model of police work.

COMMUNITY POLICING IN THE TWENTY-FIRST CENTURY

The 1980s witnessed the re-emergence of an approach to policing that focused on the community. The emergence of community policing was

Police File 8.1

The Effectiveness of the Professional Model of Police Work

Question: Does an increase in random police patrols have an impact on crime levels?

Answer: Probably not. While studies attempting to assess this dimension of police crime prevention have many methodological problems, research generally has recorded no appreciable impact from an increase in random patrol.

Q: Are police response times related to reduced crime levels?

A: Not likely. Reduced response times seem to have little impact on crime rates. However, it is possible that quick police response to serious crimes and emergencies can increase the likelihood that the offender will be apprehended, that crime scene evidence will be preserved, and that information will be gathered from witnesses and complainants. Rapid response may also protect lives and reduce the risk of serious injury to crime victims. Police services whose response times to serious incidents approach the best-practice benchmark of seven minutes may also enjoy higher levels of legitimacy in the eyes of the public (see below, and Chapter 6).

Q: Is there a relationship between the number of arrests the police make and the crime rate? In other words, do reactive arrests serve as a general deterrent to crime?

A: No. Reactive police arrests do not serve as a general deterrent to criminal activity. The exception may be in communities of fewer than ten thousand residents, but even here the research findings are inconsistent.

Q: Does any relationship exist between the reactive arrest of specific individuals and the crime rate? In other words, are reactive arrests a specific deterrent to crime?

A: Generally not, with a few possible exceptions. For many individuals, arrest increases subsequent reoffending. Unemployed people who are arrested tend to reoffend, whereas for employed people, arrest seems to act as a deterrent.

Source: "Preventing Crime: What Works, What Doesn't, What's Promising." Published by the National Institute of Justice, US Department of Justice, 1997.

precipitated in part by the recognition that the police cannot prevent and respond to crime on their own; they require the assistance of a variety of agencies and organizations as well as community residents. This is reflected in the comments of a chief constable, in response to the question: "How has your policing philosophy changed over the years?" For his response, see Police Perspective 8.1.

In a back-to-the-future move, the tenets of community reflect Peel's principles that were set out in the early 1800s (see Box 2.1, p. 29). These principles highlighted the importance of the police being connected to, rather than apart from, the community and accountable to the community.

Police Perspective 8.1

A Chief Constable Responds to the Question: "How Has Your Policing Philosophy Changed Over the Years?"

When I started 30 years ago, it was all about putting assholes in jail. It took me about five years to realize that the swinging gate is not a success story. You need the enforcement to keep the community safe, but you have to have a number of other strategies. I call the drug treatment centres the greatest crime prevention tool ever built. Every time I put someone in the treatment centre for 90 days, you're taking them off the street and the four crimes a day that they are committing. That's 360 less victims. You have to think differently than when I started in policing. So, that strategy for me has changed.

For policing overall, the strategy that has changed is the expectation we have for community engagement. I expect every officer and employee to belong to something. I have fourteen hundred employees right now who are volunteering somewhere, for something. I don't think that expectation was on me when I became a police officer. Maybe to coach a hockey team. But I have board members on both our missions, the Shepherds of Good Hope, our food bank, the Boys and Girls Club, Big Brothers and Big Sisters. I could go on. There is not an organization in this city that I don't have one or two of my people sitting on the board of directors. That wasn't originally an expectation of policing but now it's an expectation that your job doesn't end when you leave the office.

Source: Personal communication with the author, June 2011.

As a concept, community policing has the following features:[2]

1. **It is an organizational strategy and philosophy.** Community policing is based on the idea that the police and the community must work together as equal partners in order to identify, prioritize, and solve problems such as crime, drugs, fear of crime, social and physical disorder, and overall neighbourhood decay. The goal is to improve the overall quality of life in the area.
2. **It requires a department-wide commitment.** The philosophy of community policing requires all personnel in the police service—civilians and sworn members—to balance the need to maintain an effective police response to incidents of crime with the goal of exploring proactive initiatives aimed at solving problems before they arise or escalate.
3. **It requires a change in how the performance of the police is measured.** Traditionally, performance has been measured by a number of crime control/enforcement criteria, including crime rates and clearance rates. Additional measures are required to assess the performance of police services in other areas.
4. **It rests on decentralizing and personalizing police services.** Decentralization gives line officers the opportunity, freedom, and mandate to focus on community building as well as community-based problem

solving, so each and every neighbourhood can become a better place in which to live and work.

In summary, community policing involves much more than introducing new programs to a community: it requires substantial changes in how police services are organized and delivered, an expansion of the roles and responsibilities of officers, and the development of new ways to measure police performance. See the Media Link, "Saskatoon Canada Police Service – Restructure and Redeployment," at the end of this chapter.

community policing
a philosophy of policing centred on police–community partnerships and problem solving

Community policing can thus be defined as a philosophy, a management style, and an organizational strategy centred on police–community partnerships and problem solving to address the conditions that contribute to crime, social disorder, and fear of crime in communities.

The differences between community policing and the professional model of police work with respect to relationships with the community are outlined in Figure 8.1.

The Principles of Community Policing

three Ps
prevention, problem solving, and partnership—the basis of community policing

Community policing is based on the **three Ps**: prevention, problem solving, and partnership (with the community). The basic idea is that the police and the community constitute a partnership that brings together the resources and talents of each to identify and solve problems. The key principles of community policing include the following:[3]

- Citizens are responsible for becoming actively involved in identifying and responding to problems in their neighbourhoods and communities.
- The community is a source of operational information and crime-control knowledge for the police.
- Police are more directly accountable to the community.
- Police have a proactive and preventative role in the community that goes beyond traditional law enforcement.
- The cultural and gender mix of a police agency should reflect the community it serves.
- The operational structure of the police agency should facilitate broad consultation on strategic and policing issues.
- To gain the confidence and trust of the community, the police must establish and maintain their legitimacy through proactive initiatives and the fair treatment of residents.

Community policing focuses on crime and social disorder through the delivery of police services that include aspects of traditional law enforcement, as well as prevention, problem solving, and partnerships. The community policing model balances reactive responses to calls for service with proactive problem solving centred on the causes of crime and disorder.

Researchers have found that community policing can increase the job satisfaction of police officers, as well as their productivity and their commitment to the organization. It can also improve relations with co-workers. In addition, officers develop more positive attitudes toward community residents and become more knowledgeable about the communities they police.

Figure 8.1. Police–Community Relations, Community Partnership versus Justice Process

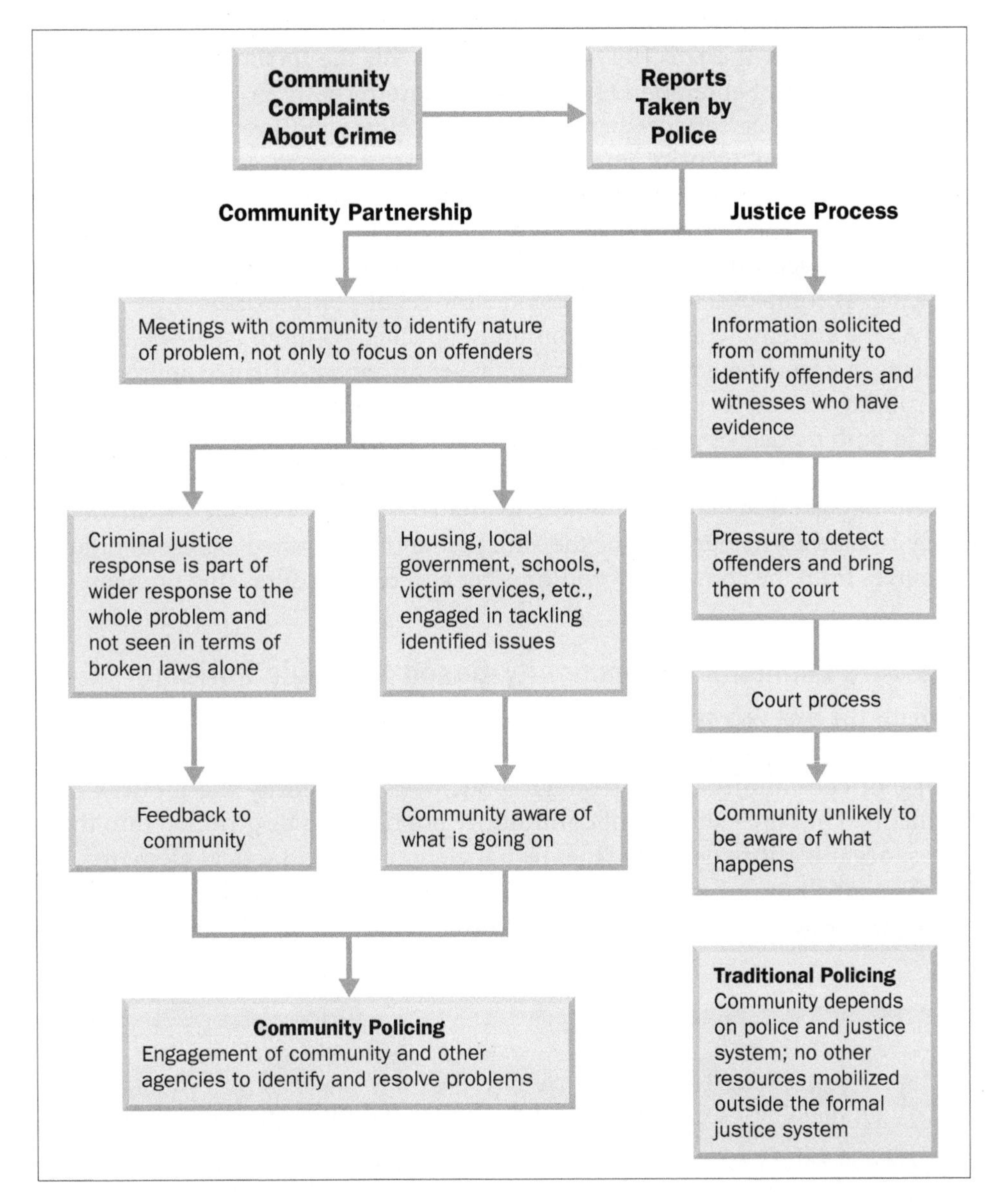

Source: C.G. Nicholl, "Community Policing, Community Justice, and Restorative Justice: Exploring the Links for the Delivery of a Balanced Approach to Public Safety" (Washington: Office of Community Oriented Policing Services, U.S. Department of Justice, 1999), 50, http://www.cops.usdoj/gov/files/ric/Publications/e09990014_web.pdf.

COMMUNITY-BASED STRATEGIC POLICING

A new model of policing has emerged in the early twenty-first century—a post–community policing model that incorporates the key principles of community policing while at the same time including a focus on security and crime response and crime attack strategies and a continuing emphasis on crime prevention. All of these approaches are discussed below.

community-based strategic policing
a model of police work that incorporates the key principles of community policing with crime prevention, crime response, and crime attack approaches

This model has been labelled **community-based strategic policing**, the title capturing the importance of community engagement and of police services being strategic in their policies and operations.[4]

Beginning in the late 1990s, accelerating with the terrorist attacks on the United States on September 11, 2001, and more recently in Canada, the U.S., and Europe, police services have been facing increasing pressure to focus on public safety and security and to be more proactive in addressing specific threats. At the same time, they are expected to continue strengthening ties with other agencies and with the communities they serve.

Table 8.1 sets out several of the key attributes of community-based strategic policing, as compared to the professional model of police work.

As the current iteration of community policing, community-based strategic policing incorporates a number of proactive, enforcement-oriented approaches in the context of strategic partnerships involving the police and the community. Note that in both models of police work, patrol officers are often reactive—responding to calls from citizens. A major difference is how the officers *approach* the calls to which they are dispatched: an officer with a community policing orientation is likely to take a broader view of the situation and, if required, access additional resources from the community and/or other agencies to address the problem.

organizational elements (of community policing)
how a police service is structured to implement community policing

external elements (of community policing)
police–community partnerships that enhance community policing and increase police legitimacy, visibility, and accessibility

tactical elements (of community policing)
the enforcement, prevention, and problem-solving strategies of a police service

The Core Elements of Community-Based Strategic Policing

Perhaps the best way to capture the wide range of organizational, operational, and community partnership activities that are now included under the general rubric of community-based strategic policing is to identify the model's core elements. The core elements of community policing can be grouped into three areas: **organizational elements**, **external elements**, and **tactical elements**.[5]

The attributes of each of these core elements and examples of the police strategies associated with each element are summarized in Table 8.2.

TABLE 8.1
Comparison of the Professional and Community-Based Strategic Models of Police Work

	Professional Model	Community-Based Strategic Policing
Administrative approach (locus of control)	Centralized/hierarchical	Decentralized with strong management and organizational support
Authority	Statute	Community/statute
Community role	Report violations of the law; passive	Strategic partnerships, formalized by protocols and agreements, which integrate into police operations
Operational focus	Crime and disorder	Crime and disorder; national security; quality of life; fear of crime and disorder
Operational strategies	Random patrol; reactive investigation; rapid response	Targeted/directed patrol focused on "hot spots"; strategic partnerships; integrated service delivery; intelligence-led policing; ongoing evaluation; problem-based deployment of personnel

TABLE 8.2
The Core Elements, Attributes, and Strategies of Community-Based Strategic Policing

Core Element	Attributes	Strategies
Organizational	Community policing philosophy adopted organization-wide and reflected in mission/vision/core value statements, policies, procedures, and operations Decentralized decision making; patrol officers given the discretion to solve problems and to make operational decisions Fixed geographic accountability; the majority of staffing, command, deployment, and tactical decisions are geographically based; personnel assigned to fixed geographic areas for extended periods of time Use of volunteers and active encouragement for citizens to become involved in police-sponsored initiatives and activities Use of technology and analytical capacities to facilitate information generation and effective allocation of departmental resources	Community police stations and storefronts Zone/turf/team policing Evidence-based policing Recruitment and deployment of volunteers Organizational reform
External	Public involvement and community partnerships Partnerships with governments and other agencies	Police partnerships with key community stakeholders Private-sector initiatives
Tactical	Enforcement of law Proactive crime prevention problem solving	Crime prevention Problem-oriented policing Intelligence-led policing/CompStat Zero-tolerance policing Quality-of-life policing Integrated service teams Neighbourhood service teams Crime attack strategies Community service approaches

Source: Adapted from G. Fisher-Stewart. (2007). *Community policing explained: A guide for local governments.* Washington, DC: U.S. Department of Justice. Retrieved from http://www.cops.usdoj.gov/pdf/vets-to-cops/cp_explained.pdf

THE CONCERN WITH SECURITY AND RISK: UNDERMINING COMMUNITY POLICING?

Concerns have been expressed that the core principles of community policing are being compromised by the increased focus on risk and security.[6]

Canadian police scholar Chris Murphy has argued that there has been a "securitization" of community policing, in the sense that community policing is increasingly being used as a security strategy. Under this approach, the community is viewed as "a strategic resource, a source of security information and intelligence."[7] In Murphy's view, this trend is undermining the local origins of community policing and is posing challenges for police and communities. Specifically, how are police to "balance the tensions between state security and local policing needs, between individual and collective rights, and community collaboration and the problematic nature of 'community' in a security context"?[8] This further highlights the tensions surrounding policing in a democratic society (see Chapter 1). See Critical Thinking Exercise 8.1 at the end of this chapter.

In recent years, a number of persons have been convicted of plotting to commit terrorist acts. The increasing concern with terrorist attacks and the threat of "homegrown terrorists" have resulted in an expansion of police powers. This has been driven in large measure by the increasing concerns with the risk of terrorism and "homegrown" extremists who may pose a threat. To date, however, there is very little information on how effective the security-oriented initiatives of police services are in countering the threat to public safety.

This trend has been accompanied by an increase in the number of specialty units operated by police services and the rise of the "warrior cop" (discussed in Chapter 2), as well as legislation expanding the powers of the police (see Chapter 7). A concern is that the trend toward securitization will accelerate.

THE POLICE AND THE COMMUNITY

The ability of the police to perform their duties depends upon public approval of their actions.

—Sir Robert Peel

The community was a focal point of Peel's principles and remains an important component of policing. There are a number of key points that must be considered in any discussion of the relationship between the police and the community. These include the following.

Police Legitimacy

Recall from Chapter 1 that a key concept in policing in the early 21st century is that of police legitimacy. The legitimacy of the police is "a measure of the extent to which the public trust and have confidence in the police, are willing to defer to the law and to police authority, and believe that police actions are morally justified and appropriate. . . . Police legitimacy is difficult to quantify and is less amenable to statistical analysis. It is not a public relations program, an initiative, or a set of policies. Legitimacy is a criterion by which every police department is judged every day."[9] Police scholar Craig Fischer has stated: "At the core of community policing is the premise that effective policing is a result of strong and positive relationships between officers and the people they serve."[10]

Achieving legitimacy is a challenge for a police service and requires continued attention. It is difficult to attain and easy to lose. Police services in which officers engage in biased policing, are involved in critical incidents, use excessive force, or are viewed as not being engaged with the community may suffer a loss of legitimacy. This, in turn, may render the police service less effective and efficient in its efforts. Conversely, a police service that is well-connected to the community, has open lines of communication and information sharing with stakeholders, and is transparent in its operations will have a higher level of legitimacy in the minds of the general public.

Police Presence

Extensive police research has established the importance of police visibility as a major factor in the public's feelings of safety and security, attitudes toward the police, and in crime prevention and deterrence. It is also closely associated with the legitimacy of the police and is a key component of what has become known as "reassurance" policing.

A recent report noted: "Previous research indicates that one of the most successful ways of increasing perceived police effectiveness is by improving the visibility of (and so familiarity with) the police foot patrols and problem solving in and with the community."[11] The report also found from an analysis of the British Crime Survey a relationship between police visibility and public confidence in the police.[12] A major consequence of the community being under-policed in relation to its size and diversity or the deployment of patrol officers in the absence of an analytically informed framework is that police officers are often not visible. This is another important dimension of policing that is not readily quantifiable, yet which is essential for effective policing.

Canadian police services operate a variety of facilities designed to increase police visibility in the community as well as to provide access to the general public. These include community police centres and storefronts, which are staffed largely by civilian employees and volunteers. These sites provide a locale for community residents to file complaints and report information on individual and community problems; they also serve as information and referral sources. Several police services also operate fully functional "mini" police stations staffed by sworn and civilian personnel. The officers assigned to a community police station are responsible for a defined territory and conduct patrol and investigative operations from these stations.

Few studies have been conducted about the impact of community police centres, and the ones that have been done have not been encouraging. There is no evidence that these centres help reduce levels of crime and social disorder. Nor is there any indication that these centres have been a catalyst for sustainable police–community partnerships. It may be more productive for these centres to focus on specific activities, such as problem solving, or to explore alternative strategies for developing police–community partnerships.

Community Engagement

A core component of policing in the early 21st century is **community engagement.** These are strategies used by the police service to facilitate citizen and community involvement in efforts to prevent and respond to crime and disorder. Police services utilize a variety of strategies to enhance community engagement. These include widely advertising strategies and plans in a variety of languages in communities with diversity; partnering with ethnic and cultural groups in the community to co-sponsor events; actively recruiting volunteers to reflect the diversity of the community; and seeking to recruit officers that

community engagement
police strategies that facilitate the involvement of citizens and communities in initiatives to address crime and social disorder

have the language skills to effectively communicate with persons who have limited English- or French-language abilities and/or are ELLs (English language learners).

Police scholars have noted: "Research indicates that community engagement can help create stronger communities by supporting the development of informal social controls, improving police–community relations and making police work more effective."[13] It has also been noted that in order to successfully engage the community requires the police to "undergo significant organizational, procedural and cultural change."[14] This requires the police service to be adaptable and to have the capacity to engage in a process of continuous improvement. It also suggests that police policies and strategies must be adapted to the needs of the community in which services are being delivered. For example, it has been stated: "Community engagement . . . needs to be flexible and tailored to meet the needs of different types of environments, not a 'one size fits all' or 'best practice' approach that fails to reflect local situations."[15]

The police can be effective only to the extent that they establish and sustain partnerships with the community. A key feature of community policing is networking with community groups and organizations as well as with the private sector and other government agencies at the municipal, provincial, and federal levels. The police must also develop strategies to involve more marginalized community residents on a permanent basis. Otherwise, these residents may feel that police interventions are targeting them, and may develop a sense that the police are intruding on their neighbourhoods. In many provinces, there are policing standards that mandate police services to consult with communities.

Police–community partnerships may have more general objectives, such as improving the quality of life in the community, or they may be directed toward issues in specific neighbourhoods, such as problem premises, street-level drug trafficking, or traffic problems. In some circumstances, as Murphy has cautioned, these relationships can also be used to gather intelligence on groups and individuals suspected of plotting to carry out terrorist attacks.[16]

Police services must also find ways to determine community priorities and to solicit feedback from community residents (including complainants and victims) regarding their experiences and satisfaction with the police.

Research studies have found that "soft policing" (e.g., community-based strategic policing, collaborative police–community relationships, and police involvement in neighbourhoods) can be effective in preventing and reducing levels of crime and disorder. Soft policing requires officers to have at least 30 percent of proactive time, which is the best-practices standard.

Communication

To be effective, police services must have the capacity to effectively communicate with local government and with community residents. This includes providing a process by which the community can have ongoing input into police plans and priorities as well as receiving timely information about crime and disorder in their neighbourhoods. Having community input enables the police "to assess if the time and effort is worthwhile and if future investment would be well spent."[17]

Police–Community Partnerships

A review of individual police service websites reveals a myriad of partnerships designed to strengthen police–community relations, enhance efforts to address problems of crime and disorder, and improve the overall quality of life in communities.

Most police services have created structures to facilitate the development of police–community partnerships and ongoing communication. The Toronto Police Service, for example, has established Community Consultative Committees (CCCs) with the city's Aboriginal, black, Asian, French, gendered, Muslim, and South and West Asian communities.[18]

The Ottawa Police Service is involved in a variety of community partnerships throughout the city, including the following:

- *Somali Youth Basketball League (SYBL).* This is a volunteer, not-for-profit basketball league intended to provide a safe environment for Somali youth, where they can develop life and leadership skills and benefit from positive role models.
- *Police Youth Centre.* This centre provides a wide range of counselling services, sports and recreation programs, and leadership programs for children and youth between 6 and 19 years of age. As well, the centre works with parents and parents' groups to address the challenges faced by youth in the community.
- *Street Ambassador Program.* In this program, volunteers, who wear shirts and name tags identifying themselves as ambassadors, serve as front-line resources for tourists in the ByWard Market area and work with community organizations. (http://www.ottawapolice.ca).

Courtesy of Ottawa Police Service.

An Ottawa Police Service officer at a community event

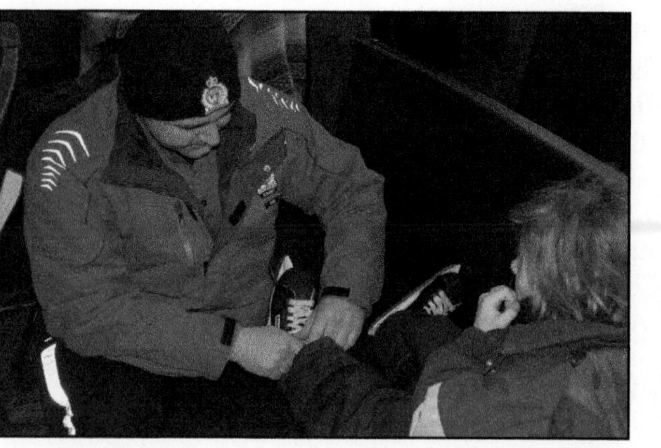
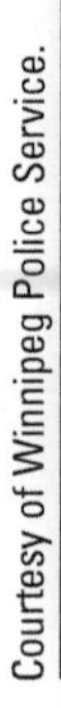
Courtesy of Winnipeg Police Service.

Winnipeg Police Service's Skates & Badges program for underprivileged children

One question is whether police services have overcommitted in developing these partnerships. A review of the Winnipeg Police Service (WPS), for example, found that the WPS had relationships with ninety-seven different agencies and organizations in Winnipeg. Some of these were required by legislation, others by policy, and others were established as part of the WPS outreach into the community. While some of the arrangements required contact on an annual basis, others were weekly or monthly. This placed an immense strain on the resources of the WPS.[19]

Police services have tried various other approaches to connecting with community organizations and residents. The Edmonton Police Service, for example, has neighbourhood empowerment teams (NETs) that operate in at-risk neighbourhoods. The NETs focus on (1) developing community partnerships and community capacities to prevent and respond to crime and social disorder, and (2) improving social development in communities. NETs operate storefront offices to provide a police presence in the communities. There is strong support for the program among community residents, and the program has resulted in improved attitudes toward the police, especially among minority groups. The impact on crime rates is less conclusive, although the NET program has improved the quality of life in the communities in which it operates.[20]

In addition, police services and officers across the country involve themselves in a wide range of charitable events. These events raise money for important causes, besides allowing officers to contribute to the community and to meet community residents in a non–law enforcement capacity. Among the more high-profile initiatives is Cops for Cancer, which involves a wide range of fundraising activities—for example, officers that allow their heads to be shaved for donations, and multi-day cycling events, during which officers stop in communities to raise funds for cancer research.

Community Consultation

The causes of crime and disorder in any community are varied and complex. It is unrealistic to expect that the police alone—or even the police acting in concert with dedicated community residents—can reduce or eliminate all of society's problems. This requires that police services partner with the community and other agencies and organizations, rather than going it alone as was the case under the professional model of police work.

For community policing to be successful, residents must be involved in the identification of problems of crime and disorder and in creating solutions to these problems. When solutions are developed by police and imposed on the community, they generally fail. The strategies that are most likely to be effective in improving confidence are those initiatives that are aimed at increasing community engagement. This includes contacts with residents and businesses through foot patrol, responding to requests for service in a professional manner, and effectively communicating information on police initiatives.[21]

The idea is for citizens to network within their communities and to assume ownership of problem-solving strategies. This requires an understanding of the factors that affect public perceptions of the police, as well as the strategies that can be utilized to develop, and sustain, police–community partnerships.

Community consultation can take a number of forms. Police–community meetings provide a forum where the problems and concerns of community residents can be identified and strategies can be developed for addressing them. However, community meetings are generally not effective in mobilizing residents and in raising confidence in the police. These meetings are often attended by only a few members of the community, including persons representing specific interests. At-risk groups and visible minorities are less likely to attend.

Community consultation committees (often called community–police liaison committees) are another strategy taken by police services to develop partnerships with the community. For example, the Toronto Police Service has liaison committees for every police division in the city. These committees include community residents and police representatives, who work together to identify and prioritize local issues and to develop solutions. These committees play an especially important role in fostering positive relationships with diverse groups in the community, including visible minorities and the LGBT.

The RCMP uses the Annual Performance Plan (APP) as a way to secure community input into policing plans and priorities at the individual detachment level. The APP is completed on a yearly basis by the detachment commander and includes information on (1) the detachment, (2) community consultation and infrastructure, (3) risk and protective factors, (4) community issues, and (5) the detachment work plan. These documents provide a running record of the initiatives that have been taken in the community and feedback from community residents.

WHAT DOES THE PUBLIC THINK ABOUT THE POLICE?

Measuring the Community's Level of Support

There are a variety of methods that are used to gauge community satisfaction with the police. Some of the more common strategies for gathering information from the community are set out in Table 8.3, along with the method used to gather the information and the challenges posed by the strategy. See Class/Group Discussion 8.1 at the end of this chapter.

For an example of a community survey, review the Community Survey administered by the Waterloo Regional Police Service; see the Media Link at the end of this chapter.

The Levels of Public Confidence in the Police

Canadians have traditionally given the police high approval ratings—in the 80 percent range—much higher than their justice system counterparts, which consistently score less than 50 percent (the National Parole Board's approval ratings

TABLE 8.3
Strategies for Gathering Information from the Community

Strategy	Method/Challenges
Community surveys	Administered by mail, by telephone, or online Questions about perceptions of crime, feelings of personal safety, victimization, satisfaction with police service Expensive; responses are of limited value Don't target high-risk/vulnerable/high–police contact groups (e.g., youth/young adults, visible/cultural minorities) Most respondents have no contact with police Limited information on police activities/outcomes Limitations of fixed choice surveys
Contact surveys	Can produce useful information Target persons who have had contact with police including victims, witnesses, and accused

Community consultation	Community "open mike" meetings generally of limited value
	  Dominated by special-interest groups
	  Generally exclude at-risk and vulnerable groups
	  May be a "legitimizer" for police
	Focus groups are a cost-effective and efficient way to gather information from communities
	  Can be tailored to specific groups and vulnerable groups
	  Provide an opportunity for community involvement in assessing police performance and identifying areas of concern
	  Opportunity to probe citizen perspectives

hover in the 4 percent range). After a period of decline in public trust between 2003 and 2011 (from 73 to 57 percent),[22] public trust is on the uptick.[23] Despite the controversy that surrounded the actions of the Toronto Police Service (TPS) during the G20 protests (discussed in Chapter 7) and the ongoing debate over "carding" by TPS officers, a survey conducted in 2014 found that Torontonians, on average, rated the TPS 7.0/10 (on a scale of 1 to 10), second only to garbage collection (7.2/10). This was a higher rating than recreation facilities (6.9/10) and public transportation (6.0/10).[24]

Research studies have generally found that persons who come into contact with the police want to be treated fairly and with respect, and that a single negative encounter with a police officer can have a significant impact on their attitudes toward the police.[25]

Similar to the notion of police legitimacy, public trust in the police is difficult to gain, but very easy to lose. One high-profile police incident can have a wide impact on the public's view of the police. It is likely that a number of high-profile incidents, including the tasering death of Robert Dziekanski at the Vancouver International Airport in 2007, the response of the Toronto Police Service to protestors during the G20 Summit in Toronto in 2010, and the shooting death of Sammy Yatim in Toronto in 2012 (all discussed in Chapter 7), contributed to a decline in public trust.

Certain segments of the community, including persons who are visible minorities or Aboriginal, may hold less positive views of the police.[26] This may be due to experiences with the police and/or concerns that the police are engaged in biased policing and racial profiling.

Less positive citizen views of the police may be due, in part, to unrealistic expectations on the part of the general public. Citizens in communities that are disordered tend to express lower levels of confidence in the police, reflecting the perception that the police are held at least partially accountable for the disorder and crime.[27] Of all the agencies in the criminal justice system, community residents tend to hold the police most responsible for neighbourhood disorder.[28] There is an expectation that police services will engage in proactive, preventative policing, as well as reactive, enforcement-related activities.[29] See Critical Thinking Exercise 8.2 at the end of this chapter.

These expectations may be exacerbated by the increased downloading onto the police of activities that are the responsibility of other agencies. Recall that downloading was identified in Chapter 1 as a key trend in Canadian policing. As well, the increasing demands on police services, combined with the fiscal challenges, have contributed to the demise of full-service policing. The reduced ability of the police to respond to all of the demands of a community or neighbourhood may lead to frustration as well as to residents "taking the law into their own hands."

On the flip side, the inability of the police alone to address issues in the community can also be a catalyst for the development of police–community partnerships, where community residents become more involved in addressing issues relating to crime prevention and the neighbourhood quality of life, instead of relying solely on the police.

WHAT'S THE ROLE OF THE "COMMUNITY" IN COMMUNITY POLICING?

Most discussions and research studies on community policing have focused on only one part of the police–community equation: the police. Little attention has been paid to the role and responsibilities of community residents in developing and implementing community policing. This lack of attention raises a number of problems, especially in terms of the *community* part of community policing.

First, it is one thing to declare that communities are actively responsible for participating in partnerships with the police, and quite another thing to bring this about. Who is responsible for ensuring that communities become involved? The police? The community? Municipal and provincial governments?

Second, while the term *community* arises quite often, the *who* and *what* of the community is rarely specified. Too often it is assumed that all of the community's residents have a common interest and live in the same neighbourhood. Little consideration is given to the opportunities and obstacles that are presented by culturally and economically diverse communities in which there are many different neighbourhoods. The boundaries of policing districts have long been established by the police alone, rather than by the police in consultation with community residents. Often these boundaries are arbitrary and are drawn to meet organizational rather than community needs. Needless to say, community residents may define the boundaries of their neighbourhoods quite differently from the way the police organization does.

Third, it is important to consider both the *level* of participation in a community and the *distribution* of that participation.[30] In any community policing initiative, some parts of the community may be underrepresented; at the same time, members of certain community interest groups—for example, business owners—may be overrepresented relative to those of lower socio-economic status.

Most often, community participants are heavily middle class. The research on citizen involvement in neighbourhood crime prevention efforts indicates that volunteers tend to have higher incomes and more education; they also tend to own their own homes and to have lived in the area for a longer time.[31] Communities that are plagued with high rates of crime and social disorder may have less capacity to mobilize and sustain involvement in crime prevention initiatives with the police. This may be particularly difficult in rural and remote communities where the available pool of interested persons may be small. Ironically, the residents who are most likely to be policed are the same ones who are the least likely to have access to the police, to affect police policy and practice, and to participate in police–community initiatives.[32]

Finally, here is a question to consider: What is the community supposed to do? Community residents may not understand clearly the principles of community policing and may, like police officers, equate it with crime prevention. Where community committees do exist, their roles and responsibilities are often not clearly defined, or they may focus on only one issue.

A key question, and one that has generally remained unaddressed in discussions of community policing, is this: Does the community *want* to become involved in police–community partnerships? Community residents may reject involvement in such partnerships for various reasons: apathy; fear of retaliation from the criminal element; hostility toward and distrust of the police; a lack of understanding as to what their role in these initiatives would be; and the diversity of needs among community residents. Furthermore, there is considerable variability among neighbourhoods in terms of their amenability to forming partnerships with the police and in terms of the resources the area can bring to efforts to address crime and disorder.

An example that illustrates the challenges of securing community involvement in policing occurred in 2014 when the Toronto Police Services Board began the process of considering a successor to a retiring chief constable. A private company was hired to hold community meetings in the city to solicit input from residents about a new chief. The meetings each attracted about ten persons, which hardly qualifies as "community consultation."[33]

Once they understand that there are different types of neighbourhoods, with different capacities and levels of interest among the residents, police services can tailor their approaches to developing police–community partnerships according to neighbourhood conditions. Unfortunately, there is in Canada a paucity of best-practice materials on this topic. See Class/Group Discussion 8.2 at the end of this chapter.

Community Volunteers

Citizen volunteers serve in a wide range of capacities—for example, they staff storefronts, victim services units, and community policing committees; they participate in special police–community projects; they conduct citizen patrols, thus serving as extra "eyes and ears" for the police; and they serve as police auxiliary constables. Volunteers help the police develop partnerships with the community and are a means for the community to take ownership of problems. They are a continual source of new energy and fresh ideas, and finally, they help reduce the workload on patrol officers. Police services generally offer a range of training programs for volunteers and have developed strategies for recruiting and retaining volunteers. In the recruiting process, police services are looking for applicants with volunteer experience, be that at a community police office, as a coach in youth sports, or in other capacities. This is a preferred qualification (see Chapter 5) and indicates that the applicant is contributing to the community.

THE IMPACT OF COMMUNITY POLICING ON THE COMMUNITY

A review of the extensive research in the United States (there are few Canadian studies) tells us that it is possible for police services to adopt the principles of community policing; that community policing strategies may increase the legitimacy of the police in the community; and that such strategies may help the police and the community identify and target specific issues relating to crime and disorder.[34]

Police File 8.2 summarizes some of what is known about the community and community policing.

The strategies that a police service develops to implement community policing vary among communities, as a function of the demands made on the police and the community's interest in and capacity for involvement. The strategies that a community employs to become an equal partner in preventing and responding to crime and disorder depend on the personal and fiscal resources it can commit to the endeavour, as well as on the levels of interest that exist among different segments of the community. How to implement community policing, how to measure whether it is a success, and how to determine which initiatives the police and the community must take—these are all questions that need to be asked and answered. But we know that those answers must be arrived at on a community-by-community basis, and that they must reflect the needs of the community in question and the outcomes of the dialogue between the police and community residents.

POLICING DIVERSE COMMUNITIES

The challenges and opportunities of policing diverse communities is a major theme of this text. Recall from Chapter 1 that Canada has a rich cultural diversity that includes visible/cultural/religious minorities, newcomers (recently arrived immigrants in Canada), Indigenous peoples, and a diversity of sexual orientation. This diversity presents challenges and opportunities for Canadian police services in the areas of recruitment and training, police–community engagement, police strategies, and police–community relationships.

Police File 8.2

Citizen Perceptions and Levels of Satisfaction

Public opinion surveys and field research studies have found the following:

- There is strong support for increased visibility and accessibility of the police.
- Foot patrols are favoured by community residents.
- Residents who have informal contacts with the police hold more favourable opinions of the police than those who have formal contact with the police, although there is no evidence that it reduces the number of complaints against the police.
- Residents who feel safe in their neighbourhoods and who have a positive feeling toward their community hold a higher opinion of the police.
- Community policing increases police legitimacy.
- Community policing has the potential to reduce fear of crime in communities.

Levels of Knowledge and Participation

- Community residents, even those who have been the victims of crime, tend not to become involved in community policing initiatives.
- Many citizens have little knowledge or understanding of the role and activities of community policing initiatives such as community police stations.
- Community residents have positive views of community police stations, but rarely use them.
- Police services have experienced considerable difficulty in generating and sustaining community interest and involvement in community policing initiatives.

Many new immigrants ("newcomers"), for example, have arrived from countries where the criminal justice system and the police are to be feared. It is understandable that these persons may be reluctant to call the police for help, or to provide eyewitness information. It has been found that the experiences that people have with the justice system in their country of origin influences their perceptions of the police and whether they will rely on the police to assist them in a time of need. This increases the importance of the officers in a police service reflecting, to the greatest extent possible, the composition of the community being policed, as well as for the police service to have a strategic plan to implement and sustain outreach programs to the newcomer community. See the Media Link, "A Guide to the Police Service in London," at the end of this chapter for an example of an initiative by a police service to reach out to newcomer communities.

In the absence of adequate training and initiatives for improving police/community relations and facilitating community engagement, the potential is high for misunderstandings, mutual suspicion, and distrust between police officers and residents. The inability of police officers to speak a second language can hinder the development of police–community partnerships, and can contribute to misunderstandings that can have serious consequences.

The Police and the LGBT Communities

Historically, the relationship between the police and the LGBT communities were characterized by conflict and mistrust. Police officers were generally drawn from the working classes and held conservative, inflexible attitudes toward non-heterosexual persons, views that were reinforced by a "macho" police culture. Recall from the discussion in Chapter 2 that historically the police have been involved in policing morality in enforcing laws that prohibited consensual homosexual conduct. This led to police raids on gay clubs, cinemas, and bathhouses and the arrests of patrons in these facilities.[35] The high-profile raids of gay bathhouses by Toronto police in the early 1980s prompted legal action and the beginning of a change in police attitudes and behaviour, as well as changes in legislation.

Officers were often unsympathetic to gay victims, and police services were slow to respond to crimes that were hate-motivated crimes. The members of these communities were often reluctant to report victimization, which was compounded by the attitudes of the investigation officers. The most common experience with the police was negative, and there is often the perception that police services are not aware of the issues in the LGBT communities.[36]

Canadian police services have made efforts to improve relationships with the LGBT communities and, at the same time, increase awareness through training programs for officers. Today, it is not uncommon for chief constables to walk in Gay Pride parades and for police services to engage with the LGBT communities on a variety of issues. The Windsor Police Service, in collaboration with the advocacy group Equality for Gays and Lesbians Everywhere (EGALE), implemented a mandatory training program (the first of its kind in Canada) for its officers and staff, designed to building awareness of homophobic violence and to facilitate the development of positive relationships with the LGBT communities. The Ottawa Police Service (OPS) has a liaison committee for the LGBT communities. The committee facilitates contact between the OPS and these communities, and advocates for issues of mutual interest.[37] See the Media Link, "Andre Goh – Building the Asian LGBT Community," at the end of this chapter.

The RCMP has produced a video featuring 20 LGBT officers directed toward "building a bridge of understanding for youth undergoing similar experiences" and "sharing the eventual joy of knowing that life, indeed, does get better." See the Media Link, "It Gets Better," at the end of this chapter.

Courtesy of Toronto Police Service.

Poster against homophobic violence, sponsored by the Toronto Police Service and a community coalition

There has also been an increased focus by police services on hate crimes committed against persons, which are defined as a criminal offence committed against a person or property that is "motivated by bias, prejudice or hate, based on race, national or ethnic origin, language, colour, religion, sex, age, mental or physical disability, sexual orientation, or any other similar factor" (Criminal Code, Section 718.2(a)(i); see also Criminal Code, Sections 318/319). The Toronto Police Service has a Hate Crime Unit as well as hate crime coordinators who are located in each police division and who are responsible for investigating hate crime occurrences.

The Police and Aboriginals

It was noted earlier that the generally high levels of public support for and confidence in the police may not be shared by some Aboriginal communities. Nearly 4 percent of Canadians are Aboriginal people. This figure includes Status and non-Status people, Métis, and Inuit. Aboriginal people are unevenly distributed across the country; figures range from 60 percent in the Northwest Territories, to 20 percent in Yukon, to 6 percent in Saskatchewan and Manitoba, to 3 percent in Alberta and British Columbia. While it is often assumed that Aboriginal people reside primarily in rural and northern areas of the country, census figures indicate that the number of Aboriginal people living in urban areas has been increasing and is now estimated to be 50 percent of the Aboriginal population. Unbeknownst to most Canadians, for example, the City of Ottawa has the largest population of Inuit of any "southern" Canadian city.

A disproportionate number of Aboriginal persons reside in low-income neighbourhoods; Aboriginal families are likely to be single-parent; and urban Aboriginals are more likely to experience domestic violence than urban non-Aboriginals. Residing in disadvantaged neighbourhoods with high crime rates may contribute to increased encounters with the police and higher arrest rates.[38]

A survey of Aboriginals, Métis, and Inuit living off-reserve found that a majority of respondents stated that they had personally experienced racism and discrimination from businesses, employers, and the police, among others.[39] There is the perception among many Aboriginal persons that non-Aboriginals have negative stereotypes of them (e.g., addiction, laziness, poverty). (Recall similar comments from Black youth in Chapter 6.)

For a variety of historical and contemporary reasons, Aboriginal peoples may have little confidence in the criminal justice system.[40] A study of community perceptions of the Regina Police Service (RPS), for example, found that among First Nations and Métis respondents, the overall levels of trust and confidence in the RPS were lower (at a statistically significant level) than for non-Aboriginal persons in the survey sample. Aboriginal respondents also rated the RPS lower on overall quality and level of satisfaction with the RPS (statistically significant). The reasons *why* there were lower levels of satisfaction among the First Nations and Métis respondents were not explored in the study.[41]

These findings suggest that even in a community where there is a high level of trust and confidence in the police, these perceptions may not extend to certain groups of residents. This requires a police service to develop strategies to address perceptions and to create a higher level of confidence and trust among special populations, including First Nations and Métis.

As part of an overall community policing strategy, and to address these issues, many police services have partnered with Aboriginal organizations. The Aboriginal and Diversity Relations Unit in the Winnipeg Police Service, for example, has developed relationships with Aboriginal organizations, including the Southern Chiefs, the Treaty Relations Commission of Manitoba, and community-based Aboriginal groups. WPS officers also attend the Indian-Métis Friendship Centre in support of programs offered for youth, and the WPS sponsors an annual Aboriginal Youth Careers Camp. The RCMP has a full-time officer working in the Friendship Centre as well as with the Assembly of Manitoba Chiefs.

Courtesy of Philippe Morin.

RCMP officers in First Nations' communities become involved in community activities to foster relationships.

An inspector in the WPS describes the efforts of the police service to break down the barriers that have traditionally existed between the police and the Aboriginal community in the city in Police Perspective 8.2.

The Toronto Police Service has established an Aboriginal Peacekeeping Unit composed of Aboriginal police officers. The unit is involved in a variety of activities designed to foster trust and understanding between the police and the Aboriginal community. This program includes an Aboriginal Youth Mentoring Program in which officers serve as role models for youth, liaise with Aboriginal social services and organizations in the city, and help with efforts to increase the numbers of Aboriginal police officers in the TPS.[42] The RCMP operates an Aboriginal Policing Program that has been successful in improving the delivery of policing services to Aboriginal communities.

There are instances in which tragic events involving Aboriginals and the police have led to significant reforms, as in the case of Raymond Silverfox in Box 8.1.

Police Perspective 8.2

A Police Inspector Comments on the Police and Aboriginal Peoples

The social issues and the history of the Aboriginal people in this country have created a situation where they don't trust the police. Unfortunately, a lot of their experiences with the police are of the police taking their dad away or arresting their mum or taking them to CFS [Child and Family Services]. So, we're trying to have our members understand the Aboriginal perspective as well as for Aboriginals to understand our perspective on things. It's all about building that relationship and putting a little bit of humanness to what you do.

Source: Griffiths, C.T. and N. Pollard. 2013. *Policing in Winnipeg. An Operational Review*. Ottawa: Canadian Police Association. http://www.curtgriffiths.com.

Box 8.1

A Death in Custody: The Case of Raymond Silverfox

On December 2, 2008, an RCMP police constable picked up Raymond Silverfox at the Salvation Army shelter in Whitehorse in the early morning hours and transported him to the RCMP detachment. Mr. Silverfox was placed in the drunk tank, where, over the next 16 hours, he continually vomited (at least 23 times) and soiled himself, until he died. At one point during this time, when Silverfox asked for a mat to sleep on, one constable stated, "Yeah, and you need a pizza too. Is there anything else I can get you?" Contrary to jail policy, only six personal checks were made on Silverfox during the time he was in the drunk tank. The required number was around 30. Nor was his cell cleaned at any point in time, contrary to jail policy. No calls were made to emergency medical personnel until it was too late.

The death of Raymond Silverfox prompted a review of the RCMP police in Yukon, including extensive consultations with communities and agencies. The review culminated in a report setting out a number of recommendations, including the creation of a Yukon Police Act, a police council, a police complaints process, and a variety of initiatives designed to improve police–community relations and community trust in the police, and to increase the skill sets of RCMP members posted to Yukon communities.

Sources: Commission of Public Complaints Against the RCMP. (2011). *Chair's final report after commissioner's notice: Chair-initiated complaint regarding the in-custody death of Mr. Raymond Silverfox.* Ottawa: Author. Retrieved from http://www.crcc-ccetp.gc.ca/en/chairs-final-report-after-commissioners-notice-chair-initiated-complaint-regarding-custody-death-mr; S. Arnold, P. Clark, and D. Cooley. (2011). *Sharing common ground: Review of Yukon's police force: Final report.* Whitehorse: Government of Yukon. Retrieved from http://www.policereview2010.gov.yk.ca/pdf/Sharing_Common_Ground_Final_Report.pdf.

IMPLEMENTING COMMUNITY-BASED STRATEGIC POLICING: RHETORIC VERSUS REALITY

Despite the emergence of community policing in the mid-1980s, and its evolution into community-based strategic policing, field research studies indicate that the professional model of police work is "alive and well" in many police services. The focus in these police services is on law enforcement and the generation of arrest statistics, and officers are provided with little incentive to become involved in proactive, problem-solving initiatives.[43]

A review of the strategic plan and annual report of many police services reveals a heavy focus on crime control and law enforcement. Performance measures for police services are still heavily weighted toward crime rates, clearance rates, and annual percentage reductions in specific types of crime. This is due to a number of factors, including growing concerns with public safety and security as well as pressure from the community for aggressive law enforcement approaches to crime and criminal organizations, such as drug traffickers.

Even these efforts may be less effective due to the absence of a robust analytical capacity in the police service.

Police organizations can face a number of obstacles in implementing community policing:

- *Resistance among line-level officers.* Police officers who do not believe in a community policing approach and/or those officers who subscribe to the principles of community policing are not provided with organizational support for community policing initiatives, which can hinder the quality of service delivery.[44] Some police officers are much more oriented toward community policing than others. Many police officers feel that community policing is nothing new and that it has always been standard police practice. This is often suggested by officers who work in smaller communities, where they have always pursued a no-call-too-small policy. Some officers remain committed to reactive, enforcement-oriented policing, even in the face of mounting evidence that this approach doesn't work. Other officers find themselves trapped in an endless cycle of calls for service from the public, which limits the time they can spend on proactive initiatives. In those police services that have designated officers to pursue community policing initiatives, there may be resentment on the part of other officers who are required to pick up the slack with respect to responding to calls for service.[45] There may also be differences between the community and the police with respect to the importance given to community-oriented policing programs, research studies suggesting that residents often assigned a higher priority to these types of programs than do officers.[46]
  Officers may struggle to carry out the priorities and plans developed by senior supervisors. In the absence of a clear framework for implementation, officers may view community policing as merely adding to their workload. While officers may contend that they don't have time to do community policing, recall from Chapter 6 that most calls for service are for order maintenance and service, rather than for law enforcement.[47] In the absence of "time and task" studies that examine how patrol officers spend their time, it is difficult to determine what officers are busy "doing." And even when the principles of community policing have been incorporated into mission and value statements as well as community development programs, the criteria for assessing officer performance may remain firmly grounded in the professional model of policing. Finally, in the absence of specific skill sets, officers may find it difficult to work directly with community residents in identifying and resolving problems, especially if they have been trained to do reactive, incident-driven police work.
- *Lack of participation by communities and neighbourhoods.* This may be a result of poor police–community relations, as characterized by mutual suspicion and distrust and by the fact that some neighbourhoods are more "amenable" to community policing than others. The likelihood of residents participating in police–community partnerships seems to increase with levels of confidence in the police and with police legitimacy in the community.[48]

- *Lack of planning and analytical capacities in the police service.* Many police services still have not developed the capacity to strategically plan, analyze, and evaluate their policies and practices on an ongoing basis. This makes it difficult for them to assess the outcomes of specific strategies and programs.
- *Failure to develop sustainable police–community partnerships.* This may be owing to a lack of police strategies to engage the community and to provide community residents and organizations with a substantive role in preventing and responding to crime and disorder. RCMP, SQ, and OPP detachments may face challenges in sustaining community-focused programs due to the frequent transfer of members.
- *Failure to identify the roles and responsibilities of communities and neighbourhoods.* It is largely unexplored just how communities and neighbourhoods can become involved in police–community partnerships, how community participation can be built and sustained, and how community performance can be assessed with regard to identifying and responding to crime and disorder. It should not be assumed that the same interventions will work in every area and in every situation: "The best practice for any community is one that fits their needs and conditions and is compatible with available resources."[49] The challenges of generating, and sustaining, community interest and involvement in community policing should not be underestimated.
- *Organizational features of police services.* Particular organizational features of specific police services can hinder the development and implementation of community policing strategies. Provisions in collective bargaining agreements (e.g., the requirement of two-officer patrol cars at certain times or as a ratio to one-officer cars) may limit the options of the senior managers when it comes to deploying officers. The transfer policy of the RCMP, the OPP, and the SQ, which results in officers being moved between detachments on a regular basis. This practice has always been at odds with the requirements of community policing, as patrol officers, supervisors, and senior officers may not remain in any one detachment long enough to develop an intimate knowledge of the communities and neighbourhoods they are policing and to create sustainable police–community partnerships. See Class/Group Discussion 8.3 at the end of this chapter.

Summary

The discussion in this chapter has explored the issues surrounding the delivery of policing services in communities. The professional model of policing that emerged following World War II was examined and contrasted with community policing, which developed in the 1980s and has now morphed into community-based strategic policing. The core elements of community-based strategic policing—internal, external, and tactical—were described. There is concern that increasing focus on security and risk, particularly related to terrorist threats, are undermining the core principles of community policing. A number of key concepts in the study of policing in the community were discussed, including the notions of police legitimacy and presence, community engagement and communication, police–community partnerships, and community consultation. The attributes toward and expectations of the police held by community residents were examined, and it was revealed that certain segments of the community may have less-than-favourable views of the police and that the public may have unrealistic expectations of the police. The role of the community in community policing was found to be complex; although citizens are supportive of police initiatives, most residents have little knowledge of the various programs and services, rarely access them, and do not participate in them. There are challenges and opportunities in policing diverse communities. The chapter concluded with a discussion of the gap that often exists between the rhetoric and the reality of community policing, and a number of reasons for the disconnect were identified.

KEY POINTS REVIEW

1. The professional model of police work, centred on random patrol, rapid response, and reactive investigation, is not effective in preventing and responding to crime and disorder in communities.
2. Community policing can be defined as a philosophy, management style, and organizational strategy centred on police–community partnerships and problem solving to address problems of crime and disorder in communities.
3. The current iteration of community policing is community-based strategic policing.
4. The core elements of community policing are organizational, external, and tactical.
5. The organizational elements of community policing are centred on how the police service itself is structured and the requirements of a community-policing police service.
6. The external elements of community policing involve the police service developing partnerships with the community and undertaking initiatives that increase police legitimacy, visibility, and accessibility.
7. The tactical elements of community policing involve enforcement, proactive crime prevention, and problem-solving approaches.
8. Key concepts in the study of the police and the community include police legitimacy, police presence, community engagement, communication, police–community partnerships, and consultation with the community.
9. Although the police have traditionally enjoyed high levels of public support, critical events can undermine public trust in the police.
10. Community residents may have unrealistic expectations of the police and this, in turn, may result in a loss of public confidence in the police.
11. There are a number of potential obstacles to the community becoming involved in partnerships with the police, including public apathy and disinterest and variations in neighbourhood capacities.
12. The overall impact of community policing on the community is positive, although many residents have little knowledge of police initiatives and programs and are rarely involved in them.

13. There are challenges and opportunities in the delivery of police services to diverse communities.
14. Attention must be given to the rhetoric versus the reality of community policing.

KEY TERM QUESTIONS

1. Describe the key features of the **professional model of policing**, including the three Rs, and then note the importance of the **Kansas City Preventive Patrol Experiment.**
2. Identify and discuss the philosophy and key principles of **community policing**, including the **three Ps** and the **community-based strategic policing** model of police work.
3. Discuss the core elements of community policing: **organizational elements, external elements**, and **tactical elements.**
4. What is **community engagement** and what role does it play in community policing?

CRITICAL THINKING EXERCISES

Critical Thinking Exercise 8.1. Security, Risk, and Community Policing

There are increasing concerns that the focus on security and risk is undermining the principles of community policing. Efforts to engage the community may be viewed by certain segments of the community—such as, Muslims in the case of concerns with terrorist threats—as overpolicing and biased policing. How is this issue best addressed?

Critical Thinking Exercise 8.2. Reconciling High Public Expectations of the Police with the Reality of Community Involvement

In the chapter discussion, it was stated: "There is an expectation that police services will engage in proactive, preventative policing, as well as reactive, enforcement-related activities." It was also noted that most community residents, particularly those in high-crime/disorder neighbourhoods (who may tend to blame the police for crime and disorder), are not involved in community policing initiatives. What is the way out of this dilemma?

CLASS/GROUP DISCUSSION EXERCISES

Class/Group Discussion 8.1. Measuring Levels of Support for the Police

Table 8.3 (p. 228) sets out the various strategies for gathering information from the community in an attempt to measure levels of support for the police. Consider each strategy and then (1) discuss how the limitations of each could be addressed, and (2) devise strategies that may more accurately gather information from the community. What are the challenges that might be encountered in gathering information from diverse communities?

Class/Group Discussion 8.2. The Community and Community Policing

In the discussion of the police and the community, it was noted that community residents often have little knowledge of police programs and initiatives, rarely access these programs, and often do not participate in them. What strategies could be devised to increase public awareness of, and involvement in, community policing initiatives?

Class/Group Discussion 8.3. Closing the Gap between the Rhetoric and Reality of Community Policing

There are a variety of factors that often create a disconnect between the pronouncements of a police service that it employs a community policing model and the reality of how the police service actually operates. How can this disconnect be addressed? Should there, for example, be national standards to which all police services must subscribe? In the U.K., the government conducts an annual review of police services and issues a report card on how well each police service is meeting a number of standardized goals and objectives. Would you support a similar protocol in Canada? Why or why not?

MEDIA LINKS

Visit www.nelson.com/canadianpolicework4 for links to these videos and other additional content available with this text.

"Saskatoon Canada Police Service – Restructure and Redeployment," WebsEdgeGovernment, October 17, 2013, youtube.com

"Community Survey 2014," Waterloo Regional Police Service, wrps.on.ca

"A Guide to Police Service in London," LM LIP, April 15, 2013, youtube.com

"Andre Goh – Building the Asian LGBT Community," OntHumanRights, August 9, 2013, youtube.com

"It Gets Better." Royal Canadian Mounted Police, youtube.com

9 Police Strategies

LEARNING OBJECTIVES

After reading this chapter, you should be able to:

- Identify and discuss primary, secondary, and tertiary crime prevention programs and their effectiveness
- Discuss the obstacles to effective crime prevention programs
- Discuss firearm amnesty programs and the D.A.R.E. program as examples of programs that may increase police legitimacy but not be effective
- Identify and discuss the various crime response strategies used by the police, including problem-solving policing, zero-tolerance policing, and the "broken windows" approach
- Identify and discuss the various crime attack strategies used by the police, including tactical-directed patrol and specific initiatives designed to target high-risk offenders
- Discuss the use and impact of foot patrols and bicycle patrols in crime response and crime prevention strategies
- Describe restorative justice and how the police are involved in the various restorative justice approaches
- Discuss the effectiveness of police crime response strategies
- Identify and discuss how technology is used to respond to and attack crime, including crime analysis, intelligence-led policing, and CompStat
- Discuss what the issues surrounding CompStat illustrate about how the police culture may influence the implementation and use of specific strategies

Police services employ a variety of strategies designed to prevent and respond to crime. These can generally be grouped into crime prevention, crime response, and crime attack strategies.

CRIME PREVENTION

The basic mission of the police is to prevent crime and disorder.

—Sir Robert Peel

Crime prevention programs are generally aimed at reducing crime, fostering community involvement in addressing crime, and strengthening citizens' perceptions of safety. Crime prevention initiatives can be categorized as (1) primary prevention programs, (2) secondary prevention programs, and (3) tertiary prevention programs. Police departments are most extensively involved in primary crime prevention programs, although they do participate in secondary and (to a lesser extent) tertiary crime prevention as well.

Crime prevention initiatives may be funded by governments, nongovernmental organizations (NGOs), and other community groups, as well as the private sector.

Primary Crime Prevention Programs

Primary crime prevention programs are the most common type of prevention program and are designed to alter the conditions that provide opportunities for criminal offences. Police services are involved in a wide variety of primary crime prevention programs. The ProAction program, for example, was created by a Toronto businessman to improve relationships between police and youth. It funds ProAction Cops & Kids programs in Toronto, Hamilton, and other urban municipalities, many of which focus on at-risk youth. Among the programs offered for at-risk youth are mountain biking, rock climbing, and a youth hockey league. The programs are led by police officers on a voluntary basis (https://www.copsandkids.ca/about-us). See the Media Link, "ProAction 20 Years of Bridging the Gap," at the end of this chapter.

primary crime prevention programs
prevention programs designed to alter the conditions that provide opportunities for criminal offences

See Police File 9.1 for a summary of several of the more high-profile initiatives and what research studies have found about their effectiveness. Note that, in this file, and in Police File 9.2 and Police File 9.3, for many of the strategies, the comments on effectiveness begins with "can" or includes the phrase "has the potential to," or "in some jurisdictions . . . ." This reflects the limitations of the research that has been conducted to date. Also, the majority of the research studies on police strategies have been conducted in urban environments. It is uncertain whether these strategies are effective in rural, remote, and northern communities. Police researchers have generally ignored these areas.[1] Finally, the majority of research studies have been conducted in other jurisdictions, most notably the U.S., the U.K., and Australia. Canada has traditionally not had a robust program of police research, the consequences of which are discussed in Chapter 11.

Police File 9.1

The Effectiveness of Selected Primary Crime Prevention Strategies

Program	Strategy	Effectiveness
Crime prevention through environmental design (CPTED)	Alter the physical environment of structures and places to reduce criminal opportunities (e.g., improved lighting). See the Media Link, "Crime Prevention Through Environmental Design," at the end of this chapter.	In some jurisdictions, altering the designs of buildings and pedestrian routes has helped to reduce levels of robberies, assaults, and residential break-and-enters. The application of CPTED principles in Glendale, Arizona, resulted in a significant decline in calls for service at convenience stores and reduced rates of theft.[2]
Closed-circuit television (CCTV)	Place cameras in business and/or residential areas to provide live images 24/7.	Pilot projects in Calgary and Toronto and cities in the U.S. and U.K. found that CCTVs are most effective when targeted at specific locales, such as drug-dealing spots and parking garages, and can assist in investigations.[3] They may be most effective in reducing levels of disorder and in providing evidence to assist police in apprehending perpetrators after a crime has been committed.[4]
Operation identification/ operation provident	Citizens and businesses mark their property with ID numbers to make it difficult to fence stolen goods and to assist in recovery by the police.	Impact on property crimes is uncertain. Identification programs do increase police–public interaction and citizens' awareness of police crime prevention activities. They may displace crime.
Neighbourhood watch	Organize residents to make them aware of strangers and criminal activities in their neighbourhood.	It is effective in reducing crime in some communities, although little is known about the factors that influence its effectiveness. Implementation most successful in low-crime, middle-class neighbourhoods.[5]
Citizen patrols	Create citizen foot and vehicle patrols under the supervision of the police.	American and European studies have found some reduction in crime levels and in citizen fear of crime. To date, there are no Canadian evaluations.
Media-based programs	Educate the public about crime and solicit public assistance in locating offenders (e.g., tip lines, Crime Stoppers), often for a monetary reward.	These programs can increase arrest rates, although with little impact on the overall crime rate. Do stimulate community involvement.[6]

Closed-circuit televisions (CCTVs) are perhaps the most controversial of the primary crime prevention programs. Although CCTV has been used extensively in Britain and the United States for many years, it is only recently that cameras have been installed in some Canadian municipalities. Critics have argued that while the expansion of surveillance cameras continues unabated and often in the absence of regulations, there are questions as to their effectiveness in deterring crime. From this perspective, the emergence of a "surveillance society" threatens the privacy and rights of citizens.[7]

While concerns over privacy have been expressed, Canadian society is well on the way to becoming a "surveillance" society. The movements and behaviour of citizens are recorded tens or perhaps hundreds of times per day as they move around the community. There are cameras on buses, in taxis, and in most private businesses, not to mention in every smartphone. See Class/Group Discussion 9.1 at the end of this chapter.

Secondary Crime Prevention Programs

Secondary crime prevention programs focus on areas that produce crime and other types of disorder. Some initiatives focus on identifying high-risk offenders and include analyses that target high-crime areas; others are designed to help vulnerable groups avoid becoming the victims of crime. See Police File 9.2 for a summary of selected secondary crime prevention programs.

secondary crime prevention programs
programs that focus on areas that produce crime and disorder

Examples of police-sponsored secondary crime prevention programs targeting at-risk youth include the following:

- *Camp Little Buffalo, Grand Prairie, Alberta RCMP Detachment.* This five-day leadership camp for at-risk youth between the ages of 11 and 13 is a collaborative effort of the RCMP, municipal agencies, not-for-profit

Police File 9.2

Selected Secondary Crime Prevention Programs

Program	Strategy	Effectiveness
Drug Abuse Resistance Education (D.A.R.E.) for youth	School-based program provides information to youth about the perils of drug use.	While the program generally has high levels of support among educators, parents, and youth, the program has no impact on student attitudes and beliefs about drugs or drug use.[8] There is some evidence that the program may improve youth attitudes toward the police, particularly among youth from minority groups.[9]
Crime prevention through social development (CPSD)	Collaborative efforts aim to reduce the risks faced by individuals, families, and communities (e.g., early intervention programs, programs to strengthen families), and to increase community capacities to prevent crime.	There is some evidence of effectiveness; the Better Beginnings, Better Futures program in Ontario reduced youth arrests and decreased grade repetitions, among other positive findings.[10] To be effective, the police, social agencies, and community groups must collaborate.[11]

(Continued)

Program	Strategy	Effectiveness
Programs for at-risk youth, such as summer camps and wilderness experience programs	Develop leadership and life skills in at-risk youth and increase positive police–youth interactions.	Few evaluations have been done. Programs may have a positive impact on youth attitudes and behaviour, but follow-up is required or results may fade over time.
Police school-liaison officer programs	Police officers are assigned to schools on a residential (full-time, in school) or non-residential (periodic officer visits) basis. Officers make class presentations and participate in school activities. Objectives are primary and secondary crime prevention.	Few evaluations have been done. Programs may increase the legitimacy of the police with students and have indirect benefits (e.g., identifying at-risk youth, providing intelligence to patrol and investigative units); no demonstrated impact on school safety or crime rates.[12] Programs may result in criminalization of disciplinary situations.
Positive youth development	This holistic strategy is based on crime prevention through social development, designed to build capacity in communities and in youth in order to improve the quality of life and decision making among youth, and to facilitate the development of positive attitudes and behaviour. Multi-agency (including the police) initiatives may be directed toward individual youth, families, and communities.	This strategy has the potential to significantly impact youth with low levels of competencies and to improve community capacities to assist at-risk youth.[13]
Crime reduction	This holistic, multi-agency approach involves the police, agencies, and NGOs. It is designed to prevent and deter crime; apprehend, prosecute, and treat offenders; and address citizens' fear of crime. It focuses on the people, places, and situations where criminal activity occurs.	It is effective in facilitating the development of police–community–agency partnerships. The absence of evaluations makes it difficult to determine program success and the factors that contribute to positive, and sustainable, outcomes.
Community mobilization	This strategy is designed to reduce crime and victimization, strengthen at-risk communities and families, and increase community wellness. It involves government agencies (health, education, social services, etc.), community groups, the police, and others working collaboratively to address larger social issues and the needs of at-risk families and individuals.	The Prince Albert, Saskatchewan, program (commonly known as "The HUB"), the first of its kind in Canada, resulted in fewer calls for police service, reduced rates of violent and property crime, and a decline in emergency room visits.[14] It is being implemented in other Canadian cities.

groups, and private businesses. Fiscal and goods-and-services donations are contributed by a wide range of businesses in Grand Prairie, including Costco and Safeway. The camp program, which is available free-of-charge to the youth participants, focuses on the development of skills in the areas of assertiveness, communication, decision making, consequences, goal setting, and problem solving. As well, there are a number of sports and outdoor activities, including canoeing, hiking, and crafts. RCMP members serve as mentors for the campers, and this is designed to foster positive interaction between the police and youth (http://www.cityofgp.com/index.aspx?page=995).

- *ECOTRIP, York Regional Police.* This ten-month-long program is directed toward at-risk youth between the ages of 14 and 17. These youth are mentored by police officers during the program, which includes a number of pre-trip training sessions and a four-day, three-night wilderness trip. Among the goals of ECOTRIP are the development of youth life and leadership skills and the development of positive police–youth relationships (http://www.yrp.ca/en/community/youth-programs.asp).
- *Community Cadet Corps Program.* The program is directed toward at-risk youths up to the age of 18. It focuses on the development of discipline and leadership skills, goal setting, and building self-esteem. Program activities include military-style drill and marching, sports and recreational activities, and cultural events. Originally developed by the RCMP in the rural First Nations community of Hobbema, Alberta, it has expanded across Canada to other First Nations communities and to urban centres, including programs operated by the Regina Police Service and the Winnipeg Police Service.

In recent years, there has been increased concern with Aboriginal gangs, and police services have developed innovative approaches designed to reduce the vulnerability of youths to being recruited into gangs, as well as to provide options for youths who want to leave the gang life.

Tertiary Crime Prevention Programs

Tertiary crime prevention programs focus on adults and youths who have already committed a crime; these programs are designed to prevent these past offenders from doing more crime. A key objective of these programs is to prevent future re-offending. Many tertiary programs are directed toward first-time, less serious offenders, typically with a high degree of success. The challenges are greater for programs that target repeat offenders, which generally involve close supervision and surveillance.

tertiary crime prevention programs
programs designed to prevent adults and youths from re-offending

Tertiary crime prevention programs are often collaborative efforts of justice and social service agencies and community groups.

OBSTACLES TO EFFECTIVE CRIME PREVENTION PROGRAMS

Despite the proliferation of crime prevention programs, evidence of their effectiveness is sketchy and often inconclusive. Among the challenges that initiatives have encountered are (1) poor planning, (2) poor implementation, (3) lack of support from the police service, and (4) an absence of community involvement.

Many crime prevention initiatives are introduced without any analysis and lack clearly stated, measurable performance objectives. There is often a failure to consider best-practice crime prevention programs as well as the "lessons learned" from past crime prevention efforts. With respect to program implementation, an important issue is *where* crime prevention initiatives are implemented: "All too often, programs are initiated in neighbourhoods that really don't need them, while less organized neighbourhoods with higher crime rates are not served by programs because local residents have not taken the initiative or do not have the capacity to start them and because programs are much more difficult to implement in high-needs communities."[15]

Police services also vary greatly in the extent to which they integrate crime prevention into their operations and resource their crime prevention initiatives. In some police services, crime prevention is an ancillary function; in others, it is a core objective. When budgets are tight, crime prevention programs may be vulnerable to resource cuts. Also, participation in crime prevention initiatives requires that patrol officers have the time to engage in proactive policing.

Among the potential obstacles to community involvement in crime prevention initiatives are residents' apathy toward, and lack of participation in, crime prevention programs; the absence of a clearly defined role for the community; community distrust of, and hostility toward, the police; and the fact that communities afflicted by high rates of crime and disorder are often the same ones where it is most difficult to interest residents.

Remember, though, that a reduced crime rate is only one indicator of success for crime prevention programs. Other important considerations are the quality of police–community relationships, the fear of crime, the experiences of crime victims and their attitudes toward the police, and the extent to which the initiatives succeeded in securing the participation of community residents in the long term.

Comprehensive crime prevention strategies hold the most promise. Two types of comprehensive initiatives are those that focus on the needs of an entire community or on high-crime neighbourhoods in the community, and those initiatives that are designed to address a particular problem, such as domestic violence or vehicle theft, on a broad scale.[16]

Police Legitimacy and Crime Prevention

The legitimacy of the police is a key theme in our study of Canadian policing. Any discussion of the effectiveness of crime prevention programs should consider whether specific initiatives are effective in preventing crime, or whether the specific strategy or program is being used to increase police legitimacy. Sometimes, police champion programs that evaluative studies have determined to be ineffective or there is no evidence as to their effectiveness. Two examples that illustrate this are police-sponsored firearm amnesty programs and the D.A.R.E. program.

Firearm amnesty programs allow residents to turn in unregistered guns without penalty. Some police services pay cash, give grocery gift cards, or provide other rewards in exchange for citizens turning in guns. These programs are designed to reduce the number of firearms and the levels of violent crime in the community. There is no evidence that these programs reduce the levels of gun-related violence in crime, particularly in the U.S. where there are more than 310 million firearms, one for every man, woman, and child in the country.[17] Yet the programs provide police services with a high-profile initiative that gives the impression that serious and violent crime is being addressed, thereby increasing the legitimacy of the police.

The D.A.R.E. (Drug Abuse Resistance Education) program for high school students is another example of an initiative that raises the profile and legitimacy of the police. Originally directed toward substance abuse—alcohol, tobacco, and drugs—the D.A.R.E. program has been expanded in many jurisdictions to include conflict resolution, gang prevention, parent education, and after-school learning and recreation.

Research studies conducted on D.A.R.E. programs have found that while there is strong support for the program among parents, educators, the police, and youth, the program has very little impact on student attitudes and beliefs about drugs or drug use behaviour. It may have other benefits that have remained unexplored. The D.A.R.E. program is a good example of a widely used program whose effectiveness is more often assumed than demonstrated and a program that many police services continue to promote because it increases their legitimacy in the community.[18] The D.A.R.E. program is often cited as an example of why there should be evidence-based crime prevention.

Sustaining Community Involvement in Crime Prevention Initiatives

In the discussion of policing in the community in Chapter 8, it was noted that generating, and sustaining, community involvement in community policing is a challenge. These challenges also exist in mobilizing community residents to participate in crime prevention initiatives.

A key question is: How is community involvement in crime prevention initiatives to be sustained? Both the police and the community must anticipate and address obstacles to community involvement. A review of crime prevention through social development initiatives in six Canadian communities identified several factors that contributed to successful sustainability. These factors are depicted in Figure 9.1. Successful programs are relevant to, and "owned" by, the community and reflect a community vision.

Figure 9.1. Key Elements in Sustaining Crime Prevention Initiatives

Source: T. Caputo, K. Kelly, W. Jamieson, and L. Hart, "A Portrait of Sustainable Crime Prevention in Selected Canadian Communities, Vol. 1, Main Report," p. iii, 2004, Carleton University.

There are several possible reasons why crime prevention strategies have not been as successful as the police and public might have hoped. One is community participation. First, the public often is not aware of police crime prevention initiatives. An environmental scan conducted by the Ottawa Police Service (OPS), for example, found that, with the exception of Neighbourood Watch and Crime Stoppers (both of which receive considerable media attention), most residents do not know much about the OPS's crime prevention programs.[19]

Second, there are low levels of community participation. It appears that only about 10 percent of households participate in crime prevention programs. Citizens who do participate in community crime prevention initiatives tend to live in neighbourhoods with few problems; in other words, they are among those *least* at risk of victimization. For the full potential of crime prevention initiatives to be realized, it is essential that there be participation by residents in those neighbourhoods affected by high rates of crime and disorder. This requires police services to develop neighbourhood-specific strategies and partnerships. A key role can be played by NGOs that have networks of relationships in the area.

Crime Prevention in Aboriginal Communities

Developing and implementing effective crime prevention programs in Aboriginal communities has proven to be a challenge both for police services (Aboriginal and non-Aboriginal) and communities. The crime prevention initiatives that have been developed to date fall into one of two categories: (1) programs that are part of an overall crime prevention strategy, developed by senior police administrators, and implemented in both Aboriginal and non-Aboriginal communities; and (2) programs that are developed by police officers at the local level in collaboration with chiefs, band councils, and community residents. Needless to say, these latter programs have been the most effective. The effectiveness of programs is increased when community residents have a significant role in the design and delivery of the interventions.

An example of a reserve-based program is the Police Athletic League for Students (PALS) and Life Skills 101 sponsored by the Six Nations Police (Ontario). This program is directed at high-risk youth and targets youths ranging in age from 6 to 12. Youths from participating schools spend one afternoon per week with police officers in a variety of athletic activities. Life Skills 101 assists youths in gaining insights into their behaviour and in avoiding future conflicts and violence. It includes field trips, drug awareness programming, and assistance with school studies (http://www.snpolice.ca/index.php/community-services/pals).

CRIME RESPONSE STRATEGIES

The crime response strategies that are used in community-based strategic policing include a range of tactical initiatives. Several of the more common ones are discussed below.

problem-oriented policing (POP)
a tactical strategy based on the idea that the police should address the causes of recurrent crime and disorder

Problem-Oriented Policing (POP)

A key tactical strategy of community policing is **problem-oriented policing (POP)**, which is based on the idea that policing should address the root causes of recurring problems of crime and disorder and then fashion solutions to those problems, often in collaboration with community residents. A central tenet of POP is the **iceberg (or 80/20) rule**, the view that crime (20 percent of the iceberg) is only a visible symptom of invisible, much larger problems (the 80 percent of the iceberg that lies below the water's surface). The 80 percent represents the underlying causes or conditions that allow the 20 percent of the problem that is visible to exist.

iceberg (or 80/20) rule
the view that crime is only a visible symptom of much larger problems

The **SARA (scanning, analysis, response, and assessment)** problem-solving model helps officers identify and respond to problems, with the assistance of various agencies and organizations and community groups.

SARA (scanning, analysis, response, and assessment)
a problem-solving model for police

There are several clearly defined stages to problem-solving policing:

- *Scanning.* Identifying the problem.
- *Analysis.* Determining the cause, scope, and effect of the problem.
- *Response.* Developing a plan to address and solve the problem.
- *Assessment.* Determining whether the response was effective.

The particular problem to be addressed may be community-wide and may require a long-term plan of action, or it may involve a single individual and a situation that can be addressed in relatively short order. A good example is what is known as "problem premises," which consume considerable police resources. Every community has them. In Vancouver, for example, one relatively small rooming house was flagged as a problem premises: police were called to the address a total of 259 times during an 18-month period. A total of 413 officers were on scene for more than 320 hours, and the overall cost to the taxpayers was $25,000. The Vancouver Police Department targeted specific individuals living in the rooming house and the number of calls for service was reduced.[20] See the Media Link, "Problem-Oriented Policing," at the end of this chapter.

Problem solving is a key component of the RCMP's **CAPRA model.** CAPRA stands for focusing on **C**lients, **A**cquiring and analyzing information, developing and maintaining **P**artnerships, generating an appropriate **R**esponse, and **A**ssessing the intervention. This model emphasizes the identification of and response to problems of crime and social disorder in the community utilizing a problem-solving approach. It also highlights the importance of consultation and collaboration with community partners.

CAPRA model
the RCMP model of problem-oriented policing that utilizes a collaborative problem-solving approach

Zero-Tolerance Policing and Quality-of-Life Policing

A policing strategy that has gained popularity in the past decade or so is **zero-tolerance policing**, also referred to as "confident policing," "proactive policing," or "community policing with the gloves off." The key principle here is that a strict order-maintenance approach by the police in a specific area, coupled with high police visibility and presence, with a focus on disorder and minor infractions, will reduce more serious criminal activity.[21]

zero-tolerance policing
a crime response strategy centred on the premise that a strict order-maintenance approach by the police will reduce more serious criminal activity

Increased police visibility is a core component of **quality-of-life policing**—efforts to improve conditions in an area by targeting annoying behaviours such as panhandling, loitering, and public drug and alcohol use. A highly visible police presence may deter and alter criminal behaviour, increase residents' sense of security, and enhance the legitimacy of the police. Recall that police presence was a key concept in the discussion of community

quality-of-life policing
police efforts to improve conditions in an area by targeting disruptive and annoying behaviour

policing in Chapter 8. These strategies are often applied in conjunction with police crackdowns, which are designed to instill in the criminal population the perception that they are more likely to be apprehended or intervened against.

This aggressive policing strategy has often resulted in charges that the police are overpolicing in certain communities and neighbourhoods, as well as practising racial profiling. Recall the discussion of racial profiling in Chapter 6. In New York City, the police employed a "stop and frisk" strategy in an attempt to reduce the levels of violent crime. Persons were stopped and frisked for weapons and other contraband. Police officers were required to have only "reasonable suspicion" that a crime was about to occur. See the Media Link, "Systematic Abuse by the NYPD: They Will Break Your Arm and Punch You in the Face for Being a F***ing Mutt," at the end of this chapter.

Critics pointed to data indicating that a disproportionate number of African-Americans and Latinos were targeted and a report by the New York State Attorney General found that only 3 percent of 2.4 million stops resulted in a conviction.[22] A federal court ruled in 2013 that the practice violated the constitutional rights of minorities in the city.[23]

Similar criticism has surrounded the practice of "carding" used by the Toronto Police Service. Patrol officers gather personal data from persons in encounters that are usually non-criminal. This information is then entered into a database to be used by the police in future investigations. Between 2008 and 2012, police officers filled out 1.8 million cards and a disproportionate number were for Blacks, in particular young Black males.[24] This led to calls for the Toronto Police Service to modify or eliminate the carding program.

In 2014, new guidelines for the use of carding by Toronto police officers were introduced. These guidelines required that officers have a valid reason for stopping persons and that officers not prolong questioning of individuals to gather information in order to justify formal questioning.[25] It was found that when the new policy was implemented in 2014, the number of cards issued fell by more than 75 percent, indicating that many officers had stopped the practice altogether.[26] In mid-2015, it was announced that the province of Ontario would develop regulations to standardize the practice of carding.

The "Broken Windows" Approach

"broken windows" approach
the view that if minor crimes are left unaddressed, an environment for more serious crime will be created

The **"broken windows" approach** emerged in New York City in the 1980s. It was a metaphor for neighbourhood deterioration and was based on the observations of patrol officers that if a window was broken in a building and not replaced, then in very short order, all of the windows would be broken.[27]

According to this approach, a broken window that remains in place is a statement that no one cares enough about the quality of life in the neighbourhood to bother fixing the little things that go wrong. While a broken window is a small thing, it triggers further neglect and results in the progressive deterioration of the entire neighbourhood and may result in more serious crime.[28]

Proponents of the broken windows approach argued that police services had neglected little things—the law-enforcement equivalent of broken windows—and that a need had arisen to reorient the efforts of police work.

The central thesis, then, is that "the existence of unchecked and uncontrolled minor incivilities in a neighbourhood—for example, panhandling, public drunkenness, vandalism and graffiti—produces an atmosphere conducive to more serious crime."[29]

To address this situation, NYPD patrol officers concentrated on quality-of-life crimes and were tasked with ridding the streets of nuisance crime—beggars, noise, vandals, and "squeegee merchants," groups of youths who approach drivers to wash their windshields—which made people fearful. This model of policing emphasized rapid deployment of officers and relentless follow-up. The implementation of the broken windows approach was associated with a significant reduction in crime levels in New York City. It has been adopted by many police services in Canada and the U.S.

Considerable controversy has surrounded the broken windows theory, and questions have been raised as to the effectiveness of the various policing strategies that are based on its tenets. Among the questions that have been raised are whether policing initiatives targeting disorder are effective in reducing the levels of crime and, if so, at what cost, including the potential of overpolicing and increases in public concern with safety.[30] There is a growing recognition, however, that an order-maintenance approach centred on preventing disorder in the community can result in a reduction in the levels of fear among citizens and a corresponding increase in their quality of life.

Police File 9.3 presents research findings on the effectiveness of selected crime response strategies.

CRIME ATTACK STRATEGIES

Crime attack strategies are proactive operations used by the police to target and apprehend criminal offenders, especially those deemed likely to re-offend, and specific areas or neighbourhoods. These strategies include increased patrol visibility, including foot patrols; proactive policing by patrol officers; and rapid patrol response.

crime attack strategies
proactive operations by the police to target and apprehend criminal offenders

Tactical-Directed Patrol

One widely used strategy is the tactical-directed patrol, which involves saturating high-crime areas (often referred to as "hot spots") with police officers, or targeting individuals engaged in specific types of criminal activity. This may include areas that generate frequent hard-crime calls (e.g., holdup alarms, shootings, stabbings, auto thefts, thefts from autos, assaults, sexual assaults) or soft-crime calls (e.g., for audible break-in alarms, disturbances, drunks, noise, unwanted individuals, vandalism, prowlers, and fights). These hot spots, which are often identified through intelligence-led policing, are plotted on crime maps.

Directed forms of patrol are usually either location- or person-oriented. Tactical patrol strategies give police managers greater control over their most valuable resource—the time and activities of patrol officers. Foot and bicycle patrols may also be used in hot spot areas. A number of police services, for example, deploy foot patrol officers in troubled areas.

Police File 9.3

The Effectiveness of Selected Crime Response Strategies

Strategy	Technique	Effectiveness
Problem-oriented policing (POP)	Police attempt to address the root causes of crime and disorder, and fashion solutions to those problems in collaboration with community residents. SARA is used.[31]	It has the potential to reduce crime and disorder and to reduce the fear of crime. It can improve police–community relations and develop skills in patrol officers.[32] In Los Angeles, the use of SARA resulted in significant reductions in gun-related violence, including violent crimes, homicide, and robbery in selected divisions.[33]
Broken windows	The existence of unchecked and uncontrolled minor infractions/incivilities in a neighbourhood produces an environment conducive to serious crime.[34]	Studies on the impact of broken windows have produced mixed results. Some studies have found no impact on crime rates, while others have found a reduction in property crime rates.[35] It is likely that the broken windows approach may work in some types of neighbourhoods and that its impact may be increased if it is combined with other community policing initiatives. There is concern that in adopting the broken windows approach, the increased police activity may result in elevated levels of fear in the community. The legitimacy of the police may be compromised if certain segments of the community perceive they are being targeted.[36]
Zero-tolerance/quality-of-life policing	Influenced by the broken windows approach, this strict order-maintenance approach in a specific area includes high police visibility and a focus on disorder and minor infractions. Often involves police crackdowns on specific criminal activities, such as drug dealing.	Police presence may alter offender's behaviour. Increased police visibility may increase citizens' sense of security, may deter criminal behaviour, and enhances police legitimacy.[37]

Targeting High-Risk Offenders

Many police services have developed initiatives designed to target high-risk offenders. Examples include the following:

- *Calgary Police Service Serious Habitual Offender Program (SHOP) and Multi-Disciplinary Resource Team (MDRT).* SHOP is a multi-agency (police, probation, Crown, social services agencies, and corrections) information and case-management program for youths and adults designated as serious habitual offenders. SHOP monitors the activities of offenders both during custody and upon release in an attempt to reduce serious crime. The MDRT initiative is designed for early intervention and support for high-risk youths in the city.

- *Repeat Offender Program Enforcement (ROPE) squad.* The ROPE squad, in Ontario, with officers from a number of municipal, provincial, regional, and federal police services, locates and apprehends criminal offenders who are unlawfully at large because they have violated the conditions of their release from custody, have failed to return to custody, or have escaped from correctional authorities.
- *Integrated Police-Parole Initiative (IPPI).* This program places police officers in parole offices of Correctional Service Canada (CSC). These officers work alongside patrol officers to monitor the activities of high-risk offenders released into the community. A preliminary evaluation of the program found that there was a reduction in technical violations of condition release by offenders in those CSC offices participating in the IPPI program, suggesting that this approach may assist with the reintegration of offenders.[38] This is a good example of a tertiary crime prevention program, as the efforts of the police and their partners are directed toward preventing re-offending.

Police services have become more involved in multi-agency efforts to assist with reintegration and the reduction of re-offending among persons released from incarceration, expanding their role beyond that of enforcement.[39]

These types of police strategies have not been without controversy. The Toronto Police Service Anti-Violence Intervention Strategy (TAVIS) was created to reduce the high levels of gun violence and to enhance public safety

Robyn Doolittle/Getstock.com

Toronto Police Rapid Response TAVIS unit makes an arrest.

in high-crime neighbourhoods in Toronto. Its strategies include intervention, prevention, and community support and mobilization. A key strategy is building relationships with the residents in at-risk neighbourhoods. Community meetings, high-profile police patrols, and the identification of crime hot spots and individuals involved in gun violence are all components of TAVIS (http://www.torontopolice.on.ca/tavis/). See the Media Link, "@TorontoPolice Neighbourhood TAVIS Initiative 2014," at the end of this chapter.

In recent years, criticism has been directed toward TAVIS for allegedly engaging in overpolicing of Black neighbourhoods. This includes concerns that officers arbitrarily stop and search Blacks and the perception that Black youth are harassed and criminalized. Support for this view is provided by an analysis of police records indicating that Black males are stopped disproportionately in comparison to white males.[40] TAVIS provides a good example of how police initiatives may reduce the levels of crime and violence in a community while at the same time undermining the legitimacy of the police among community residents, a challenging paradox. See the Media Links, "TAVIS: Police unit faces criticism as it tries to bridge gaps in Toronto neighbourhoods," and "Toronto police TAVIS stop of four teens ends in arrests, captured on video," at the end of this chapter. There are concerns that officers engage in racial profiling and biased policing, as discussed in Chapter 6.

There are similar concerns surrounding the Bar Watch and Restaurant Watch programs operated by many police services. This proactive initiative is designed to reduce the levels of gang violence and to keep patrons safe. See Critical Thinking Exercise 9.1 at the end of this chapter.

Targeting Specific Types of Crime

Police services may also develop strategies to address specific types of crime. The "bait car" program, for example, is designed to reduce auto thefts and to apprehend offenders involved in committing this crime.

The program involves rigging police-owned vehicles with audio and visual equipment and a GPS navigation system, as well as with technology that allows the vehicle to be stopped remotely. The bait car program has resulted in significant decreases in the rates of auto theft in the jurisdictions where it is used. Live videos taken inside bait cars can be viewed at http://www.baitcar.com. See the Media Link, "Bait Car – Censored Montage," at the end of this chapter.

Police services have also been very proactive in attempts to suppress gang activity and its associated violence. This has included targeted investigations, the development of integrated gang task forces, and other initiatives.

Community Notification

Another proactive strategy that many Canadian police services use to manage high-risk offenders is community notification. This practice involves advising the media, crime victims, and the public when certain offenders are released (generally from federal correctional facilities). Research studies have consistently found that community notification does not increase public safety.

Tony Caldwell, Ottawa Sun

Police in Ottawa use a bait car program to help reduce auto theft.

The strategy, technique, and effectiveness of selected crime response and crime attack strategies are set out in Police File 9.4.

THE POLICE AND RESTORATIVE JUSTICE APPROACHES

Restorative justice is based on the principle that criminal behaviour injures not only the victim but also the community and the offender, and that any effort to resolve the problems created by criminal behaviour should involve all parties. Among the more common restorative justice initiatives are victim–offender mediation, circle sentencing, community holistic healing programs, and family group conferences. These programs vary in the types of offences and offenders processed; the procedures for hearing cases, reaching dispositions, and imposing sanctions; and the extent to which justice system professionals, including police officers, are involved. Box 9.1 compares retributive justice and restorative justice principles.

restorative justice
an approach based on the principle that criminal behaviour injures the victim, the community, and the offender

A key feature of all of these approaches is that the response to criminal behaviour addresses not only the offender and the offence but also the crime victims and their families, the offender's family, community residents, and justice personnel, including police officers. Together, they formulate a sanction that addresses the needs of all parties.

Among the better-known restorative justice programs in which police officers play a key role are circle sentencing and community and family group conferencing. Circle sentencing was first used in Yukon; family group conferencing originated in New Zealand and has been exported to Australia, Canada, and the United States.

In circle sentencing, all of the participants—including judge, defence lawyer, prosecutor, police officer, victim and family, offender and family, and community residents—sit facing one another in a circle. The discussions within the circle are intended to reach a consensus about the best way to dispose of the case, taking into account the need to protect the community as

Police File 9.4

The Effectiveness of Selected Crime Attack Strategies

Strategy	Technique	Effectiveness
Tactical-directed patrol	This is proactive, aggressive patrol in high-crime areas. Patrol officers use unallocated time to engage in purposeful activities directed by analysis of crime data. May be location-focused or person (offender)-oriented. Often applied in conjunction with crackdowns, focusing on specific types of criminal activities (e.g., drug dealing).	Increasing the number of uniformed police officers in patrol cars in hot spots and during hot times (crime peaks) may significantly reduce levels of criminal activity. Proactive police arrests, including zero-tolerance arrest policies that focus on high-risk people and offences, can reduce the levels of serious violent crime. The impact of crackdowns may depend upon the community. They are resource-intensive, and it is difficult to sustain positive results over the long term. May undermine the legitimacy of the police, particularly among young men and other groups who are more likely to be the targets of police attention.[41]
Hot spots policing	Police focus on areas that have a high concentration of crime and/or disorder and a high risk of criminal victimization.[42]	It can reduce crime and disorder without displacing crime to surrounding areas;[43] long-term effectiveness is enhanced by the use of POP and the continued presence of officers in specific locations.[44] There is no evidence that hot spots policing reduces the legitimacy of the police; U.S. studies have found that residents often welcome the concentration of police.[45] Whether these findings apply to Canada is unknown. There is no evidence as to whether hot spots policing reduces overall crime rates in a municipality.[46]
Focusing on high-risk offenders	Special police units monitor chronic and violent offenders. Often involves collaboration of multiple police services and other agencies.	It can result in high levels of arrest and incarceration, and reduction in violent crime incidents. A study in Philadelphia found that an offender-focused strategy outperformed both foot patrol and problem-solving strategies and that a focus on "problem people" in "problem places" can result in significant decreases in violent crime.[47]
Bike patrols	Officers on bikes are often deployed to areas of high crime and disorder. Provide excellent mobility in an urban environment.	They can be an effective component of community policing. Bike patrol officers can have much more personal contact with citizens than patrol car officers.[48]

(*Continued*)

Foot patrols	Officers walk a "beat" in a neighbourhood or district. Some police services have dedicated foot patrols, while others encourage officers to park their patrol cars and walk when they have the opportunity.	Evidence is emerging that strategically directed foot patrols can reduce the levels of crime and disorder in neighbourhoods.[49] Reduce citizens fear of crime and calls for service. Improve officer's familiarity with neighbourhoods. To be effective, must be deployed as part of a comprehensive community policing strategy rather than as an add-on.
Community notification	The act of advising the media, crime victims, and the general public when certain offenders are released from confinement. Used most frequently with sex offenders.	There is no evidence that it reduces re-offending. May increase citizen fear of crime and further marginalize offenders released from confinement. Raises issues of public security versus individual privacy.

Box 9.1

Comparison of Retributive and Restorative Justice Principles

Retributive Justice	Restorative Justice
Crime violates the state and its laws.	Crime violates people and relationships.
Justice focuses on establishing guilt so that doses of pain can be meted out.	Justice aims to identify needs and obligations so that things can be made right.
Justice is sought through conflict between adversaries in which the offender is pitted against the state.	Justice encourages dialogue and mutual agreement, and gives victims and offenders central roles.
Rules and intentions outweigh outcomes; one side wins and the other loses.	The outcome is judged by the extent to which responsibilities are assumed, needs are met, and healing (of individuals and relationships) is encouraged.

Source: Zehr, H., *Changing Lenses: A New Focus for Crime and Justice*, © 1990, Herald Press. Reprinted by permission of the publisher.

well as the punishment and rehabilitation of the offender. Circle sentencing is generally available only to offenders who plead guilty. Offenders who have their cases heard in a sentencing circle may be sent for a period of incarceration; however, many other sanctions are available, including banishment (for Aboriginal offenders, generally to a wilderness location), house arrest, and community service.

Police officers apply community conferencing in a variety of settings. For example, school liaison officers (SLOs) often use conferencing to address conflicts between students, or groups of students, that arise in school settings.

THE EFFECTIVENESS OF POLICE STRATEGIES

The absence of evaluation studies, especially in Canada, makes it difficult to determine the extent to which police crime response strategies reduce the levels of crime and disorder in communities and improve the quality of life for community residents. Studies conducted so far (primarily in the U.K. and U.S.) have produced mixed findings.

The innumerable differences in how individual police services plan and implement crime response strategies, variations in the extent to which police services have established productive collaborative relationships with other agencies and organizations and with community groups, and the specific challenges confronting individual neighbourhoods, combine to make it difficult to reach definitive conclusions about the effectiveness of police crime response strategies. It does appear that many of the strategies function to increase police legitimacy, a critical component of the police role in the community.

The Issue of Crime Displacement

crime displacement
the relocation—due to effective crime prevention and crime response initiatives—of criminal activity from one locale to another

In attempting to determine the effectiveness of crime prevention programs and of crime response and attack strategies, there is the slippery issue of **crime displacement**—"the relocation of crime from one place, time, target, offense, or tactic to another as a result of some form of crime initiative."[50]

Crime displacement can take a number of forms: (1) *geographic,* which involves offenders moving their criminal activity to another area; (2) *temporal,* in which criminals alter the times they commit offences; (3) *tactical,* in which offenders develop different strategies to commit crimes; (4) *target,* in which offenders select different places to commit crimes or different people to victimize; and (5) *functional,* in which changes in technology reduce criminal opportunities in some areas but open them up in others (e.g., bank robberies are declining as we move toward a cashless society, while wire fraud is growing as a new criminal opportunity).[51]

Techniques Designed to Improve the Effectiveness of Police Strategies

Police services are making increasing use of techniques designed to improve the effectiveness of crime prevention and crime response. Many of these are based on analytics and the use of *big data*—large amounts of information that require sophisticated analytical hardware and software but provide unprecedented opportunities to improve the effectiveness and efficiency of the police. See the Media Link, "VPD Uses Big Data Analytics to Fight Crime," at the end of this chapter.

A number of jurisdictions have also created fusion centres, centralized facilities designed to integrate and promote information and intelligence sharing between police services in a region. There is a particular emphasis on preventing and detecting specific types of crime, including gang-related activity and terrorism. See the Media Link, "Intelligence-Led Policing Fusion Centers, part 1," at the end of this chapter.

The first Canadian police fusion centre was opened in the Vancouver area in 2014, based on the U.S. model, at a cost of $5.8 million per year. While it is too soon to evaluate the effectiveness of the fusion centre, results from the U.S. have been mixed, and questions have been raised as to whether the costs of the centres outweigh their benefits.[52]

THE USE OF SOPHISTICATED TECHNOLOGY TO RESPOND TO AND ATTACK CRIME

Police services are increasingly adopting new technologies to improve their effectiveness and efficiency. Crime analysts use sophisticated statistical programs to create crime maps and to provide intelligence to police officers in patrol and investigative units. A key issue is how this technology will be managed to ensure that the rights of citizens are protected, another example of the ongoing tension between the efforts to ensure public safety and security while protecting citizens' rights. This tension was illustrated in the issues surrounding police body-worn cameras, discussed in Chapter 6. A new challenge is posed by the availability of unmanned aerial vehicles (more commonly referred to as *drones*; see Box 9.2). See also Class/Group Discussion 9.2 and the Media Link, "Police Surveillance Drones Coming Soon to Local Law Enforcement," both at the end of this chapter.

The Role of Crime Analysis

Crime analysis plays a central role in the various techniques that are used to improve the capacities of a police service to prevent and respond to crime. **Crime analysis** is a systematic approach to crime prevention and crime response that is designed to allow police services to deploy its resources effectively and to assist case investigation. This information is used by management, patrol, and investigative units to deploy resources effectively and efficiently. Crime analysts, many of them civilians, use sophisticated statistical tools not only to "mine" data gathered by the police service but also to inform decision making and strategic planning.[56] There is considerable evidence that crime analysis can assist in crime reduction and can increase the effectiveness and efficiency of police service delivery.[57]

crime analysis
a systematic approach to crime prevention and crime response based on the analysis of statistical and other data

There are several different types of crime analysis:[58]

- *Tactical.* Focuses on the "when, where, and how" of crimes and is used to assist patrol officers and investigators.
- *Strategic.* Examines long-term crime patterns and trends, including seasonal variations in crime; this information can be used by the police and community groups to develop crime prevention and crime response strategies.
- *Administrative.* This analysis is conducted to provide information to police managers, including comparative figures for police services.

Box 9.2

Here Come the Drones!

Since the terrorist attacks on the U.S. in 2001, unmanned aerial vehicles (UVAs), or drones, have been used by the U.S. military to track and attack persons identified as terrorists. This technology has been adapted to develop small drones that can be used by police services. These drones can be fitted with cameras, licence-plate readers, radar, and thermal-imaging devices.[53] Some models are equipped with Tasers, automatic shotguns, and grenade launchers. See the Media Link, "'ShadowHawk' Police Drone Armed with Tasers, Automatic Shotguns, Grenade Launchers," at the end of this chapter.

David Bloom/Edmonton Sun/QMI Agency

Police officer with drone

Among the potential uses for drones in policing are surveying accident scenes, photographing crime scenes, monitoring crowds, searching for lost persons, and, of course, surveillance of people and suspected criminals. Many drones are small enough to fit in a backpack and can be deployed by patrol officers. For cash-strapped police services, drones are viewed as a cost-effective alternative to helicopters and even police personnel.[54]

Drones are now being used by Canadian and U.S. police services. The Halton Regional Police is using drones to locate marijuana grow-ops, while the RCMP is using drones for a variety of tasks. Officials have been quick to state that drones will not be used for surveillance, although there is currently no regulation prohibiting the use of drones for that purpose. Transport Canada has issued flight certificates for drones used by police, which require them to be flown within eyesight of the operator and only during daylight hours. There are, however, no policies in place to regulate the use of drones by police, and critics have raised privacy concerns and argued for legislated limitations on their use that would address privacy and other issues.[55] There are also concerns about "mission creep"—that is, expanding the use of drones to include the surveillance of persons.

- *Investigative.* Profiling suspects and crime victims for police investigators, including chronic offenders and specific types of offenders (e.g., car thieves).
- *Intelligence.* Criminal intelligence analysis, focusing on linkages between offenders and crime groups and the identification of patterns.
- *Operations.* Focuses on how the police service is utilizing its resources, including patrol deployment, the activities of specialty units, and other expenditures.

A key component of crime analysis is *crime maps*, which are computer-generated maps of specific geographic areas that depict the incidence and patterns of specific types of criminal activity. This information can then be used to identify certain crime hot spots, to which patrol and investigative units can then be deployed. Statistical programs are also used to generate matrices that depict the links among various crime elements. Crime maps are created using a geographic information system (GIS), which can be used to plot crime trends and locations in an area, including crime hot spots.

Perhaps the most sophisticated analytical approach that is in the early stages of development is **predictive policing.** Predictive policing uses statistical analysis to identify the time and location of criminal activity that is likely to occur and, in some instances, which offenders will be committing them.[59]

predictive policing
the use of statistical analysis to identify the time and location of criminal activity that is likely to occur

Patrol units are directed to specific places where it is predicted the crime will occur. This increases the likelihood that an offender will be apprehended. Predictive policing has the potential to fundamentally alter how police resources are deployed and to increase the effectiveness and efficiency of patrol units.[60] See the Media Links, "Predictive Policing" and "Predictive Policing: Don't Even Think About It," at the end of this chapter.

Intelligence-Led Policing

Intelligence-led policing (ILP) involves applying criminal intelligence analysis in order to reduce and prevent crime. ILP is one example of how police services use technology to generate information and deploy resources. ILP is policing that is guided by the collection and analysis of information that is used to inform police decision making at both the tactical and strategic levels. As noted in Chapter 6, patrol officers are an important source of information that may not be included in official incident reports.

intelligence-led policing (ILP)
the application of criminal intelligence analysis to facilitate crime reduction and prevention

A number of police observers have cautioned that translating the concept of ILP into actual practice will encounter a number of challenges.[61] Concerns have been expressed that ILP represents a move away from community-based strategic policing and a return to the crime control orientation. Another concern is that there is often a disconnect between the analyses that are conducted and police operations. However, the ILP model does provide for problem identification and problem solving as well as for consultation with communities. Furthermore, a key component of ILP models is an assessment of the impact of specific strategic interventions.

CompStat

CompStat, derived from the words "computer statistics," is a strategy designed to increase the effectiveness and efficiency of police services while at the same time holding police personnel and the police service accountable for achieving objectives in crime reduction. CompStat provides the police with a mechanism to implement effective initiatives to address problems of crime and disorder, while at the same time retaining a focus on the key elements of community policing.[62]

CompStat
a strategy designed to increase the effectiveness and efficiency of police services while holding police personnel accountable for achieving crime reduction objectives

CompStat has been a key part of the movement of police services toward results-oriented police management and is a good example of how community policing has transformed with the increasing use of analytics.

CompStat is based on four general principles:[63]

1. **Timely and accurate intelligence.** District commanders, supervisors, and patrol officers are provided with information regarding where crimes are occurring, how crimes are being committed, and who is committing the crimes.
2. **Effective tactics.** Based on a careful analysis of crime data, tactical options are considered, including the effectiveness of various strategies. These tactics not only focus on the apprehension of criminal offenders but also consider the social and environmental contexts within which crime is occurring.
3. **Rapid deployment.** A proactive response to crime is developed, which involves a coordinated effort of patrol officers, investigative units, and support personnel.
4. **Relentless follow-up and assessment.** The effectiveness of tactical strategies in preventing and reducing crime is evaluated on an ongoing basis. A constant stream of information flows from patrol officers and supervisors to senior management on the outcomes of specific strategies and tactics.

The effective implementation of CompStat requires that a police service assess on a regular basis the results from the strategies and tactics that are deployed and understand why specific strategies were effective or not effective. This is a process of continuous learning for the police service and can be incorporated into the development of specific interventions.

CompStat meetings, attended by district commanders, supervisors, and selected support personnel, may be held weekly or monthly. A key focus is on crime trends and patterns in the different areas and the development of specific strategies and tactics. The expectation is that district commanders will have specific knowledge of crime and crime trends committed in their districts, and apply tactical solutions in response. District commanders must set forth plans for utilizing resources within their districts to respond to and prevent crime. CompStat provides the police with a mechanism for implementing effective initiatives to address problems of crime and disorder; at the same time, it keeps the focus on the key elements of community policing.[64]

Some version of CompStat is being used in many Canadian police services and is used to determine the deployment of patrol and the use of specific strategies. One patrol supervisor noted: "Whether it's giving an area special attention, deploying undercover surveillance teams, or having teams develop their own projects, it's almost always driven by CompStat."[65]

CompStat is a key feature of community-based strategic policing and illustrates how this model of policing has evolved from the original foci of community policing that developed in the 1980s (see Police Perspective 9.1).

There is considerable debate about CompStat that has centred on the effectiveness of this strategy in reducing levels of crime and how it interfaces with community policing. This highlights the often "uneasy fit" of tactical strategies within the community policing model.

There is concern, for example, that CompStat places too heavy of an emphasis on crime fighting and generally does not include measures of other strategies within the community policing model.[66] Field research has also found that there is often a disconnect between the managerial level in the

Police Perspective 9.1

A Patrol Sergeant Speaks to the Value of CompStat

In the past two decades, one of the biggest changes in patrol philosophy has been the move from reactive to proactive. Our focus is on the CompStat model: using statistical analysis to identify hot spots in your patrol area. We are less focused today on POP than we were a decade ago. With POP, there was an attempt to bring together all of the potential stakeholders to solve a problem. It was very time-consuming, and often the stakeholders had different ideas. And it was not always clear as to who was going to take responsibility for the problem. Initiatives would often die on the vine.

CompStat is much more about solving problems by focusing on hot spots. It identifies the problems, and the managers are required to come up with strategies to address these problems. In so doing, managers are held accountable for the activities of their patrol officers. You can involve community volunteers and provide a framework for directing resources to a specific problem. We not only target problem areas, but we target problem people—persons who are committing a high number of criminal offences. The focus is week to week rather than on long-term projects, which was the case with POP.

Source: Personal communication with author, 2013.

police service and the line-level officers with respect to CompStat objectives. This is reflected in the following exchange between a researcher and a foot patrol officer:

> Officer: "Everybody feels the pressure to make bodies, to lock people up."
>
> Researcher: "Is that because you feel like you are evaluated at the end of the week?"
>
> Officer: "Yup."[67]

District commanders are often under considerable pressure to show decreases in crime levels, which could lead officers to make "statistical adjustments" in crime reports. A survey of retired NYPD officers ($N = 1{,}770$) found that during the 1990s, when CompStat was introduced, there were pressures on officers from management to manipulate crime statistics to lower the crime rate. The performance management culture placed significant pressures on commanding officers, with one officer stating: "The pressure and humiliation attributed to CompStat was too much for most commanding officers. The vast majority of them played the numbers game to some degree to avoid being embarrassed and degraded in front of their peers."[68] This is an example of how the police culture, discussed in Chapter 5, can have a less-than-positive impact on the behaviour of officers.

FINAL THOUGHTS ON EFFECTIVE POLICE STRATEGIES

To be effective, and to achieve the objectives of specific projects, police strategies must be implemented on the basis of a careful analysis and evaluation of crime data. If the strategy involves proactive patrol—including zero-tolerance enforcements, car stops and person checks, and other crackdowns—officers must ensure that their actions do not violate the rights of citizens as guaranteed by the Charter of Rights and Freedoms. Strategies that combine tactical patrol with longer-term problem-solving approaches may ultimately be more effective and have more impact over time.

It is important to note that the strategies discussed in this chapter have the *potential* to prevent crime and reduce levels of crime and disorder in communities. The extent to which these objectives are achieved depends in large measure on how specific interventions are designed and implemented and on the quality of the relationship between the police and the community.

Merely adopting a community policing model is not an effective crime prevention and crime response approach. Rather, police services must make efforts to "personalize" community policing through strategies that strengthen their legitimacy, increase personal contacts with community residents, and ensure that police–citizen interactions are positive and respectful. Police are more effective when they combine enforcement with a variety of other approaches, such as problem-oriented policing, intensive enforcement, and hot spots patrols.

There is considerable evidence that "service-oriented" models of policing, including procedural fairness in encounters with citizens, high-visibility patrol, a problem-solving approach, and engagement with the community, contribute to higher levels of public confidence in the police.[69] Furthermore, two critical ingredients for success appear to be (1) utilizing a diversity of approaches, and (2) applying strategies that focus on specific crime and disorder problems. The least effective interventions use neither of these. Further, it should not be assumed that the same interventions will work in every area and in every situation: "The best practice for any community is one that fits their needs and conditions and is compatible with available resources."[70]

Summary

This chapter has examined the various strategies that the police use to prevent and respond to crime, with particular emphasis on the efforts of police services to build sustainable partnerships with communities and to utilize the latest technologies for detecting crimes and investigating cases. The traditional professional model of policing has evolved into community-based strategic policing, which incorporates elements of community policing with crime prevention, crime response, and crime attack strategies. This model of police work makes extensive use of data analysis, which allows police policies and operations to be intelligence-led. A number of these have been found to be effective in preventing and reducing levels of crime and social disorder, although some of the more aggressive police tactics have been criticized for being disproportionately focused on visible minorities, in particular, Blacks. Crime analysis, intelligence-led policing, predictive policing, and CompStat are examples of how police services are using sophisticated technologies to prevent and respond to crime. There are concerns, however, that some technology, including drones, pose a risk to the rights of citizens and highlight the ongoing tension between the need to ensure the safety of the community while ensuring the rights of citizens.

KEY POINTS REVIEW

1. Police services utilize a variety of strategies to prevent, respond to, and attack crime.
2. The police are involved in primary, secondary, and tertiary crime prevention programs.
3. There are few evaluations of crime prevention programs in Canada.
4. Crime prevention programs have been shown to reduce calls for service, to reduce crime, and to have a positive impact on at-risk youth.
5. There are a number of factors that may influence the effectiveness of crime prevention initiatives, including the level of legitimacy of the police in the community and a lack of community participation.
6. Among the more-common crime response strategies are problem-oriented policing, zero-tolerance policing, and the "broken windows" approach.
7. Critics argue that some crime response strategies disproportionately target visible minorities.
8. Studies of the effectiveness of crime response strategies have produced mixed results, with problem-oriented policing showing potential to reduce crime and citizen fear of crime, the broken windows approach producing mixed results, and zero-tolerance policing having the potential to alter the behaviour of offenders.
9. Crime attack strategies include targeting high-risk offenders and specific types of crime and include tactical-directed patrol, hot spots policing, and foot patrols, among other strategies.
10. Research studies have found that crime attack strategies can have a significant impact on the levels of crime and disorder in a community.
11. Many police services are involved in various restorative justice approaches.
12. Police services are making increasing use of sophisticated technologies to respond to and attack crime, including crime analysis, intelligence-led policing, CompStat, and predictive policing.
13. Some new approaches, including the use of drones, have stirred controversy and raise issues about the expansion of surveillance.

KEY TERM QUESTIONS

1. Define and discuss **primary**, **secondary**, and **tertiary crime prevention programs**, provide examples of each, and note their effectiveness.

2. Describe **problem-oriented policing (POP)** and discuss how the **iceberg (80/20) rule** and the **SARA** and **CAPRA** models are related to this crime response strategy.
3. Describe the crime response strategies of **zero-tolerance policing**, **quality-of-life policing**, and the **"broken windows"** approach, and discuss their effectiveness in reducing crime and disorder.
4. Describe the **crime attack strategies** used by police and the effectiveness of these approaches.
5. Identify and discuss the key principles of **restorative justice** and compare these with the principles of retributive justice.
6. What role does **crime displacement** play in discussions of measuring police performance?
7. Define and describe the role that **crime analysis**, **predictive policing**, **intelligence-led policing (ILP)**, and **CompStat** play in police strategies to prevent, respond to, and attack crime.

CRITICAL THINKING EXERCISES

Critical Thinking Exercise 9.1. Bar Watch and Restaurant Watch: Protecting Patrons or Violating Their Civil Liberties?

In an attempt to reduce the presence of gangs and associated gang violence in bars and restaurants and to protect patrons, a number of police services across the country have implemented the Bar Watch and Restaurant Watch programs. This program is a partnership between the police and drinking and dining establishments. Participation is voluntary, and bars and restaurants operate the program through an association to which the police do not belong. This program has been adopted by a number of cities in British Columbia and Alberta and also in Halifax, Nova Scotia.

Common components of the programs include the following: (1) participating establishments are required to install a CCTV and metal scanners at the entrance; (2) signs are posted, advising patrons that they are entering a premise that is participating in the Bar Watch (or Restaurant Watch) program; (3) patrons are advised that the tapes from the CCTV may be turned over to police; (4) patrons are required to "swipe" their driver's licence into a scanner that collects personal information, which is retained in a master database; and (5) this information can be shared with other establishments and the police. "Undesirable persons" (persons who are gang-affiliated and/or who have a criminal record) can be refused entry or removed from the premises by staff or the police.

The program has not been without controversy. Provincial privacy commissioners have expressed concerns with violations of civil liberties and, more specifically, with the gathering of personal information from patrons, how the data are stored and accessed. Patrons have also expressed concerns, as reflected in the comments on Internet discussion forums regarding the adoption of a Bar Watch program in Calgary:

> "I think bar watch is a good idea, to keep everyone safe of course, but . . . I don't think it's necessary for Police to be walking around removing

> patrons from a local establishment when there are plenty more crimes going on just in the streets. This is what our taxpayers money is going to?"
>
> "Calgarians are contributing taxes to run this city, why do the Police have the right to harass and defame citizens, when these citizens are NOT breaking any laws? They are merely just out trying to have fun?"

Supporters of Bar Watch/Restaurant Watch counter that it increases the safety of law-abiding citizens and that the program is not coercive:

> "The last time I checked, it wasn't your RIGHT to go into a bar/lounge . . . places like that are private establishments & the owners/operators have the RIGHT not to service (or not to serve) of admit (or not to admit) whoever they choose to."
>
> "Entertainment spots are supposed to be placed where you can go and have a good time. The last thing someone wants to worry about is getting caught in the middle of a violent incident."

Your Thoughts?

1. Have you ever been to a Bar Watch or Restaurant Watch premise?
2. If yes, what did you think about having to scan your driver's licence?
3. What are your views on the issues that surround the Bar Watch/Restaurant Watch program?
4. Would you be in support of, or opposed to, the adoption of the Bar Watch/Restaurant Watch program in your community?
5. Would you not patronize a bar or restaurant that participated in the program? Or did not participate in the program?

CLASS/GROUP DISCUSSION EXERCISES

Class/Group Discussion 9.1. CCTVs in the Neighbourhood?

Many municipalities across Canada are debating whether to install police-monitored CCTVs. Concerns have been raised about privacy issues and the location of the cameras, for example, whether CCTVs should be limited to specific high-crime areas and business centres or located throughout the municipality. An issue that is likely to emerge in the coming years is whether facial recognition technology should be incorporated into the cameras, allowing monitoring personnel to identify persons in the video images.

Your Thoughts?

Assume that you are a member of a subcommittee of the municipal council that is considering installing police-monitored CCTVs. What would be your position on the following?

1. Should the municipality install police-monitored CCTVs?
2. If yes, should the CCTVs be installed (a) only in specific high-crime areas, (b) in the business centre of the municipality, or (c) throughout the municipality, including in residential neighbourhoods?
3. If yes, should facial recognition technology be incorporated into the CCTVs?
4. As a community resident, would you support the installation of CCTVs in your neighbourhood?

Class/Group Exercise 9.2. To Drone or Not to Drone. . .

Recalling the discussion of drones in this chapter, consider the following:

1. Assume that your municipality is holding a referendum on whether the local police service should be allowed to use drones in police operations. Would you vote in favour of allowing the police to use drones, or against?
2. If you would vote in favour, what restrictions, if any, would you place on how drones were used? What oversight structures would you put in place?
3. If you voted against the police being able to use drones, what are the primary reasons for your position?

MEDIA LINKS

Visit www.nelson.com/canadianpolicework4 for links to these videos and other additional content available with this text.

"ProAction 20 Years of Bridging the Gap," ProAction Cops & Kids," n.d., copsandkids.ca/about-us

"Crime Prevention Through Environmental Design," cpschilliwack, August 16, 2012, youtube.com

"Problem-Oriented Policing," policenz, August 3, 2014, youtube.com

"Systematic Abuse by the NYPD: They Will Break Your Arm and Punch You in the Face for Being a F***ing Mutt," 8bitRicky, October 16, 2012, youtube.com

"@TorontoPolice Neighbourhood TAVIS Initiative 2014," Toronto Police Service, October 10, 2014, youtube.com

"TAVIS: Police unit faces criticism as it tries to bridge gaps in Toronto neighbourhoods," by James Armstrong and Sean Mallen, Global News, October 23, 2013, globalnews.ca

"Toronto police TAVIS stop of four teens ends in arrests, captured on video," by Jim Rankin, *Toronto Star,* August 7, 2012, thestar.com

"Bait Car – Censored Montage," Integrated Municipal Provincial Auto Crime Team (IMPACT), n.d., baitcar.com/video

"VPD Uses Big Data Analytics to Fight Crime," BlueBuzzCanada, July 17, 2013, youtube.com

"Intelligence-Led Policing Fusion Centers, part 1," J. Cazares, August 17, 2011, youtube.com

"Police Surveillance Drones Coming Soon to Local Law Enforcement T-Hawk," Big Brother Is Watching, January 25, 2011, youtube.com

"'ShadowHawk'" Police Drone Armed with Tasers, Automatic Shotguns, Grenade Launchers," seattlepatriot1776, August 25, 2011, youtube.com

"Predictive Policing," Richland CityView, July 3, 2013, youtube.com

"Predictive policing: Don't even think about it," *The Economist,* July 19, 2013, youtube.com

10 Case Investigation

LEARNING OBJECTIVES

After reading this chapter, you should be able to:

- Discuss the role of patrol officers, specialty units, and detectives in case investigations
- Discuss the role of police informants and the issues that surround their use in case investigations
- Describe the fundamentals of case investigation, including the crime scene search, police note-taking, and the various types of evidence
- Discuss the issues that surround the use of eyewitnesses in case investigation
- Describe how DNA is used in case investigations
- Discuss the work of cold case squads and forensic specialists
- Describe the use of the "Mr. Big" strategy in case investigation and why the technique is surrounded by controversy
- Discuss the issues that surround the interrogation of crime suspects and false confessions
- Identify the various analytical tools that are used by the police in case investigations

The investigation of criminal offences is an important, yet understudied, feature of Canadian police work. Depending on the circumstances of the case, investigations may involve patrol officers, detectives, undercover officers, informants, and surveillance teams, as well as special techniques such as wiretaps and the use of sophisticated analytical techniques. A case (or criminal) investigation is intended to form reasonable grounds so that an arrest can be made, or at least suspects identified.

Improperly conducted case investigations are a major contributor to wrongful convictions.[1] Among the factors that have contributed to innocent persons being found guilty are false confessions, improperly conducted photo lineups, erroneous information provided by informants, and investigator "tunnel vision"—becoming so focused on certain pieces of evidence and/or suspects that critical evidentiary clues and other potential perpetrators are overlooked.

This chapter focuses on case investigation and examines the strategies that police use to investigate crimes. This includes the analytical techniques that the police use to respond to increasingly complex and specialized forms of crime that often extends into the global arena. There has been an exponential growth in the use of sophisticated technologies by police services, including the use of facial recognition technologies, body-worn cameras, and drones.[2]

The fight against cybercrime, Internet-based child exploitation, and illegal activities on the "dark net" has required police services to develop specialized expertise and investigative techniques. The rise of specialized policing has been driven by the increasing globalization of crime and the complexity of criminal networks. Police services have developed the capacity to gather and analyze large amounts of information that can be used in case investigations. This was discussed in Chapter 9. These developments, however, have been accompanied by increasing concerns about privacy issues and ensuring that the rights of Canadians are protected.

PATROL OFFICERS: THE FIRST RESPONDERS

Most case investigations are conducted by patrol officers, who learn the fundamentals of case investigation during their initial years working the street. In later years, they will apply these skills in more-complex investigations when they become part of specialized investigative units.

In their daily activities, front-line patrol officers gather a considerable amount of raw criminal intelligence. For example, an officer may stop a vehicle for speeding and, while issuing a summons to the driver, obtain the identity of three other individuals in the car. This information is important because it establishes a relationship among all four parties. Crime analysts and investigators from specialized investigation units can use this information to help them identify suspects in a criminal conspiracy. This information may also be vital for obtaining judicial authorization to install a wiretap or listening devices in a dwelling.

The patrol officers who are the first to arrive at a crime scene usually have little information, or conflicting information, about what has occurred. The most important duties of first responders include ensuring that emergency medical personnel have access to and from the scene; securing and protecting the crime scene, and establishing the continuity of the scene and the evidence. Patrol officers must also attend to the needs of victims, including mobilizing victim services personnel.

SPECIALTY UNITS

Most of the larger police services have a number of specialized units to deal with serious and complex crimes, including homicide, child abuse, sex crimes, robbery/holdups, commercial crime, drug trafficking, Internet crime, and property offences. Smaller police departments across Canada often seek investigative support from larger municipalities or have established their own protocols for investigations.

In most police services, there has been exponential growth in the number of specialized investigative units. There are two general types of special units in police services: **problem-oriented special units** and **method-oriented special units.**[3]

problem-oriented special units
investigative units that focus on specific types of offenders or criminal activities

method-oriented special units
police units that are distinguished by specialized equipment and tactics

Problem-oriented special units focus on specific types of offenders or criminal activities and include outlaw motorcycle gang units, financial crime units, and sex offence units. Problem-oriented special units are created to address a particular problem that is perceived to be beyond the capacity of patrol officers or general investigators. Method-oriented special units are distinguished by specialized equipment and tactics. These include Emergency Response Teams (ERTs), strike force units, and bomb squads.

Recent years have seen a rapid proliferation of problem-oriented special units, many of which bring together officers from a number of police services and, in some instances, personnel from other criminal justice agencies, such as corrections. Examples of integrated units are the Integrated Market Enforcement Teams (IMETs), which operate in urban financial centres and focus on capital markets fraud and market-related crime, and the Combined Forces Special Enforcement Units (CFSEUs) which operate in Toronto, Montreal, Quebec City, and British Columbia. In Ontario, the unit is composed of the Toronto Police Service, Ontario Provincial Police, York Regional Police, Peel Regional Police, Royal Canadian Mounted Police, Citizenship and Immigration Canada, and Criminal Intelligence Service Ontario.

THE CANADIAN PRESS/Darryl Dyck

Problem-oriented special units focus on specific types of offenders, such as outlaw motorcycle gangs.

The Detectives

Detectives staff the various specialty units in a police service. The more common units include homicide, fraud, auto theft, and robbery. In recent years, many police services have added specialty units for high-risk offenders, cybercrime, and sex offences, including identifying sexual predators involved in luring on the Internet.

The work of police detectives is both preventative and reactive. In investigating crimes, there is an attempt to apprehend the offender(s) before additional offences are committed. Investigators, for example, may be proactive in identifying online predators, in some instances posing as young girls in order to apprehend sex offenders.

In a reactive role, these officers arrive on the scene once it has been secured, having been called by supervisory personnel already in attendance. The detective often takes over management of the crime scene(s) and ensures that witnesses are interviewed. Once the detectives have been briefed by patrol officers and have had an opportunity to gather facts from witnesses, they assign investigative follow-up roles or conduct further inquiries themselves. For serious crimes, identification section officers come to collect evidence at the scene. The Canadian Criminal Code and provincial legislation give police officers the authority to freeze or hold a crime scene for a prescribed length of time.

The Challenges of Working in Specialty Units

The discussion in Chapter 6 revealed that patrol officers experience a number of stressors that may have an impact on their mental and physical well-being. Little attention has been given to the challenges experienced by police officers who work in specialty units, including those who are involved in high-risk and traumatic events such as Emergency Response Teams and homicide units. It can be anticipated that the officers may experience considerable stress in their professional and personal lives. Officers in specialty units often work in high-demand, high-stress environments that place them at high risk of burnout. Homicide investigations, for example, are intense and take a toll on officers, professionally and personally. Officers may work as many as one hundred hours a week. As one homicide investigator stated: "This is not the type of work that you can leave at the end of the day and come back to tomorrow morning."[4] See the Media Link, "Inside the Luka Magnotta Case," at the end of this chapter for an inside look at the investigation of a particularly heinous crime.

The stress on specialty unit members may be exacerbated by insufficient resources, with officers being asked to do more with less, including high case loads, the increasing complexity of criminal investigations, and the challenges of meeting the requirements of legislation and court decisions. Homicides, for example, often occur on weekends, and to respond to these incidents and begin the case investigation can cost as much as $10,000 a day in overtime. It is not unusual for an investigation to cost $1 million. In addition to investigating the crime, homicide detectives may be responsible for witness management—that is, ensuring that the witnesses in the case are available to provide testimony if the case proceeds to trial. This can be a challenging task particularly if the witness is involved in a criminal lifestyle.

The Effectiveness of Specialty Units

Despite their proliferation, little is known about the effectiveness of police specialty units, including whether these units are cost-effective or are guided by best practices, and the operational strategies that contribute to high clearance rates. This is unfortunate, as these units are costly and often require participating police services to second experienced investigators. Integrated units may also be created by provincial governments in response to public pressure following a critical event

Sue Reeves, London Free Press

A police seizure in London, Ontario

or series of events (e.g., gangland shootings). It is important to determine whether a specialty unit has been created for what might be termed "ceremonial" purposes (i.e., to give the appearance of accomplishment and to preserve the legitimacy of the police service), or to make the police service more effective.[5]

Specialty units do provide the police with a source of legitimacy in the community, "providing the appearance of, if not an effective response to, the special or intense problems in the community."[6] A good example are the frequent "photo-ops" in the media that the police use to display their prize seizures, most often drugs and weapons. While quite photogenic, the questions that one might ask are: So what? What impact do these seizures have on the flow of illicit weapons and drugs, and on the crime rate? Was the investigation that led to the seizures an effective use of police resources? These questions are rarely, if ever, asked by the media and the general public and remain largely unexplored by researchers.

FUNDAMENTALS OF MAJOR CASE INVESTIGATION

A case (or criminal) investigation is intended to form reasonable grounds to make an arrest, or at least identify suspects. This relatively simple objective can result in a highly complex and time-consuming process. Recall from the discussion in Chapter 1 that legislation, case law, public policy, and the increasing sophistication of criminal activity have led to significant increases in police workloads. Contrary to the images presented on television and in movies, many criminal investigations do not result in the arrest of suspects. Both time and the odds are on the side of the criminal offender, especially in non-violent offences, where clearance (catch) rates may be quite low. Case investigations can be costly and require the commitment of significant resources. This often requires investigators to prioritize cases on the basis of potential "solvability."

Police officers involved in case investigations must be aware of changes in the Criminal Code, provincial statutes, court decisions, and internal police policies and procedures, among others. In Canada, evidence obtained in a manner that breaches the Charter is not automatically excluded.

There is pressure on case investigators to gather evidence that will withstand scrutiny and challenges in court. It has been suggested that there may be a "CSI effect" attributable to the popular television show *CSI: Crime Scene Investigation*, whereby jurors expect clear and unequivocal scientific evidence to be presented by the prosecutor.[7] There is some evidence to suggest that the *CSI* effect may exist among jurors. In one U.S. case, jurors asked the judge whether a cigarette butt had been tested for a DNA match with the defendant. It had been, but the defence lawyer, quite inexplicably, had failed to introduce the test results as evidence. The DNA results were introduced, and the defendant was acquitted.[8]

A Canadian study, based on interviews with police detectives ($N = 31$), found that the majority of the officers felt that programs such as *CSI* led the public to "Monday morning quarterbacking," wherein citizens questioned how an investigation was being conducted. The officers also expressed concerns that the general public would lose confidence in the police when the discrepancy between the well-resourced TV-based investigators was contrasted with the under-resourced investigative units in the real world.[9]

A number of factors affect the case investigation process, including the ingenuity, skills, and motivation of the investigator(s); the priorities of the police service; the level of sophistication of the crime; and the willingness of Crown counsel to proceed with the case. Police services make extensive use of the Internet in their attempts to solve crimes and other types of cases. Many police websites include sections on "most wanted," unsolved crimes, missing persons, and unidentified bodies/remains (see, for example, the OPP website at http://www.opp.ca).

Investigations must be both strategic (as in determining when to execute search warrants, interview suspects, and make arrests) and tactical (as in deciding on approaches to establishing reasonable grounds). There are two types of investigations, one at each end of the spectrum. In **smoking gun investigations**, either the accused is found at the scene of a crime or circumstantial evidence clearly points to the accused (e.g., the accused leaves his driver's licence at the crime scene). In **whodunit investigations**, the suspect is unknown, and investigations require considerable time and usually rely heavily on circumstantial and forensic evidence gathered at the scene. These latter investigations are resource intensive, may take several years to conduct, and may never result in an arrest.

smoking gun investigations
cases in which the perpetrator is readily identifiable

whodunit investigations
cases in which the suspect is unknown and extensive investigation is required

Notwithstanding the development of high technology as part of the investigator's tool kit, the fundamental role of investigators is encapsulated in the acronym GOYAKOD (get off your ass—knock on doors). The process of solving crimes still depends on this basic premise, which highlights the importance of community assistance. This may be challenging in a multicultural society where language barriers and mistrust of the police may hinder police investigations.

Investigators of serious crime in Canada are guided by the **major case management model**, which sets out a protocol for conducting investigations. The model is designed to facilitate the collection, management, retrieval, and

major case management model
the protocol for conducting investigations

Figure 10.1. The Major Case Management Model

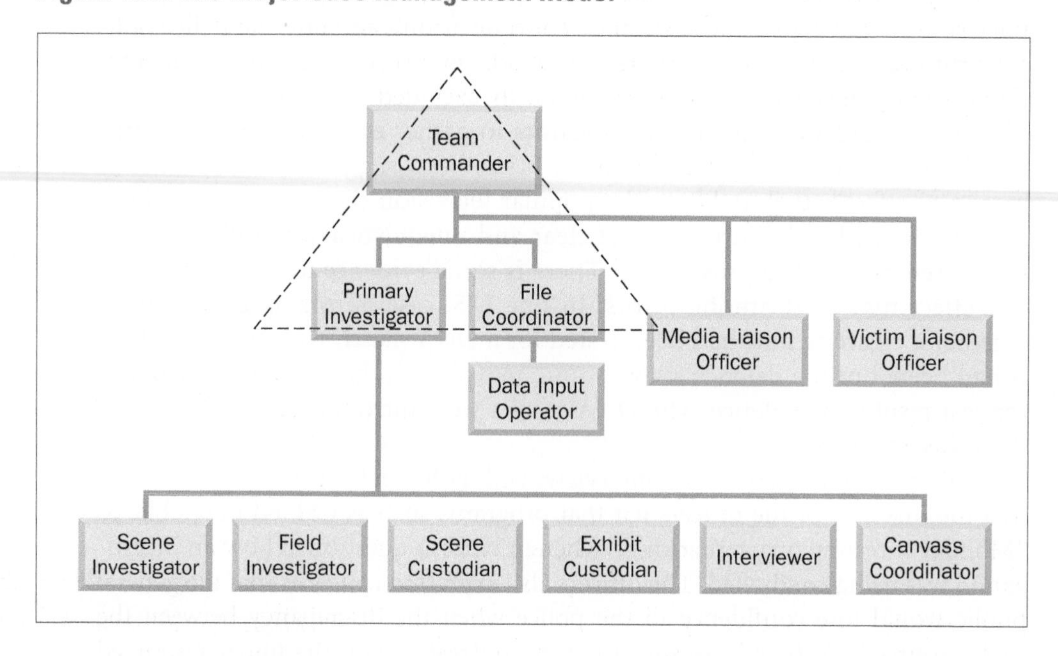

Source: Campbell and LePard (2007), 20. Reprinted by permission of Doug LePard.

analysis of large volumes of data that are gathered in major crime investigations (see Figure 10.1). The failure to follow this model may affect the quality of a police investigation and reduce the likelihood that the offender will be apprehended.

The Use of Informants in Case Investigation

An important tool for police investigators are informants, who inhabit a grey and under-studied area of Canadian police work. Informants can provide the police with valuable information that can assist in preventing and solving crimes. However, if not properly managed, they can compromise an investigation, seriously affect the reputation and legitimacy of a police service, place the lives of officers and others at risk, and lead to wrongful convictions.[10] See the Media Link, "Informants," at the end of this chapter.

Police officers are trained to consider that all of the offenders with whom they have contact are potential informants.[11] The responsibility for policies and procedures for managing informants resides largely with individual police services. There are no national standards or protocols for the recruitment and management of informants, although in Quebec, there are ad hoc committees composed of representatives from police services and the public prosecution office that supervise the use of informants.[12]

In legal terms, it is important to distinguish between "informants" and "agents." Both are covert human assets, but they differ in the privilege they enjoy legally. Informants only provide information to the police. The Supreme Court of Canada (SCC) has held that informants have a privilege that exists with the

Crown and them. This means that the identity of the informant can only rarely be exposed. One police investigator stated that the police feel so strongly about the protection of the informant that rather than expose the identity of the informant, an appeal will be made by the police to the Crown counsel to enter a stay of proceedings rather than risk the exposure of the asset.[13]

Police agents, on the other hand, work for the police. They do not have privilege and can be directed by the police to do things in support of an investigation. The agent is well aware that at some point they will have to testify in open court. This often means that after an agent has been used in a large operation, the agent is given the option of witness protection and a change of identity.

See Police Perspective 10.1 for a police investigator's comments on the role of informants and agents in policing.

Informants may be used at the street level by patrol officers and by major case investigators. In some instances, the informant is the alleged offender who offers

Police Perspective 10.1

A Police Investigator Comments on the Role of Informants in Police Work

Covert human assets are essential for police officers like me who work gangs and/or organized crime. The level of sophistication that these types of criminals have has made them immune to many traditional investigative methods. In order to be successful against this level of criminality, police officers must be able to recruit, manage, and protect covert human assets. Snitches, stool pigeons, rats, and informants are key ingredients to the battle against the violence that organized crime brings. With that said, while they are valuable assets to the police, they can also be very dangerous for an officer's career if mismanaged, and often the covert human asset can be treacherous. Many police officers have been terminated and/or disciplined for the mishandling of covert human assets.

Managing covert human assets requires complete professionalism at all times, with excellent note-keeping and commitment to the asset's safety. Meetings must be scheduled in a manner that is always cognizant of the fact that the covert human asset's life could be ended if his/her relationship with the police is ever exposed. Police officers who mismanage covert human assets run the risk of being responsible for their asset's death, their asset's forced relocation, and the abandonment of large and costly criminal investigations. That said, a well-placed covert human asset can be very destructive to a criminal gang and/or organization. Covert human assets save lives and are often motivated by nothing more than trying to turn their own life around and be the good guy. Often they are motivated by revenge, a desire to eliminate competition, and often money. The police will pay covert human assets for providing information. All information must be corroborated, and there must be an insulation process put between the covert human asset and the information.

Source: Personal communication with author, December 2014.

to provide details of the crimes, including the location of the deceased victim(s) for remuneration. There have been instances in which the police have paid "cash for bodies" to crime suspects and convicted offenders in order to locate deceased victims and to secure crime scene evidence that would assist in securing a conviction. The most high-profile case occurred in the early 1980s in British Columbia when the RCMP made a series of payments totalling thousands of dollars to a serial child killer (placed in a trust fund for his son) for this type of information. See Critical Thinking Exercise 10.2, "Should the Police Pay Offenders for Bodies?" at the end of this chapter.

Remuneration can range from no monetary benefit for the informant to millions of dollars. For higher-dollar amounts, a formal contract is generally signed between the police service and the informant. In one investigation into the criminal activities of the Hells Angels, the RCMP paid $1 million to an informant who had connections with Hells Angels in Vancouver to wear a "wire" and gather incriminating evidence. During the months he was on the payroll, the informant was a big-time spender on women and in the clubs. The informant's testimony in several court cases resulted in the convictions of several Hells Angels, and he was subsequently relocated to an undisclosed location under an assumed name. There are also instances of "rogue" informants, who, while working for the police, continue to be involved in criminal behaviour or who do not follow the instructions of their police handlers.

Police informants played a critical role in a 2006 case that foiled what would have been the largest terrorist attack on Canadian soil. In a case that came to be known as the "Toronto 18," the RCMP paid out over $4 million to two informants who infiltrated a group of individuals who intended to carry out a series of attacks, including storming Parliament Hill in Ottawa and beheading politicians and bombing the Toronto Stock Exchange and other prominent buildings. The intent of the Al Qaeda–inspired group was to force the Canadian government to withdraw from the conflict in Afghanistan. Several individuals were subsequently convicted of a variety of offences under the Anti-Terrorism Act and received lengthy prison terms.

Section 25 of the Criminal Code contains a controversial provision that allows undercover officers and informants to commit acts that are criminal (except violence), including drug dealing. There are also concerns with the motivations of informants—whether they are in it for the money or for a higher moral purpose—and with the quality and validity of the information gathered. Much more research remains to be conducted on the role of informants in police work.

While the use of informants has become an integral part of police work, critics argue that the effectiveness of this practice has not been documented and, further, that paying persons who are often associated with criminal activities compromises the principles of the justice system.[14]

THE CRIME SCENE SEARCH

A crime scene search is conducted in order to gather evidence that will

- determine the facts of the crime committed;
- establish the methods used to commit the crime; *and*
- identify the perpetrator(s) of the crime.

Two basic approaches are used to search a crime scene: (1) a *cautious search* of visible areas, taking steps to avoid evidence loss or contamination, followed by (2) a *vigorous search* for hidden/concealed areas. Case investigators may also gather photographic evidence that can be presented in court in the place of actual evidence. Photographs are often taken of physical evidence that is too large to move or store, or in situations in which the owner of the evidence would experience hardship by losing possession of it. Witnesses may also be able to help the investigator locate evidence.

Police Note-Taking

The notes made by officers at the scene are an important source of evidence and may assist in identifying suspects who might otherwise go undetected, establishing patterns of criminal activity from seemingly unrelated events, linking suspects who might otherwise not be connected, and providing a source of recall for the officer, who may be required to testify months or even years after an incident. Despite this, police notes are often incomplete, too brief, and insufficiently detailed.

Officers who attend court are often asked to refer to their notes. Both the prosecution and the defence ask whether the officer recorded the notes at the time of the incident or as soon as practical thereafter. If the answer is yes and no challenges are made, the officer is free to refer to the notes. Generally, a police officer's notes remain in the possession of the investigating officer, although copies of the notes accompany all arrest reports and are routinely disclosed to defence counsel. There are cases in which officers have "backfilled" their notebooks in order to cover for mistakes in an investigation. This was discussed in Chapter 4.

An internal audit of a sample of RCMP notebooks ($N = 217$) from across the country found non-compliance with regulations. Many of the notebooks had missing pages, improper handwritten corrections, and no indication that the notebook had been reviewed by a supervisor. It was also found that there was no clear policy as to whether RCMP officers can retain their notebooks following their resignation or retirement from the force.[15] Similar findings had been reported in audits of notebooks conducted in 2005 and 2011, suggesting that there is a need for proper oversight of this most important facet of police work.

TYPES OF EVIDENCE

At a crime scene, investigators look for four general types of evidence:

- *Oral (or testimonial) evidence* provided by witnesses, suspects, and victims. May be provided in written form or verbally. Includes confessions by suspects and sworn statements.
- *Real evidence,* which includes physical objects such as weapons, paint chips, and broken glass.
- *Documentary evidence,* such as written materials and records, including letters, invoices, bank records, and accounting ledgers.
- *Social media sources,* including Facebook and images on cellphones and PDAs. The "crime scene" may not be a physical place but instead may be

direct evidence
evidence in criminal investigations that is detected through at least one of the five senses

circumstantial evidence
evidence not directly observed but that can implicate an offender

located on the Internet (cybercrime) or on a cellphone or other electronic device. Social media is playing an increasing role as a source of evidence for police investigations. See Police File 10.1 below, and then consider Critical Thinking Exercise 10.1 at the end of this chapter.

Crime scene investigators also distinguish between direct and circumstantial evidence. **Direct evidence** is information detected through at least one of the five senses: sight, touch, hearing, smell, and taste. Eyewitness accounts are a form of direct evidence. **Circumstantial evidence** is not directly observed; even so, it links

Police File 10.1

The Role of Social Media in Case Investigation: The Vancouver Hockey Riot, 2011

Following the Vancouver Canucks' loss to Boston in Game 7 of the Stanley Cup playoffs in June 2011, a riot ensued that resulted in millions of dollars in property damage. The riot erupted after as many as 100,000 people crowded into the downtown area, many of whom were watching the game on big screens that had been erected. Fights broke out, cars (including two police cruisers) were set afire, and stores were looted. It took police over three hours to restore order. During the melee, thousands of photos and videos were taken on cellphones, some posted on Twitter and Tumblr, and the media shot footage. The Vancouver Police Department (VPD) put out a general call for the public to send in their images of perpetrators. There were so many responses that the VPD computer server crashed. Images were posted on Facebook, and many of the rioters who looted and caused damage were "outed" by friends and associates. The images were used by investigators to identify and arrest persons who had committed criminal offences, many of whom were subsequently convicted. An offer was also made to the police by the provincial insurance agency to use facial recognition technology to assist in identifying persons involved in the riot, matching this with driver's licence photos.

© Sergei Bachlakov/ZUMA Press/Corbis

An image from the post–Game 7 Stanley Cup riot in Vancouver, 2011

Observers commented that these events indicate that society may be entering a new arena of "citizen surveillance," and concerns have been raised that this may, ironically, undermine a sense of community rather than solidify it. Consider the issues raised in Critical Thinking Exercise 10.1 at the end of this chapter.

offender, victim, and accused by inference. In *R. v. John,* 1971, S.C.R. 781, the trial judge explained the distinction between direct and circumstantial evidence:

> If a witness gives evidence that he saw A stab B with a knife, that is direct evidence that A stabbed B. If a witness gives evidence that he found a dagger with an unusually long blade in the possession of A and another witness testified that such a dagger could have caused B's wounds, that is circumstantial evidence tending to prove that A did in fact stab B.

Eyewitnesses: An Unreliable Source of Evidence

Information gathered from individuals who have witnessed events surrounding the commission of a crime is often used in forming reasonable grounds in case investigations, especially in the absence of physical evidence. This evidence, however, is notoriously unreliable and must be used with caution.

It has been found that mistaken eyewitness identification accounts for more convictions of innocent people than all other factors combined.[16] The ability of an eyewitness to accurately describe an offender may be hindered by a number of factors, including light conditions, weather conditions, the chaos surrounding the incident, the speed with which an offence occurred, and the attributes of the eyewitness, including age (young children and the elderly are, generally, less reliable eyewitnesses than are young adults).[17] For a test of your eyewitness capacities, do an Internet search—keyword "Gary Wells Eyewitness Test"—for an exercise prepared by one of the leading experts in eyewitness testimony (https://public.psych.iastate.edu/glwells/theeyewitnesstest.html). Then consider the implications of the results of the test. Also, surprise or distraction may interfere with an eyewitness's ability to notice important information such as the offender's height, weight, and clothing; the colour, make, and licence plate number of a vehicle; and even the number of suspects involved. See the Media Link, "When Eyes Deceive – Eyewitness Testimony," at the end of the chapter.

For a powerful and moving story of a man who was wrongfully convicted based on faulty eyewitness testimony by the victim of the crime, read *Picking Cotton: A Memoir of Injustice and Redemption* (2009).[18] The book was co-authored by Jennifer Thompson-Cannino, the victim, and Ronald Cotton, the man who was wrongfully convicted and spent eleven years behind bars before being exonerated by a DNA test. See the Media Link, "Eyewitness Misidentification," at the end of this chapter.

Specific criticisms have been directed toward police lineups, which involve placing a suspect (or a picture of a suspect) among other individuals (or pictures of other individuals) and presenting the array to eyewitnesses to see whether they select the suspect.

"It's so hard to choose just one—can't I pick two?"

Many experimental studies have illustrated the unreliability of eyewitness evidence. This should alert criminal investigators to the need to search for physical evidence whenever possible. In one field study, two researchers went to various convenience stores posing as customers. They stayed in each store for three to four minutes, drawing attention to themselves intentionally by displaying certain behaviour, such as paying for the entire amount of their purchase in pennies and making lengthy searches for money. The researchers also asked for directions that required lengthy explanations by the clerks. Two hours after the researchers left, two individuals entered the store posing as police officers searching for the two customers. A photo lineup consisting of six mug shots was presented to each store employee. Only 32 percent of the witnesses accurately identified either customer.[19]

Closed-circuit televisions (CCTVs) are electronic eyewitnesses and can provide a more accurate record of events than human eyewitnesses. The Supreme Court of Canada has ruled that videotape evidence can be used in criminal trials, although any electronic image, including videos and photographs taken by cellphones, can be misleading. The lighting and camera angle may present an inaccurate picture of the incident, and the images often do not capture the entire incident. Recall from the discussion in Chapter 9, however, that the expansion of CCTVs has been accompanied by concerns that a surveillance state is being created that threatens the civil liberties of citizens.

POLICE INTERVIEWS WITH VICTIMS AND WITNESSES

A critical component of all case investigations is interviews with victims and witnesses. The police interviewer must take particular care with vulnerable groups, including children, to ensure that "leading" questions are not posed and that the information gathered in the interview is accurate. It is also important to ensure that the victim is not traumatized ("revictimized") by the interview. Interviewing skills are a key component of police recruit training and in-service training.

LINKAGE IN CRIMINAL INVESTIGATIONS

A primary objective in case investigations is to link the various facets of the crime scene, the victim, the physical evidence, and the suspect. Each of these components must be connected if the case is to be resolved successfully. The basis for conducting such a four-way linkage rests on the **principle of transfer and exchange**.

principle of transfer and exchange
the assumption that physical evidence is transferred during the commission of a criminal offence

Perhaps the most fundamental of all assumptions made by investigators is that physical evidence is transferred during the commission of a criminal offence. The offender may well have *left* something at the scene and may well have *taken* something from the scene. The key is to find or recognize the evidence. For example, a residential break and enter may involve the transfer of physical evidence

- *from the offender to the crime scene* (fingerprints, footprints, palm prints, treadmarks from footwear or tires, blood, saliva, hair, dirt from footwear); *and*

- *from the crime scene to the offender* (carpet fibre; victim's blood, hair, or saliva; drywall dust; glass).

linkage blindness
the investigative failure to recognize a pattern linking one crime with one or more others

Linkage blindness is the investigative failure to recognize a pattern linking one crime with one or more others. For example, investigators may fail to notice similar crimes in other jurisdictions, or the offender's signature or modus operandi.[20] Linkage blindness is a major cause of police failures to solve major serial crimes in a timely manner. The absence of interoperability (i.e., the failure to share information) among police services may also hinder police investigations. The lack of interoperability is often a key feature of failed police investigations, including the case of the serial killer Robert Pickton discussed below. A central objective of the major case management model is to ensure that investigators make the proper linkages in case investigations.

THE MISSING WOMEN IN BRITISH COLUMBIA: MASS MURDER AND A FAILURE OF POLICE INVESTIGATION

During the mid- to late 1990s, a number of sex trade workers from Vancouver's Downtown Eastside began to go missing. These women, many of whom were addicted, disappeared and did not make contact with family or friends. One suspect who emerged was a pig farmer, Robert "Willie" Pickton, whose property was in the rapidly developing suburban municipality of Coquitlam, a few kilometres from Vancouver. Coquitlam is policed under contract by the RCMP. Both the Vancouver Police Department and the Coquitlam RCMP were slow to initiate investigations, and there were ongoing issues between the two police services, including a lack of communication and information sharing.

Pickton was finally arrested in 2002, and the search for evidence on his property over the next several years became the largest and most expensive police investigation in Canadian history. Over a two-year period, 235,000 pieces of DNA evidence were gathered, and the remains of thirty women were identified. It is estimated that Pickton killed sixty-five women over a fifteen-year period on his farm. In 2007, Pickton was convicted of second-degree murder of six women and given a life sentence with no possibility of parole for twenty-five years.

The Vancouver Police Department conducted an extensive internal review of its handling of the Pickton investigation and identified a number of organizational factors that had hindered the investigation.[21] The provincial government subsequently appointed a retired judge to conduct an examination of the missing women's investigation. Among the findings of the final report were that the police had failed to act to protect marginalized women and that there were systematic failures in the investigative process that delayed the apprehension of Pickton.[22] More specifically, the police were criticized for a failure of leadership, a failure to consider and pursue all investigative strategies, and inadequate staffing and resources. Compounding these were the lack of a regional police service that would have facilitated communication and the sharing of information among police investigators.

Similar concerns have surrounded police investigations of missing and murdered Aboriginal women in Canada. The Native Women's Association of Canada estimates that, as of 2010, there were 582 cases of missing and murdered Aboriginal women and girls.[23] This figure is disputed by the RCMP, which places the number at less than one hundred. From its investigation, Human Rights Watch concluded: "The failure of law enforcement authorities to deal effectively with the problem of missing and murdered indigenous women and girls in Canada is just one element of the dysfunctional relationship between the Canadian police and indigenous people."[24] The report, based on eighty-seven interviews that included forty-two indigenous women and eight indigenous girls, documented their experiences of abuse at the hands of the police and the absence of police action to investigate cases of domestic abuse and of missing and murdered women.

Across the country, a number of police task forces are investigating missing persons cases as well as "cold case" homicides. This includes the area along Highway 16 (christened "The Highway of Tears"), which runs across the northern part of British Columbia. Since 1969, thirty-two women have been murdered or gone missing on this stretch of highway, most while hitchhiking. An RCMP special unit is conducting an ongoing review of the cases, although the majority remain unsolved. See the Media Link, "Highway of Tears," at the end of this chapter. In Manitoba, a joint RCMP–Winnipeg Police Service task force was, as of 2015, examining a number of missing persons and homicide cases dating back to 1961.

The issues of missing and murdered women is viewed by many as one of Canada's top human rights issues. Although a United Nations human rights investigator as well as Aboriginal leaders and organizations have called for a national inquiry into missing and murdered women, as of mid-2015, the federal government had not acted on these calls.

THE ANALYSIS OF SPECIFIC TYPES OF EVIDENCE

Evidence gathered at a crime scene must be analyzed to determine its usefulness in solving the crime and identifying suspects. In forensic analysis, trained personnel and laboratory technicians examine this evidence. They play a critical role in case investigations and provide laboratory analyses and examinations of physical evidence. They also prepare reports and arrange expert court testimony on the results of their analyses. Forensic scientists and technologists can be civilians or sworn police officers.

Specific types of evidence are regularly subjected to forensic analysis as part of case investigations. Fingerprints are useful in placing an individual at a crime scene, although they cannot be lifted from all surfaces. Once fingerprints are lifted, the investigators may access the national Automated Fingerprint Identification System (AFIS). AFIS is a system of fingerprint workstations and databases across Canada, many of which are networked together and to the RCMP national system in Ottawa. Evidence can also be gathered from firearms, bullets, and casings. Hair can be used in DNA analysis, and fibres found at a crime scene can be positively compared to fibres found on the suspect or in the suspect's car or home.

DNA: The Genetic Fingerprint

DNA
genetic information that can be used in case investigations

DNA is the acronym for deoxyribonucleic acid, which is often referred to as the blueprint of the body and the basic building blocks of life. Human bodies have trillions of cells. Each cell contains a nucleus, within which are 46 chromosomes divided into 23 pairs. These chromosomes are inherited from both parents. Chromosomes consist of two long, twisted strands of DNA, called a double helix. Human DNA is divided into about 100,000 clusters called genes. Genes determine such human characteristics as height, eye colour, and hair colour. Each gene is composed of molecules called nucleotides, which occur in four different shapes—adenine, cytosine, guanine, and thymine—and which are arranged in pairs along the strands of DNA. Sources of forensic DNA evidence include blood, semen, tissue, hair (root), saliva, tooth (pulp), and bone (marrow).

The DNA of every person is unique (except in the case of identical twins, who receive the same genetic material from both parents). DNA analysis, or genetic fingerprinting, involves various molecular biological techniques and allows perpetrators to be identified through direct analysis of specific sites on the DNA molecule.

The use of DNA evidence by investigators has increased significantly over the past decade, especially since 1995, when the Criminal Code was amended, allowing police to obtain warrants for bodily substances that enable DNA analysis. Acting under the authority of a search warrant, police can obtain either blood (by a simple finger lancet) or saliva (by swabbing the inside of the mouth). The Supreme Court of Canada held in *R. v. Stillman*, 1997, 1 S.C.R. 607, that the police can use DNA evidence collected from discarded items, such as chewing gum, drink containers, and cigarettes and that gathering such evidence does not violate a person's privacy rights and does not breach a person's Charter rights.[25] Box 10.1 presents information on the types, location, and sources of DNA evidence.

Box 10.1

Identifying DNA Evidence: Selected Examples

Evidence	Possible Location of DNA on the Evidence	Source of DNA
Bandana, hat, mask	Anywhere (inside or outside)	Dandruff, hair, saliva, sweat
Bite mark	Clothing, skin	Saliva
Blanket, pillow, sheet	Surface area	Blood, hair, saliva, semen, sweat, urine
Bottle, can, glass	Mouthpiece, rim, sides	Saliva, sweat
Fingernail, partial fingernail	Scrapings	Blood, sweat, tissue
Used cigarette	Cigarette butt	Saliva
Used condom	Inside/outside surface	Rectal or vaginal cells, semen

Source: National Institute of Justice, 2012. "DNA Evidence Basics," Washington: U.S. Department of Justice, http://www.dna.gov/basics/evidence_collection/identifying.

Under Section 487.04 of the Criminal Code, the police can obtain DNA warrants only for certain offences. These include murder, manslaughter, assault, sexual assault, and sexual exploitation, as well as a number of other specifically identified crimes.

DNA testing has been accepted by Canadian courts since 1988. DNA analysis is most commonly used to identify suspects in violent crimes using biological samples (e.g., semen, saliva, hair, blood) found at crime scenes.

DNA analysis serves a number of important functions in case investigations. For example, it can

- establish the association between the victim and the suspect in a murder, a sexual assault, or another violent crime;
- identify the weapon used;
- identify where the crime took place;
- determine whether a series of murders or sexual assaults has been committed by the same person or whether a copycat offender is involved;
- exonerate the wrongly accused; *and*
- identify the remains of victims.

DNA enables crime investigators to solve crimes that would, in many cases, go unsolved (see Police File 10.2).

Police File 10.2

DNA Helps Solve a Home Invasion

In 2012, in Saskatoon, Saskatchewan, two masked men forced their way into a home around 1 a.m. and demanded drugs and cash from the residents, a young man and woman, who later told police that one of the invaders had been carrying a collapsible baton, the other, a machete. The male victim was held in the living room while the young woman locked herself in a bedroom. The two men fled after the woman told them she had called the police. When police arrived, the victims gave descriptions of the suspects, indicating that one of the men had been wearing a black neck warmer. Police used dogs to conduct a search and found the neck warmer. They also noted a distinct shoe print in the snow that matched a shoe print found in the home. The DNA profile developed from the neck warmer matched the DNA of one of the perpetrators, who was already registered in the National DNA Data Bank as a result of a previous conviction. The man was later arrested, and his shoe was found to match the prints left at the scene. He accepted responsibility for the home invasion and indicated that his accomplice that night had since died. In 2013, he was sentenced to four years in prison for the home invasion.

Source: Royal Canadian Mounted Police, "The National DNA Data Bank of Canada: Annual Report 2009–2010" (Ottawa: 2010), p. 9, http://www.rcmp-grc.gc.ca/nddb-bndg/index.htm. Reprinted with the permission of the RCMP.

DNA analysis can also be used to exonerate people who have been wrongfully convicted. There are a number of cases in which wrongfully convicted persons spent years in prison before being exonerated by DNA evidence. Many of them had been convicted prior to the development of DNA analysis.

However, contaminated or improperly collected DNA has also led to wrongful convictions. When confronted with DNA evidence, defence lawyers have generally counselled their clients to accept a plea bargain. Concerns have centred on cross-contamination and mislabelling of DNA samples, a lack of quality control in testing procedures, and, in some instances, DNA analysts who falsify test results. Gregory Turner, convicted of killing an elderly woman in Newfoundland, spent 27 months in prison before it was determined that the technician who analyzed the DNA sample in the laboratory had contaminated the evidence.[26]

New advances in DNA technology will allow the identification of a suspect's ancestors, and this has raised concerns about genetic profiling. In the U.S. and the U.K., familial DNA matches are used to identify a suspect: police in L.A. had the DNA of the suspect in the "Grim Reaper" serial killer case, but couldn't find a match on any DNA database. They found a near match in the DNA databank from a young man who had been recently convicted of a weapons charge. The investigators followed his father and lifted a DNA sample from a discarded slice of pizza. His father turned out to be the Grim Reaper.[27] The use of familial DNA is controversial, and it remains to be seen whether the legal provisions will be put in place for this practice to be used by Canadian police services. See Figure 10.2 on page 299 for a diagram on how DNA fingerprinting works.

The National DNA Data Bank

The National DNA Data Bank (http://www.nddb-bndg.org) was established under the DNA Identification Act (1998, c. 37) and a legislative amendment (Bill C 13). This legislation defines the procedures for collecting, storing, using, and destroying DNA samples taken from criminal offenders, as well as for identifying those offenders who are required to submit a DNA sample. The bank is managed by the RCMP and holds the genetic profiles of more than three thousand offenders. The objective here is to link unsolved crimes and determine whether DNA from a person matches DNA found at these crime scenes. The bank also contains DNA evidence obtained from the scene of unsolved crimes.

The DNA samples are taken from people who have been convicted of certain serious crimes, including murder and sexual assault. These samples are matched with samples of blood, hair, bone, or semen taken from crime scenes or from the bodies of crime victims. With the approval of a judge, DNA samples can be taken from convicted offenders without their consent.

In recent years, there has been an effort to expand the collection of DNA evidence from persons who have not been convicted of a crime. See Class/Group Discussion 10.1 at the end of this chapter.

COLD CASE SQUADS

cold case squads
specialized units that focus on unsolved serious crimes

Many urban police services have created **cold case squads**, which focus exclusively on unsolved serious crimes. Sophisticated techniques for gathering and

Police File 10.3

DNA Closes a Cold Case

On July 17, 1984, Denise Morelle, a popular performer in a children's theatre in Montreal, was found strangled in a vacant apartment in Montreal. The actress had gone to the apartment during a search for new accommodation. The owner had indicated that it was unlocked and that she could visit it anytime. Her body, with small burn marks, was found the next day. Initially, investigators believed that she had surprised vagrants who may have been in the apartment. However, the case went cold and remained unsolved for 23 years.

In 2006, Montreal police announced that they had arrested 49-year-old Gaetan Bissonnette and charged him with first-degree murder. Bissonnette had been convicted of break and enter in 2006 and was required to submit a DNA sample to the National DNA Data Bank. His DNA matched that found on Denise Morelle years earlier. Bissonnette was subsequently convicted of second-degree murder with no possibility of parole for 20 years.

Source: The Gazette (Montreal), 2007

analyzing DNA specimens, and computer-based systems such as ViCLAS, now allow police investigators to revisit—and often solve—crimes that are years or even decades old. A cold case that was solved through the use of DNA is presented in Police File 10.3.

FORENSIC SPECIALISTS

A number of other forensic specialists may be called on to assist in criminal investigations. These include forensic anthropologists who help identify bones and skeletal remains. These specialists focus on identifying the deceased person (gender, race, age) and determining the cause of death as well as the circumstances surrounding the death. Forensic entomology is the study of insects associated with a human body. It is used in death investigations to determine time of death, but it can also be used to determine other factors, such as whether a body has been moved or disturbed after death, the position of the body at death, and the presence of wounds (see Police File 10.4).

"Mr. Big" technique
an investigative strategy designed to secure confessions from crime suspects through the creation of an elaborate scenario

THE "MR. BIG" TECHNIQUE: A CONTROVERSIAL INVESTIGATIVE STRATEGY

A particularly controversial investigation technique used by Canadian police is known as the **"Mr. Big" technique**. The technique has been used in hundreds of investigations over the past twenty-five years. This is referred to as

Police File 10.4

The Use of Forensic Entomology to Solve a Crime

On June 4, the partially clad body of a young female was found alongside a rural highway in the northwestern United States. An autopsy revealed that she died of multiple head and neck wounds inflicted by a heavy, sharp object. She was later identified as a 14-year-old prostitute. Her brother had reported her as missing approximately four days before her corpse was discovered.

She was last seen alive on the morning of May 31 in the company of a 30-year-old army sergeant, the primary suspect. While strong circumstantial evidence supported the theory that the sergeant had murdered her, an accurate estimation of time of death was crucial to establishing a possible link between the suspect and the victim at the time the death occurred.

Several estimates of postmortem interval were offered by medical examiners and investigators. These were based largely on the physical appearance of the body and on the extent to which decompositional changes had occurred in various organs. They were not based on any quantitative scientific methodology.

Numerous fly larvae (maggots), adult flies, and other insects were observed and collected in and around the victim's wounds. Some were placed alive in small containers and later reared to produce adult flies. Others were placed immediately in a liquid preservative. Additional specimens collected at the autopsy were processed in a similar manner. Numerous photographs of the crime scene, the surrounding vegetation and terrain, and the corpse were taken. These photographs included enlargements illustrating the adult flies and maggots present at the time the body was discovered.

Reports describing the condition of the body when found and detailing autopsy procedures and results were reviewed. Climatological data, including maximum and minimum temperatures, incidence of rainfall, cloud cover, wind speed and direction, and relative humidity, were obtained from a government weather station a short distance from where the victim was found. These data indicated the environmental conditions to which the remains and its insect associates were exposed.

Based on this array of evidence, entomologists determined that the first insects to colonize the remains had arrived on May 31. The insect evidence indicated a PMI (postmortem interval: the time elapsed since a person has died). Based on this evidence, the army sergeant with whom the victim had last been seen alive was arrested and charged with first-degree murder. On questioning, he admitted to having murdered the girl by striking her six to eight times with a small hatchet sometime around noon on May 31. Subsequently, he pled guilty to the murder charge and was sentenced to life in prison without parole.

Source: Forensic investigations: Case Studies. (2013, June). The University of Western Australia. Retrieved from http://www.clt.uwa.edu.au/__data/assets/word_doc/0020/2332316/FSE09.doc

a "non-custodial" interrogation strategy and is prohibited in the U.S. and in Europe where it is considered entrapment and a contributor to false confessions.

The technique involves police undercover officers befriending crime suspects who are subsequently introduced to "Mr. Big," a purported organized crime boss. The target(s) are then invited to join the crime group, but only if they admit to having committed a major crime.[28]

While police services have pointed out that the Mr. Big technique has a 75 percent confession rate and a 95 percent conviction rate, this has not silenced critics. There are concerns that Mr. Big stings are really dirty tricks that lead to false confessions and the conviction of innocent persons. Critics have argued that the practice raises legal, moral, and ethical issues.[29] Of concern is that suspects who are questioned about crimes in a Mr. Big scenario have none of the legal safeguards of persons who are interrogated in a "custodial" setting. And there is little documentation on when the strategy fails and the consequences of this failure (e.g., false confessions, wrongful convictions).

The technique has been successful in securing the conviction of many offenders, and the convictions were subsequently corroborated by other evidence and upheld on appeal. There have also been instances in which suspects who confessed to police in a Mr. Big operation were later exonerated by DNA evidence. See Police Files 10.5 and 10.6.

In previous cases, Canadian courts had ruled that the police may engage in deception to catch criminals, and this included the Mr. Big strategy (e.g., *R. v. Mentuck*, 2000, MBQB 155; *R. v. Bonisteel*, 2009, NSSC 30). In July 2014, however, in the case of *R. v. Hart*, 2014, SCC 52, the Supreme Court placed restrictions on the admissibility of evidence, including suspect confessions, garnered through the use of the Mr. Big technique. Mr. Hart, who has a Grade 5 level of education and was on social assistance, was the prime suspect in the drowning deaths of his twin daughters in Newfoundland in 2002. In 2005, the RCMP spent over $400,000 to construct an elaborate Mr. Big operation, wherein officers posed as gangsters and recruited Hart to join their crime network. Mr. Hart participated in activities, including moving what he thought was stolen property. In addition to being wined and dined at restaurants and casinos, he was paid nearly $16,000. To remain part of the gang, Mr. Hart was required to "confess" to any previous crimes. The court concluded that the scenario required Mr. Hart to confess to a crime.

On the basis of his "confession," Hart was found guilty of first-degree murder and received a life sentence with no possibility of parole for twenty-five years. In 2012, the Newfoundland Court of Appeal overturned the conviction, finding that the lengths to which the RCMP went in the Mr. Big operation violated Mr. Hart's rights and that the tactics were excessive and unjust. The SCC agreed, noting that Mr. Hart had been subjected to physical and psychological harm. At the time of the SCC decision, Hart had served nine years in prison.

In its decision, the SCC ruled that confessions obtained via the Mr. Big strategy rely on coercion, threats, and financial inducements and should be presumed to be inadmissible in court. However, the court left open the possibility that evidence gathered from Mr. Big stings could be admitted in court if the prosecutors are able to convince the presiding judge that the reliability of the evidence outweighs any prejudicial effects of the strategy. This will require the police and prosecutors to gather corroborating evidence to support the suspect's confession.[30]

Also in 2014, an Ontario Superior Court judge acquitted a man who had been charged as a result of an elaborate Mr. Big sting, which involved him

Police File 10.5

Mr. Big and a False Confession

On June 24, 1990, the body of 16-year old Brigitte Grenier was found on the grounds of a ski resort in Roseilse, Manitoba. She had been strangled and her body mutilated. One of two suspects in the killing was 19-year-old Kyle Unger, who had been seen with Grenier at a rock concert near where the body was located. Unger and his friend were charged and arrested for first-degree murder. The Crown entered a stay of proceedings. However, while being held in custody awaiting bail, Unger made statements to his cellmate (a jailhouse informant) that implicated him in the murder.

Based on this, the RCMP developed a Mr. Big scenario in order to gather more evidence from Unger. Two undercover agents pretended to have their vehicle break down near a farm where Unger was working. The two officers befriended Unger and led him to believe that they were part of a criminal organization. Unger was invited to join the group, but he was told that he would have to be truthful about his past criminal activities in order to become part of the gang. Unger stated that he had killed Brigitte Grenier. At trial, Mr. Unger recanted his confession, stating that during what turned out to be a Mr. Big scenario, he had been offered employment, the potential to earn a lot of money, and membership in the gang. He indicated that although he initially denied having killed the victim, he subsequently confessed to the crime for financial gain. He was convicted on the basis of his Mr. Big confession and two pieces of corroborative evidence: hair consistent with his found on the victim's sweater and comments he had made to the jailhouse informant.

Mr. Unger appealed his conviction to the Manitoba Court of Appeal on the grounds that the Mr. Big sting involved entrapment. This appeal was rejected and leave to appeal to the Supreme Court of Canada was also denied. He then spent 14 years in prison. In 2004, the hair comparison evidence used at trial was called into question by a forensic review committee. DNA testing found no trace of Mr. Unger on any of the exhibits used at trial and did not link him to the crime scene.

He was released on bail in 2005 pending a ministerial review of his case. In 2009, the Crown dropped murder charges against him, admitting that there was not sufficient evidence for a retrial.

When asked by a reporter following his acquittal why he would have confessed to a crime that he had not committed, Unger replied, "When you're young, naïve and desperate for money, they hold a lot of promises to you, so you say and do what you have to do to survive . . ." In 2011, Mr. Unger filed a $14.5 million wrongful-conviction lawsuit against federal and Manitoba justice officials, the RCMP, and prosecutors. The defendants have all filed documents in court denying the allegations. As of 2015, the case was still before the courts.

Sources: T.E. Moore. (2009, November 29). Eliciting wrongful convictions by Mr. Big lies - the Unger case. Law Enforcement Accountability Project [blog]. Retrieved from http://windsorlaw-leap.blogspot.ca/2009/11/eliciting-wrongful-convictions-by-mr.html; T. Riddell and K. Puddister. (2014, August 6). Who's in charge of Mr. Big? *National Post*. Retrieved from http://fullcomment.nationalpost.com/2014/08/06/riddell-puddister-whos-in-charge-of-mr-big/

Police File 10.6

The Successful Use of the Mr. Big Strategy

On March 22, 1992, in Sydney, Nova Scotia, convenience store clerk Marie Dupe was stabbed to death during a robbery. The assailant fled the store with cash and cartons of cigarettes and then disappeared into a snowstorm, which prevented police dogs from picking up his trail. Left behind at the scene were several pieces of evidence, including a coffee cup and several cigarette butts. Owing to the state of forensic science at the time, the items could not be analyzed for DNA, but were put into an evidence storage locker. The crime remain unsolved for a decade. In 2001, advances in forensic technology made it possible to conduct a DNA analysis on the evidence. Using the National DNA Data Bank, the police scored a hit on Gordon Strowbridge, who had provided DNA after being convicted of an assault. The DNA matched that found on one of the cigarette butts outside the convenience store where Marie Dupe had been killed. This placed him at the scene, but did not prove that he had committed the crime.

While being processed for an outstanding warrant, Strowbridge was befriended by an undercover police officer who posed as a criminal and offered him a job. In the following months, Strowbridge was involved in a number of car thefts that were set up by the police. He was then offered a chance to meet "Mr. Big" and to move higher in the criminal organization. During the interview with Mr. Big, he admitted to killing Marie Dupe. This was recorded on a hidden camera and led to Strowbridge pleading guilty and being sent to prison.

Source: S.M. Smith, V. Stinson, and M.W. Patry. (2009). Using the "Mr. Big" technique to elicit confessions: Successful innovation or dangerous development in the Canadian legal system? *Psychology, Public Policy, and Law, 15*(3), 168–93.

believing he was enmeshed in a crime ring and the dumping of a bloody corpse (in reality a mannequin) off a cliff. In his ruling, the judge stated that admitting the evidence would "shock the sense of trial fairness to Canadian society."[31] View the documentary film, "Mr. Big Stings: Cops, Criminals and Confessions," listed in the Media Links at the end of this chapter.

THE INTERROGATION OF CRIME SUSPECTS

The tools and techniques discussed so far in this chapter are intended to identify an individual (or individuals) who may have committed the crime. Once this has been done, the police interrogate the suspect in an attempt to confirm the results of their analysis of the evidence. Despite the importance of this phase of the investigation, the interrogation of crime suspects is one of the least studied features of police work.

Interrogations are usually conducted with four objectives: (1) to obtain a confession or at least a partial admission of guilt; (2) to eliminate innocent people from the investigation; (3) to identify the guilty party (even if a confession is not obtained, the interrogator may become aware of the guilty party and follow up with other investigative options such as surveillance, undercover operatives, or wiretaps); and (4) to gather information regarding other crimes and/or suspects. A considerable amount of skill is involved in conducting interviews, and investigating officers use various techniques to obtain information from suspects, witnesses, and victims.

Officers rely mainly on psychological persuasion to obtain confessions. In an era of Charter rights, extreme interview tactics are seldom used. However, the Supreme Court of Canada has ruled that the Charter does not confer a right of suspects to have a lawyer present during interrogation (see *R. v. Sinclair*, 2010, SCC 35; *R. v. McCrimmon*, 2010, SCC 36; and *R. v. Willier*, 2010, SCC 37).

An experienced police investigator will attempt to "bond" with the suspect and to gain their trust and confidence. There are even instances in which the suspect has re-enacted the crime for the interrogator.

For an inside look at a police interrogation in a high-profile case involving heinous crimes, see the police interviews with Colonel Russell Williams, a commanding officer in the Canadian Air Force who was subsequently convicted of a series of brutal sexual assaults and murders. See the Media Link, "The Confession," at the end of this chapter. The interview with Williams was conducted by an OPP detective-sergeant, a specialist in the police service's Behavioural Sciences and Analysis Services unit, which works on violent and sexual crimes. Williams subsequently pleaded guilty to a total of eighty-eight crimes: two counts of first-degree murder, two counts of sexual assault, and two counts of forcible confinement, and eighty-two counts of break and enter and attempted break and enter. He received two life sentences, with no eligibility for parole for twenty-five years.

For another interrogation, see the Media Link, "Byron Sonne Interview with Detective Bui, June 23," at the end of this chapter. Mr. Sonne faced a number of charges related to the G20 protests in Toronto but was found not guilty on all counts at trial in 2012.

The Right of Suspects to Remain Silent

Under Canadian law, police officers have no formal powers to compel crime suspects to answer their questions. Suspects have a right to remain silent, and police officers must inform them of that right. They must also inform suspects that any statements they do make may be used against them in a criminal trial. (In reality, remaining silent may only make things worse for the suspect: when a person refuses to answer some general questions asked by the officer, this may raise suspicions and result in an arrest.) The right to remain silent does not extend to situations where a citizen would thereby be able to obstruct a police officer from carrying out his or her duties. Suspects who have low levels of intelligence or other impairment may not understand their right to silence and its implications.

The courts have also taken a dim view of the use of trickery by police to obtain confessions. The classic case involves placing an undercover police officer in a cell with a suspect; the officer then encourages the suspect to make incriminating statements. The Supreme Court of Canada has established strict limits on the extent to which police can use this tactic to obtain a confession from a suspect who has refused to make a formal statement to the police. However, voluntary statements made by a suspect to a cellmate (who may be an undercover police officer) may not violate the suspect's right to remain silent and may be admissible at trial if the admission does not bring the administration of justice into disrepute.

Interrogation and False Confessions

Innocent people confess to crimes they did not commit for a variety of reasons, including a desire to escape the psychological pressures of the interview room, sleep deprivation, an attempt to cover for another suspect, a desire to the police, mental impairment, and drug or alcohol addiction or withdrawal.[32] This, in turn, may lead to a person being wrongfully convicted.

While false confessions are rare, investigating officers must always carefully assess the reliability of a suspect's statement or confession against all other known facts. Actual innocence may not protect individuals from being wrongfully convicted. Innocent people often waive their right to legal assistance, and certain interview techniques can elicit false confessions. It has been stated that "innocence puts innocents at risk."[33]

Officers must be cognizant that the way in which questions are asked may induce a suspect to falsely confess. In the words of a man who (along with two others) falsely confessed to the rape and murder of a fourteen-year-old girl in Regina (and was later exonerated when DNA evidence convicted another man):

> I'm not even sure how to explain it because I'm not sure how it happened to me . . . All I know is for hours on end I said 'No, I had nothing to do with it.' Next thing you know I'm sitting there going 'Sure, why not. I did it.' More or less it's like they kill your spirit or something."[34]

ANALYTICAL TOOLS

To assist in case investigations, police services use sophisticated analytical techniques. Some systems combine behavioural science research with computer analysis to generate profiles of crime scenes and perpetrators; others apply forensic science to evidence gathered during the investigation. Among the more commonly used analytical tools are the following.

Criminal Profiling

criminal profiling
a strategy to identify suspects by constructing biographical and psychological sketches based on crime scene evidence

Criminal profiling has been described as "the practice of predicting a criminal's personality, behavioral and demographic characteristics based on crime scene evidence."[35] The typical profile involves preparing a biographical sketch based on information taken from the crime scene as well as victim-related materials.

The objective of criminal profiling is to provide the investigation with a personality composite of the unknown suspect(s). The profiler studies a crime scene from a psychological standpoint, interpreting evidence there for clues to the personality of the individual who committed the crime.

A criminal profile attempts to determine the attributes of the offender, which may include age, gender, ethnicity, marital status/adjustment, intelligence, education level, lifestyle, the environment in which the person was raised, social adjustment, personality style/characteristics, demeanour, appearance and grooming, emotional adjustment, evidence of mental decomposition, pathological behavioural characteristics, employment/occupational history and adjustment, work habits, residency in relation to the crime scene, socioeconomic status, sexual adjustment, type of sexual perversion or disturbance (if applicable), and motive. The profiler is also able to analyze the scene in terms of emotions such as rage, hate, love, fear, and irrationality.

Despite its use in case investigations, concerns have been raised about the validity and effectiveness of criminal profiling. Police scholars have argued that the approach lacks a scientific basis and that there is no evidence that it works.[36] Evaluative research is required to test the assumptions upon which criminal profiling is premised, as well as the concerns that have been expressed about its use.

Violent Crime Linkages Analysis System (ViCLAS)

Canadian police services collaborated in the development of a system to track serial killers and violent offenders and link their crimes. Known as the **ViCLAS** (Violent Crime Linkages Analysis System), this system combines current findings from behavioural research with sophisticated computer technology.

ViCLAS
the Violent Crime Linkages Analysis System, used by investigators that includes information on predatory and sexual crimes of violence

ViCLAS is designed to capture information on all homicides that are sexual or predatory in nature and/or that are apparently random, motiveless, or suspected of being part of a series, as well as all sexual assaults or attempted assaults of a predatory nature, including stranger-to-stranger assaults, date rapes, and pedophilia crimes. It also captures information on missing persons when the circumstances indicate a strong possibility of foul play, and when the victim is still missing; on unidentified bodies when the manner of death is unknown or suspected to be a homicide; and on all non-parental abductions and attempts at abduction. The underlying premise of ViCLAS is that repeat offenders follow similar patterns and that homicidal and sexual offenders have identifiable and often predictable characteristics and motives.

Geographic Profiling

Geographic profiling is related to the broader investigative strategy of criminal or psychological profiling. Essentially, geographic profiling involves analyzing behavioural patterns that relate to space or geography and incorporating the findings as they relate to the journey to crime, or crime-trip distance. This is the distance that offenders travel from their residence or place of work to commit crimes.

geographic profiling
the analysis of behaviour patterns that relate to space or geography, with particular reference to the journey to crime

Geographic profiling is based on a number of key findings with respect to patterns of criminal offending, including that most crimes occur in relatively close proximity to the offender's place of residence or work, often referred to as the offender's "comfort zone"; that the number of crimes committed by an offender decreases as the distance from the offender's residence increases; and that the distance that offenders travel often increases as their criminal career develops. For example, the first murder committed by a serial killer is the one most likely to be closest to the offender's home.[37]

Geographic profilers often apply computer technology to create a Geographic Information System (GIS; see Chapter 9). These systems can be used to generate foot patrol maps and to plan patrol strategies. The sources of information required to conduct geographic profiling include data on the crimes, the locations where the crimes were committed, data on the victims, a criminal profile, and data on the suspect.[38]

Through spatial analysis, high-volume crimes often associated with career criminals (e.g., break and enters, auto theft, and armed robbery) can be charted, and three-dimensional computer maps can be generated that indicate the areas most likely to be associated with the residence, worksite, social venue, and travel routes of offenders.

Criminal Intelligence Analysis

criminal intelligence analysis
the use of sophisticated computer programs to analyze information gathered on suspected criminal activity

Case investigation is often assisted by **criminal intelligence analysis**, which utilizes sophisticated computer programs to analyze information gathered on suspected criminal activity.

These analyses attempt to identify relationships between criminal groups and among individuals and are utilized by case investigators on an operational level. Criminal intelligence analysis can also be used to inform strategic decision making in a police service about potential threats and emerging criminal issues. Figure 10.2 provides an example of the type of information that can be generated by criminal intelligence analysts.

There is also mapping software such as ArcGIS. This uses sophisticated techniques in identifying offenders and their "journey to crime"; conducting "hot spot" analysis where the events were taking place; as well as applying geo-profiling variables to offenders and how they choose where to "hunt" and commit their offences in relation to where they live and work.

Social Network Analysis

social network analysis
an analytical technique that is designed to show the relationships between individuals in a criminal network

Social network analysis is an analytical technique that is designed to show the relationships between individuals in a criminal network. It is able to determine the level of cohesion amongst the key leaders in the crime group, and is a way for the police to focus its resources (see Police Perspective 10.2).

There is also *call frequency analysis*, which examines the call patterns and frequencies related to certain events: who is calling whom, time and days of the week and with what frequency, and the duration of calls. Call analysis can assist in identifying who the key stakeholders are, who the key leaders are, and which people are in positions of responsibility for taking action. In the case of an extortion, for example, the crime analysts can historically go back and look at the calls between persons. Every time someone ordered an activity, the gang leader may call his lieutenants. This may involve running hundreds of thousands of phone records over a period of months.

Figure 10.2. How DNA Fingerprinting Works

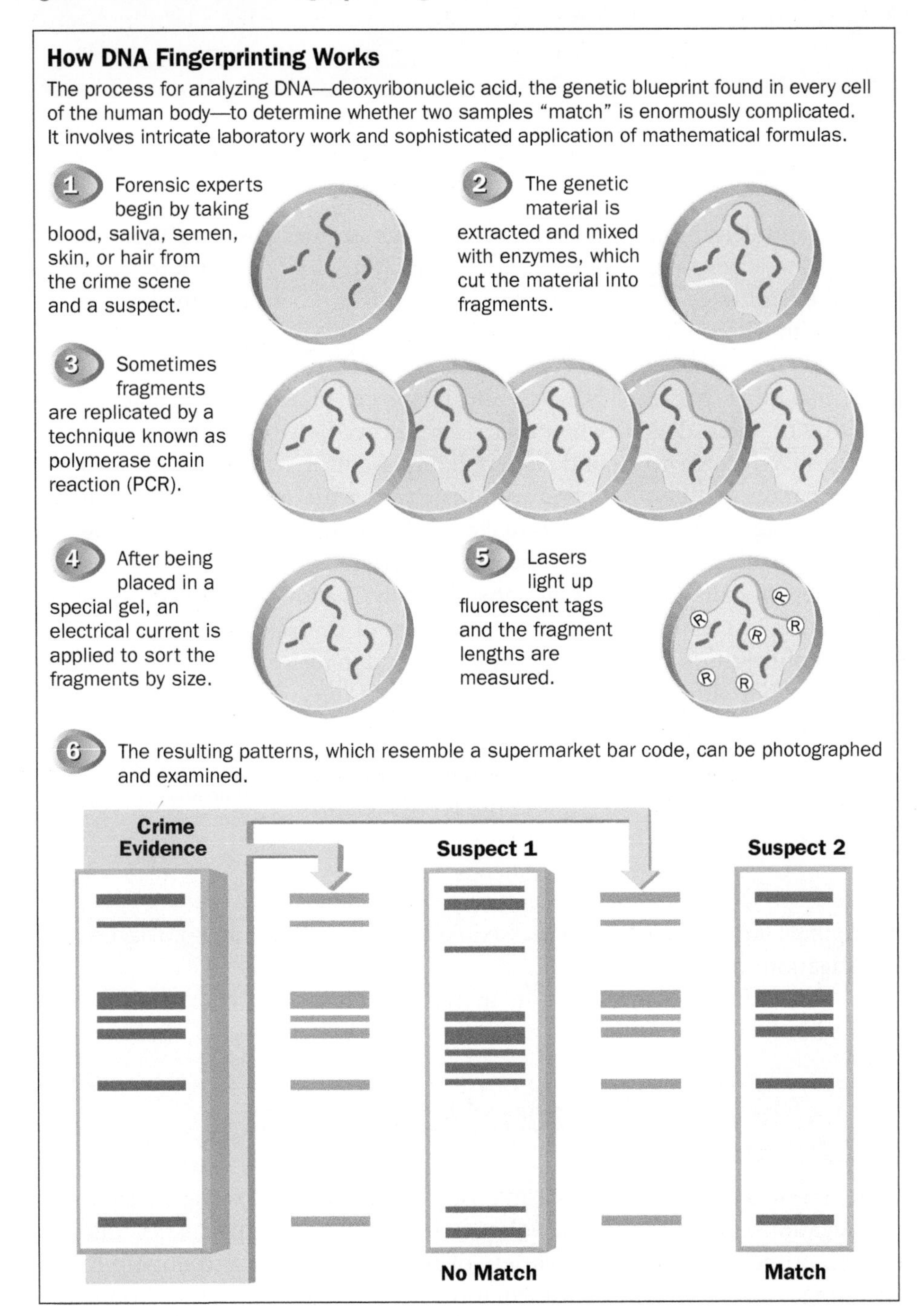

Source: S. Strauss, "Fingerprints Leaving Fingerprints of Their Own," *Globe and Mail*, June 19, 1997, A1, A3. Created from material by Cellmark Diagnostics, Lifecodes Corp., and Cetus Corp.

A key objective of these and other analytical techniques is to break down the information "silos" that have traditionally existed in police services and to create large data sets that can be subjected to sophisticated analysis. Police services must ensure that sworn officers and civilian staff have the expertise to

Police Perspective 10.2

A Crime Analyst Describes the Use of Social Network Analysis

Social network analysis allows us to determine where to do surveillance on persons involved in criminal networks—what their routines are, where they go, who is meeting with whom. The data that are used in the analysis are gathered from a variety of sources, including patrol officers and specialty units. All of these data are pulled in, analyzed, and distilled down to the important kernels of information that you need to focus on. Twenty years ago, people would do this on a wall chart or a pad of paper. They would sketch out a small network analysis. Now the amount of information on crime groups would fill rooms. The sophistication of the crime groups and the relationships among the crime groups are much more complex. Different crime groups will come together and cooperate on a specific project, such as the movement of drugs or firearms, and then go their separate ways. The ability of track this and make sense of it, this is where the intelligence analysts really shine.

We can put surveillance teams on them, in vehicles, and in spotter planes. It's a challenge when there is a massive network of 300 people and a surveillance team of 20 people. You can spend months chasing the wrong people. You better make certain you are focusing on the right people, otherwise you waste resources. Social network analysis allows you to come up with measurements of centrality and cohesion among the group and to identify the key people who have a leadership role.

Source: Personal communication with author, May 2014.

manipulate large data sets, and be flexible enough to adopt an approach to case investigations based on analysis.

A successful case investigation that used various analytical techniques is profiled in Police File 10.7.

THE USE OF MEDIA AND SOCIAL MEDIA IN CASE INVESTIGATIONS

Police services are making increasing use of the media and social media in case investigations. For many years, police have made public appeals for information on crimes and operated a variety of reward programs and hot-tip lines to encourage citizens to provide information, even anonymously, that would assist in identifying suspects. See the Media Link, "Mike Pimentel Homicide Witness Appeal to Call Toronto Police Wayne Banks at 416-808-7411," at the end of the chapter.

A recent phenomenon is "Serial." See the Media Link, "Serial: The podcast everyone's talking about," at the end of this chapter. "Serial" was originally developed in the U.S. in relation to the 1999 murder of a young woman in Baltimore. Her boyfriend was subsequently arrested, charged, and convicted

Police File 10.7

A Successful Case Investigation

Between 1995 and 2009, a series of violent sexual assaults on young girls on their way home from school occurred in Vancouver and in the surrounding municipalities of Delta and Surrey. The attacks were premeditated, and the girls were targeted when they were in secluded areas. A joint forces operation (JFO), Project Scourge, comprising the Vancouver Police Department and two other police services in the region, was established to investigate the cases and apprehend the offender.

The investigation revealed that a single offender was responsible for all of the attacks. A total of 561 potential suspects were identified, and each was investigated through the examination of castoff DNA and interviews. The team also sought the assistance of an FBI profiler. Despite months of investigation, however, the team had been unable to identify a suspect. During the investigation into the initial attacks, the offender committed another violent sexual assault. The victim was younger than the previous victims and the attack more violent than the previous assaults. A concern was that if the offender was not apprehended, the next attack might result in the death of the victim.

A challenge for the investigators was the high level of sophistication exhibited by the offender in planning and carrying out the attacks. It was determined that the offender was likely a highly educated individual who carefully planned each attack.

Eighteen months into the investigation, a new inspector was placed in charge of the investigation. One of his first actions was to question why a crime analyst had not been part of the investigative team. A special constable in the Vancouver Police Department, who had expertise in crime analysis, was subsequently assigned to the team. He began working on the investigation with a sergeant from the Rotterdam (Netherlands) police who had been seconded to the VPD to learn about crime analysis.

The two investigators took a new approach to the case that departed from the traditional case investigation approach of tracking the suspect's modus operandi and developing an inventory of known offenders with similar offence patterns.

Over the course of eight weeks, the two analysts had gathered data on geographical patterns, including residential tenancy changes based on housing sales, movements of renters, driver's licence change histories, and the offender's methods, hunting paradigms, and movements from geographic location to geographic location. The data analysis included predictive algorithms using the Vancouver Police Department's GIS system (the geography-based program that enables the creation and organization of link geographic information) to see where the attacks occurred to try to isolate the most likely places where the offender might have lived based on common locations and a comfort zone of operating. At the time, this type of data was not traditionally examined and police investigations.

These data were combined with information from the Vancouver Police Department's CRIME system, the provincial data warehouse repository, and the system began to crunch through the numbers. The system provided the name of a man who hit on 98 percent of the criteria that the two analysts had set out. They were subsequently able to locate the individual on Facebook and obtained his picture, which corresponded with the sketches that had been compiled on descriptions provided by the victims of his assaults.

The senior VPD crime analyst was able to overcome the skepticism of his supervisor about the validity of the analytical techniques that had been employed, which were quite different from traditional police investigative practices. The investigative team subsequently obtained castoff DNA from a disposed coffee cup used by the suspect. The subsequent DNA analysis was a match of one in six quadrillion.

A man named Ibata Hexamer was arrested in December 2010 and charged with four counts of sexual assaults and two counts of unlawful confinement. He pleaded guilty to the charges in August 2012, but subsequently sought to withdraw his guilty plea. As of early 2015, he remained in custody awaiting sentencing.

Hexamer was not previously known to police, which made the investigation that much more difficult. By all appearances, he was an upstanding citizen in the community. He was the financial manager for a Vancouver political party and ran a successful business. He did not fit the profile of a traditional offender. The success of the investigation revealed the potential of sophisticated crime analysis and the importance of incorporating these techniques into criminal case investigation.

Source: Personal communication with author, May 2014.

of the murder and given a life sentence. Episodes on the case were podcasted weekly, the narratives covering all facets of the investigative, prosecution, and conviction of the boyfriend who continues to profess his innocence.[39] The series quickly became a hit on iTunes.[40]

In Canada, police services are using Twitter to extend the reach of their investigations, and a Toronto detective has used the "Serial" podcast format to release clues in an unsolved murder case.[41]

See the Media Link, "Toronto police take to Twitter to help solve 2012 murder," at the end of this chapter.

Summary

The discussion in this chapter has centred on police case investigations. It was noted that, as first responders, patrol officers play a key role in case investigations—securing the scene, identifying witnesses, and gathering evidence. Most police services have specialized units composed of detectives who conduct investigations, which can be arduous and stressful. Informants play an important, yet sensitive role in case investigations. There are many types of evidence that are gathered in case investigations, including eyewitness testimony, which is one of the most unreliable investigative tools and is responsible for many cases of wrongful convictions. While there are a number of high-profile cases of police investigative failure, there are many examples of successful case investigations, assisted in many instances by the collection and use of DNA evidence. The Mr. Big technique is a made-in-Canada investigative strategy that has been surrounded by controversy, and the Supreme Court of Canada has set out limits for its use. A key component of case investigation is the interrogation of suspects, and care must be taken to ensure that suspects do not falsely confess to crimes they did not commit. Police services employ a variety of analytical strategies to assist in case investigations, including criminal profiling, geographic profiling, criminal intelligence analysis, and social network analysis. Recently, police services have been expanding the use of social media in case investigations.

KEY POINTS REVIEW

1. While most case investigations are conducted by patrol officers, more serious crimes and criminal incidents require the involvement of specially trained police officers.
2. There has been exponential growth in the number of specialty investigative units in police services, although the effectiveness and efficiency of these units has rarely been studied.
3. Detectives play a key role in case investigation.
4. A case (or criminal) investigation is intended to form reasonable grounds so that an arrest can be made, or at least so that suspects can be identified.
5. Informants play an essential, yet controversial, role in case investigation.
6. A variety of types of evidence are gathered at the crime scene and through other methods, including through the work of forensic specialists.
7. Eyewitnesses are an unreliable source of evidence.
8. The missing women's case in British Columbia and the numbers of missing and murdered Aboriginal women raise questions about the effectiveness of police investigations.
9. DNA is an important type of evidence that is gathered in case investigations, although care must be exercised in its use to avoid wrongful convictions.
10. The Mr. Big strategy is an investigative technique that has resulted in successful convictions but has also been surrounded by controversy and, in some instances, has led to wrongful convictions.
11. Police investigators must ensure that suspects do not falsely confess to crimes they did not commit.
12. Police investigators use a variety of analytical tools, including criminal profiling, geographic profiling, and social network analysis.
13. Interrogation of suspects is an important component of case investigation.
14. Police investigators must ensure that interrogation techniques do not result in false confessions.

KEY TERM QUESTIONS

1. Distinguish between **problem-oriented special units** and **method-oriented special units** in police services.
2. Compare and contrast **smoking gun investigations** and **whodunit investigations.**
3. What is the **major case management model**?
4. Compare and contrast **direct evidence** and **circumstantial evidence.**
5. Define the **principle of transfer and exchange** and **linkage blindness**, and discuss their role in case investigations?
6. Describe the various types of **DNA** and note how it is used in case investigations.
7. What do **cold case squads** do?
8. Describe the **"Mr. Big" technique** and the issues that surround its use in case investigation.
9. Define and discuss **criminal profiling**, **ViCLAS**, **geographic profiling**, **criminal intelligence analysis**, and **social network analysis** in relation to how these techniques are used in case investigations.

CRITICAL THINKING EXERCISES

Critical Thinking Exercise 10.1. The Vancouver Hockey Riot, 2011: The "Name and Shame" Phenomena

In the days following the Stanley Cup riot in Vancouver in 2011, a campaign of "name and shame"—posting images and names of rioters on the web, or images asking for identification—emerged. The posting of images taken by smartphones resulted in many of the rioters losing their jobs. In one instance, the family of a youth who was photographed lighting a police car on fire was forced to flee after their home address was posted on the Internet. Significantly, much of the name and shame was conducted by younger persons, and this process raced ahead of the police investigation.

Concerns were raised about "vigilante justice" and the violation of individual civil liberties. Many of the persons identified issued apologies and admitted their criminal actions in online postings or in public statements to the media.

Your Thoughts?

1. If you had been at the riot and had taken photos of persons involved in the riot (e.g., looting, setting vehicles on fire), would you have submitted them to the police?
2. Would you submit the digital images and/or identify a photo of
   a. a family member?
   b. a close friend?
   c. a neighbour?
   d. a fellow employee?

Critical Thinking Exercise 10.2. Should the Police Pay Offenders for "Bodies"?

It was noted that police services have, in certain cases, paid offenders for providing information on the location of deceased persons whom they have killed. Consider the following questions:

1. If you were in a position of authority and were asked to approve a payment to a convicted offender for information on the location of their victims, would you approve such a payment?
2. If you would approve a payment, what factors would you consider in your decision?
3. What moral and ethical issues would be raised by making payments?

CLASS/GROUP DISCUSSION EXERCISES

Class/Group Discussion 10.1. Should the Police Be Allowed to Collect DNA Samples from Arrested Persons Who Have Not Been Convicted?

In 2013, several Canadian police chiefs advocated for the powers of the police to be expanded to collect DNA evidence from arrested persons. At the time, the police were allowed to gather DNA only from certain convicted offenders (i.e., sex offenders). In the words of the chief of the Ottawa Police Services, "I think if we're expected to solve crimes and to do a better job at solving more crimes, this is using science to our advantage to ensure that those individuals who are responsible for committing these types of crimes are brought to justice" (Bell, p. 1). The federal government indicated that it was considering expanding the use of DNA, the justice minister stating: "I maintain that, you know, a genetic fingerprint is no different [from traditional fingerprinting] and could be used in my view as an investigative tool" (Mackrael, p. 1).

This news item generated considerable controversy and debate. The online comments to the justice minister's statement trended heavily toward opposing the idea and a reiteration that in the Canadian criminal justice system, a person is innocent until proven guilty, including the following:

> Take DNA if charged and convicted of a crime. I would agree. Taking it from everyone arrested rightfully or wrongfully who are still innocent until proven guilty is a gross violation. What's next, a chip in your head to track movement?
>
> This latest idea from law enforcement officials should be rejected immediately if not sooner. This notion that the police must have all possible information about you prior to even being charged, let alone convicted, is simply not acceptable in a free society.

Supporters of the practice contend that it will assist the police in solving crime.

Your Thoughts?

1. Would you be prepared to give the police the power to collect DNA evidence from crime suspects who have been arrested but have not yet been convicted?
2. If you are opposed to giving police this power, what if it was shown that this practice would increase the clearance rate for criminal offences, would you change your position?

Sources: D. Bell. (2013, October 4). Ottawa police chief supports taking DNA from anyone arrested. *Ottawa Sun*. Retrieved from http://www.ottawasun.com/2013/10/04/ottawa-police-chief-supports-taking-dna-records-from-anyone-arrested; K. Mackrael. (2013, October 2). Feds look at plan to collect DNA from suspects upon arrest. *The Globe and Mail*. Retrieved from http://www.theglobeandmail.com/news/politics/ottawa-looks-at-plan-to-collect-dna-from-suspects-upon-arrest/article14652881/

MEDIA LINKS

Visit www.nelson.com/canadianpolicework4 for links to these videos and other additional content available with this text.

"Inside the Luka Magnotta Case," *The Fifth Estate*, CBC, July 6, 2014, cbc.ca/fifth

"Informants," The Innocence Project, n.d., innocenceproject.org

"When Eyes Deceive – Eyewitness Testimony," thibs44, January 19, 2009, youtube.com

"Eyewitness Misidentification," The Innocence Project, n.d., innocenceproject.org

"Highway of Tears," *48 Hours*, CBS News, December 21, 2013, cbsnews.com/48-hours

"Mr. Big Stings: Cops, Criminals and Confessions," *The Fifth Estate*, CBC, January 9, 2015, cbc.ca/fifth

"The Confession," *The Fifth Estate*, CBC, October 22, 2010, cbc.ca/fifth

"Bryon Sonne Interview with Detective Bui, June 23," Christopher Olah, November 25, 2011, youtube.com

"Mike Pimentel Homicide Witness Appeal to Call Toronto Police Wayne Banks 416-808-7411," Toronto Police Service, January 4, 2012, youtube.com

"Serial: The podcast everyone's talking about," *BBC Newsnight*, October 31, 2014, youtube.com

"Toronto police take to Twitter to help solve 2012 murder," *CityNews*, December 16, 2014, citynews.ca

11 Going Forward: Critical Issues in Canadian Policing

LEARNING OBJECTIVES

After reading this chapter, you should be able to:

- Identify and discuss some of the critical issues facing Canadian policing in the early 21st century
- Discuss the challenges presented by the increasing sophistication and globalization of crime
- Discuss the darknet as an example of the challenges of policing in the global context
- Discuss the issues that surround the use of technology in policing
- Discuss the challenges of developing and implementing evidence-based policies and practice in policing
- Discuss the challenges of maintaining the balance between risk, safety, and security
- Discuss the debate over the economics and sustainability of policing
- Provide examples of key questions that surround Canadian police work

In this, the final chapter, we take a step back and consider a number of the critical issues that are facing Canadian policing. The topics discussed should be taken only as illustrative; doubtless, new challenges and opportunities will emerge during the life of this edition of the text. While there are challenges, there are also opportunities.

DEVELOPING AND IMPLEMENTING EVIDENCED-BASED POLICIES AND PRACTICE

> *"If the medical profession used research the way that the police use research, we'd still be using leeches."*[1]
>
> —John DeCarlo, professor, John Jay College of Criminal Justice; former police chief, Branford, Connecticut

Recall that throughout the text, the term "evidence-based practice" was used in discussions of the various facets of police work. An ongoing challenge in the criminal justice system is to ensure that police work is informed by the findings of evaluation research. This includes cost-benefit analysis that examines whether the investment of resources produces effective outcomes and improves the efficiency of the justice system.[2]

Unfortunately, this is currently not the case. Most police initiatives do not include an evaluation component, and in those relatively few instances in which programs and strategies are evaluated, the impact on operational practice may be minimal. As one scholar noted: "Evaluation research . . . has reached industrial proportions but remains feudal in its capacity to create change."[3] Police services have been slow to adopt evidence-based strategies and to discard policies and programs that are not effective.

The challenges to developing evidence-based practices are numerous and include the resistance of policymakers to new strategies, concerns among politicians that research findings may compromise political agendas, concerns about the costs of new initiatives, and a general fear of the unknown. Historically, police services have lacked the capacity to incorporate best practices into their operations. Even policies and programs that have been proven by research to be ineffective (e.g., the D.A.R.E. program discussed in Chapter 9) may be continued purely because they are "known." Traditional "that's the way we've always done it" practice is still prevalent in many police services.

Another example is the persistence of the two-days/two-nights/four-off shift schedule that, while administratively convenient, does not provide for the effective use of patrol resources. The shifting of patrol officers should be determined by an analysis of the demands for service, which, we have seen, vary throughout the week and in different jurisdictions. Similarly, officers are deployed in eight-, ten-, and twelve-hour shifts, despite research indicating that the ten-hour shift is most optimal for officer productivity and work/life balance.[4]

In the early 21st century, governments are far more reluctant than in previous decades to provide police services with additional resources without supporting documentation indicating what the resources will be used for, the anticipated impact of the resource expenditures, and an evaluative component measuring performance outcomes. Whether a police service is requesting additional sworn or civilian positions, or asking for monies for special projects, or if a police union is negotiating for additional benefits, all of these monetary requests will receive close scrutiny that may have been absent in previous years. This has been the catalyst for police services to develop capacities to document their activities, to develop performance metrics, and to begin to capture the wide variety of activities that officers are involved in that are not related to law enforcement. This includes the demands made on officers in responding to persons with mental illness.

The increasing fiscal accountability of police services may provide the catalyst for significant reforms in police policy and practice. The term **smart policing** can be used to describe the efforts of police services to "do more with less" and to reform traditional police practice.

smart policing
an approach to policing that, through the use of best practices and evidence-based strategies, maximizes resources to increase the effectiveness and efficiency of police policies and operations

Key to these reforms is effective police leadership.[5] Police leaders may remain mired in traditional practices and resistant to change. They may be adverse to adopting private-sector practices and may be out of touch with the new generation of officers.[6]

To consider further the role of evidence-based and best practices in policing, see Class/Group Discussion 11.1.

The State of Canadian Police Research

Contributing to the absence of evidence-based practice is a lack of research on Canadian policing. A university-based police scholar described the state of police research in this country as "disjointed, incoherent, fragmented, and inconsistent."[7] This is due in large measure to the absence of structures and processes to facilitate funding, collaboration, and dissemination of research findings.

The consequences of this are significant and include the fact that much of the research cited in this text is not Canadian. On more than one occasion, your author has had to offer the caveat that the research findings on a specific topic might not apply to Canada as the projects were carried out in other countries, most notably the U.S.

Much of the academic research that has been conducted on Canadian policing remains "hidden in plain sight," published in professional journals that are rarely accessed by police services and not written in a manner that is understandable and actionable by police leaders.[8] This lack of access to police research extends to the members of police service boards, municipal councillors, and government policymakers. Other observers have noted that ". . . the everyday problems of police have little status in the universities," highlighting the fact that there is often little interface between academic research and policing.[9]

Noticeably absent are collaborative partnerships that would increase access to expertise in the field of policing.[10] There is also no national strategic plan to coordinate police research. There is only a limited capacity among the key stakeholder groups in Canadian policing—including police service boards, municipal councils, and police associations—to conduct research; and there is often little communication between academics and these groups.

This increases the likelihood that funding decisions for police by municipal and provincial governments will not be informed by the research literature and best practices in policing, but rather by political expediency.

In other countries, the federal government plays a major role in funding police research. Governments in these nations are involved in assisting with establishing portals and platforms through which research findings on criminal justice and policing are made accessible to a broad audience, and collaboration and networking between academics, police services, and other stakeholder groups is encouraged. Two of the more prominent sites are the Campbell Collaboration (www.campbellcollaboration.org) and CrimeSolutions.gov (www.crimesolutions.gov). Public Safety Canada sponsors the Policing and Community Safety Research website, which features the Canadian Policing Research Catalogue, a central repository for accessing policing research in Canada (http://www.publicsafety.gc.ca/cnt/cntrng-crm/plcng/plcng-rsrch/index-eng.aspx).

THE INCREASING SOPHISTICATION AND GLOBALIZATION OF CRIME

The increasing interdependence of the world's nations and the rapid expansion of high technology have created new and more sophisticated forms of criminal activity, as well as new channels for more traditional types of crime. Police services must now consider the world beyond their immediate jurisdictions and collaborate with other police organizations, both national and international.

A major challenge is tracking criminal activity on the Internet, which requires the use of leading-edge technologies and highly trained sworn and civilian police personnel. One example is the emergence of the **darknet**, also often referred to as the *deep net* or *dark web*.

darknet
also known as the deep net or dark web, an anonymized Internet space originally designed to protect Internet users from surveillance and reprisals

The dark web was originally developed by scientists to ensure the anonymity of computer users from government surveillance and reprisals.[11] Using a program called Tor, people could host websites without revealing their location. The use of bitcoins, a decentralized online currency, made transactions difficult to trace. See the Media Link, "Inside the Dark Web," at the end of this chapter. For a demonstration on how computer users can access the darknet, see the Media Link, "The Hidden Internet – Exploring the Deep Web," also at the end of this chapter.

The darknet provides a safe place for persons in countries with repressive governments and victims of crime to communicate without fear of reprisal. However, the darknet has also become a host for virtual marketplaces selling drugs and weapons; stolen financial data, including credit cards; stolen and fake passports; and counterfeit money, among other items. The darknet also hosts forums for persons engaged in criminal activity, including pedophiles and persons who post photos of women hacked from their Facebook accounts that can be used for blackmail. See the Media Link, "Buying Guns and Drugs on the Deep Web," at the end of this chapter. New websites appear as fast as law enforcement agencies raid and shut down the sites. Activists contend that increasing government surveillance of the darknet threatens free speech and places persons in countries with repressive governments at risk.[12] Observers have also noted that since one of the original darknet sites was shut down

(Silk Road, which was relatively tame), this has created a vacuum that has been filled by sites that are much more dangerous.[13] The founder of Silk Road went on trial in the U.S. in January 2015, charged with drug trafficking, money laundering, and operating a criminal enterprise.[14] See Critical Thinking Exercise 11.1 at the end of this chapter.

globalization of policing
the development of collaborative partnerships among police services at the international level

These developments have contributed to the **globalization of policing**, the development of collaborative partnerships between police services across the world.

There has also been the emergence of a new international policing that involves Canadian police officers and police officers from other countries, serving in conflict and post-conflict countries. These officers play a multifaceted role, including providing security to communities in crisis, training local police services in community policing and case investigation strategies, and assisting in the transformation to post-conflict stability.[15] Recall the discussion of Canadian police peacekeepers in Chapter 3.

The Terrorist Threat

An increase in the number of terrorist attacks, and planned attacks foiled by police services, has led to increasing concerns with terrorism. This has required police services to develop the capacities to identify and monitor persons who may pose a threat to commit criminal acts.

There are increasing concerns about *extremist travellers*, Canadians who go abroad to participate in terrorist-related activities. Figure 11.1 illustrates the cases of six extremist travellers with Canadian connections.

There is also concern that these individuals may return to Canada with the intent to do harm. As of early 2014, 130 individuals (citizens, permanent residents, or others who have connections to Canada) were abroad and had been identified as participating in terrorist activities.[16] In addition, eighty individuals who had been abroad and suspected to have been involved in terrorist activity and had returned to Canada were being monitored. The so-called "lone wolf" terrorists—persons who have been radicalized but who act alone—are also very challenging for law enforcement agencies. Monitoring their activities is resource intensive, and ironically, these individuals may be more difficult to identify and monitor than larger groups of conspirators.

These efforts are all very resource intensive, and it remains to be seen what the overall impact is on police budgets and expenditures. Police officials have estimated that it can require thirty to sixty police officers and cost up to $8 million a year to maintain 24/7 surveillance of one suspected terrorist.[17] The Montreal police indicated that as of late 2014, they had launched one hundred terror-related investigations in a two-month period, while other police services have seen a significant increase in terror-related tips.[18] Police services are also providing in-service training to officers to deal with radicalized persons.

THE TECHNOLOGICALIZATION OF POLICING

Technology can be a two-edged sword: it has the potential to assist the police in preventing and responding to crime; on the other hand, there may be

Figure 11.1. Cases of Extremist Travellers with Canadian Connections

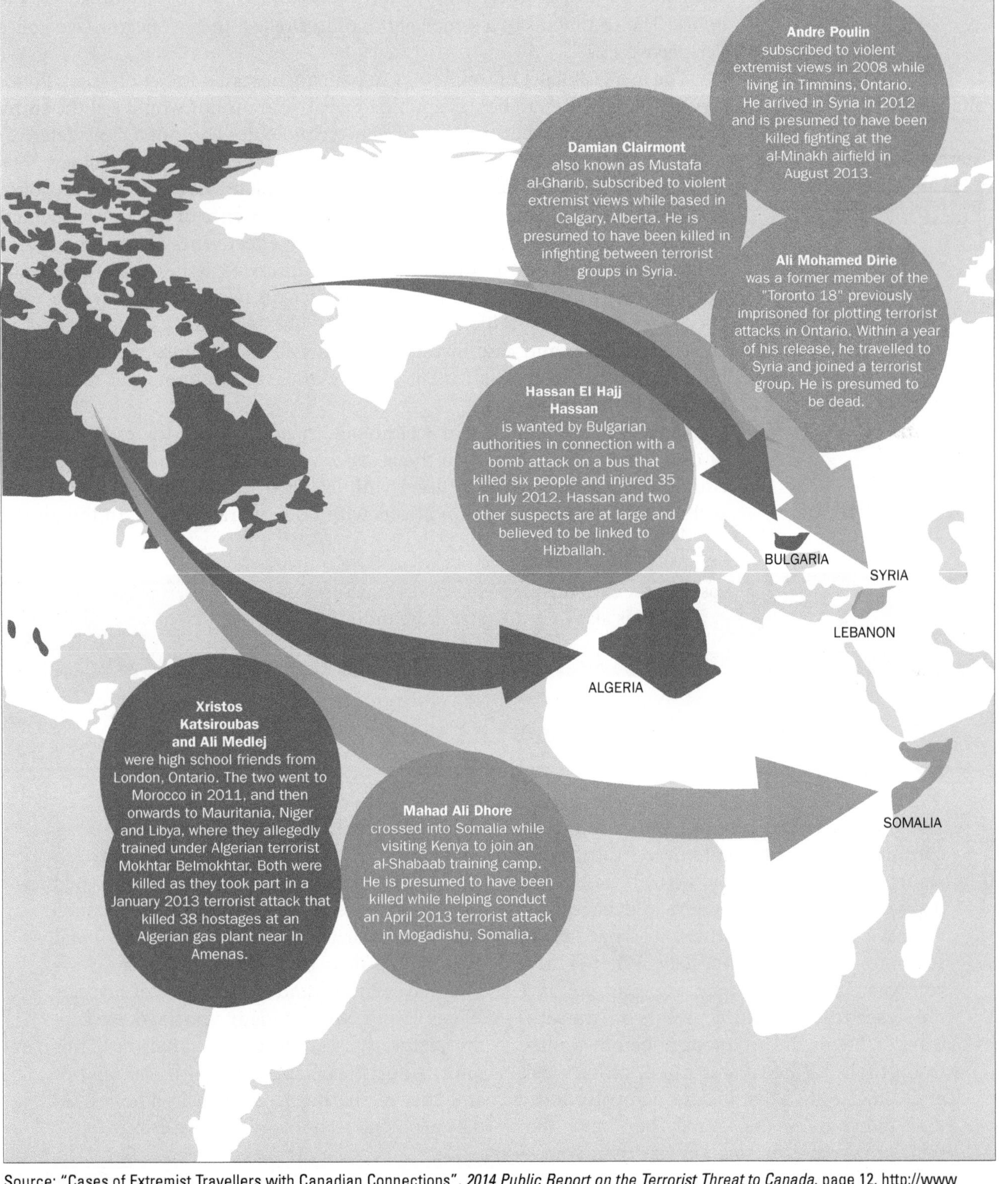

Source: "Cases of Extremist Travellers with Canadian Connections", *2014 Public Report on the Terrorist Threat to Canada*, page 12, http://www.publicsafety.gc.ca/cnt/rsrcs/pblctns/2014-pblc-rpr-trrrst-thrt/2014-pblc-rpr-trrrst-thrt-eng.pdf. Reprinted with the permission of the Minister of Public Safety and Emergency Preparedness Canada, 2015.

unanticipated consequences. Police officers who come to overrely on technology may lose their ability to communicate effectively in encounter situations and subsequently misuse force. This, in turn, may undermine the legitimacy of the police. The comments of a senior police officer reflect these concerns (see Police Perspective 11.1).

The increasing use of technology in policing raises a number of issues. Police services have proven to be susceptible to what your author would call the **shiny new toy syndrome**, the adoption of new technologies without a clear determination of the potential, limitations, and impact of the specific technology.

shiny new toy syndrome
the adoption of new technologies in the absence of a clear determination of their potential, limitations, and impact

The late 20th and early 21st centuries are replete with examples of police services rushing to incorporate technology in the absence of research that could be used to create guidelines to ensure that the effectiveness and efficiency of police service delivery is improved, while addressing issues that these technologies may create. This includes the impact on police legitimacy, the cost-effectiveness of the specific technology, and the technology's effectiveness in crime prevention and case investigation, as well as any impact related to the preservation of citizens' rights. The positive impact of technology is more often assumed than demonstrated.

More notable examples of technology in policing are the expanding use of drones by police services, in the absence of any guidelines on their use; the issuing of Tasers to police officers without clear guidelines for deployment; and in 2015, the rush to equip officers with body-worn cameras. In the case of

Police Perspective 11.1

A Deputy Chief Constable Reflects on the Use of Technology in Police Work

The officers I learned from were such good communicators. They did not feel the need to resort to tools often. Now we have Tasers and pepper spray and computers and handhelds. We have a generation where it is natural for them to resort to technology. When I hear younger officers say they are glad to have the Taser to deal with a person on transit, I wonder, "How did we manage before we had those tools?" When I was hired, officers generally had only a baton and a revolver, and they didn't often use them. They knew that their most powerful weapon was their voice—communication.

Now in policing generally, there is sometimes a tendency to resort to the tools. There are definitely officers out there who "get it," but I would say that we have more officers who are inclined to rely on their technology. On the other hand, they do use their technology in effective ways. They have iPhones and share photos of suspects. When I was in patrol many years ago, we kept the picture of a suspect in our hat; now this information is available on their in-car laptops and they're sharing it with their iPhones. So they are using technology to solve crimes.

Source: Personal communication with author, October 2014.

body-worn cameras, this technology is being deployed without full consideration of how it will affect police–citizen encounters, how the privacy of citizens will be protected, the costs of the equipment and the storage and retrieval of information, and the impact of the availability of massive amounts of video recordings on Crown counsel, among other issues.

This can result in a "snap-back" effect, wherein the use of the technology has a number of unanticipated consequences resulting in critical incidents that then may limit the potential of the technology. This occurred with the rapid adoption of Tasers by police services during the 1990s, often in the absence of any guidelines on their use. As a result, Tasers were overused and inappropriately used. Fare evaders in transit stations were Tasered, as were non-compliant persons sitting passively on the street. Many officers came to overrely on the Taser to "resolve" a situation that would have in previous times been managed by verbal judo and good communication skills. Recall, for example, the discussion of the Taser death of Robert Dziekanski at Vancouver International Airport in Chapter 7.

The danger is that the increasing use of technology will come at the expense of developing human and helping relationships that have been demonstrated to be a core component of successful criminal justice interventions. The increasing use of high technology may significantly impact the quality of police–community interaction and raise issues of police legitimacy and citizens' rights, among other concerns. An overreliance on criminal intelligence analysis, for example, may result in officers spending less time in the community, developing sources and becoming familiar with the areas they police. Officers wearing cameras may be reluctant to engage in informal dispute resolution and creative problem solving, knowing that their every action is being recorded for future review by their superiors, Crown counsel, defence lawyers, judges, and juries. The use of drones by police services without strict guidelines presents challenges related to ensuring citizen privacy. For a look at the application of technology in policing going forward, see the Media Link, "10 Future Law Enforcement Technologies," at the end of this chapter.

The heretofore science fictional "robo-cop" machines are certain to appear in the not-too-distant future, potentially reducing police engagement with the community and raising a plethora of issues, including ethics, privacy, and the balance of citizen rights versus public security. Futurists have proposed that robots could be used for situations too dangerous for human police officers, including protests, riots, and peacekeeping duties.[19] See the Media Links, "DARPA's Police Robot" and "C.R.A.B. Robot (London Riot Police – Prototype Sentry Mech)," at the end of this chapter.

© J. Emilio Flores/CORBIS

Police officer of the future?

A number of police observers have cautioned that a fixation on technology as the way forward in policing may come at the expense of imagination, judgment, and a focus on building trust and legitimacy in the community and ensuring accountability.[20] In considering the role of technology in policing, the reader should remain mindful of the words of police scholar Peter Manning that "the primary technology is verbal—the words used to persuade and control others in interaction."[21]

RISK, SAFETY, AND SECURITY IN A DEMOCRATIC SOCIETY: MAINTAINING THE BALANCE

> *"The question is whether European societies would like to be free, and live more dangerously because they can't arrest everyone, or whether they want less freedom and more security."*[22]
>
> —Farhad Khosrokhavar, School for Advanced Studies in the Social Sciences, Paris

The above comment was made by a Paris-based expert on radical Islam in the immediate aftermath of the terrorist attacks that occurred in Paris in early January 2015. The attacks resulted in the deaths of most of the cartoonists on the staff of a Parisian satire magazine that had published controversial cartoons depicting the prophet Mohammed. Two police officers were also killed. Subsequent standoffs with police resulted in the deaths of the attackers and a number of hostages.

These attacks accelerated the plans of the Canadian federal government to enact legislation expanding the authority of law enforcement and security services. This includes increased powers of surveillance, detention, and arrest. Plans had been underway since two lone-wolf terrorist attacks in October 2014 resulted in the deaths of two soldiers and, in one instance, an armed attack on Parliament Hill. Critics cautioned against a legislative overreaction that would serve only to compromise the rights of citizens without increasing their safety and security, and that the courts might ultimately determine its provisions to be unconstitutional.[23]

Among the Canadian public, there is considerable concern with home-grown terrorism. A national online survey ($N = 1{,}609$) conducted in 2014 found that 62 percent of respondents felt that there was a "serious threat of home-grown terrorism in Canada." The threat was most likely to be perceived as serious among respondents who were aged 55 and older (74 percent), although high rates of concern were also expressed by those in the age ranges of 35 to 54 (63 percent) and 18 to 34 (47 percent).[24] Interestingly, concern was highest (70 percent) in Saskatchewan rather than in more populated urban centres in the country.[25] One-third of persons in the sample residing in British Columbia believed that there were radicals living in their community.[26] Of concern is that 55 percent of the respondents indicated that they had no confidence in the ability of security services to prevent home-grown acts of terror.[27] See Class/Group Discussion 11.2 at the end of this chapter.

Recall from Chapter 2 that there is a history in Canada of the police conducting surveillance on groups and individuals who were deemed to be a threat to the government. Since the terrorist attacks on the U.S. in September 2001, there has been an exponential growth in the number agencies that have as some portion of their mandate "national security," a generally ill-defined term that may create conditions for expanded surveillance of Canadian citizens.

THE ECONOMICS OF POLICING: ARE THE POLICE WORTH THE MONEY?

It was noted early in the text that the costs of policing comprise a significant portion of municipal budgets and that these costs have been increasing. Critics argue that these costs are not sustainable in the climate of fiscal restraint and declining crime rates. However, research studies have found that there can be significant cost-benefits of policing. Investing in street-level policing and strategies such as hot spots policing, for example, can reduce prison populations and curb the increasing costs of corrections (which are escalating, particularly in Canada).[28]

Researchers in the U.S. have calculated that money diverted from correctional institutions to policing would buy at least four times as much reduction in crime. Shrinking the prison population by one-quarter would result in sufficient savings to hire an additional 100,000 police officers. The former commissioner of corrections for the State of New York stated: "If you had a dollar to spend on reducing crime, and you looked at the science instead of the politics, you would never spend it on the prison system."[29] Ironically, in Canada in recent years, there have been increasing discussions about reducing the number of sworn police officers while committing more money to constructing additional prison cells.[30]

Conversely, reducing the numbers of police officers may result in increased rates of crime. As noted in Chapter 1, reductions in the size of a typical police service were found to lead to increases in crime.[31]

Specific concerns have been expressed about the salaries of police officers. However, figures show that, after controlling for cost-of-living increases, police officers earned an average hourly wage of $27.12 in 2012, the fourth highest among the occupations analyzed. The highest earners in 2012 were secondary school teachers, at an average wage of $28.92 per hour, followed by registered nurses at $27.61 and elementary school and kindergarten teachers at $27.47. These wage differences were found throughout the period of 2002 to 2012, as reflected in the percentage change in wages for registered nurses (+14 percent), firefighters (+12 percent), ambulance attendants and paramedical occupations (+21 percent) and counsellors (+15 percent), and police officers (+7 percent).[32]

KEY QUESTIONS GOING FORWARD

As noted at the outset of this text, policing is a dynamic enterprise that is often surrounded by controversy. The informed observer should bring to discussions of policing an open mind and a critical eye. Key questions surrounding Canadian policing in the early 21st century that should be addressed include the following:

- Are police policies and operations evidence-based and informed by best practices?
- Are the police cost-effective?
- What are the potential and limitations of tiered policing?
- Are there limits to the role that private security companies can play in communities?
- What impact is downloading onto the police having on police resources and the ability of the police to prevent and respond to crime and disorder?
- What is the impact of the transfer policy in the RCMP, the SQ, and the OPP on the ability of these police services to provide effective policing; to engage communities; and to sustain crime prevention, crime response, and crime attack strategies?
- What action can be taken to ensure that the police do not become politicized?
- How can it be determined that police provide value for money?
- How will police services respond to the increasing globalization of crime?
- What are the implications of the growing threat of terrorism for the costs of policing?
- How will the increasing focus on security affect community policing programs?
- How will the increasing pressures to adopt high technology in policing be managed so as to ensure that the rights of citizens are protected?
- How can the unique challenges of delivering police services in northern and remote communities be best addressed?
- What structures and processes need to be put in place to ensure that police policy and practice are driven by best practices and are evidence-based?
- How can police services best address the needs of diverse communities?

See Class/Group Discussion 11.3 at the end of this chapter.

In reflecting on the materials presented in this text, it is important to recall Peel's principles of policing, first set out in the early 1800s. These establish the importance of a close relationship between the public and the police, that is, "the police are the public and the public are the police." Amidst the quickening pace of life and the rise and impact of technology on all facets of modern life and on policing, it is important to remember that policing is first and foremost a human enterprise that requires that there be a close connection between the police and the communities they serve. Despite the massive social changes that have occurred over the past 150 years, Peel's principles still provide a framework within which police services can meet these challenges.

Summary

This chapter has identified and discussed several of the challenges and opportunities in Canadian policing. Police services in the early 21st century are confronted by a myriad of demands, including the increasing complexity of crime,

Class/Group Discussion 11.2. Should Law Enforcement and Security Agencies Be Given Additional Powers of Surveillance in Order to Combat Home-Grown Terrorism?

A key issue surrounding the threat of home-grown terrorism is how much power law enforcement and security agencies should have to conduct surveillance and other operations to combat the threat of terrorist acts. This again raises one of the key themes in this text: how to balance the need for safety and security with the rights of citizens. In an online survey of 1,609 Canadians across the country, nearly 50 percent of the sample indicated that they would support giving additional powers of surveillance to the Canadian Security Intelligence Service (CSIS), while 27 percent said that legislation proposed by the federal government in 2014 (Bill C-44) would diminish the rights of Canadians. Additional levels of support were found for suspending the passports of home-grown terrorists who wanted to travel abroad to join terrorist movements (60 percent), deporting radicalized persons (82 percent), and legislation blocking access to Internet sites that promote extremist views and groups (83 percent).

Your Thoughts?

1. Had you been asked to answer the survey questions reported above, what would have been your answer?
2. What are the potential benefits and concerns of giving law enforcement and security agencies additional powers of surveillance?
3. What would be effective strategies for altering Canadians perceptions of the threat of home-grown terrorism and their lack of confidence in law enforcement and security agencies to effectively combat this threat?

Class/Group Discussion 11.3. For Further Consideration

The discussion in this chapter concluded with a number of questions that could be asked about policing. Reflecting on the materials presented in the text, what additional questions should be asked?

MEDIA LINKS

Visit www.nelson.com/canadianpolicework4 for links to these videos and other additional content available with this text.

"Inside the Dark Web – Documentary," Doc Film, November 8, 2014, youtube.com

"The Hidden Internet – Exploring the Deep Web," Takedownman, March 1, 2014, youtube.com

"Buying Guns and Drugs on the Deep Web," Motherboard, November 14, 2013, youtube.com

"10 Future Law Enforcement Technologies," Alltime10s, February 9, 2012, youtube.com

"DARPA's Police Robot," Mara Jade, August 25, 2009, youtube.com

"C.R.A.B. Robot (London Riot Police – Prototype Sentry Mech)," jamiefmartin, June 14, 2010, youtube.com

Glossary

allocated patrol time the amount of time that patrol officers spend responding to calls from the general public (p. 149)

arrest warrant a document that permits a police officer to arrest a specific person for a specified reason (p. 181)

basic qualifications the minimum requirements for candidates applying for employment in policing (p. 106)

best practices organizational, administrative, and operational strategies that are effective in preventing and responding to crime (p. 65)

bias-free policing the requirement that police officers make decisions on the basis of reasonable suspicion and probable grounds rather than stereotypes (p. 169)

blue-light syndrome an attitudinal set that emphasizes the high risk and action component of police work (p. 121)

"broken windows" approach the view that if minor crimes are left unaddressed, an environment for more serious crime will be created (p. 252)

call shedding a strategy to discard or divert calls for service to match available police resources (p. 147)

call stacking prioritizing calls for service (p. 147)

Canadian Charter of Rights and Freedoms a component of the Constitution Act that guarantees basic rights and freedoms (p. 4)

Canadian Police Information Centre (CPIC) the centralized, computer-based information system used by police services (p. 144)

CAPRA model the RCMP model of problem-oriented policing that utilizes a collaborative problem-solving approach (p. 251)

circumstantial evidence evidence not directly observed but that can implicate an offender (p. 282)

Civilian Review and Complaints Commission for the RCMP (CRCC) an independent civilian body that receives complaints made by citizens against RCMP officers who are policing under contract (p. 90)

clearance rates the proportion of the actual incidents known to the police that result in the identification of a suspect, whether or not that suspect is ultimately charged and convicted (p. 70)

code of ethics policies that establish standards of behaviour for police officers (p. 75)

code of silence officers protecting one another from outside scrutiny and criticism (p. 121)

cold case squads specialized units that focus on unsolved serious crimes (p. 289)

collaborative policing the cooperation between public and private police (p. 45)

community-based strategic policing a model of police work that incorporates the key principles of community policing with crime prevention, crime response, and crime attack approaches (p. 220)

community engagement police strategies that facilitate the involvement of citizens and communities in initiatives to address crime and social disorder (p. 223)

community policing a philosophy of policing centred on police–community partnerships and problem solving (p. 218)

competency-based training recruit training that focuses on the acquisition of specific skills and knowledge (p. 115)

CompStat a strategy designed to increase the effectiveness and efficiency of police services while holding police personnel accountable for achieving crime reduction objectives (p. 263)

Constitution Act, 1867 legislation that includes provisions that define the responsibilities of the federal and provincial governments in the area of criminal justice (p. 4)

contract policing an arrangement whereby the RCMP and the Ontario Provincial Police provide provincial and municipal policing services (p. 55)

crime analysis a systematic approach to crime prevention and crime response based on the analysis of statistical and other data (p. 261)

crime attack strategies proactive operations by the police to target and apprehend criminal offenders (p. 253)

crime displacement the relocation—due to effective crime prevention and crime response initiatives—of criminal activity from one locale to another (p. 260)

Crime Severity Index (CSI) the method used in Canada to denote the levels of violent and property crime and to measure the effectiveness of a police service (p. 160)

Criminal Code federal legislation that sets out criminal law, procedures for prosecuting federal offences, and sentences and procedures for the administration of justice (p. 5)

criminal intelligence analysis the use of sophisticated computer programs to analyze information gathered on suspected criminal activity (p. 298)

criminal profiling a strategy to identify suspects by constructing biographical and psychological sketches based on crime scene evidence (p. 296)

critical incident stress the physiological, psychological, physical, and emotional rections that may occur in an individual who has been involved in a traumatic incident (e.g., patrol officers involved in a fatal shooting) (p. 206)

dark figure of crime the difference between how much crime occurs and how much crime is reported to or discovered by the police (p. 17)

darknet also known as the deep net or dark web, an anonymized Internet space originally designed to protect Internet users from surveillance and reprisals (p. 311)

demonstrated threat the level of potential danger posed by a person confronted by police officers, generally in the form of weapons or levels of resistance (p. 192)

dependent model (of investigation) the practice of police investigating themselves (p. 90)

differential police response (DPR) categorizing calls for service based on the response required, such as patrol car or no patrol car (p. 147)

direct evidence evidence in criminal investigations that is detected through at least one of the five senses (p. 282)

discretion the power or right to decide or act according to one's own judgement (p. 153)

Division Staff Relations Representative (DivRep) Program in lieu of a union, a program that provides RCMP officers with a way to express their concerns to management (p. 57)

DNA genetic information that can be used in case investigations (p. 286)

environmental scans studies designed to identify trends that may impact demands on the police (p. 65)

ethical dilemma a situation in which a person has to make a decision or take a course of action in the face of two or more conflicting ethical principles or values (p. 75)

ethics how behaviour is defined as right or wrong (p. 75)

external elements (of community policing) police–community partnerships that enhance community policing and increase police legitimacy, visibility, and accessibility (p. 220)

First Nations Policing Policy a framework that allows First Nations to negotiate a policing arrangement suitable to their needs (p. 59)

force options model provides police officers with a working model that sets out the course of action to be taken in use-of-force situations (p. 192)

frankpledge system an early system of maintaining order in early England (p. 25)

geographic profiling the analysis of behaviour patterns that relate to space or geography, with particularly reference to the journey to crime (p. 297)

globalization of policing the development of collaborative partnerships among police services at the international level (p. 312)

high-visibility/high-consequence policing police work in the North that places officers under constant scrutiny and the high impact of their decisions (p. 164)

hue and cry in early England, the requirement that able-bodied men assist the police (p. 25)

hypervigilance elevated alertness about potential dangers in the environment (p. 121)

iceberg (or 80/20) rule the view that crime is only a visible symptom of much larger problems (p. 251)

independent model (of investigation) a complaint procedure in which civilians conduct all phases of the investigation (p. 93)

information a written statement sworn by an informant alleging that a person has committed a specific criminal offence (p. 181)

in-service training training courses for serving police officers (p. 119)

intelligence-led policing (ILP) the application of criminal intelligence analysis to facilitate crime reduction and prevention (p. 263)

interdependent model (of investigation) a procedure for complaint investigation with varying degrees of civilian involvement (p. 92)

Justice of the Peace Act centralized peacekeeping duties under justices of the peace (p. 27)

Kansas City Preventive Patrol Experiment a study of the effectiveness of random mobile patrol, which found no impact on reported crime, victimization, fear of crime, or citizen satisfaction with the police (p. 215)

learning organization the notion that a police service is constantly seeking improvement, learning from successes as well as from initiatives that did not achieve their intended goals (p. 66)

less-lethal (or lower lethality) force option a control technique that is highly unlikely to cause death or serious injury (p. 195)

linkage blindness the investigative failure to recognize a pattern linking one crime with one or more others (p. 285)

major case management model the protocol for conducting investigations (p. 277)

method-oriented special units police units that are distinguished by specialized equipment and tactics (p. 274)

Metropolitan Police Act established a full-time, unarmed police force in London (p. 28)

"Mr. Big" technique an investigative strategy designed to secure confessions from crime suspects through the creation of an elaborate scenario (p. 290)

noble cause corruption a view by police officers that the ends justify the means (misconduct) (p. 78)

one-plus-one the generally accepted use-of-force standard that says police officers have the authority to use one higher level of force than that with which they are confronted (p. 194)

operational field training instructing the recruit on how to apply principles from the training academy in the community (p. 120)

organizational elements (of community policing) how a police service is structured to implement community policing (p. 220)

organizational wisdom an in-depth understanding of the community and its residents, crime and disorder, and agencies and organizations that can be mobilized to prevent and respond to crime (p. 66)

overpolicing a disproportionate police focus on a racialized population or neighbourhood (p. 170)

para-police unarmed officers who generally have special constable status (p. 61)

performance measurement the collective actions taken by a police service to assess the efficiency and effectiveness of its activities and interventions (p. 69)

pluralization of policing the expansion of policing beyond the public police to include para-police and private security (p. 45)

police acts the legislative framework for police services (p. 85)

police boards and police commissions bodies that provide oversight of police (p. 85)

police governance the structures that guide the policies, strategic direction, and goals of a police service (p. 84)

police legitimacy the collective actions taken by the police to enhance the levels of trust and confidence that citizens have in the police (p. 18)

police oversight the processes that are in place to receive and respond to citizen complaints about the police (p. 84)

policing the activities of any individual or organization acting legally on behalf of public or private organizations or persons to maintain security or social order (p. 4)

policing standards provisions that set out how police services are to be maintained and delivered (p. 85)

political policing secretive police investigative activities and surveillance of persons and groups deemed to be a threat to the stability and status quo of the state (p. 7)

post-traumatic stress disorder (PTSD) an extreme form of critical incident stress that includes nightmares, hypervigilance, intrusive thoughts, and other forms of psychological distress (p. 133)

predictive policing the use of statistical analysis to identify the time and location of criminal activity that is likely to occur (p. 263)

preferred qualifications requirements that increase the competitiveness of applicants seeking employment in policing (p. 106)

pretext policing police stops or searches for a minor reason that lead to more intrusive intervention (p. 170)

previously experienced officers (PEOs) in-service police officers who are interested in leaving their current police service (p. 118)

primary crime prevention programs prevention programs designed to alter the conditions that provide opportunities for criminal offences (p. 243)

principle of transfer and exchange the assumption that physical evidence is transferred during the commission of a criminal offence (p. 284)

problem-oriented policing (POP) a tactical strategy based on the idea that the police should address the causes of recurrent crime and disorder (p. 250)

problem-oriented special units investigative units that focus on specific types of offenders or criminal activities (p. 274)

professional model of policing a model of police work that is reactive, incident-driven, and centred on random patrol (p. 215)

quality-of-life policing police efforts to improve conditions in an area by targeting disruptive and annoying behaviour (p. 251)

racial profiling police targeting of members of a particular racial group on the basis of the supposed criminal propensity of the entire group (p. 169)

radical perspective (on the role of the police) a perspective that views the police as an instrument used by governments and powerful interests to suppress dissent, stifle protest, and help maintain the status quo (p. 5)

RCMP External Review Committee an oversight body of the RCMP that hears appeals from RCMP officers who have been disciplined (p. 90)

recipes for action the actions taken and decisions made by patrol officers in various types of encounter situations (p. 158)

restorative justice an approach based on the principle that criminal behaviour injures the victim, the community, and the offender (p. 257)

rotten apples individual police officer misconduct (p. 77)

rotten barrels group misconduct by police officers (p. 77)

rotten orchards misconduct by a police service (p. 77)

Royal Canadian Mounted Police Act federal legislation that provides the framework for the operation of the RCMP (p. 5)

SARA (scanning, analysis, response, and assessment) a problem-solving model for police (p. 251)

search warrant a document that permits the police to search a specific location and take items that might be evidence of a crime (p. 186)

secondary crime prevention programs programs that focus on areas that produce crime and disorder (p. 245)

selective (or situational) enforcement discretionary enforcement due to the inability of police officers to enforce all of the laws at all times (p. 154)

shiny new toy syndrome the adoption of new technologies in the absence of a clear determination of their potential, limitations, and impact (p. 314)

Sir Robert Peel founded the first organized police service (p. 28)

smart policing an approach to policing that, through the use of best practices and evidence-based strategies, maximizes resources to increase the effectiveness and efficiency of police policies and operations (p. 310)

smoking gun investigations cases in which the perpetrator is readily identifiable (p. 277)

social contract perspective (on the role of the police) a perspective that considers the police to be a politically neutral force that acts primarily to enforce the law and protect the public (p. 5)

social network analysis an analytical technique that is designed to show the relationships between individuals in a criminal network (p. 298)

soft skills patrol officer skills sets centred on information collection, communication, and conflict resolution (p. 152)

Statute of Winchester a statute that made policing a community responsibility (p. 27)

strategic planning the identification of police priorities and objectives and associated resource requirements for the use of setting goals and resources (p. 64)

symbolic assailants individuals encountered by patrol officers who display mannerisms and behaviours that suggest the potential for violence (p. 158)

tactical elements (of community policing) the enforcement, prevention, and problem-solving strategies of a police service (p. 220)

task environment the organizational context and the community and areas in which police officers carry out their activities (p. 159)

tertiary crime prevention programs programs designed to prevent adults and youths from re-offending (p. 247)

three Ps prevention, problem solving, and partnership—the basis of community policing (p. 218)

tiered policing a model of police work involving a mix of traditional sworn police officers with new types of police and private security personnel (p. 45)

tired cop syndrome a jet-lag state of police officers, primarily due to shift work (p. 130)

typification how patrol officers depict or categorize the people and situations they encounter (p. 158)

unallocated patrol time the amount of time that patrol officers have that is not committed to responding to calls for service (p. 149)

ViCLAS the Violent Crime Linkages Analysis System, used by investigators that includes information on predatory and sexual crimes of violence (p. 297)

victim-precipitated homicides incidents in which the victim acts in a manner calculated to provoke the use of deadly force on the part of the police (p. 204)

whodunit investigations cases in which the suspect is unknown and extensive investigation is required (p. 277)

working personality of police officers a set of attitudinal and behavioural attributes of police officers (p. 121)

W system the approach used by police dispatchers to determine key facts about a call (p. 145)

zero-tolerance policing a crime response strategy centred on the premise that a strict order-maintenance approach by the police will reduce more serious criminal activity (p. 251)

Chapter Notes

CHAPTER 1

1. Goldsmith, A.J. (2010). Policing's new visibility, *British Journal of Criminology, 50*, 914–934.
2. Clarke, C., & Murphy, C. (2002). *In search of security: The roles of public police and private agencies* (discussion paper). Ottawa: Law Reform Commission of Canada. Retrieved from http://publications.gc.ca/collections/Collection/JL2-19-2002E.pdf
3. Polite Ire. (2012, January 5). The police: The case against [Blog post]. Retrieved from https://politeire.wordpress.com/2012/01/05/the-police-the-case-against/
4. Jochelson, R., Kramer, K., & Doerksen, M. (2014). *The disappearance of criminal law: Police powers and the Supreme Court.* Black Point, NS: Fernwood Publishing, p. 10.
5. ActivistRights.org.au. (n.d.). Role of police in society. Retrieved from http://www.activistrights.org.au/handbook/print/ch01s06.php
6. Corbett, J. (2011, November 30). Police state Canada: From the McDonald Commission to the G20. The Corbett Report. Retrieved from http://www.corbettreport.com/police-state-canada-from-the-mcdonald-commission-to-the-g20/
7. Whitaker, R., Kealey, G.S., & Parnaby, A. (2012). *Secret service: Political policing in Canada from the Fenians to Fortress America.* Toronto: University of Toronto Press.
8. Law Reform Commission of Canada. (2006). *In search of security: The future of policing in Canada.* Ottawa: Minister of Public Works and Government Services, pp. 120–121.
9. Bayley, D.H. (2005). What do the police do? In T. Newburn (Ed.), *Policing: Key readings* (pp. 141–149). Portland: Willan Publishing.
10. Murphy, C. (2012). Canadian police and policing policy, post 9/11. In K. Ismaili, J. Sprott, & K. Varma (Eds.), *Canadian criminal justice policy: Contemporary perspectives* (pp. 5–29). Toronto: Oxford University Press, p. 15.
11. Manning, P.K. (2005). The police: Mandate, strategies, and appearances. In T. Newburn (Ed.), *Policing: Key readings* (pp. 191–214). Portland: Willan Publishing.
12. Miller, S., & Blackler, J. (2005). *Ethical issues in policing.* Aldershot, UK: Ashgate Publishing Limited.
13. Institute for Canadian Urban Research Studies. (2014, November 27). *Economics of policing: Complexity and costs in Canada, 2014.* Burnaby, BC: Author, p. 1. Retrieved from http://capg.ca/wp-content/uploads/2014/12/Economics-of-Policing-Summary-ICURS-2014.pdf
14. Toronto Police Service. (2011). *Planning for the future...scanning the Toronto environment.* Toronto: Author, p. 14. Retrieved from http://www.torontopolice.on.ca/publications/files/reports/2011envscan.pdf
15. Quan, D. (2014, June 27). Canada at 147: Is it time to drop "visible minorities" from our lexicon? Canada.com. Retrieved from http://o.canada.com/news/national/visible-minorities-for-friday-june-27-online-28-print
16. Canadian Human Rights Act. (1986). Government of Canada, Department of Justice, p. 1. Retrieved from http://laws-lois.justice.gc.ca/eng/acts/h-6
17. Easton, S., Furness, H., & Brantingham, P. (2014). *The cost of crime in Canada.* Vancouver: The Fraser Institute. Retrieved from https://www.fraserinstitute.org/uploadedFiles/fraser-ca/Content/research-news/research/publications/cost-of-crime-in-canada-2014.pdf
18. Ibid., p. 62.
19. Jones, N.A., Ruddell, R., & Leyton-Brown, K. (2014). *The duty to disclose: The challenges, costs and possible solutions: Final report.* Regina: University of Regina, Collaborative Centre for Justice and Safety. Retrieved from http://www.justiceandsafety.ca/rsu_docs/duty-to-disclose-final-with-cover-to-ps.pdf
20. Malm, A., Pollard, N., Brantingham, P., Tinsley, P., Plecas, D., Brantingham, P., Cohen, I., & Kinney, B. (2005). *A 30 year analysis of police service delivery and costing: "E" Division.*

Abbotsford, BC: Centre for Criminal Justice Research, University College of the Fraser Valley. Retrieved from http://www.oldsruralcrimewatch.ca/pdfs/analysis.pdf

21. Brean, J. (2014, December 1). Canada's homicide rate falls to lowest level in half a century. *Ottawa Citizen.* Retrieved from http://ottawacitizen.com/news/local-news/canadas-homicide-rate-falls-to-lowest-level-in-half-a-century
22. Statistics Canada. (2014, July 23). Police-reported crime statistics, 2013. *The Daily.* Retrieved from http://www.statcan.gc.ca/daily-quotidien/140723/dq140723b-eng.pdf
23. Boyce, J., Cotter, A., & Perrault, S. (2014). Police-reported crime statistics in Canada, 2013, *Juristat, 34*(1). Ottawa: Minister of Industry. Retrieved from http://www.statcan.gc.ca/pub/85-002-x/2014001/article/14040-eng.pdf
24. Easton et al., *The cost of crime in Canada,* p. 33.
25. Statistics Canada. (2014, September 25). Police-reported cybercrime in Canada, 2012. *The Daily.* Retrieved from http://www.statcan.gc.ca/daily-quotidien/140925/dq140925-eng.pdf
26. Easton et al., *The cost of crime in Canada,* p. 1.
27. Ibid, p. iii.
28. Heaton, P., & Jackson, A. (2012, November 12). Short-term savings, long-term losses: When police departments respond to economic pressure by cutting their forces [Blog post]. The RAND Blog. Retrieved from http://www.rand.org/blog/2012/11/short-term-savings-long-term-losses-when-police-departments.html
29. Griffiths, C.T., & Murdoch, D. (2014). *Canadian corrections,* Fourth Edition. Toronto: Nelson.
30. Sparrow, M.K. (2014). *Managing the boundary between public and private policing.* Cambridge, MA: Harvard Kennedy School, p. 1. Retrieved from http://www.ncjrs.gov/pdffiles1/nij/247182.pdf
31. Ibid., p. 7.
32. Goldsmith, *Policing's new visibility.*
33. Bruemmer, R., & Laframboise, K. (2014, August 19). Dozens of Montreal firefighters storm city hall, throw water at councillors to protest pension reforms. *National Post.* Retrieved from http://news.nationalpost.com/2014/08/19/dozens-of-montreal-firefighters-storm-city-hall-throw-water-at-city-councillors-to-protest-pension-reforms; Gurney, M. (2014, June 18). In Montreal, It's one law for you, and another for fire-setting civil servants. *National Post.* Retrieved from http://fullcomment.nationalpost.com/2014/06/18/matt-gurney-in-montreal-its-one-law-for-you-and-another-for-fire-setting-civil-servants
34. Sutherland, A. (2014, October 14). Head of Montreal firefighters union suspended six months without pay for his part in trashing City Hall. *National Post.* Retrieved from http://news.nationalpost.com/news/canada/head-of-montreal-firefighters-union-suspended-six-months-without-pay-for-his-part-in-trashing-city-hall

CHAPTER 2

1. Stenning, P.C. (1981). *Legal status of the police.* Ottawa: Law Reform Commission of Canada.
2. Critchley, T.A. (1978). *A history of the police in England and Wales.* London: Constable, p. 6.
3. Berkley, G. (1969). *The democratic policeman.* Boston: Beacon Press, p. 5.
4. Ignatieff, M. (2005). Police and people: The birth of Mr. Peel's "Blue Locusts." In T. Newburn (Ed.), *Policing: Key Readings* (pp. 25–29). Portland: Willan Publishing, p. 25.
5. Berkley, *The democratic policeman,* p. 5.
6. Styles, J. (2005). The emergence of the police—explaining police reform in eighteen and nineteenth century England. In T. Newburn (Ed.), *Policing: Key Readings* (pp. 80–87). Portland: Willan Publishing.
7. Reith, C. (1956). *A new study of police history.* London: Oliver and Boyd.

8. Murphy, C. (2005). Securitizing community policing: Towards a Canadian public policing model. *Canadian Review of Policing Research, 2,* 25–31 (p. 26).
9. Fox, J.A. (1971). *The Newfoundland Constabulary*. St. John's: Robinson Blackmore, p. 4.
10. Dickinson, J.A. (1987). Reflexions sur la police en Nouvelle-France. *McGill Law Journal, 32,* 497–522.
11. Juliani, T.J., Talbot, C.K., & Jayewardene, C.H.S. (1984). Municipal policing in Canada: A developmental perspective. *Canadian Police College Journal, 8,* 315–385 (p. 326).
12. Ibid.
13. Halifax Regional Municipality. (n.d.). Police: History. Retrieved from http://www.halifax.ca/police/AboutHRP/history.php
14. Juliani et al., Municipal policing in Canada: A developmental perspective, p. 326.
15. Vronsky, P. (2003–2004a). History of the Toronto Police 1834–1860. Part 1. Toronto Police in 1834–1860, "Formidable Engines of Oppression." Retrieved from http://www.russianbooks.org/crime/cph3.htm, p. 2.
16. Weaver, J.C. (1995). *Crimes, constables, and courts*. Montreal and Kingston: McGill-Queen's University Press, p. 101.
17. Vronsky, History of the Toronto Police 1834-1860. Part 1.
18. Vronsky, P. (2003–2004b). History of the Toronto Police, 1870–1920. Part 4. "Constables as Urban Missionaries," p. 2. Retrieved from http://www.russianbooks.org/crime/cph6.htm
19. Weaver, *Crimes, constables, and courts,* p. 89.
20. Juliani et al., Municipal policing in Canada: A developmental perspective, p. 326.
21. Vancouver Police Department. (n.d.). History of the VPD. Retrieved from http://www.vancouver.ca/police/about/history/index.html
22. Templeman, J. (1992). Women in policing: History 1916–1992. Retrieved from http://www.winnipeg.ca/police/WomeninPolicing/history.stm
23. Schmidt, B.R. (2011). "The greatest man-catcher of all": The first female Mounties, the media, and the Royal Canadian Mounted Police. *Journal of the Canadian Historical Association, 22,* 201–243.
24. Weaver, *Crimes, constables, and courts*, p. 337.
25. Jenkins, M. (2005). Bloody falls of the coppermine: Madness, murder, and the collision of cultures in the Arctic, 1913. New York: Random House.
26. Smandych, R., & Linden, R. (1996). Administering justice without the state: a study of the private justice system of the Hudson's Bay Company to 1800. *Canadian Journal of Law and Society, 11,* 21–61.
27. Anderson, F.W. (1972). *Saskatchewan's provincial police*. Calgary: Frontier Publishing, p. 18.
28. Murphy, C., & McKenna, P. (2007). *Rethinking police governance, culture & management.* Ottawa: Public Safety Canada, p. 11. Retrieved from http:/publicsafety.gc.ca/cnt/cntrng/tsk-trc-rcmp-grc/_fl/archive-rthnk-plc-eng.pdf
29. Morton, D. (1977). Cavalry or police: Keeping the peace on two adjacent frontiers, 1870–1900. *Journal of Canadian Studies, 12,* 27–37 (p. 32).
30. Graybill, A.R. (2007). Policing the Great Plains: Rangers, Mounties, and the North American frontier, 1875–1920. Lincoln: University of Nebraska Press.
31. Morgan, E. (1973). The North-West Mounted Police: Internal problems and public criticism, 1874–1883. *Saskatchewan History, 26*(2), 41–62.
32. Morton, Cavalry or police: Keeping the peace on two adjacent frontiers, p. 31.
33. MacLeod, R.C. (1994). The RCMP and the evolution of provincial policing. In R.C. MacLeod & D. Schneiderman (Eds.), *Police Powers in Canada: The Evolution and Practice of Authority* (pp. 44–56). Toronto: University of Toronto Press, p. 45.
34. Ibid., p. 46.
35. Morgan, The North-West Mounted Police: Internal problems and public criticism, p. 60.

36. Morrison, W.R. (1985). *Showing the flag: The Mounted Police and Canadian sovereignty in the North, 1894-1925.* Vancouver: University of British Columbia Press, p. 13.
37. Roberts-Moore, J. (1987). Review of *Showing the Flag: The Mounted Police and Canadian Sovereignty in the North, 1894-1925. Archivaria, 25,* 138–140 (p. 138). Retrieved from http://journals.sfu.ca/archivar/index.php/archivaria/article/view/11470/12413
38. Morrison, W.R. (1974). The North-West Mounted Police and the Klondike Gold Rush. *Journal of Contemporary History, 9*(2), 93–105 (p. 102).
39. Personal communication with author, 1995.
40. Ibid.
41. Baker, W.M. (1993). Superintendent Deane of the Mounted Police. *Alberta History, 4*(4), 20-26; Betke, C. (1974). The Mounted Police and the Doukhobors in Saskatchewan, 1899–1909. *Saskatchewan History, 28*(1), 1–14.
42. Talbot, C.K., Jayewardene, C.H.S., & Juliani, T.J. (1983). *The thin blue line: A historical perspective of policing in Canada.* Ottawa: Crimcare, p. 22.
43. Hewitt, S. (2006). *Riding to the rescue: The transformation of the RCMP in Alberta and Saskatchewan, 1914–1939.* Toronto: University of Toronto Press.
44. Hewitt, S. (2000). "Information believed true": RCMP security intelligence activities on Canadian university campuses and the controversy surrounding them, 1961–1971. *Canadian Historical Review, 81,*191–228; Hewitt, S. (2002). *Spying 101: The RCMP's secret activities at Canadian universities, 1917–1997.* Toronto: University of Toronto Press; and Hewitt, *Riding to the rescue: The transformation of the RCMP in Alberta and Saskatchewan.*
45. Martel, M. (2009). "They smell bad, have diseases, and are lazy": RCMP officers reporting on hippies in the late sixties. *The Canadian Historical Review, 90,* 215–245 (pp. 215–216).
46. Ibid., p. 229.
47. Sethna, C., & Hewitt, S. (2009). Clandestine operations: The Vancouver Women's Caucus, the Abortion Caravan, and the RCMP. *The Canadian Historical Review, 90,* 463–495.
48. See Kinsman, G.W., & Gentile, P. (2009). *The Canadian war on queers: National security as sexual regulation.* Vancouver: UBC Press.
49. Murphy, C., & Clarke, C. (2005). Policing communities and communities of policing: A comparative study of policing and security in two Canadian communities. In D. Cooley (Ed.), *Re-Imagining Policing in Canada* (pp. 209–259). Toronto: University of Toronto Press, p. 21.
50. McKenna, P.J. (2014). *Tiered policing: An alternative model of police service delivery.* Ottawa: Canadian Police College, pp. 7–8. Retrieved from http://www.cpc.gc.ca/sites/default/files/pdf/tieredpolicing-eng.pdf
51. Bayley, D.H., & Shearing, C.D. (1996). The future of policing. *Law and Society Review, 33,* 585–606.
52. Reiss, A.J. (1992). Police organization in the twentieth century. In M. Tonry & N. Morris (Eds.), *Modern Policing: Crime and Justice,* Volume 15 (pp. 51–95). Chicago: University of Chicago Press.
53. American Civil Liberties Union. (2014). *War comes home: The excessive militarization of American policing.* New York: Author, p. 3. Retrieved from https://www.aclu.org/criminal-law-reform/war-comes-home-excessive-militarization-american-police-report
54. New Glasgow Regional Police Service. (2013). ERT (emergency response team). Retrieved from http://www.newglasgow.ca/departments/police-service/ert-emergency-response-team
55. Nova Scotia Finance and Treasury Board. (2014). Crime prevention and reduction policy view (for New Glasgow). Retrieved from www.novascotia.ca/finance/communitycounts/profiles/crime/default.asp?gnew=&table=&acctype=3&acctype2=&chartid=&mapid=&dcol=&sub=&gsel=3&ptype=geo&tid=&gview=4&glevel=juc&gnum=jpd10&gnum2=juc8
56. Spratt, M. (2014, August 15). The creeping militarization of the police. *iPolitics* [Blog post]. Retrieved from http://www.ipolitics.ca/2014/08/15/the-creeping-militarization-of-the-police

57. Quan, D. (2014, August 29). Canadian forces donate surplus military hardware to police agencies. Canada.com. Retrieved from http://www.o.canada.com/news/national/rcmp-defends-acquisition-of-surplus-military-hardware
58. Cited in Simmie, R. (2014, August 14). America's thick blue line. Toronto Star. http://www.thestar.com/news/world/2014/08/14/critics_decry_militarization_of_police_in_wake_of_missouri_death.html
59. Polite Ire. (2012, January 5). The police: The case against [Blog post]. Retrieved from https://politeire.wordpress.com/2012/01/05/the-police-the-case-against/

CHAPTER 3

1. Mounted Police Professional Association of Canada. (n.d.). Our mission. Retrieved from http://mppac.ca/about/
2. Donais, T. (2004). Peacekeeping's poor cousin: Canada and the challenge of post-conflict policing. *International Journal, 59,* 943–963; Dupont, B., & Tanner, S. (2008). *What happens before and after: The organizational and human resources challenges of deploying Canadian police peacekeepers abroad* (paper). Retrieved from https://papers.ssrn.com/sol3/papers.cfm?abstract_id=141525; Dupont, B., & Tanner, S. (2009). Not always a happy ending: The organizational challenges of deploying and reintegrating civilian peacekeepers (a Canadian perspective). *Policing & Society, 19,* 134–146; and Salahub, J.E. (2013, January 14). Forget peacekeeping: Canada should focus on policing. *Vancouver Sun.* Retrieved from http://www.vancouversun.com/business/Forget+peacekeeping+Canada+should+focus+policing/7818884/story.html
3. McLeod, R. (2002). Parapolice: A revolution in the business of law enforcement. Toronto: Boheme Press; Rigakos, G.S. (2003). The new parapolice: Risk markets and commodified social control. Toronto: University of Toronto Press.
4. Burbidge, S. (2005). Governance deficit: Reflections on the future of public and private policing in Canada. *Canadian Journal of Criminology and Criminal Justice, 47,* 63–86.
5. Walker, S. (2014). *What a good police department looks like: Professional, accountable, transparent, self-monitoring.* Omaha: University of Nebraska. Retrieved from http://samuelwalker.net/wp-content/uploads/2014/10/WHAT-A-GOOD-POLICE-DEPARTMENT-Final.pdf
6. Amendola, K.L., Weisburd, D., Hamilton, E.E., Jones, G., & Slipka, M. (2011). *The shift length experiment: What we know about 8-, 10- and 12-hour shifts in policing.* Washington, DC: The Police Foundation. Retrieved from http://www.policefoundation.org/sites/g/files/g798246/f/ShiftLengthExperiment_0.pdf
7. Orchowsky, S. (2014). *An introduction to evidence-based practices.* Washington, D.C.: Bureau of Justice Administration, p. 12. Retrieved from http://www.jrsainfo.org/projects/ebp_briefing_paper_april2014.pdf
8. Hutchins, H. (2014). *Police resources in Canada, 2013.* Ottawa: Minister of Industry, p. 26. Retrieved from http://www.statcan.gc.ca/pub/85-002-x/2014001/article/11914-eng.pdf
9. Artley, W., Ellison, D.J., & Kennedy, B. (2001). *The performance-based management handbook, volume 1: Establishing and maintaining a performance-based management program.* Washington, DC: U.S. Department of Energy, p. 4. Retrieved from http://www.orau.gov/pbm/pbmhandbook/volume%201.pdf
10. Roberts, D.J. (2006). *Law enforcement tech guide for creating performance measures that work: A guide for executives and managers.* Washington, DC: Office of Community Oriented Policing Services, U.S. Department of Justice. Retrieved from http://ric-zai-inc.com/Publications/cops-p120-pub.pdf
11. Lilley, D., & Hinduja, S. (2006). Officer evaluation in a community policing context. *Policing, 29(1),* 19–37.
12. Bratton, W.J. (1999). Great expectations: How higher expectations for police departments can lead to a decrease in crime. In R.H. Langworthy (Ed.), *Measuring What Matters: Proceedings From the Policing Research Institute Meetings* (pp. 11–26). Washington, DC:

Office of Community Oriented Policing Services, U.S. Department of Justice. Retrieved from https://www.ncjrs.gov/pdffiles1/170610-1.pdf; Langworthy, R.H. (1999). *Measuring what matters: Proceedings from the Policing Research Institute meetings.* Washington, DC: Office of Community Oriented Policing Services, U.S.Department of Justice. Retrieved from https://www.ncjrs.gov/pdffiles1/170610-1.pdf

13. Robertson, N. (2012). Policing: Fundamental principles in a Canadian context. *Canadian Public Administration, 55,* 343–363.
14. Paré, P.-P., Felson, R.B., & Ouimet, M. (2007). Community variation in crime clearance: A multilevel analysis with comments on assessing police performance. *Journal of Quantitative Criminology, 23,* 243–258.

CHAPTER 4

1. Ellwanger, S.J. (2012). How police officers learn ethics. In M.C. Braswell, B.R. McCarthy, & B.J. McCarthy (Eds.), *Justice, Crime, and Ethics* (pp. 45–69). Cincinnati, OH: Anderson Publishing, p. 45.
2. Pollock, J.M. (2005). Ethical issues in policing. In Q.C. Thurman & A. Giacomazzi (Eds.), *Controversies in Policing* (pp. 119–138). New York: LexisNexis.
3. Justice Institute of British Columbia. (2005). *British Columbia police code of ethics.* New Westminster, BC: Author. Retrieved from http://www.jibc.ca/sites/default/files/police_justice/pdf/JIBC_signing_final_web.pdf
4. Evans, D.R., & MacMillan, C.S. (2014). *Ethical reasoning in criminal justice and public safety,* 4th ed. Toronto: Emond Montgomery, p. 14.
5. Braswell, M.C., McCarthy, B.R., & McCarthy, B.J. (2002). *Justice, crime, and ethics*, 4th ed. Cincinnati: Anderson Publishing, p. 91.
6. Dean, G., Bell, P., & Lauchs, M. (2010). Conceptual framework for managing knowledge of police deviance. *Policing & Society, 20*, 204–222.
7. Petrovich, C. (2013, January 13). RCMP failed to track internal misconduct for years. CBC News. Retrieved from http://www.cbc.ca/news/canada/rcmp-failed-to-track-internal-misconduct-for-years-1.1353537
8. Perkel, C. (2014, June 27). Sex in cruisers, lying under oath, assault, drunk driving, porn – a historic year of Mountie misconduct. *National Post.* Retrieved from http//news.nationalpost.com/2014/06/27/sex-in-cruisers-lying-under-oath-assault-drunk-driving-porn-a-historic-year-of-mountie-misconduct
9. Murphy, C., & McKenna, P.F. (2007). *Rethinking police governance, culture and management: A summary review of the literature.* Ottawa: Task Force on Governance and Cultural Change in the RCMP, Public Safety Canada, p. 7. Retrieved from http://www.publicsafety.gc.ca/cnt/cntrng-crm/tsk-frc-rcmp-grc/_fl/archive-rthnk-plc-eng.pdf
10. Wright, B. (2010). Civilianising the "blue code"? An examination of attitudes to misconduct in the extended police family. *International Journal of Police Science and Management, 12,* 339–356.
11. Bronskill, J. (2014, May 20). RCMP study finds 322 incidents of corruption within force during 11-year period. *Vancouver Sun.* Retrieved from http://www.vancouversun.com/news/RCMP+study+finds+incidents+corruption+within+national+force/9854635/story.html
12. Dean, et al., Conceptual framework for managing knowledge of police deviance.
13. House of Commons, Canada. (2007). *Restoring the honor of the RCMP: Addressing problems in the administration of the RCMP's pension and insurance plans.* Report of the Standing Committee on Public Accounts. Ottawa: Government of Canada, p. 3. Retrieved from http://www.publications.gc.ca/collections/collection_2008/parl/XC16-392-1-1-01E.pdf
14. Rothlein, S. (2008). Noble cause corruption. Public Agency Training Council (PATC) newsletter. Retrieved from http://www.patc.com/weeklyarticles/noble-cause-corruption.shtml
15. Adapted from Rothlein, Noble cause corruption.

16. Martinelli, T.J. (2006). Unconstitutional policing: The ethical challenges in dealing with noble cause corruption. *The Police Chief, 73*(10), 16–22. Retrieved from http://www.policechiefmagazine.org/magazine/index.cfm?fuseaction=display&article_id=1025&issue_id=102006
17. Hutchinson, B. (2009, December 12). What does the force do with a wayward Mountie?" *National Post,* p. A9. Retrieved from http://www.bcpolicecomplaints.org/rcmp_discipline.html
18. Braidwood, Mr. Justice T.R. (Commissioner). (2010). *WHY? The Robert Dziekanski tragedy.* Victoria: Attorney General of British Columbia. Retrieved from http://www.ag.gov.bc.ca/public_inquiries/docs/BraidwoodPhase2Report.pdf
19. U.S. Department of Justice. (2011). Investigation of the New Orleans Police Department. Washington, DC: Civil Rights Division. Retrieved from http://www.justice.gov/crt/about/spl/nopd_report.pdf
20. Martinelli, T.J. (2007). Minimizing risk by defining off-duty police misconduct. *The Police Chief. 74*(6), 40–45. Retrieved from http://www.policechiefmagazine.org/magazine/index.cfm?fuseaction=display&article_id=1208&issue_id=62007
21. High-ranking Quebec police charged with fraud, (2014, January 28). *Toronto Star.* Retrieved from http://www.thestar.com/news/canada/2014/01/28/former_quebec_provincial_police_chief_charged_with_fraud.html
22. Pollock, J.M., & Williams, H.W. (2012). Using ethical dilemmas in training police. In M.C. Braswell, B.R. McCarthy, & B.J. McCarthy (Eds.), *Justice, Crime, and Ethics* (pp. 91–109). Cincinnati, OH: Anderson Publishing, p. 93.
23. Papenfuhs, S. (2011, April 6). Ethical dilemmas cops face daily. PoliceOne.com. Retrieved from http://www.policeone.com/legal/articles/3467115-Ethical-dilemmas-cops-face-daily
24. Wolfe, S.E., & Piquero, A.R. (2011). Organizational justice and police misconduct. *Criminal Justice and Behavior, 38*, 332–353.
25. East, K., & Kaustinen, F. (2014). *Independent citizen governance of police – reasons and principles.* Brampton, ON: Ontario Association of Police Service Boards, p. 1. Retrieved from http://www.oapsb.ca/news/2014/11/11/indep_cit_gov_police_oapsb_4_nov_2014_final.pdf
26. The Police Foundation. (2006). *Police governance and accountability* (report). Oxford Policing Policy Forum. Oxford, UK: Oxford University. Retrieved from http://www.police-foundation.org.uk/uploads/holding/oppf/oppf2.pdf
27. Law Reform Commission of Canada. (2006). *In search of security: The future of policing in Canada.* Ottawa: Minister of Public Works and Government Services, pp. 88–89. Retrieved from http://www.policingsecurity.ca/wp-content/uploads/2013/05/In-Search-of-Security.pdf
28. Pollock, J.M. (2010). *Ethical dilemmas and decisions in criminal justice.* Belmont, CA: Wadsworth/Cengage Learning, p. 182.
29. See Miller, S., & Blackler, J. (2005). *Ethical issues in policing.* Aldershot, UK: Ashgate.
30. Stenning, P. (2009). Governance and accountability in a plural policing environment—the story so far. *Policing, 3*(1), 22–33.
31. Law Reform Commission of Canada, *In search of security: The future of policing in Canada.*
32. Stenning, Governance and accountability in a plural policing environment, p. 29.
33. Murphy, C., & McKenna, P.F. (2010). *Police investigating police: A critical analysis of the literature.* Ottawa: Commission for Public Complaints Against the RCMP. Retrieved from https://www.crcc-ccetp.gc.ca/en/police-investigating-police-critical-analysis-literature
34. Smith, G. (2009). Citizen oversight of independent police services: Bifurcated accountability, regulation creep, and lesson learning. *Regulation & Governance, 3,* 421–441.
35. See Oppal, W.T. (2012). *Forsaken: The Report of the Missing Women Commission of Inquiry: Executive Summary.* Victoria: Ministry of Justice and Attorney General of British Columbia. Retrieved from http://www.ag.gov.bc.ca/public_inquiries/docs/Forsaken-ES.pdf

36. See Griffiths, C.T., & Murdoch, D. (2014). *Canadian Corrections,* 4th ed. Toronto: Nelson.
37. London Police Service. (2013). *2012 annual report.* London, ON: Author, p. 36. Retrieved from http://www.police.london.ca/About_Us/PDFs/2012AnnualReport.pdf
38. Lloyd, K., & Foster, J. (2009). *Citizen focus and community engagement: A review of the literature.* London, UK: The Police Foundation, p. 7. Retrieved from http://www.police-foundation.org.uk/uploads/catalogerfiles/citizen-focus-and-community-engagement-a-review-of-the-literature/citizen_focus.pdf
39. Leuprecht, C. (2007). Reforming security management: Prospects for the RCMP. *Policy Options, 28*(8), 67–72 (p. 69).
40. Walker, S., & Kreisel, B.W. (1996). Varieties of citizen review: The implications of organizational features of complaint review procedures for accountability of police. *American Journal of Police, 15*(3), 65–88.
41. Bobb, M. (2005). Internal and external police oversight in the United States. In C. Stone (Ed.), *Police Accountability and the Quality of Oversight: Global Trends in National Context (Conference Proceedings).* The Hague: Ministry of Foreign Affairs.
42. Alberta Urban Municipalities Association. (2009). *Policing in Alberta.* Edmonton: Author. Retrieved from http:///www.auma.ca/live/digitalAssets/26/26798_Task_Force_Policy_Paper_on_Policing_06102009.pdf
43. Arnold, S., Clark, P., & Cooley, D. (2010). *Sharing common ground: Review of Yukon's police force: Final report.* Whitehorse: Government of Yukon. Retrieved from http://www.policereview2010.gov.yk.ca/pdf/Sharing_Common_Ground_Final_Report.pdf; and Nixon, M., Massie, R., & Clark, P. (2012). *Sharing Common Ground: Review of Yukon's Police Force: Year One Progress Report.* Whitehorse: Government of Yukon. Retrieved from http://www.policereview2010.gov.yk.ca/pdf/Sharing_Common_Ground_Implementation_One_Year_Update-_May_2012.pdf. See also http://www.yukonpolicecouncil.gov.yk.ca.
44. Commission for Public Complaints Against the Police. (2009). *Police investigating police: Final public report.* Ottawa: Author. Retrieved from http://www.cpc-cpp.gc.ca/prr/rep/chair-pre/pipR/pip-finR-eng.pdf
45. Cf. Commission on First Nations and Metis Peoples and Justice Reform. (2004). *Legacy of hope: An agenda for change, volume 1: Final report.* Regina: Department of Justice. Retrieved from http://www.justice.gov.sk.ca/justicereform/volume1.shtml
46. MacDonald, R. (2010). *Review of Yukon's police force: The views of clients of the Salvation Army in Whitehorse, Yukon.* Whitehorse: Government of Yukon, p. 29. Retrieved from http://www.policereview2010.gov.yk.ca/pdf/Salvation_Army_Clients_Submission.pdf
47. Marin, A. (2012, April 22). *Effective police oversight in Ontario: Myth or reality.* Presentation of Andre Marin to Civil Liberties Association – National Capital Region. April 22. Retrieved from http://www.ombudsman.on.ca/Resources/Speeches/2012/Effective-police-oversight-in-Ontario--Myth-or-Rea.aspx
48. Murphy and McKenna, *Police Investigating Police,* p. 22.

CHAPTER 5

1. Foley, P.F., Guarneri, C., & Kelly, M.E. (2007). Reasons for choosing a police career: Changes over two decades. *International Journal of Police Science & Management, 10*(1), 2–8.
2. Ipsos Public Affairs. (2010). *Trends in youth perceptions of the police and police recruitment (2007, 2009, 2010).* Ottawa: Police Sector Council. Retrieved from http://www.publicsafety.gc.ca/lbrr/archives/cnmcs-plcng/cn79233308-eng.pdf
3. Campbell, M. (2012, March 20). Would you reveal your Facebook password for a job? *Toronto Star.* Retrieved from http://www.thestar.com/business/2012/03/20/would_you_reveal_your_facebook_password_for_a-job.html; Ontario Human Rights Commission. (2014, December 5). Ontario Human Rights Commission issues statement on employer requests for Facebook passwords [Blog post]. Law of Work. Retrieved from http://lawofwork.ca/?p=5026

4. Toronto Police Service. (2011). *Planning for the future…scanning the Toronto environment.* Toronto: Author, p. 198. Retrieved from http://www.torontopolice.on.ca/publications/files/reports/2011envscan.pdf
5. Toronto Police Service. (n.d.). Latest recruit class a diverse group. Retrieved from http://www.torontopolice.on.ca/modules.php?op=modload&name=new&file=article&sid-3820
6. Royal Canadian Mounted Police. (2012). *Gender-based assessment.* Ottawa: National Program Evaluation Services, p. 1. Retrieved from http://www.rcmp-grc.ca/aud-ver/reports-rapports/gba-eces/gba-eces-eng.pdf
7. Quan, D. (2014, October 19). RCMP sets an "ambitious" new goal: Recruit as many women as men. *National Post.* Retrieved from http://news.nationalpost.com/news/canada/rcmp-sets-an-ambitious-new-goal-recruit-as-many-women-as-men
8. Ontario Provincial Police. (n.d.) Recruiting resources. Retrieved from http://www.opp.ca/ecms/index.php?id=132
9. Rockliffe, A. (2014, March 14). Aboriginal police officer recruitment in Saskatoon grows. Global News. Retrieved from http://globalnews.ca/news/1209749/aboriginal-police-officer-recruit-in-saskatoon-grows/
10. OACP, & Kirkup, K. (2013). *Best practices in policing and LGBTQ communities in Ontario.* Toronto: OACP. Retrieved from http://www.oacp.on.ca/Userfiles/Files/NewAndEvents/OACP%20LGBTQ%20final%20Nov2013.pdf
11. Colvin, R. (2009). Shared perceptions among lesbian and gay police officers: Barriers and opportunities in the law enforcement work environment. *Police Quarterly, 12*(1), 86–101.
12. Griffiths, C.T. (2015). *Canadian Criminal Justice,* 5th ed. Toronto: Nelson.
13. Peritz, I. (2010, September 16). Fitness tests, intelligence tests and, now, "suitability" tests. *The Globe and Mail*, pp. A1, A9.
14. Middleton-Hope, J. (2004). Misconduct among previously experienced officers: Issues in the recruitment and hiring of "gypsy cops." *Canadian Review of Policing Research, 1*, 178–188.
15. Henson, B., Reyns, B.W., Klahm, C.F., & Frank, J. (2010). Do good recruits make good cops? Problems predicting and measuring academy and street-level success. *Police Quarterly, 13*(1), 5–26.
16. Chan, J.B.L. (2003). *Fair cop: Learning the art of policing.* Toronto: University of Toronto Press.
17. Chappell, A.T., & Lanza-Kaduce, L. (2009). Police academy socialization: Understanding the lessons learned in a paramilitary-bureaucratic organization. *Journal of Contemporary Ethnography, 39*, 187–214.
18. Personal communication with author, September 2013.
19. Personal communication with author, 2012.
20. Haarr, R.N. (2001). The making of a community policing officer: The impact of basic training and occupational socialization on police recruits. *Police Quarterly, 4*, 402–433.
21. Novakowski, M. (2004). Police field training officers: It's the singer, not the song. *The Canadian Review of Policing Research, 1*, 220–230.
22. Skolnick, J. (1966). *Justice without trial: Law enforcement in a democratic society.* New York: John Wiley.
23. Murphy, C., & McKenna, P. (2007). *Rethinking police governance, culture & management.* Ottawa: Public Safety Canada. Retrieved from http://publicsafety.gc.ca/cnt/cntrng-crm/tsk-frc-rcmp-grc/_fl/archive-rthnk-plc-eng.pdf; and Paoline, E.A. (2004). Shedding light on police culture: An examination of officers' occupational attitudes. *Police Quarterly, 7*, 205–236.
24. Wood, R.L., Davis, M., & Rouse, A. (2004). Diving into quicksand: Program implementation and police subcultures. In W.G. Skogan (Ed.), *Community Policing: Can It Work?* (pp. 136–161). Belmont: Wadsworth/Thomson Learning (p. 139).
25. Cockcroft, T. (2013). *Police culture: Themes and concepts.* New York: Routledge.

26. Twersky-Glasner, A. (2005). "Police personality: What is it and why are they like that?" *Journal of Police and Criminal Psychology, 20*(1), 56–67 (p. 66).
27. Paoline, Shedding light on police culture.
28. Burke, R.J. (1989). Career stages, satisfaction, and well-being among police officers. *Psychological Reports, 65*, 3–12.
29. Cited in Egan, K. (2014, September 30). What price policing? The aftershock of Kal Ghadban's tragic end. *Ottawa Citizen*, p. 3. Retrieved from http://ottawacitizen.com/opinion/columnists/egan-what-price-policing-the-aftershock-of-kal-ghadbans-tragic-end
30. Morash, M., Haarr, R., & Kwak, D.-H. (2006). Multilevel influences on police stress. *Journal of Contemporary Criminal Justice, 22*(1), 26–43; and Parsons, J.R.L. (2004). *Occupational health and safety issue of police officers in Canada, the United States, and Europe: A review essay.* Retrieved from http://www.mun.ca/safetynet/library/OHandS/OccupationalHS.pdf
31. Cited in Yogaretnam, S. (2014, October 10). Walking the thin blue line: How stigma is silencing police officers. *Ottawa Citizen*, p. 1. Retrieved from http://ottawacitizen.com/news/local-news/walking-the-thin-blue-line-how-stigma-is-silencing-officers
32. D.P. Rosenbaum, Schuck, A.M., & Cordner, G. (2011). *The National Police Research Platform: The life course of new officers* (research review). Washington, DC: National Institute of Justice, p. 13. Retrieved from http:// www.nationalpoliceresearch.org/storage/Recruits%20Life%20Course.pdf
33. Cited in Yogaretnam, Walking the thin blue line, p. 3.
34. Cited in Egan, What price policing?, p. 2.
35. Duxbury, L., & Higgins, C. (2012). *Summary of key findings: Caring for and about those who serve: Work-life and employee well being within Canada's police departments* (p. 7). Retrieved from http://sprott.carleton.co/wp-content/files/Duxbury-Higgins-Police2012_keyfindings.pdf
36. Buttle, J., Fowler, C., & Williams, M.W. (2010). The impact of rural policing on the private lives of New Zealand police officers. *International Journal of Police Science & Management, 12*, 596–606.
37. Dowler, K., & Arai, B. (2008). Stress, gender and policing: The impact of perceived gender discrimination on symptoms of stress. *International Journal of Police Science & Management, 10*, 123–135.
38. Hassell, K.D., & Brandl, S.G. (2009). An examination of the workplace experiences of police patrol officers: The role of race, sex, and sexual orientation. *Police Quarterly, 12*, 408–430; and Maher, T.M. (2010). Police sexual misconduct: Female police officers' views regarding its nature and extent. *Women & Criminal Justice, 20*, 263–282.
39. Royal Canadian Mounted Police. (2009). *Results – RCMP employee opinion survey 2009.* Ottawa: Author. Retrieved from http://www.rcmp-grc.gc.ca/surveys-sondages/2009/index-main-accueil-eng.htm
40. Royal Canadian Mounted Police, *Gender-based assessment.*
41. Maher, Police sexual misconduct: female police officers' views regarding its nature and extent, p. 276.
42. CBC News. (2013, June 11). 282 join RCMP sexual harassment class-action lawsuit. Retrieved from http://www.cbc.ca/news/canada/british-columbia/282-join-rcmp-sexual-harassment-class-action-lawsuit-1.1346440
43. Goodwin, S. (1999.) *The experience of combining motherhood with career for members of the Royal Canadian Mounted Police* (unpublished MA thesis). Vancouver: Department of Educational and Counselling Psychology, University of British Columbia, p. 65.
44. Shane, J.M. (2010). Organizational stressors and police performance. *Journal of Criminal Justice, 38*, 807–818.
45. Royal Canadian Mounted Police, *Results – RCMP employee opinion survey 2009.*
46. Commission for Public Complaints Against the RCMP. (2013). Public interest investigation into workplace harassment within the Royal Canadian Mounted Police. Ottawa. https://www.crcc-ccetp.gc.ca/pdf/rep-rap-eng.pdf

47. LeBlanc, D. (2012, September 18). Female Mounties fear backlash over reporting harassment, report shows. *The Globe and Mail.* Retrieved from http://www.theglobeandmail.com/news/national/female-mounties-fear-backlash-over-reporting-harassment-report-shows/article4550565/

48. McCarty, W.P., Schuck, A., Skogan, W., & Rosenbaum, D. (2011). *Stress, burnout, and health.* Chicago: National Police Research Platform. Retrieved from http://www.nationalpoliceresearch.org/storage/updated-papers/Stress%20Burnout%20%20and%20Health%20FINAL.pdf

49. McDonald, J.M. (2006). *Gold medal policing: Mental readiness and performance excellence.* New York: Sloan Associate Press; and Vila, B. (2009). *Sleep deprivation: What does it mean for public safety officers?* Washington, DC: U.S. Department of Justice, Office of Justice Programs. Retrieved from https://www.ncjrs.gov/pdffiles1/nij/225762.pdf

50. Senjo, S.R., & Dhungana, K. (2009). A field data examination of policy constructs related to fatigue conditions in law enforcement personnel. *Police Quarterly, 12,* 123–136.

51. Marquie, J.-C., Tucker, P., Folkard, S., Gentil, C., & Ansiau. D. (2014, November 20). Chronic effects of shift work on cognition: Findings from the VISAT longitudinal study. *Occupational and Environmental Medicine.* Published online.

52. Vila, B. (2010). The effects of officer fatigue on accountability and the exercise of police discretion. In C. McCoy (Ed.), *Holding Police Accountable* (pp. 161–185). Washington, DC: The Urban Institute Press.

53. Cited in Rockliffe, Aboriginal police officer recruitment in Saskatoon grows, pp. 2–3.

54. OACP & Kirkup, *Best practices in policing and LGBTQ communities in Ontario.*

55. Royal Canadian Mounted Police, *Results – RCMP employee opinion survey 2009.*

56. Duxbury and Higgins, *Summary of key findings: Caring for and about those who serve,* p. 5.

57. Duxbury and Higgins, as cited in Marin, A. (2012). *In the line of duty: Investigation into how the Ontario Provincial Police and the Ministry of Community Safety and Correctional Services have addressed operational stress injuries affecting police officers.* Toronto: Ombudsman of Ontario, p. 33. Retrieved from http://www.ombudsman.on.ca/Ombudsman/files/c4/c43aef71-b2ac-4008-ac89-124f56d8dd75.pdf

58. Austin-Ketch, T.L., Violanti, J., Fekedulegn, D., Andrew, M.E., Burchfield, C.M., & Hartley, T.A. (2012). Addictions and the criminal justice system: What happens on the other side? Post-traumatic stress symptoms and cortisol measures in a police cohort. *Journal of Addictions Nursing, 23*(1), 22–29.

59. Varvarigou, V., Farioli, A., Korre, M., Sato, S., Dahabreh, I.J., & Kales, S.N. (2014). Law enforcement duties and sudden cardiac death among police officers in the United States: Case distribution study. *British Medical Journal,* 349.

60. Arter, M.L. (2008). Stress and deviance in policing. *Deviant Behavior, 29*(1), 43–69; and Regehr, C., Johanis, D., Dimitropoulos, G., Bartram, C., & Hope, G. (2003). The police officer and the public inquiry: A qualitative inquiry into the aftermath of workplace trauma. *Brief Treatment and Crisis Intervention, 3,* 383–396.

61. Marin, *In the line of duty: Investigation into how the Ontario Provincial Police and the Ministry of Community Safety and Correctional Services have addressed operational stress injuries affecting police officers.*

62. Patterson, G., Chung, I., & Swan, P.G. (2012). The effects of stress management interventions among police officers and recruits. *Campbell Collaboration, 8* (7). Retrieved from http://www.campbellcollaboration.org/lib/project/150/

63. See Gilmartin, K.M. (2002). *Emotional survival for law enforcement: A guide for officers and their families.* Tucson: E-S Press.

64. Austin-Ketch et al., Addictions and the criminal justice system, What happens on the other side?

65. McCanlies, E.C., Mnatsakanova, A., Andrew, M.E., Burchfiel, C.M., & Violanti, J.M. (2014). Positive psychological factors associated with lower PTSD symptoms among police officers: Post Hurricane Katrina. *Stress and Health, 30,* 405–415.

66. McCarty, W.P., & Skogan, W.G. (2013). Job-related burnout among civilian and sworn police personnel. *Police Quarterly, 16*(1), 66–84.
67. Pearsall, B. (2012, June). Sleep disorders, work shifts, and officer wellness. *NIJ Journal, No. 270*. Retrieved from http://www.ncjrs.gov/pdffiles1/nij/238487.pdf
68. Skogstad, M., Skogstad, M., Lie, A., Conradi, H.S., Heir, T., & Weisaeth, L. (2013). Work-related post-traumatic stress disorder. *Occupational Medicine, 63*, 175–182.
69. Marin, *In the line of duty: Investigation into how the Ontario Provincial Police and the Ministry of Community Safety and Correctional Services have addressed operational stress injuries affecting police officers.*
70. McGinn, D. (2010, February 27). The untold perils of policing: Post-traumatic stress disorder quietly affects many officers. *The Globe and Mail*, p. M4.
71. Rades, A. (2014, May 19). 7 jobs with the highest suicide rates [Blog post], daddu.net. Retrieved from http://daddu.net/7-jobs-highest-suicide-rates
72. Ibid.
73. Violanti, J.M. (2007). Homicide-suicide in police families: Aggression full circle. *International Journal of Emergency Mental Health, 9*, 97–104.
74. Leenaars, A.A. (2014). *Municipal police: A sworn member's risk for suicide* (conference presentation). Calgary Police Symposium, "A National Symposium: A Sworn Member's Risk for Suicide." Retrieved from http://www.calgary.ca/cps/Documents/Municipal%20Police%20Sworn%20Member%27s%20%20Risk%20for%20Suicide.pdf; and Leenaars, A.A., Collins, P., & Sinclair, S. (2008). *Report to the London Police Service and London community on the deaths of David Lucio and Kelly Johnson*. London, ON: London Police Service. Retrieved from http://www.police.london.ca/Newsroom/PDFs/luciojohnsonreport.pdf
75. City of Calgary. (2014, November 12). Calgary Police Service is first policing agency in Canada to adopt mental health program (news release). Retrieved from http://newsroom.calgary.ca/news/calgary-police-service-is-the-first-policing-agency-in-canada-to-adopt-mental-health-program
76. Armstrong, J. (2014, July 18). "I was scared of appearing weak": First responders speak out on PTSD. Global News. Retrieved from http://globalnews.ca/news/1460326/i-was-scared-of-appearing-weak-first-responders-speak-out-on-ptsd
77. Marin, *In the line of duty: Investigation into how the Ontario Provincial Police and the Ministry of Community Safety and Correctional Services have addressed operational stress injuries affecting police officers*, p. 8.
78. Ibid.

CHAPTER 6

1. Bullock, K. (2013). Community, intelligence-led policing and crime control. *Policing & Society, 23*, 125–144.
2. Van Maanen, J. (1973). Observations on the making of policemen. *Human Organization, 32*, 407–418.
3. McDonald, J.M. (2006). *Gold medal policing: Mental readiness and performance excellence.* New York: Sloan Associate Press, p. 82.
4. Amendola, K.L., Weisburd, D., Hamilton, E.E., Jones, G., & Slipka, M. (2011). *The shift length experiment. What we know about 8-, 10-, and 12-hour shifts in policing.* Washington, DC: Police Foundation. Retrieved from http://www.policefoundation.org/sites/g/files/g798246/f/ShiftLengthExperiment.pdf
5. Dunn, S. (2010). *Police officers murdered in the line of duty, 1961 to 2009.* Ottawa: Statistics Canada. Retrieved from http://www.statcan.gc.ca/pub/85-002-x/2010003/article/11354-eng.htm
6. Demers, S., Prox, R., Palmer, A., & Griffiths, C.T. (2007). *Vancouver Police Department patrol deployment study.* Vancouver: Vancouver Police Department. Retrieved from http://www.city.vancouver.bc.ca/police/assets/pdf/studies/vpd-study-patrol-deployment.pdf

7. Edmonton Police Service. (2014). *2013 annual policing plan: Report card*. Edmonton: Author, p. 6. Retrieved from http://www.edmontonpolicecommission.com/wp-content/uploads/2014/04/2013-Annual-Policing-Plan-Report-Card_Final_web.pdf
8. Plecas, D., McCormick, A.V., & Cohen, I.M. (2010). *RCMP Surrey ride along study: General findings*. Abbotsford, BC: Centre for Public Safety and Criminal Justice Research, University of the Fraser Valley, p. 7. Retrieved from https://www.ufv.ca/media/assets/ccjr/reports-and-publications/Surrey_General_Findings.pdf
9. Personal communication with author, 2013.
10. Cf. Toronto Police Service. (2011). *Planning for the future…scanning the Toronto environment*. Toronto: Author, p. 174. Retrieved from http://www.torontopolice.on.ca/publications/files/reports/2011envscan.pdf
11. Edmonton Police Service, *2013 annual policing plan*, p. 6.
12. London Police Service. (2012). *Annual report 2012*. London, ON: Author, p. 11. Retrieved from http://www.police.london.ca/About_US/PDFs/2012AnnualReport.pdf
13. McDonald, *Gold medal policing*, p. 83.
14. Ibid., p. 57.
15. Cited in Egan, K. (2014, September 30). What price policing? The aftershock of Kal Ghadban's tragic end. *Ottawa Citizen*, p. 2. Retrieved from http://ottawacitizen.com/opinion/columnists/egan-what-price-policing-the-aftershock-of-kal-ghadbans-tragic-end
16. Pollock, J.M. (2014). *Ethical dilemmas and decisions in criminal justice*, 8th ed. Belmont, CA: Wadsworth, p. 2.
17. Davis, K.C. (1975). *Police discretion*. Minneapolis: West Publishing.
18. Terrill, W., & Paoline, E.A. (2007). Nonarrest decision making in police-citizen encounters. *Police Quarterly, 10*, 308–331.
19. Pollock, J.M., & Williams, H.W. (2012). Using ethical dilemmas in training police. In M.C. Braswell, B.R. McCarthy, and B.J. McCarthy (Eds.), *Justice, Crime, and Ethics*, 7th ed. (pp. 91–109). Cincinnati, OH: Anderson Publishing, p. 97.
20. Braswell, M.C., McCarthy, B.R., & McCarthy, B.J. (2012). *Justice, crime, and ethics*, 7th ed. Cincinnati: Anderson Publishing, p. 92.
21. Terrill and Paoline, Nonarrest decision making in police-citizen encounters.
22. Cooper, C. (1997). Patrol police officer conflict resolution processes. *Journal of Criminal Justice, 25*, 87–101.
23. Lundman, R.J. (1980). *Police and policing—an introduction*. New York: Holt, Rinehart, and Winston, p. 110.
24. Van Maanen, Observations on the making of policemen, p. 413.
25. Skolnick, J. (1966). *Justice without trial: Law enforcement in a democratic society.* New York: John Wiley and Sons, p. 45.
26. McDonald, *Gold medal policing*, p. 98.
27. Dunn, *Police officers murdered in the line of duty*, pp. 98–99.
28. Bayley, D.H. (2005). What do the police do? In T. Newman (Ed.), *Policing: Key Readings* (pp. 141–149). Portland: Willan Publishing, p. 144.
29. Dunn, *Police officers murdered in the line of duty.*
30. Gifford, D. (2014). *Hamilton Police Service patrol officer workload study 2011–2013.* Hamilton, ON: Hamilton Police Service. Retrieved from http://www.hamiltonpolice.on.ca
31. Hutchins, H. (2014). *Police resources in Canada, 2013.* Ottawa: Minister of Industry, p. 26. Retrieved from http://www.statcan.gc.ca/pub/85-002-x/2014001/article/11914-eng.pdf
32. Ruddell, R. (2011). Boomtown policing: Responding to the dark side of resource development, *Policing, 5*, 328–342.
33. Boyd, N. (2014). *Crime in the Regional Municipality of Wood Buffalo*. Ft. McMurray: Regional Municipality of Wood Buffalo. Retrieved from http://www.woodbuffalo.ab.ca/Assets/OOassets/living/Crime+Study/PDF/Crime+Report.pdf

34. Hassell, K.D. (2007). Variation in police patrol practices: The precinct as a sub-organizational level of analysis. *Policing: An International Journal of Police Strategies & Management, 30,* 257–276.
35. Bayley, What do the police do? p. 144.
36. Rydberg, J., & Terrill, W. (2010). The effect of higher education on police behavior. *Police Quarterly, 13*(1), 92–120.
37. Gau, J.M. (2010). A longitudinal analysis of citizens' attitudes about police. *Policing: An International Journal of Police Strategies & Management, 33,* 236–252; and Hinds, L. (2009). Public satisfaction with the police: The influence of general attitudes and police-citizen encounters. *International Journal of Police Science and Management, 11*(1), 54–66.
38. Bradford, B., Jackson, J., & Stanko, E.A. (2009). Contact and confidence: Revisiting the impact of public encounters with the police. *Policing & Society: An International Journal of Research and Policy, 19*(1), 20–46.
39. Sherman, L.W., Gottfredson, D., MacKenzie, D., Eck, J., Reuter, P., & Bushway, S. (1997). *Preventing crime: What works, what doesn't, what's promising.* Washington, DC: Department of Justice, Office of Justice Programs, p. 81. Retrieved from http://www.ncjrs.gov/works
40. Poteyeva, M., & Sun, I.Y. (2009). Gender differences in police officers' attitudes: Assessing current empirical evidence. *Journal of Criminal Justice, 37,* 512–522.
41. Dunham, R.G., & Alpert, G.P. (2009). Officer and suspect demeanor: A qualitative analysis of change. *Police Quarterly, 12*(1), 6–21.
42. Jones, N.A., Ruddell, R., & Leyton-Brown, K. (2014). *The duty to disclose. The challenges, costs and possible solutions: Final report.* Regina: University of Regina, Collaborative Centre for Justice and Safety, p. 3. Retrieved from http://www.justiceandsafe.ca/rsu_docs/duty-to-disclose-final-with-cover-to-ps.pdf
43. Statistics Canada. (2014, July 23). Police-reported crime statistics, 2013. *The Daily,* p. 7. Retrieved from http://www.statcan.gc.ca/daily-quotiden/140723/dq140723b-eng.pdf
44. CBC News. (2012, July 24). Crime rates in North still higher than in rest of Canada. Retrieved from http://www.cbc.ca/news/canada/north/crime-rates-in-north-still-higher-than-in-rest-of-canada-1.1221263
45. Griffiths, C.T., Saville, G., Wood, D.S., & Zellerer, E. (1995). *Crime and justice among Inuit in the Baffin Region, N.W.T, Canada.* Burnaby, BC: Criminology Research Centre, Simon Fraser University.
46. Ibid., pp. 50–51.
47. Ibid., p. 30.
48. Galloway, G. (2010, October 16). Mounties pulled from Cape Dorset after rash of gunplay. *The Globe and Mail,* p. A10.
49. Higenbottam, J. (2014). *Into the future: The Coquitlam Health Campus. A vision for the Riverview Lands.* Coquitlam, BC: City of Coquitlam, pp. 9–10. Retrieved from http://coquitlam.ca/Libraries/Community_Planning_Documents/Into_the_Future_-_the_Coquitlam_Health_Campus.sflb.ashx
50. Wilson-Bates, F. (2008). *Lost in transition: How a lack of capacity in the mental health system is failing Vancouver's mentally ill and draining police resources.* Vancouver: Vancouver Police Department. Retrieved from http://vancouver.ca/police/assets/pdf/reports-policies/vpd-lost-in-transition.pdf
51. Iacobucci, F. (2014). *Police encounters with people in crisis.* Toronto: Toronto Police Service. Retrieved from http://www.torontopolice.on.ca/publications/files/reports/police_encounters_with_people_in_crisis_2014.pdf
52. Ibrahim, M. (2013, August 21). Police Stuck "Babysitting" in Hospitals, Chief Says. *Edmonton Journal.* Retrieved from http://www2.canada .com/edmontonjournal/news/story.html?id=91c06643-2f41-4735-bf75 -9fb8e42893f6
53. Engel, R.S., & Silver, E. (2001). Policing mentally disordered suspects: A reexamination of the criminalization hypothesis. *Criminology, 39,* 225–252.

54. Cotton, D. (2004). The attitudes of Canadian police officers toward the mentally ill." *International Journal of Law and Psychiatry, 27*, 135–146.
55. Johnson, R.R. (2011). Suspect mental disorder and police use of force. *Criminal Justice and Behavior, 38*, 127–145.
56. Butler, A. (2014). *Mental illness and the criminal justice system: A review of global perspectives and promising practices.* Vancouver: International Centre for Criminal Law Reform and Criminal Justice Policy. Retrieved from http://www.icclr.law.ubc.ca; Coleman, T., & Cotton, D. (2014). *A comprehensive review of the preparation and learning necessary for effective police interactions with persons with a mental illness.* Toronto: Mental Health Commission of Canada. Retrieved from http://www.mentalhealthcommission.ca/English/system/files/private/document/effective_police_interaction_-_exec_summary_0.pdf; and Livingston, J. D., Weaver, C., Hall, N., & Verdun-Jones, S. (2008). *Criminal justice diversion for persons for mental disorders: A review of best practices.* Vancouver: The Law Foundation of British Columbia, B.C. Mental Health & Addiction Services, Canadian Mental Health Association, BC Division. Retrieved from http://www.cmha.bc.ca/files/DiversionBestPractices.pdf
57. Franz, S., & Borum, R. (2010). Crisis intervention teams may prevent arrests of people with mental illness. *Police Practice and Research, 12*, 265–272.
58. Roth, P. (2013, March 18). Edmonton police using less force with the mentally ill after University of Alberta course. *Edmonton Sun.* Retrieved from http://www.edmontonsun.com/2013/03/18/edmonton-police-using-less-force-with-mentally-ll-after-university-of-alberta-course
59. Cotton, D., & Coleman, T.G. (2010). Canadian police agencies and their interactions with persons with a mental illness: A systems approach. *Police Practice and Research, 11*, 301–314 (p. 310).
60. Steadman, H.J., Morrissey, J.P., Deane, M.W., & Borum, R. (1999). *Police response to emotionally disturbed persons: Analyzing new models of police interactions with the mental health system.* Washington, DC: U.S. Department of Justice. Retrieved from http://www.ncjrs.gov/pdffiles1/nij/grants/179984.pdf
61. Kisely, S., Campbell, L.A., Peddle, S., Hare, S., Psyche, M., Spicer, D., & Moore, B. (2010). A controlled before-and-after evaluation of a mobile crisis partnership between mental health and police services in Nova Scotia. *Canadian Journal of Psychiatry, 55*, 662–668.
62. Thompson, D., & Taylor, J. (2013). *Police and Crisis Team (PACT): Pilot evaluation report, December, 2011 to March, 2013.* Red Deer, AB: City of Red Deer. Retrieved from http://www.reddeer.ca/media/reddeerca/about-red-deer/social-well-being-and-community-initiatives/Police-and-Crisis-Team-PACT-Pilot-Evaluation-Report---December-2011-to-March-2013.pdf
63. Canadian Association of Chiefs of Police. (2004). Bias-free policing. *Resolutions adopted at the 99th Annual Conference.* Ottawa: Author, p. 7. Retrieved from https://www.cacp.ca/resolution.html?asst_id=318
64. Fridell, L., Lunney, R., Diamond, D., & Kubu, B. (2001). *Racially biased policing: A principled response.* Washington, DC: Police Executive Research Forum, p. 5. Retrieved from http://www.cops.usdoj.gov/files/RIC/Publications/raciallybiasedpolicing.pdf
65. Human Rights Tribunal of Ontario. (2011) *McKay v. Toronto Police Services Board,* 2011 HRTO 499, 15. Toronto: Author, p. 15. Retrieved from http://www.canlii.org/en/on/onhrt/doc/2011/2011hrto499/2011hrto499.html
66. Rubin, cited in ibid., p. 16.
67. Assets Coming Together Youth Project. (2010). *Jane-Finch youth speak out: turf, violence, well-being.* Toronto: York University, p. 5. Retrieved from http://www.yorku.ca/act/reports/Jane-FinchYouthSpeakOut.pdf
68. Ontario Provincial Police. (2011). *Destination diversity. The Ontario Provincial Police diversity journey.* Toronto: Strategic Initiatives Office, p. 10. Retrieved from http://www.opp.ca/ecms/files/270341239.pdf

69. Miller, K. (2009). The institutionalization of racial profiling policy. *Crime & Delinquency, 59*(1), 32–58.
70. Danville Police Department. (2012). *Officer-worn camera program.* Danville, VA: Author. Retrieved from http://www.theiacp.org/Portals/0/pdfs.LEIM/2012Persentations/OPS-Officer-WornCameras.pdf; and National Institute of Justice. (2012). *A primer on body-worn cameras for law enforcement.* Washington, DC: U.S. Department of Justice. Retrieved from http://www.justnet.org/pdf/00-body-Worn-Cameras-508.pdf
71. 10 limitations of body cams you need to know for your protection. (2014, September 23). PoliceOne.com. Retrieved from http://www.policeone.com/police-products/body-cameras/articles/7580663-10-limitations-of-body-cams-you-need-to-know-for-your-protection
72. Clissold, P., Tuson, R., & Stratton, M. (2014). *Edmonton Police Service body worn video project, 2011–2014.* Edmonton: Edmonton Police Service. Retrieved from http://www.cacole.ca/confere-reunion/pastCon/presentations/2014/maryS.pdf
73. Katz, C., Kurtenbach, M., Choate, D., & Ready, J. (2014). *Evaluating the impact of officer worn cameras in the Phoenix Police Department.* Washington, DC: Smart Policing Initiative and Bureau of Justice Administration. Retrieved from http://www.smartpolicinginitiative.com/sites/all/files/SPI%20Body%20Worn%20Cameras%20Phoenix%20Webinar%20Slides%20FINAL.pdf
74. Satzewich, V., & Shaffir, R. (2009). Racism versus professionalism: Claims and counter-claims about racial profiling. *Canadian Journal of Criminology and Criminal Justice,* 51, 199–226.
75. Ibid., p. 209.
76. Ibid., p. 210.
77. Ibid.

CHAPTER 7

1. Maloney, R. (2015, April 11). Bill C-51: Support for anti-terror legislation still dropping, poll suggests. *The Huffington Post Canada.* Retrieved from http://www.huffingtonpost.ca/2015/04/10/bill-c-51-poll-anti-terror-legislation_n_7042460.html
2. Boutilier, A. (2014, October 29). Police and security agencies have enough powers to combat terrorism: Therrien. *Toronto Star.* Retrieved from http://www.thestar.com/news/canada/2014/10/29/new_terror_laws_must_respect_privacy_watchdogs_warn_federal_government.html
3. Braga, M. (2014, November 20). New documents show thousands of unreported wiretaps by Canadian cops [Blog post]. *Motherboard.* Retrieved from http://www.motherboard.vice.com/read/new-documents-show-thousands-of-unreported-wiretaps-by-Canadian-cops
4. Bronskill, J. (2014, July 16). Rogers, Telus won't give customer info to police without a warrant, *Toronto Star.* Retrieved from http://www.thestar.com/news/canada/2014/07/16/rogers_says_it_wont_hand_customer_info_to_police_without_a_warrant.html
5. Plaxton, M. (2012). Police powers after Dicey. *Queen's Law Journal, 38*(1), 99–136.
6. Bolton, P.M. (1991). *Criminal procedure in Canada,* 10th ed. North Vancouver, BC: Self-Counsel Press, p. 24.
7. Supreme Court muzzles sniffer dogs. (2008, April 25). CanWest News Service. Retrieved from http://www.canada.com/globaltv/national/story.html?id=7cef5f97-7bfa-48bb-97db-05e8754897eb
8. Quoted in Fine, S. (2013, September 27). Supreme Court allows wider use of "sniffer dogs." *The Globe and Mail.* Retrieved from http://www.theglobeandmail.com/news/national/police-within-their-rights-to-use-sniffer-dogs-supreme-court-rules/article14564884/
9. Ibid.
10. Canadian Civil Liberties Association. (2013, November 8). R v Vu: Privacy rights protected in recent SCC ruling. *CCLA Rights Watch.* Retrieved from http://www.ccla.org/rightswatch/2013/11/08/r-v-vu-privacy-rights-protected-in-recent-scc-ruling/

11. MacNeil, A. (2014). *Independent review – Moncton shooting – June 4, 2014.* Ottawa: Royal Canadian Mounted Police. Retrieved from http://www.rcmp-grc.gc.ca/pubs/moncton/moncton-macneil-eng.htm
12. Leung, M. (2013, August 27). Ontario to allow police officers to carry stun guns. CTV News. Retrieved from http://www.ctvnews.ca/canada/ontario-to-allow-police-officers-to-carry-stun-guns-1.1428226
13. Gau, J.M., Mosher, C., & Pratt T.C. (2010). An inquiry into the impact of suspect race on police use of Tasers. *Police Quarterly, 13*(1), 27–48.
14. Smith, M.R., Fridell, L.A., MacDonald, J., & Kabu, B. (2006). *A multi-method evaluation of police use of force outcomes.* Washington, DC: National Institute of Justice. Retrieved from http://www.ncjrs.gov/pdffiles1/nij/grants/231176.pdf
15. Terrill, W., & Paoline, E.A. (2012). Conducted energy devices (CEDs) and citizen injuries: The shocking empirical reality. *Justice Quarterly, 29*, 153–182.
16. Meissner, D. (2012, October 9). BC police Taser use down by 87 per cent since Robert Dziekanski's death. *The Huffington Post Canada.* Retrieved from http://www.huffingtonpost.ca/2012/10/09/bc-taser-use-police-down-87-per-cent_n_1952239.html
17. RCMP Taser usage declines for 3rd straight year. (2012, September 19). CBC News. Retrieved from http://www.cbc.ca/news/canada/rcmp-taser-usage-declines-for-3rd-straight-year-1.1128535
18. Blackwell, T. (2011, July 16). Excessive force a rarity for police. *National Post.* Retrieved from http://news.nationalpost.com/2011/07/16/excessive-force-a-rarity-for-police-study/
19. Butler, C., & Hall, C. (2008). *Public-police interaction and its relation to arrest and use of force by police and resulting injuries to subjects and officers: A description of risk in one major Canadian urban city.* Calgary: Calgary Police Service. Retrieved from http://www.nletc.com/files/Calgary-Police-Study.pdf
20. Bazley, T.D., Lersch, K.M., & Mieczkowski, T. (2006). Police use of force: Detectives in an urban police department. *Criminal Justice Review, 31*, 213–229.
21. Harris, C.J. (2009). Police use of improper force: A systematic review of the evidence. *Victims & Offenders, 4*(1), 25–41.
22. McElvain, J.P., & Kposowa, A.J. (2008). Police officer characteristics and the likelihood of using deadly force. *Criminal Justice and Behavior, 35*, 505–521; and Rydberg, J., & Terrill, W. (2010). The effect of higher education on police behavior. *Police Quarterly, 13*(1), 92–120.
23. Harris, "Police use of improper force: A systematic review of the evidence."
24. Ibid.
25. National Institute of Justice. (1999). *Use of force by police: Overview of national and local data.* Washington, DC: National Institute of Justice and Bureau of Justice Statistics, U.S. Department of Justice. Retrieved from https://www.ncjrs.gov/pdffiles1/nij/176330-1.pdf
26. Klinger, D. (2010). Can police training affect the use of force on the streets? The Metro-Dade violence reduction field experiment. In C. McCoy (Ed.), *Holding Police Accountable* (pp. 95–107). Washington, DC: The Urban Institute Press.
27. Wortley, S. (2006). *Police use of force in Ontario: An examination of data from the Special Investigations Unit.* Toronto: Attorney General of Ontario. Retrieved from https://www.attorneygeneral.jus.gov.on.ca/inquiries/ipperwash/policy_part/projects/pdf/AfricanCanadianClinicIpperwashProject_SIUStudybyScotWortley.pdf
28. Murphy, J.J. (2014). *Beyond a split-second: An exploratory study of police use of force and use of force training in Canada* (unpublished MA thesis). Burnaby, BC: School of Criminology, Simon Fraser University, p. 34.
29. Ibid., p. 35.
30. Phillips, S.W., & Sobol, J.J. (2011). Police attitudes about the use of unnecessary force: An ecological examination. *Journal of Police and Criminal Psychology, 26*(1), 47–57; and Terrill, W., & Reisig, M.D. (2003). Neighborhood context and police use of force. *Journal of Research in Crime and Delinquency, 40*, 291–321.

31. Brean, J. (2013, August 19). Virtually every case similar to that of Sammy Yatim has seen charges against law officers dismissed. *National Post.* Retrieved from http://news.nationalpost.com/2013/08/19/yatim-history-charges/
32. British Columbia Civil Liberties Association. (2014). *Clear statement – no charges against the R.C.M.P. in Terrace case.* Vancouver: Author. Retrieved from https://bccla.org/wp-content/uploads/2012/11/20121106-Criminal-Justice-Branch-Summary-Robert-Wright.pdf
33. McElvain and Kposowam, "Police officer characteristics and the likelihood of using deadly force."
34. Kane, L. (2014, February 12). Toronto police shootings inquest rules deaths as homicides: Recommends training changes. *Toronto Star.* Retrieved from http://www.thestar.com/news/crime/2014/02/12/police_shootings_inquest_rules_deaths_as_homicides.html
35. Personal communication with author, 2012.
36. Cited in Muir, B. (2014). *Community surveillance of police-citizen encounters: Canadian police officers in YouTube* (unpublished honour's thesis). Burnaby, BC: School of Criminology, Simon Fraser University, p. 49.
37. Harris, "Police use of improper force: A systematic review of the evidence."
38. Cited in Gurney, M. (2014, July 23). If crime is consistently down, why does it sometimes seem that the police can't be bothered to enforce the law? *National Post.* Retrieved from http://fullcomment.nationalpost.com/2014/07/23/matt-gurney-if-crime-is-consistently-down-why-does-it-sometimes-seem-that-the-police-cant-be-bothered-to-enforce-the-law/
39. Polite Ire. (2012, January 5). The police: The case against [Blog post]. Retrieved from https://politeire.wordpress.com/2012/01/05/the-police-the-case-against/
40. Parent, R.B. (2006). The police use of deadly force: International comparisons. *Police Journal, 79,* 230–237 (p. 235).
41. Lord, V.B., & Sloop, M.W. (2010). Suicide by cop: Police shooting as a method of self-harming. *Journal of Criminal Justice, 38,* 889–895.
42. Addis, N., & Stephens, C. (2008). An evaluation of a police debriefing programme: Outcomes for police officers five years after a police shooting. *International Journal of Police Science and Management, 10,* 361–373.
43. Klinger, D. (2001). *Police responses to officer-involved shootings.* Washington, DC: National Institute of Justice. Retrieved from https://www.ncjrs.gov/pdffiles1/nij/grants/192286.pdf
44. Regehr, C., Johanis, D., Dimitropolous, G., Bartram, C., & Hope, G. (2003). The police officer and the public inquiry: A qualitative inquiry into the aftermath of workplace trauma. *Brief Treatment and Crisis Intervention, 3,* 383–396.
45. Hart, P., Wearing, A., & Headey, B. (1995). Police stress and well-being: Integrating personality, coping, and daily work experiences. *Journal of Occupational and Organizational Psychology, 68,* 133–136; and Regehr, C., Hill, J., Goldberg, G., & Hughes, J. (2003). Postmortem inquiries and trauma responses in paramedics and firefighters. *Journal of Interpersonal Violence, 18,* 607–622.

CHAPTER 8

1. Kelling, G.L., Pate, T., Dieckman, D., & Brown, C.E. (1974). *Kansas City preventive patrol experiment: A summary report.* Washington, DC: Police Foundation. Retrieved from https://ncjrs.gov/pdffiles1/Digitization/42537NCJRS.pdf
2. Trojanowicz, R., & Bucqueroux. B. (1998). *Community policing: How to get started,* 2nd ed. Cincinnati: Anderson Publishing.
3. Fisher-Stewart, G. (2007). *Community policing explained: A guide for local governments.* Washington, DC: U.S. Department of Justice. Retrieved from http://www.cops.usdoj.gov/pdf/vets-to-cops/cp_explained.pdf
4. Whitelaw, B., & Parent, R. (2013). *Community-based strategic policing in Canada,* 4th ed. Toronto: Nelson.

5. U.S. Department of Justice. (2005). Community policing defined. Washington, DC: Office of Community Oriented Policing Services [COPS].
6. Dubal, V. (2012). The demise of community policing? The impact of post-9/11 federal surveillance programs on local law enforcement. *Asian American Law Journal, 19,* 35–59; Jones, C., & Supinski, S.B. (2010). Policing and community relations in the Homeland Security era. *Journal of Homeland Security and Emergency Management, 7*(1), 1–14.
7. Murphy, C. (2005). Securitizing community policing: Towards a Canadian public policing model. *Canadian Review of Policing Research, 2,* 25–31 (pp. 25, 27).
8. Ibid., p. 29.
9. Fischer, C. (2014). *Legitimacy and procedural justice: A new element of police leadership.* Washington, DC: Police Executive Research Forum, pp. 33–34. Retrieved from http://www.policeforum.org/assets/docs/Free_Online_Documents/Leadership/legitimacy%20and%20procedural%20justice%20-%20a%20new%20element%20of%20police%20leadership.pdf
10. Ibid., p. 8.
11. Her Majesty's Inspectorate of the Constabulary. (2011). *Demanding times: The front line and police visibility.* London, UK: Author, p. 23. Retrieved from http://www.justiceinspectorates.gov.uk/hmic/media/demanding-times-062011.pdf
12. Ibid., p. 7.
13. Rogers, B., & Robinson, E. (2004). *The benefits of community engagement: A review of the evidence.* London: Home Office, p. 1. Cited in Lloyd, K., & Foster, J. (2009). *Citizen focus and community engagement: A review of the literature.* London, UK: The Police Foundation, p. 30. Retrieved from http://www.police-foundation.org.uk/uploads/catalogerfiles/citizen-focus-and-community-engagement-a-review-of-the-literature/citizen_focus.pdf
14. Lloyd & Foster, *Citizen focus and community engagement,* p. 39.
15. Ibid., p. 40.
16. Murphy, Securitizing community policing: Towards a Canadian public policing model.
17. Lloyd & Foster, *Citizen focus and community engagement,* p. 41.
18. Toronto Police Service. (n.d.). Community consultative process. Retrieved from http://www.torontopolice.on.ca/community/ccc.php
19. Griffiths, C.T., & Pollard, N. (2013). *Policing in Winnipeg. An operational review.* Ottawa: Canadian Police Association. Retrieved from http://www.curtgriffiths.com
20. Pauls, M. (2005). An evaluation of the neighbourhood empowerment team (NET): Edmonton Police Service. *Canadian Review of Policing Research, 2,* 19–23.
21. Rix, A., Joshua, F., Maguire, M., & Morton, S. (2009). *Improving public confidence in the police: A review of the evidence.* Research Report 28. London, UK: Research, Development, and Statistics Directorate, Home Office. Retrieved from https://www.gov.uk/government/publications/improving-public-confidence-in-the-police-a-review-of-the-evidence
22. Ipsos Reid. (2011, January 11). A matter of trust (press release). Retrieved from http://www.ipsos-na.com/news-polls/pressrelease.aspx?id=5100
23. Cf. Jones, N., & Ruddell, R. (2014). *Community perceptions of the Regina Police Service, 2013.* Regina: Department of Justice Studies, University of Regina. Retrieved from https://www.reginapolice.ca/resource/communitysurvey2013.pdf
24. Cross, J.S. (2014, December 8). Toronto police among highest-rated city services: City matters. *MetroNews*. Retrieved from http://metronews.ca/news/toronto/1232286/toronto-police-among-highest-rated-city-services-city-matters/
25. Cf. Rosenbaum, D.P., Schuck, A., Lawrence, D., & Harnett, S. (2011). *Community-based indicators of police performance: Introducing the platform's public satisfaction survey.* Washington, DC: National Institute of Justice. Retrieved from http://uicclj.squarespace.com/community-based-indicators-of/
26. O'Connor, C.D. (2008). Citizen attitudes toward the police in Canada. *Policing: An International Journal of Police Strategies & Management, 31,* 578–595.
27. Cao, L. (2011). Visible minorities and confidence in the police. *Canadian Journal of Criminology and Criminal Justice, 53*(1), 1–26.

28. Sprott, J., & Doob, A.N. (2009). The effect of urban neighborhood disorder on evaluations of the police and courts. *Crime and Delinquency, 55*, 339–362.
29. Cf. Malatest, R.A. et al. (2013). *OPP community satisfaction survey 2013. Provincial Report.* Orillia, ON: Ontario Provincial Police. Retrieved from http://www.opp.ca/media/2013-provincial-css-report-24jun2013-en.pdf; Royal Canadian Mounted Police. (2012). *Core surveys 2012: British Columbia (E Division) results.* Ottawa. Retrieved from http://www.rcmp-grc.gc.ca/surveys-sondages/2012/result-ediv12-eng.htm; and Jones & Ruddell, *Community perceptions of the Regina Police Service.*
30. Skogan, W.G. (1995). *Community participation and community policing.* Chicago: Center for Urban Affairs and Policy Research, Northwestern University, p. 15.
31. Skogan, W.G. (2004). *Community policing: Can it work?* Belmont, CA: Wadsworth/Thomson Learning, p. 62.
32. Ren, L., Zhao, J. S., Lovrich, N.P., & Gaffney, M. (2006). Participation in community crime prevention: Who volunteers for police work? *Policing: An International Journal of Police Strategies and Management, 29*, 464–481.
33. Toronto Police Accountability Coalition. (2014, November 20). *Bulletin No. 87.* Retrieved from http://www.tpac.ca/show_bulletin.cfm?id=188
34. Skogan, *Community policing: Can it work?*
35. Cherney, A. (1999). Gay and lesbian issues in policing, *Current Issues in Criminal Justice, 11*(1), 35–52.
36. Radford, K., Betts, J., & Ostermeyer, M. (2006). *Policing, accountability and the lesbian, gay and bisexual community in Northern Ireland.* Belfast: Institute for Conflict Research. Retrieved from http://www.nipolicingboard.org.uk/lgb_book1-2.pdf; and Wolff, K.R., & Cokely, C.L. (2007). "To protect and to serve?": An exploration of police conduct in relation to the gay, lesbian, bisexual, and transgender community. *Sexuality & Culture, 11*(2), 1–23.
37. Ottawa Police Service. (n.d.). GLBT Liaison Committee. Retrieved from http://www.ottawapolice.ca/en/news-and-community/glbt-liaison-committee.asp
38. Fitzgerald, R.T., & Carrington, P.J. (2008). The neighbourhood context of urban Aboriginal crime. *Canadian Journal of Criminology and Criminal Justice, 50*, 523–557.
39. Ekos Research Associates & Anishinabek Consultants, Inc. (2006). *Survey of First Nations people living off-reserve, Metis and Inuit.* Ottawa: Indian and Northern Affairs Canada. Retrieved from http://knet.ca/documents/OFF_RESERVE_SURVEY_E1.pdf
40. Environics Institute. (2011). *Urban Aboriginal peoples study.* Toronto: Author. Retrieved from http://www.environicsinstitute.org/institute-projects/completed-projects/urban-aboriginal-peoples-study
41. Jones & Ruddell, *Community perceptions of the Regina Police Service.*
42. Toronto Police Service. (n.d.). Aboriginal Peacekeeping Unit. Retrieved from http://www.torontopolice.on.ca/community/aboriginal.php
43. Wells, W. (2009). Problem solving. In E.R. Maguire and W. Wells (Eds.), *Implementing Community Policing: Lessons from 12 Agencies.* Washington, DC: U.S. Department of Justice, Office of Community Oriented Policing Programs, p. 31.
44. Rix et al., *Improving public confidence in the police: A review of the evidence,* p. 1.
45. Maguire, E., & Gantley, M. (2009). Specialist and generalist models. In E.R. Maguire and W. Wells (Eds.), *Implementing Community Policing: Lessons from 12 Agencies.* Washington, DC: Office of Community Oriented Policing Services, pp. 45–55.
46. J. Liederbach, Fritsch, E.J., Carter, D.L., & Bannister, A. (2008). Exploring the limits of collaboration in community policing: A direct comparison of police and citizen views. *Policing: An International Journal of Police Strategies and Management, 31*, 271–291.
47. Maguire, E., & Wells, W. (2009). The future of community policing. In E.R. Maguire and W. Wells (Eds.), *Implementing Community Policing: Lessons from 12 Agencies.* Washington, DC: Office of Community Oriented Policing Services, pp. 173–183.

48. Wehrman, M.M., & DeAngelis, J. (2011). Citizen willingness to participate in police-community partnerships: Exploring the influence of race and neighborhood context. *Police Quarterly, 14*(1), 25–47.
49. Rix et al., *Improving public confidence in the police: A review of the evidence,* p. 1.

CHAPTER 9

1. Weisburd, D., & Telep, C.W. (2014). Hot spots policing: What we know and what we need to know. *Journal of Contemporary Criminal Justice, 30,* 200–220 (p. 208).
2. White, M.D., & Balkcom, F. (2012). *Glendale, Arizona smart policing initiative: Reducing convenience theft.* Washington, DC: Bureau of Justice Administration. Retrieved from http://www.cna.org/sites/default/files/research/GlendaleSiteSpotlight.pdf
3. Barkley, M. (2009). *CCTV pilot project evaluation report.* Toronto: Toronto Police Service. Retrieved from http://geeksandglobaljustice.com/wp-content/TPS-CCTV-report.pdf; Welsh, B.C., & Farrington, D.P. (2009). Public area CCTV and crime prevention: An updated systematic review and meta-analysis. *Justice Quarterly, 26,* 716–745; and Ratcliffe, J.H., Taniguchi, T., & Taylor, R.B. (2009). The crime reduction effects of public CCTV cameras: A multi-method spatial approach. *Justice Quarterly, 26,* 746–770.
4. McLean, S.J., Worden, R.E., & Kim, M. (2013). Here's looking at you: An evaluation of public CCTV cameras and their effects on crime and disorder, *Criminal Justice Review, 38,* 303–334; and Ratcliffe, J.H. (2009). *Video surveillance of public places.* Washington, DC: U.S. Department of Justice, Center for Problem-Oriented Policing. Retrieved from http://www.cops.usdoj.gov/pdf/pop/e02061006.pdf
5. Bennett, T., Holloway, K., & Farrington, D.P. (2006). Does neighborhood watch reduce crime? A systematic review and meta-analysis. *Journal of Experimental Criminology, 2,* 437–458.
6. Challinger, D. (2004). *Crime Stoppers: Evaluating Victoria's program.* Canberra: Australian Institute of Criminology. Retrieved from http://www.aic.gov.au/media_library/publications/tandi2/tandi272.pdf
7. Cf. Lyon, D., Doyle, A., & Lippert, R. (2012). Introduction. In A. Doyle, R. Lippert, and D. Lyon (Eds.), *Eyes Everywhere: The Global Growth of Camera Surveillance.* New York: Routledge.
8. Rosenbaum, D.P. (2007). Just say no to D.A.R.E. *Criminology and Public Policy, 6,* 815–824.
9. A.M. Schuck. (2013). A life-course perspective on adolescents' attitudes to police : DARE, delinquency, and residential segregation. *Journal of Research in Crime and Delinquency, 50,* 579–607.
10. Corter, C., & Peters, R.D. (2011). Integrated early childhood services in Canada: Evidence from the Better Beginnings, Better Futures (BBBF) and Toronto First Duty (TFD) projects. *Encyclopedia of Early Childhood Development.* Retrieved from http://www.child-encyclopedia.com/sites/default/files/textes-experts/en/456/integrated-early-childhood-services-in-canada-evidence-from-the-better-beginnings-better-futures-bbbf-and-toronto-first-duty-tfd-projects.pdf
11. MacRae, L., Paetsch, J.J., Bertrand, L.D., & Hornick, J.P. (2005). *National police leadership survey on crime prevention through social development.* Calgary: Canadian Research Institute for Law and the Family. Retrieved from http://www.publicsafety.gc.ca/cnt/rsrcs/lbrr/ctlg/shwttls-eng.aspx?d=PS&i=23299672
12. Na, C., & Gottfredson, D.C. (2013). Police officers in schools: Effects on school crime and the processing of offending behaviors. *Justice Quarterly 30,* 619–650.
13. Anderson, S.A., Sabatelli, R.M., & Trachtenberg, J. (2007). Community police and youth programs for positive youth development. *Police Quarterly, 10*(1), 23–40.
14. Public Safety Canada. (2013). Community mobilization Prince Albert. Retrieved from http://www.publicsafety.gc.ca/cnt/cntrng-crm/plcng/cnmcs-plcng/ndx/snpss-eng.aspx?n=152
15. Linden, R., & Chaturvedi, R. (2005). The need for comprehensive crime prevention planning: The case of motor vehicle theft. *Canadian Journal of Criminology and Criminal Justice, 47*: 251–270 (p. 252).

16. Ibid.
17. Horn, D. (2013, January 13). Gun buy-backs popular but ineffective, experts say. *The Cincinnati Enquirer*. Retrieved from http://www.usatoday.com/story/news/nation/2013/01/12/gun-buybacks-popular-but-ineffective/1829165/
18. Rosenbaum, Just say no to D.A.R.E.
19. Ottawa Police Service. (2012). *Environmental scan: 2012*. Ottawa. Retrieved from http://www.ottawapolice.ca/en/news-and-community/resources/enviroscan.pdf
20. Cited in Griffiths, C.T. (2013). *Canadian police work*, 3rd ed. Toronto: Nelson, p. 228.
21. Romeanes, T. (1998). A question of confidence: Zero tolerance and problem-oriented policing. In R. Hopkins Burke (Ed.), *Zero Tolerance Policing* (pp. 39–48). Leicester, UK: Perpetuity Press.
22. Gabbat, A. (2013, November 14). Stop and frisk: Only 3% of 2.4m stops result in conviction, report finds. *The Guardian*. Retrieved from http://www.theguardian.com/world/2013/nov/14/stop-and-frisk-new-york-conviction-rate
23. Goldstein, J. (2013, August 12). Judge rejects New York's stop and frisk policy. *The New York Times*. Retrieved from http://www.nytimes.com/2013/08/13/nyregion/stop-and-frisk-practice-violated-rights-judge-rules.html?pagewanted=all&_r=0
24. Rankin, J. (2013, September 27). As criticism piles up, so do the police cards. *Toronto Star*. Retrieved from http://www.thestar.com/news/gta/knowntopolice2013/2013/09/27/as_criticism_piles_up_so_do_the_police_cards.html
25. Winsa, P. (2014, November 12). Improper police "carding" continues in Jane-Finch area, survey finds. *Toronto Star*. Retrieved from http://www.thestar.com/news/crime/2014/11/12/improper_police_carding_continues_in_janefinch_area_survey_finds.html
26. Ibid.; Toronto Police Accountability Coalition. (2014, November 20). *Bulletin No. 87*. Retrieved from http://www.tpac.ca/show_bulletin.cfm?id=188; and personal communication with author, 2014.
27. Wilson, J.Q., & Kelling, G.L. (1982, March). Broken windows: The police and neighborhood safety. *Atlantic Monthly*, pp. 29–38.
28. Burke, R.H. (1998). The socio-political context of zero tolerance policing strategies. *Policing, 21*: 666–682.
29. Ibid.
30. Harcourt, B.E. (2001). *Illusions of order—the false promise of broken windows*. Cambridge: Harvard University Press; and Hinkle, J.C., & Weisburd, D. (2008). The irony of broken windows policing: A micro-place study of the relationship between disorder, focused police crackdowns and fear of crime. *Journal of Criminal Justice, 36*, 503–512.
31. Eck, J.E. (2004). Why don't problems get solved? In W.G. Skogan (Ed.), *Community Policing: Can It Work?* (pp. 185–206). Belmont: Wadsworth/Thomson Learning.
32. Durlauf, S.N., & Nagin, D.S. (2011). The deterrent effect of imprisonment. In P.J. Cook, J. Ludwig, and J. McCrary (Eds.), *Controlling Crime: Strategies and Tradeoffs* (pp. 43–94). Chicago: University of Chicago Press.
33. Uchida, C.D., Swatt, M., Gamero, D., Lopez, J., Salazar, E., King, E., Maxey, R., Ong, N., Wagner, D., & White, M.D. (2012). *Los Angeles, California smart policing initiative: Reducing gun-related violence through operation LASER*, Washington, DC: Bureau of Justice Administration. Retrieved from http://www.smartpolicinginitiative.com/sites/all/files/spotlights/LA%20Site%20Spotlight%20FINAL%20Oct%202012.pdf
34. Burke, The socio-political context of zero tolerance policing strategies.
35. Harcourt, B.E., & Ludwig, J. (2006). Broken windows: New evidence from New York City and a five-city social experiment. *The University of Chicago Law Review, 73*(1), 271–320; Hyunseok, J., Hoover, L.T., & Lawton, B.A. (2008). Effect of broken windows enforcement on clearance rates. *Journal of Criminal Justice, 36*, 529–538.
36. Hinkle & Weisburd, The irony of broken windows policing.
37. Scott, M.S. (2003). *The benefits and consequences of police crackdowns*. Washington, DC: Office of Community Oriented Policing Services, U.S. Department of Justice. Retrieved from http://www.popcenter.org/responses/police_crackdowns

38. Axford, M., & Ruddell, R. (2010). Police-parole partnerships in Canada: A review of a promising programme. *International Journal of Police Science and Management, 12,* 274–286.
39. Cf. Travis, J., Davis, R., & Lawrence, S. (2012). *Exploring the role of the police in prisoner reentry*. Washington, DC: National Institute of Justice. Retrieved from https://ncjrs.gov/pdffiles1/nij/238337.pdf
40. Armstrong, J., & Mallen, S. (2013, October 23). TAVIS: Police unit faces criticism as it tries to bridge gaps in Toronto neighbourhoods. Global News. Retrieved from http://www.globalnews.ca/news/920979/following-tavis-officers-on-walkabout-of-jamestown-neighbourhood/
41. Gau, J.M., & Brunson, R.K. (2010). Procedural justice and order maintenance policing: A study of inner-city young men's perceptions of police legitimacy. *Justice Quarterly, 27,* 255–279.
42. Eck, J.E., Chainey, S., Cameron, J.G., Leitner, M., & Wilson, R.E. (2005). *Mapping crime: Understanding hot spots*. Washington, DC: National Institute of Justice. Retrieved from http://discovery.ucl.ac.uk/11291/1/11291.pdf
43. McElvain, J.P., Kposowa, A.J., & Gray, B.C. (2013). Testing a crime control model: Does strategic and directed deployment of police officers lead to lower crime? *Journal of Criminology,* 1–11.
44. Durlauf & Nagin, The deterrent effect of imprisonment; and Weisburd & Telep, Hot spots policing: What we know and what we need to know.
45. Corsaro, N., Brunson, R.K., & McGarrell, E.F. (2010). Evaluating a police strategy intended to disrupt an illicit street-level drug market. *Evaluation Review, 34,* 513–548.
46. Weisburd & Telep, Hot spots policing: What we know and what we need to know.
47. Ratcliffe, J.H. (2013). *Philadelphia, Pennsylvania smart policing initiative: Testing the impacts of differential strategies on violent crime hotspots,* Washington, DC: Bureau of Justice Administration. Retrieved from http://www.cna.org/sites/default/files/research/Philadelphia_Site_Spotlight.pdf
48. Menton, C. (2008). Bicycle patrols: An underutilized resource. *Policing: An International Journal of Police Strategies & Management, 31*(1), 93–108.
49. Ratcliffe, J.H., Taniguchi, T., Goff, E.R., & Wood, J. (2011). The Philadelphia foot patrol experiment: A randomized controlled trial of police patrol effectiveness in violent crime hotspots. *Criminology, 49,* 795–831.
50. Guerette, R.T. (2009). *Analyzing crime displacement and diffusion*. Washington, DC: U.S. Department of Justice, Office of Community Oriented Policing Services. Retrieved from http://www.popcenter.org/tools/pdfs/displacement.pdf
51. Rossmo, D.K. (1995). Strategic crime patterning: Problem-oriented policing and displacement. In C.R. Block, M. Dabdoub, and S. Fregly (Eds.), *Crime Analysis Through Computer Mapping* (pp. 1–14). Washington, DC: Police Executive Research Forum, pp. 5–6.
52. Monahan, T., & Palmer, N.A. (2009). The emerging politics of DHS fusion centers, *Security Dialogue, 40,* 617–636.
53. Mertl, S. (2013, November 12). Privacy, intrusion issues dog rollout of unmanned drones by police. *Daily Brew*. Retrieved from https://ca.news.yahoo.com/blogs/dailybrew/privacy-intrusion-issues-dog-rollout-unmanned-drones-police-215353890.html
54. Guma, G. (2013, April 12). Drones and law enforcement in America: The unmanned police surveillance state [Blog post]. *Global Research*. Retrieved from http://www.globalresearch.ca/drones-and-law-enforcement-in-america-the-unmanned-police-surveillance-state/5330984
55. Bronskill, J. (2013, November 12). Study urges privacy policy before widespread use of drones. *MetroNews*. Retrieved from http://www.metronews.ca/news/canada/8576181/study-urges-privacy-policy-before-widespread-use-of-drones/; Cavoukian, A. (2012). *Privacy and drones: Unmanned aerial veh*icles. Ottawa: Information and Privacy Commissioner. Retrieved from http://www.ipc.on.ca/images/Resources/pbd-drones.pdf; and Parsons, C., & Molnar, A. (2013). *Watching below: Dimensions of surveillance by UAVs*. Toronto: Block G Privacy and Security Consulting.

56. Osborne, D., & Wernicke, S. (2003). *Introduction to crime analysis: Basic resources for criminal justice practice.* New York: The Haworth Press, p. 5.
57. Santos, R.B. (2014). The effectiveness of crime analysis for crime reduction: Cure or diagnosis? *Journal of Contemporary Criminal Justice, 30*, 147–168.
58. Osborne & Wernicke, *Introduction to crime analysis: Basic resources for criminal justice practice.*
59. Pearsall, B. (2010, June). Predictive policing: The future of law enforcement? *NIJ Journal, 266*, 16–19. Retrieved from http://www.ncjrs.gov/pdffiles1/nij/230414.pdf
60. Perry, W.L., McInnis, B., Price, C.C., Smith, S.C., & Hollywood, J.W. (2013). *Predictive policing: The role of crime forecasting in law enforcement operations.* Santa Monica, CA: RAND. Retrieved from https://www.rand.org/content/dam/rand/pubs/research_reports/RR200/RR233/RAND_RR233.pdf
61. Cope, N. (2004). Intelligence led policing or policing led intelligence? Integrating volume crime analysis into policing. *British Journal of Criminology 44*: 188–203; and Ratcliffe, J.H. (2002). Intelligence-led policing and the problems of turning rhetoric into practice. *Policing & Society, 12*(1), 53–66.
62. Willis, J.J., Mastrofski, S.D., & Kochel, T. (2010). The co-implementation of CompStat and community policing. *Journal of Criminal Justice, 38*, 969–980.
63. Parshall-McDonald, P. (2002). *Managing police operations—implementing the New York crime control model—CompStat.* Belmont, CA: Wadsworth/Thomson Learning.
64. Willis et al., The co-implementation of CompStat and community policing.
65. Personal communication with author, June 2013.
66. Willis et al., The co-implementation of CompStat and community policing.
67. Dabney, D. (2009). Observations regarding key operational realities in a CompStat model of policing. *Justice Quarterly, 27*(1), 28–51.
68. Cited in Eterno, J.A., Verman, A., & Silverman, E.B. (2014). Police manipulations of crime reporting: Insiders' revelations, *Justice Quarterly*, published online November 17, 1–25 (pp. 19–20).
69. Myhill, A., & Quinton, P. (2010). What is trust and confidence in the police? *Policing, 4*, 241–248.
70. Rix, A., Joshua, F., Maguire, M., & Morton, S. (2009). *Improving public confidence in the police: A review of the evidence.* Research Report 28. London, UK: Research, Development, and Statistics Directorate, Home Office, p. 1. Retrieved from https://www.gov.uk/government/publications/improving-public-confidence-in-the-police-a-review-of-the-evidence

CHAPTER 10

1. Campbell, E., & LePard, D. (2007). How police departments can reduce the risk of wrongful convictions. In R. Bajer, et al. (Eds.), *Wrongful Convictions in Canada* (pp. 12–39). Vancouver: International Society for the Reform of the Criminal Law. Retrieved from http://www.isrcl.org/Papers/2007/YMC.pdf
2. Hutchins, H. (2014). *Police resources in Canada, 2013.* Ottawa: Minister of Industry, p. 5. Retrieved from http://www.statcan.gc.ca/pub/85-002-x/2014001/article/11914-eng.pdf
3. Phillips, P.W. (2005). *Policing and special units.* Upper Saddle River, NJ: Prentice-Hall.
4. Personal communication with author, October 2013.
5. Rubenser, L.R. (2005). Special units in policing: Functionality v legitimacy maintenance. In P.W. Phillips (Ed.), *Policing and Special Units* (pp. 24–53). Upper Saddle River, NJ: Prentice-Hall.
6. Ibid., p. 26.
7. Shelton, D.E. (2008). The "*CSI* effect": Does it really exist? *NIJ Journal, 259*, 1–6. Retrieved from https://www.ncjrs.gov/pdffiles1/nij/221501.pdf
8. The "CSI effect." (2010, April 27). *The Economist*, p. 78. Retrieved from http://www.economist.com/node/15949089

9. Stinson, V., Patry, M.W., & Smith, S.M. (2007). The CSI effect: Reflections from police and forensic investigators. *The Canadian Journal of Police & Security Services, 5*(3–4), 125–133.
10. Lieberman, B. (2007). Ethical issues in the use of confidential informants for narcotic operations. *Police Chief, 74*(6), 62, 64–66.
11. Turcotte, M. (2008). Shifts in police-informant negotiations. *Global Crime, 9*, 291–305.
12. Ibid.
13. Personal communication with author, November 2014.
14. Turcotte, Shifts in police-informant negotiations.
15. Beeby, D. (2014, November 29). RCMP officers break rules on note-taking: Internal audit. CBC News. Retrieved from http://www.cbc.ca/news/politics/rcmp-officers-break-rules-on-note-taking-internal-audit-1.2852796
16. Wells, G.L., Memon, A., & Penrod, S.D. (2006). Eyewitness evidence: Improving its probative value. *Psychological Science in the Public Interest, 7*(2): 45–75.
17. Wells, G.L., & Olson, E.A. (2003). Eyewitness testimony. *Annual Review of Psychology, 54*, 277–295.
18. Thompson-Cannino, J., R. Cotton, and E. Torneo. 2009. *Picking Cotton: Our Memoir of Injustice and Redemption*. New York: St. Martin's Press.
19. Brigham, J.C., Maass, A., Snyder, L.D., & Spaulding, K. (1982). Accuracy of eyewitness identifications in a field setting. *Journal of Personality and Social Psychology, 42*, 673–681.
20. Geberth, V.J. (1996). *Practical homicide investigation: Tactics, procedures, and forensic techniques*, 3rd ed. New York: Elsevier.
21. LePard, D. (2010). *Missing women investigation review*. Vancouver: Vancouver Police Department. Retrieved from http://www.cbc.ca/bc/news/bc-100820-vancouver-police-pickton-investigation-review.pdf
22. Oppal, W.T. (2012). *Forsaken: The Report of the Missing Women Commission of Inquiry: Executive Summary*. Victoria: Ministry of Justice and Attorney General of British Columbia. Retrieved from Retrieved from http://www.ag.gov.bc.ca/public_inquiries/docs/Forsaken-ES.pdf
23. Human Rights Watch. (2013). *Those who take us away: Abusive policing and failures in protection of indigenous women and girls in northern British Columbia, Canada.* Toronto: Author, p. 7. Retrieved from http://www.hrw.org/reports/2013/02/13/those-who-take-us-away, p. 7.
24. Ibid.
25. Burchill, J. (2008). Mr. Stillman, DNA and discarded evidence in criminal cases. *Manitoba Law Journal, 32*(2), 5–33.
26. Makin, K. (2010, March 13). The dark side of DNA. *The Globe and Mail*, p. A4. Retrieved from http://www.theglobeandmail.com/technology/science/the-dark-side-of-dna/article4310360/?page=all; and Thompson, W.C. (2006, January/February). Tarnish on the "gold standard": Recent problems in forensic DNA testing. *Champion Magazine.* National Association of Criminal Defense Lawyers. Retrieved from http://www.nacdl.org/Champion.aspx?id=1537
27. Kirchner, L. (2013, August 13). The flaws of familial DNA matching. *Pacific Standard*. Retrieved from http://www.psmag.com/science/the-flaws-of-familial-dna-matching-64736
28. Smith, S.M., Stinson, V., & Patry, M.W. (2009). Using the "Mr. Big" technique to elicit confessions: Successful innovation or dangerous development in the Canadian legal system? *Psychology, Public Policy, and Law, 15*, 168–193.
29. Keenan, K.T., & Brockman, J. (2011). *Mr. Big: Exposing undercover investigations in Canada.* Halifax and Winnipeg: Fernwood Publishing, p. 9.
30. Riddell, T., & Puddister, K. (2014, August 6). Who's in charge of Mr. Big? *National Post.* Retrieved from http://fullcomment.nationalpost.com/2014/08/06/riddell-puddister-whos-in-charge-of-mr-big/
31. Gillis, W. (2014, July 28). Man acquitted in neighbour's 1974 killing after judge throws out evidence from "Mr. Big" sting. *Toronto Star*. Retrieved from http://www.thestar.com/news/crime/2014/07/28/man_acquitted_of_murder_in_neighbours_1974_killing.html

32. Kassin, S.M., Drizin, S.A., Grisso, T., Gudjosson, G.H., Leo, R.A., & Redlich, A.D. (2010). Police-induced confessions: Risk factors and recommendations. *Law and Human Behavior, 34*(1), 3–38.
33. Kassin, S.M. (2005). On the psychology of confessions: Does innocence put innocents at risk? *American Psychologist, 60*, 215–228.
34. Widely used police interrogation technique can result in false confession: Disclosure. (2003, January 28). CBC News. Retrieved from http://www.cbc.ca/news/canada/widely-used-police-interrogation-technique-can-result-in-false-confession-disclosure-1.389125
35. Snook, B., Cullen, R.M., Bennell, C., Taylor, P. J., & Gendreau, P. (2008). The criminal profiling illusion: What's behind the smoke and mirrors? *Criminal Justice and Behavior, 35*, 1257–1276 (p. 1257).
36. Ibid.
37. Rossmo, D.K. (1999). *Geographic profiling.* Boca Raton, FL: CRC Press.
38. Wang, F. (2005). *Geographic Information Systems and crime analysis.* Hershey, PA: Idea Group Publishers.
39. Larson, S. (2014, December 18). What "Serial" really taught us. *The New Yorker.* Retrieved from http://www.newyorker.com/culture/sarah-larson/serial-really-taught-us?currentPage=all
40. Serial (podcast). (2014). Wikipedia. Retrieved from http://en.wikipedia.org/wiki/Serial_%28podcast%29
41. Serial-like Toronto police investigation releases final clue. (2014, December 31). CBC News. Retrieved from http://www.cbc.ca/news/canada/toronto/serial-like-toronto-police-investigation-releases-final-clue-1.2887663; Dutta, K. (2014, December 21). "Serial" fans have a new murder to unravel as Canadian detective crowd-sources investigation. *The Independent.* Retrieved from http://www.independent.co.uk/news/world/americas/serial-fans-have-a-new-murder-to-unravel-as-canadian-detective-crowdsources-investigation-9939069.html

CHAPTER 11

1. Cited in Bennett, D. (2014, December 11). Building a better police department. *Bloomberg Business Week,* p. 25. Retrieved from http://www.bloomberg.com/bw/articles/2014-12-11/from-ferguson-to-new-york-building-a-better-police-department
2. Roman, J. (2013, September). Cost-benefit analysis of criminal justice reforms, *NIJ Journal, 272.* Retrieved from http://nij.gov/journals/272/pages/cost-benefit.aspx
3. Pawson, R. (2006). *Evidence-based policy.* London: Sage, p. 7.
4. Amendola, K.L., Weisburd, D., Hamilton, E.E., Jones, G., & Slipka, M. (2011). *The shift length experiment: What we know about 8-, 10- and 12-hour shifts in policing.* Washington, DC: The Police Foundation. Retrieved from http://www.policefoundation.org/sites/g/files/g798246/f/ShiftLengthExperiment_0.pdf
5. Batts, A.W., Smoot, S.M., & Scrivner, E. (2012, July). Police leadership challenges in a changing world, *New Perspectives in Policing.* Washington, DC: National Institute of Justice. Retrieved from https://ncjrs.gov/pdffiles1/nij/238338.pdf
6. Ibid.
7. Griffiths, C.T., Murphy, J., & Snow, S.R. (2014). *Economics of policing: Baseline for policing research in Canada.* Ottawa: Public Safety Canada, p. 11. Retrieved from http://www.publicsafety.gc.ca/cnt/rsrcs/pblctns/bsln-plcng-rsrch/index-eng.aspx
8. Ibid.; and Heaton, P. (2010). *Hidden in plain sight. What cost-of-crime-research can tell us about investing in police* (occasional paper). Santa Monica, CA: RAND. Retrieved from http://www.rand.org/content/dam/rand/pubs/occasional_papers/2010/RAND_OP279.pdf
9. Bradley, D., & Nixon, C. (2009). Ending the "dialogue of the deaf": Evidence and policing policies and practices: An Australian case study. *Police Practice and Research, 10*, 423–435;

and Weisburd, D., & Neyroud, P. (2011, January). Police science: Toward a new paradigm. *New Perspectives in Policing.* Washington, DC: National Institute of Justice, p. 5. Retrieved from https://ncjrs.gov/pdffiles1/nij/228922.pdf

10. Griffiths et al. *Economics of policing: Baseline for policing research in Canada.*
11. Chacos, B. (2013, August 12). Meet Darknet, the hidden, anonymous underbelly of the searchable web. *PCWorld.* Retrieved from http://www.pcworld.com/article/2046227/meet-darknet-the-hidden-anonymous-underbelly-of-the-searchable-web.html; and Griffin, A. (2014, December 11). Dark net: What is it, and what are the dangers of the government's secret browsing crackdown? *The Independent.* Retrieved from http://www.independent.co.uk/life-style/gadgets-and-tech/news/dark-net-what-is-it-and-what-are-the-dangers-of-the-governments-secret-browsing-crackdown-9917649.html
12. Griffin, Dark net: What is it, and what are the dangers of the government's secret browsing crackdown?
13. Koebler, J. (2014, December 19). After Silk Road raid, the dark net is "darker than ever" [Blog post]. *Motherboard.* Retrieved from http://motherboard.vice.com/read/after-silk-road-raid-the-dark-net-is-darker-than-ever
14. Bitcoin buccaneers. (2015, January 17). *The Economist.* Retrieved from http://www.economist.com/news/united-states/21639525-one-dread-pirate-trial-what-about-others-bitcoin-buccaneers
15. Greener, B.K. (2009). *The new international policing.* London: Palgrave MacMillan.
16. Public Safety Canada. (2014). *2014 public report on the terrorist threat to Canada.* Ottawa: Author. Retrieved from http://www.publicsafety.gc.ca/cnt/rsrcs/pblctns/2014-pblc-rpr-trrrst-thrt/2014-pblc-rpr-trrrst-thrt-eng.pdf
17. Crane, E., & Dean, S. (2014, August 7). It will cost $8 million a year just to monitor just ONE jihadist who returns to Australia as the government cracks down to prevent home-grown terrorism. *Daily Mail.* Retrieved from http://www.dailymail.co.uk/news/article-2719118/It-cost-8-million-year-monitor-just-ONE-Australian-jihadist-returns-government-cracks-prevent-home-grown-terrorism.html; Moutot, M. (2015, January 9). It's incredibly difficult to track the movements of known extremists. *Business Insider.* Retrieved from http://www.businessinsider.com/afp-known-jihadists-slip-through-hands-of-overstretched-french-police-2015-1; and Solomon, L. (2015, January 16). To minimize the mass-casualty attacks that are coming, we need to get tougher on crime. *National Post.* Retrieved from http://business.financialpost.com/2015/01/16/lawrence-solomon-to-minimize-the-mass-casualty-attacks-that-are-coming-we-need-to-get-tougher-on-crime
18. Robertson, D. (2014, December 1). Canadian police directing more resources to terror fight. *Ottawa Citizen.* Retrieved from http://ottawacitizen.com/news/politics/canadian-police-directing-more-resources-to-terror-fight
19. Posel, S. (2013, May 31). Synthetic police are coming: DARPA engineering autonomous robots. *Investigative Headline News.* Retrieved from http://www.occupycorporatism.com/synthetic-police-are-coming-darpa-engineering-autonomous-robots/
20. Sklansky, D.A. (2011, March). The persistent pull of police professionalism. *New Perspectives in Policing.* Washington, DC: National Institute of Justice, p. 10. Retrieved from https://ncjrs.gov/pdffiles1/nij/232676.pdf
21. Cited in ibid., p. 9.
22. Cited in MacKinnon, M., & Slater, J. (2015, January 10). A global fight to fortify democracy and security after deadly French attacks, *The Globe and Mail.* Retrieved from http://www.theglobeandmail.com/news/world/a-global-right-to-fortify-democracy-security/article22390683
23. Robertson, D. (2014, November 28). Counter-terrorism: Two bills poised to pass. *Ottawa Citizen.* Retrieved from http://ottawacitizen.com/news/politics/counter-terrorism-two-bills-poised-to-pass
24. Quan, D. (2014, November 24). Majority fear threat of homegrown terrorism, *Vancouver Sun,* p. A7.

25. Pacholik, B. (2014, November 24). Fear of home-grown terrorism is high, *The Leader-Post*, p. A1.
26. McIntyre, G. (2014, November 24). Terror on your doorstep: A third of B.C.ers believe radicals are living on their block. *The Province*. Retrieved from http://www.theprovince.com/news/Terror+your+doorstep+third+believe+radicals+living+their+block/10407813/story.html
27. Angus Reid Institute. (2014, October 24). Just over half of Canadians not confident in ability of security services to prevent home-grown acts of terror (news release). Retrieved from http://angusreid.org/just-over-half-of-canadians-not-confident-in-ability-of-security-services-to-prevent-home-grown-acts-of-terror
28. Austin, J., & Jacobson, M.P. (2013). *How New York City reduced mass incarceration: A model for change?* New York: Brennan Center for Justice and the Vera Institute of Justice. Retrieved from http://www.brennancenter.org/sites/default/files/publications/How_NYC_Reduced_Mass_Incarceration.pdf; and Tierney, J. (2013, January 25). Prison population can shrink when police crowd streets. *The New York Times*, p. A1. Retrieved from http://www.nytimes.com/2013/01/26/nyregion/police-have-done-more-than-prisons-to-cut-crime-in-new-york.html?pagewanted=all&_r=0
29. Tierney, Prison population can shrink when police crowd streets.
30. Griffiths, C.T., & Murdoch, D. (2014). *Canadian corrections*, 4th ed. Toronto: Nelson.
31. Heaton, P., & Jackson, B.A. (2012, November 12). Short-term savings, long-term losses: When police departments respond to economic pressure by cutting their forces [Blog post]. The RAND Blog. Retrieved from http://www.rand.org/commentary/2012/11/12/RAND.html
32. Hutchins, H. (2014). *Police resources in Canada, 2013*. Ottawa: Minister of Industry, p. 16. Retrieved from http://www.statcan.gc.ca/pub/85-002-x/2014001/article/11914-eng.pdf
33. Hansen, A., Alpert, G.P., & Rojek, J.J. (2014). The benefits of police practitioner-researcher partnerships to participating agencies, *Policing, 8*, 307–320.
34. Goudge, Hon. Stephen (Chair). (2014). *Policing Canada in the 21st century: New policing for new challenges*. Ottawa: Council of Canadian Academies. Retrieved from http://www.scienceadvice.ca/uploads/eng/assessments%20and%20publications%20and%20news%20releases/policing/policing_fullreporten.pdf
35. Sklansky, The persistent pull of police professionalism.

Index

Note: Page numbers followed by *f* and *t* denote figures and tables, respectively.